TRACTATE
ON THE JEWS

´TRACTATE ON THE JEWS,

The Significance of Judaism for Christian Faith

FRANZ MUSSNER

Translated and with an Introduction by
LEONARD SWIDLER

FORTRESS PRESS
Philadelphia

SPCK
London

First published in Great Britain 1984   First published in the USA 1984
SPCK   Fortress Press
Holy Trinity Church   2900 Queen Lane
Marylebone Road   Philadelphia
London NW1 4DU   Pennsylvania 19129

Translated from the German *Traktat über die Juden,* copyright © 1979 by
Kösel-Verlag GmbH & Co., München, Federal Republic of Germany

English translation copyright © 1984 by Fortress Press

Biblical quotations, unless otherwise noted, are from the Revised Standard
Version of the Bible, copyright 1946, 1952, © 1971, 1973 by the Division of
Christian Education of the National Council of the Churches of Christ in
the U.S.A., and are used by permission.

Library of Congress Cataloging in Publication Data

Mussner, Franz.
    Tractate on the Jews.

    Translation of: Traktat über die Juden.
    Includes bibliographical references and indexes.
    1. Christianity and other religions—Judaism.
2. Judaism—Relations—Christianity. I. Title.
BM535.M8713 1984   261.2′6   83-5699
ISBN 0–8006–0707–4

British Library Cataloguing in Publication Data

Mussner, Franz
    Tractate on the Jews.
    1. Judaism
    I. Title   II. Traktat über die Juden.
    English
    296   BM561

ISBN 0–281–04086–9

K130D83   Printed in the United States of America   1–707

Contents

Translator's Foreword

For almost two thousand years Christianity has been plagued by a peculiar kind of self-hatred which has manifested itself in one form or another as hatred of Judaism. In the last century or so, with the secularization of much of Christendom and Jewry as well, this psychological disease has not abated; in fact it has intensified into that secular form of anti-Judaism euphemistically called anti-Semitism (the word, which was coined in the middle of the nineteenth century, has never meant hatred of Semites in general, but rather always and only hatred of Jews and things Jewish). However, throughout the millennia-long history of anti-Judaism the major constitutive element has been religious, and for the vast majority of that period, specifically Christian religious prejudice. The horrendous climax of this horrible history was the Holocaust, the Nazi murder of six million Jews. Only after the Holocaust did Christians slowly begin to realize what their anti-Judaic theology ("the teaching of contempt," as Jules Isaac put it) had prepared the way for. Responsible Christians then began to think that if "by their fruits shall you know them," their theology and teaching had indeed been poisoned—perhaps even at its source. Until the last few years no Christian would have thought that the Christian tradition might have been contaminated by anti-Judaism (which we now know can have such ghastly consequences) even at its source, the New Testament.

Even when the question was at first boldly raised by some Christian theologians, as in Gregory Baum's book *Is the New Testament Anti-Semitic?* (New York, 1965), the answer was no. But once the question was publicly raised by responsible theologians, it could not be so simply laid to rest. More and more Christian biblical scholars and theologians probed different aspects of the question—and often came up with increasingly disturbing answers. A sort of *ne plus ultra* was reached in this direction with Rosemary Ruether's book *Faith and Fratricide* (New York, 1974), in which she as a Christian theologian argued forcefully that anti-Judaism was woven into the very beginning of Christianity, that it was the other side of the coin of Christology: Because Judaism did not accept the Christian claim that Jesus is the Messiah, the Christ, Judaism had to be put down in order to sustain the Christian assertion. On the basis of this penetrating ideological critique—which, incidentally, persuaded Gregory Baum, as is clear from the introduction he wrote to *Faith and Fratricide*—Ruether called Christian theologians to a radical rethinking of the core of Christianity, Christology, and related teachings. Moreover, Ruether was not alone in seeing the *mene mene tekel* on the wall and demanding a thoroughgoing thinking anew of Christian teaching. Others have been doing so in an increasing crescendo.

Franz Mussner is a Roman Catholic New Testament scholar and theologian who has over the years built a reputation of careful, solid, thorough biblical scholarship, as we have long since become accustomed to expect from the best of German *Wissenschaft*. However, in regard to the Christian relationship to Judaism, he was no different from the vast majority of the rest of Christian scholars, namely, filled with undisturbed prejudices against Judaism. Then, with Vatican II and its aftermath, he underwent a *metanoia* and ventured forth on the rereading of the Scriptures, which are at the basis of Christian teaching, with new eyes as far as Judaism is concerned. What we have in *Tractate on the Jews* is the result of Professor Mussner's penetrating scholarship and new probing questions regarding the Christian relationship to Judaism applied to the Scriptures.

In *Tractate on the Jews*, Mussner has produced a comprehensive scholarly analysis of all relevant biblical issues concerning the relationship between Christianity and Judaism; none of them are sidestepped or blurred. The critique of Christian teaching is at times severe, but the author is clearly still a committed Christian (or perhaps better, *because* the author is a committed Christian . . .). At times the issues are not resolved to the author's satisfaction, despite his vigorous wrestling, but he never flinches in facing them. However, for the author and the reader, many issues are indeed resolved and are convincingly presented, as only clear-eyed scholarship and profound faith commitment can do.

Of course not all of Mussner's positions will be accepted by all Christians. But a foundation is laid here that is basically so solid that much of the work of Christian theological rethinking can be built on it in great confidence. The small but growing number of Christian theologians working in the area of Jewish-Christian dialogue are already doing this. But the greatest merit of Mussner's work is that it pulls together the best of contemporary biblical and theological scholarship, and integrates and focuses it on the fundamental issue of the relationship between Christianity and Judaism and the implications for Christian teaching and self-understanding in a way that cannot be overlooked by the masses of Christian thinkers, teachers, preachers, and eventually the faithful in general.

Because this is so, *Tractate on the Jews* is also a book that Jewish readers will find not only in many ways relieving, but also reliable. It represents the liberated thought of pioneer Christian theologians today but also in my judgment, the position of most Christians tomorrow.

LEONARD SWIDLER

Preface

"Tractates *against* the Jews" were written in the time of the church fathers, and the anti-Jewish spirit of these tractates has its effect even in our own times; thus, as the churches undertake a comprehensive rethinking of their relationship to Judaism, it is appropriate and timely for us to produce a "tractate *for* the Jews." That is what I have attempted here. Behind this book lies a learning process of many years, a true changing of the mind, and I would like to invite the reader to enter into this learning process and to think newly and differently about Israel, the elder brother and "the root" of the Church. In the first instance, then, this book is written for Christians. If Jewish readers find the book an insightful and honest account, I will be filled with joy. Nevertheless, I believe that the book will meet with as much opposition as agreement. I hope many may come to agree with me. This is my first wish. My second is that someone will soon be found who can do this work better. In any case, every attentive reader will affirm that the concern here is not with some fringe topic of theology, but rather with an issue that leads to the center of theology.

Happily this attempt is not the first or the only one. The reader is expressly directed to the knowledgeable book by Clemens Thoma, *Christian Theology of Judaism* (New York: Paulist Press, 1980). Whoever compares the two books will see that they complement one another. For additional works by Catholics, the reader is directed to the following publications: Augustin Cardinal Bea, *The Church and the Jewish People* (New York: Harper & Row, 1966); H. Spaemann, *Die Christen und das Volk der Juden* (Munich: Kösel-Verlag, 1966); Josef Blank, "Das Mysterium Israel," in *Jüdische Hoffnungskraft und christlicher Glaube*, ed. Walter Strolz (Freiburg: Herder, 1971), pp. 133–190.

There remains only the obligation of expressing thanks. I would like to thank all those who have time and again encouraged me to write this work. I would further like to thank those who stood at my side with counsel and assistance. Above all I must mention the working group for questions of Judaism of the Ecumenical Commission of the German Bishops' Conference under the direction of Auxiliary Bishop Karl Flügel of Regensburg; they offered critical comments on several portions of the manuscript. Joseph Cardinal Ratzinger's colloquium of doctoral students also provided much stimulating criticism. I also wish to thank my assistant, Michael Theobald, for many kinds of assistance and my secretary, Else Schneider, for production of the manuscript. I owe special thanks to Archbishop Joseph Cardinal Höffner, President of the Plenary of the Association of the German Dioceses. Upon the recommendation of Auxiliary Bishop Professor Dr. P.-W. Scheele (Paderborn), President of the Ecumenical Commission, Archbishop Höffner made available a significant printing subsidy for the original edition of this book. I also thank the Bavarian Bishops and their finance directors who provided additional financial assistance.

Regensburg/Passau, August 1979   FRANZ MUSSNER

For this English translation textual oversights have been remedied, several corrections made, and bibliographical references added. In these matters the author is indebted to Dr. E. L. Ehrlich.

1

Outline of a Christian Theology
of Judaism

AUSCHWITZ AS AN OCCASION
FOR RETHINKING

"Auschwitz" will be used here as a symbol for all the concentration camps in which Jews lost their lives. The terrible things that happened there became known throughout the world after the Second World War.[1] Humanity was horrified, and Christendom was likewise horrified. People reflected. Christians asked themselves the question: Are we perhaps jointly responsible for the catastrophe which has overtaken the Jews? Not simply by our silence, but also by our speech? In the final analysis, everyone who lived through the Nazi era knows how helpless we were in the face of the "Jewish problem." Except for an introduction to the Old Testament in courses on the Bible, almost the only thing we heard in religious instruction about the Jews was: The Jews killed Jesus. This sentence was almost the only content of a "Christian theology of Judaism." Through it we saw Christian and theological anti-Semitism as justified. We did not think further; there was very little stimulation to do so. In the petitions of Good Friday we even prayed for the "perfidious Jews"; we uttered the prayer in the best of conscience. In Passau there were only three Jewish stores; still, in the bishop's minor seminary we were told: "Do not buy from Jews!" We slipped by the Jewish stores with the oppressive feeling that very bad people must live inside! Among the few periodicals we were allowed to receive and read in the upper classes was the *Schönere Zukunft,* a Catholic periodical certainly, but definitely anti-Semitic in its orientation. Thus in no way were we prepared for the catastrophic event. Also, the Nazis knew well how to maintain absolute silence about the concentration camps so that it was only after the war that many learned of the horrors that took place there. There had been only vague rumors here and there.

However, after the war people were horrified and began to reflect. Eventually, a rethinking set in that bore much fruit within the spheres of Church and theology. Still, it took a rather long time before this fruit became ripe. The major result in Catholic circles is without doubt the

1

section on the Jews in the 1965 Declaration *Nostra Aetate* of Vatican
Council II. Number 4 of the Declaration on the Relation of the Church to
Non-Christian Religions reads as follows:

> Sounding the depths of the mystery which is the Church, this sacred
> Council remembers the spiritual ties which link the people of the New Cove-
> nant to the stock of Abraham.
> The Church of Christ acknowledges that in God's plan of salvation the
> beginning of her faith and election is to be found in the patriarchs, Moses and
> the prophets. She professes that all Christ's faithful, who as men of faith are
> sons of Abraham (cf. Gal. 3:7), are included in the same patriarch's call and that
> the salvation of the Church is mystically prefigured in the exodus of God's
> chosen people from the land of bondage. On this account the Church cannot
> forget that she received the revelation of the Old Testament by way of that
> people with whom God in his inexpressible mercy established the ancient
> covenant. Nor can she forget that she draws nourishment from that good olive
> tree onto which the wild olive branches of the Gentiles have been grafted (cf.
> Rom. 11:17–24). The Church believes that Christ who is our peace has through
> his cross reconciled Jews and Gentiles and made them one in himself (cf. Eph.
> 2:14–16).
> Likewise, the Church keeps ever before her mind the words of the apostle
> Paul about his kinsmen: "They are Israelites, and to them belong the sonship,
> the glory, the covenants, the giving of the law, the worship, and the promises;
> to them belong the patriarchs, and of their race, according to the flesh, is the
> Christ" (Rom. 9:4–5), the son of the virgin Mary. She is mindful, moreover,
> that the apostles, the pillars on which the Church stands, are of Jewish
> descent, as are many of those early disciples who proclaimed the Gospel of
> Christ to the world.
> As holy Scripture testifies, Jerusalem did not recognize God's moment when
> it came (cf. Luke 19:42). Jews for the most part did not accept the Gospel; on
> the contrary, many opposed the spreading of it (cf. Rom. 11:28). Even so, the
> apostle Paul maintains that the Jews remain very dear to God, for the sake of
> the patriarchs, since God does not take back the gifts he bestowed or the choice
> he made. Together with the prophets and that same apostle, the Church awaits
> the day, known to God alone, when all peoples will call on God with one voice
> and "serve him shoulder to shoulder" (Zeph. 3:9; cf. Isa. 66:23; Ps. 65:4; Rom.
> 11:11–32).
> Since Christians and Jews have such a common spiritual heritage, this sacred
> Council wishes to encourage and further mutual understanding and apprecia-
> tion. This can be obtained, especially, by way of biblical and theological
> enquiry and through friendly discussions.
> Even though the Jewish authorities and those who followed their lead
> pressed for the death of Christ (cf. John 19:6), neither all Jews indiscriminately
> at that time, nor Jews today, can be charged with the crimes committed during
> his passion. It is true that the Church is the new people of God, yet the Jews
> should not be spoken of as rejected or accursed as if this followed from holy
> Scripture. Consequently, all must take care, lest in catechizing or in preaching

the Word of God, they teach anything which is not in accord with the truth of the Gospel message or the spirit of Christ.

Indeed, the Church reproves every form of persecution against whomsoever it may be directed. Remembering, then, her common heritage with the Jews and moved not by any political consideration, but solely by the religious motivation of Christian charity, she deplores all hatreds, persecutions, displays of antisemitism leveled at any time or from any sources against the Jews.

The Church always held and continues to hold that Christ out of infinite love freely underwent suffering and death because of the sins of all men, so that all might attain salvation. It is the duty of the Church, therefore, in her preaching to proclaim the cross of Christ as the sign of God's universal love and the source of all grace. [English in Austin Flannery, ed., *Vatican Council II* (Collegeville, Minn.: Liturgical Press, 1975), pp. 740–742.]

The dramatic prehistory of this section of the Declaration has been comprehensively presented by John Oesterreicher.[2] Here I only wish to recall that the German bishops who gathered together at that time in Rome at the beginning of the debate made the following Declaration:

> We German bishops welcome the conciliar decree on the Jews. When the Church in council makes a statement about itself, it cannot remain silent concerning its connection with the people of God of the Old Testament. We are convinced that this conciliar Declaration provides the occasion for a renewed contact and a better relationship between the Church and the Jewish people.
>
> We German bishops, therefore, especially welcome the decree because we are conscious of the grave injustice that has been perpetrated on the Jews in the name of our people.[3]

As is known, a single "decree on the Jews" could not be agreed upon; resistance was too great. We have only No. 4 in the Declaration, but it contains important impulses and released a train of effects which is just beginning and includes the Roman document, "Vatican Guidelines and Suggestions for the Implementation of the Conciliar Declaration 'No. 4,'" of 3 January 1975.[4] The rethinking is in process on a worldwide basis, not only within Catholicism[5] but also among the churches of the Reformation.[6] Likewise the Joint Synod of the Dioceses of the Federal Republic of Germany has in a fortunate way taken up the theme in its "Hoffnungs-papier" (IV: 2):

> Our country's recent political history is darkened by the systematic attempt to wipe out the Jewish people. Apart from some admirable efforts by individuals and groups, during the time of National Socialism the Church community as a whole lived a life that permitted itself to be preoccupied with the threat to its own institutions. We turned our backs to the fate of this persecuted Jewish people and were silent about the crimes perpetrated on Jews and Judaism. Many became guilty from sheer fear for their lives. We feel particu-

larly distressed about the fact that Christians even took active part in these persecutions. The honesty of our intention to renew ourselves depends on the admission of this guilt, incurred by our country and our Church. Our German Church, in particular, must be alert to all tendencies that might diminish human rights and misuse political power. We must assist all those who are now persecuted for racist or other ideological reasons. On our Church falls the special obligation of improving the tainted relationship between the Church as a whole and the Jewish people and its religion.

We Germans, in particular, must not deny or water-down the redemptive link between the people of the Old Covenant and that of the New, as interpreted and acknowledged by the apostle Paul. For it was in that sense, too, that we became debtors of the Jewish people. Our speaking of the "God of hope" in the presence of the hopeless horrors of Auschwitz gains credibility only by the fact that innumerable persons, Jews and Christians, spoke of and called upon this God, even while living in that hell and after escaping from it. Here lies the task of our people, especially in view of the attitude of other nations and world public opinions vis-à-vis the Jewish people. We deem it the particular duty of the German Church within the Church as a whole to work toward a new relationship between Christians on the one hand, and Jews and their history of faith on the other.[7]

One can say that Auschwitz has exercised a hermeneutic function. The rethinking implies a new understanding. What is newly understood? Here are just a few important examples:

1. The Old Testament as the continuing source for the faith of Israel.
2. Israel as the enduring "root" of the Church.
3. The continuance of the covenant of God with his people Israel, whom he has chosen for himself.
4. The special role of the "land" in the thought of Israel.
5. The Jewishness of Jesus.
6. Specific statements of the New Testament.[8]

The book *Im Windschatten der Massengräber* by J. Bloch bears the fruits of this rethinking in exegesis and systematics.[9] The rethinking at last makes possible an honest dialogue between Jews and Christians.[10] It makes possible the development of a Christian theology of Judaism. It makes possible a tractate on the Jews in the sense of a *tractatus pro Judaeis,* whereas in the patristic and to some extent also in the medieval period of the Church "tractates against the Jews" were written.[11] The call for a "tractate on the Jews" has been repeatedly heard from both Christian and Jewish sides.[12] What is presented in this book, now that Clemens Thoma has courageously shown the way, is a response to this call.

THE ELECTION OF ISRAEL

Christians who take the Bible seriously must understand YHWH's election of Israel as his own people. Not to do so is to miss from the very beginning the meaning of Israel.

God chose Israel.[13] The Old Testament speaks of this in many places. This election of a people by God forms "a novum within the religious history of the ancient orient."[14] How far back in the history of Israel the notion of the election goes can be made out only with difficulty. The most significant witness for it is the Book of Deuteronomy. Important passages therein are the following: "For you are a people holy to YHWH your God; YHWH your God has chosen you to be a people for his own possession, out of all the peoples that are on the face of the earth. It was not because you were more in number than any other people that YHWH set his love upon you and chose you, for you were the fewest of all peoples; *but it is because YHWH loves you,* and is keeping the oath *which he swore to your fathers,* that YHWH has brought you out with a mighty hand, and redeemed you from the house of bondage, from the hand of Pharaoh king of Egypt. Know therefore that YHWH your God is God, the faithful God who keeps covenant and steadfast love with those who love him and keep his commandments, to a thousand generations" (Deut. 7:6–9). "Behold, to YHWH your God belong heaven and the heaven of heavens, the earth with all that is in it; yet YHWH set his heart in love upon your fathers and *chose* their descendants after them, you above all peoples, as at this day" (Deut. 10:14–15). "For you are a people holy to YHWH your God, *and YHWH has chosen you* to be a people for his own possession, out of all the peoples that are on the face of the earth" (Deut. 14:2).

According to these texts, Israel is the people chosen by God for his own possession, chosen however out of his pure, unfathomable love. With this election Israel is set apart from all other peoples: "Lo, a people dwelling alone, and not reckoning itself among the nations!" (Num. 23:9). This election and setting apart of Israel is unique: "Or has any god ever attempted to go and take a nation for himself from the midst of another nation?" (Deut. 4:34). With this election, God laid his hand on Israel forever—a fact which Israel itself, not only the nations, should take notice of; you can and may not be like the other peoples: "What is in your mind shall never happen—the thought, 'Let us be like the nations, like the tribes of the countries, and worship wood and stone' " (Ezek. 20:32). The election established forever the "specialness" of the Jewish people. Even when Israel shows itself a "stiff-necked people" with a view to its "fathers," God does not revoke the election (cf. Pss. 105:6; 135:4: "For YHWH has chosen Jacob for himself, Israel as his own possession").

During the exile, the so-called Deutero-Isaiah answered the question about whether there was any future at all for Israel with the prophetic statement:

But you, Israel, my servant,
    Jacob, whom I have chosen,
    The offspring of Abraham, my friend;
You[15] whom I took from the ends of the earth,
    and called from its farthest corners,
saying to you, "You are my servant,
    I have chosen you and not cast you off";
fear not, for I am with you,
    be not dismayed, for I am your God;
I will strengthen you, I will help you,
    I will uphold you with my victorious right hand. (Isa. 41:8–10)

Again, it states: "'You are my witnesses,' says YHWH, 'and my servant *whom I have chosen*, that you may know and believe me and understand that I am He'" (Isa. 43:10). This refers to the witness of Israel to the nations.

In the present context it is not possible to present the entire Old Testament theology of election—one must go to the appropriate literature for this. In any case, an important consequence of this theology is Israel's understanding of itself as "people of his [YHWH's] possession" and YHWH's "inherited people," to whom also the promise of "the land" belongs.

An important question is whether the New Testament also knows and recognizes the election of Israel. In answer, the following passages are to be borne in mind:

Acts 13:17–19: "The God of this people Israel chose our fathers and made the people great during their stay in the land of Egypt, and with uplifted arm he led them out of it. And for about forty years he bore with them in the wilderness. And when he had destroyed seven nations in the land of Canaan, he *gave them their land as an inheritance*." Six topics which belong together appear in this text: (1) God as the one choosing; (2) the fathers of Israel as the ones chosen by God; (3) Israel as the "people" of God; (4) reference to the Exodus; (5) reference to the taking of the land; (6) the land as an inheritance. The whole passage could be designated as a summary of the Old Testament theology of election.

Rom. 9:11–13: "Though they [the children of Isaac and Rebecca] were not yet born and had done nothing either good or bad, in order that God's *purpose of election* might continue, not because of works but because of his call, she was told, 'The elder will serve the younger.' As it is written 'Jacob I loved, but Esau I hated.'" In Rom. 9—11 Paul is concerned with the problem of what will happen to the Israel that rejects the gospel. Has it rejected God forever? Why does only "a remnant" of Israel believe the gospel while "[the] Gentiles who did not pursue righteousness have attained it, that is, righteousness through faith" (9:30)? The apostle explains this mystery with a reference to the decision of God to keep to his election (9:11). The God who acts throughout the course of the salvation history, to which Israel belongs by essence, acts according to his sovereign choice, upon which no human being has any influence. "God acts always and everywhere the same" (Ernst Käsemann); as he did in the story of Rebecca, so now he acts with the Jews and Gentiles. Of course his contemporary action does not signify an ultimate rejection of Israel (11:1), but only the temporary setting back of Israel: "Until the full number of Gentiles come in [to the number of those to be saved set by God beforehand]" (11:25). However, in the end "*all* Israel will be saved" (11:26).[16]

Rom. 11:28–29: "As regards the gospel they [the Jews] are enemies of God, for your sake [for the sake of the Gentiles]; but *as regards election* [in view of their previous election] *they are beloved for the sake of their forefathers.* For the gifts and the call of God are irrevocable." The "gifts of God" to Israel show themselves first of all in its election, and this is irrevocable (literally, "unrepented"; God does not repent that he at one time chose Israel); the Jews remain the beloved of God "for the sake of their forefathers."

The election therefore endures; God does not reject Israel which he "foreknew" (knew earlier) (11:2), and therefore in the end even "all Israel will be saved." According to Paul, the election of Israel will never be revoked by God. It is something that will remain, as has been shown. Therefore Christianity must take notice if it wishes to speak and judge correctly about Israel. That is the teaching of the Holy Scriptures.

ISRAEL AS PEOPLE, POSSESSION, AND HERITAGE OF GOD[17]

"YHWH the God of Israel"—"Israel the people of YHWH." This sentence has been designated as the very center of the Old Testament.[18] God has chosen Israel so that it might be his "people," his "special possession," his "inheritance." The Book of Deuteronomy has particularly developed these theologumena. And Moses and the Levitical priests said to all Israel, " 'Keep silence and hear, O Israel: this day you have become the people of YHWH your God' " (Deut. 27:9). The text continues: "You shall therefore obey the voice of YHWH your God, keeping his commandments and his statutes which I command you this day." This is reminiscent of the promulgation of the Law on Sinai and its renewal "today," that is, in the cultic "making present" at the covenantal feast. With the promulgation of the Law, Israel became the people of God; it remains the people of God, but it "always needs a new realization through the living word of YHWH; his address makes the people into the people of YHWH." This concept of people is "therefore neither sociologically nor biologically but rather clearly theologically grounded."[19]

Yet even this is not a sufficient determination, for through the encounter with YHWH Israel became above all "a holy people" (Deut. 7:6; 14:2, 21; 26:19; 28:9). The whole "people theology" (*Volkstheologie*) is grounded in Deut. 7:6b–11 as follows: "YHWH your God has chosen you to be a people for his own possession, out of all the peoples that are on the face of the earth. It was not because you were more in number than any other people that YHWH set his love upon you and chose you, for you were the fewest of all peoples; but it is because YHWH loves you, and is keeping the oath which he swore to your fathers, that YHWH has brought you out with a mighty hand, and redeemed you from the house of bondage, from the hand of Pharaoh king of Egypt. . . . You shall therefore be careful to do the commandment, and the statutes, and the ordinances which I command you this day." Israel is therefore the people of God because God chose it in his unfathomable love. Why Israel? The answer to that question is a mystery known only to God.

Israel is therefore God's "people of possession" (*am segullāh*); cf. Exod. 19:5; Deut. 7:6; 14:2, 26:18. "For YHWH has chosen Jacob for himself, Israel as his own possession" (Ps. 135:4). According to Mal. 3:17, God promises that on the "day" which he will bring about, "they shall be mine, says YHWH of hosts, *my special possession* on the day when I act, and I will spare them as a man spares his son who serves him." That is the eschatological promise to Israel! At the final judgment it will be shown that Israel has always remained God's "possession." Israel, as God's own people," is a "precious, personal possession."[20]

Here also belongs the notion that Israel is YHWH's "possession" (inheritance) (*am nachalah*); cf. Deut. 4:20; 9:26, 29; 1 Kings 8:51; Isa. 47:6, Jon. 2:17; 4:2; Mic. 7:14; Pss. 28:9; 78:62, 71; 94:5, 14; 106:4f., 40. "The close connection of the words *nachalah* and *am* in this connection as the foundation of the YHWH-*nachalah* underscores the particular personal relationship between YHWH and Israel as well as the particular position of Israel among the nations."[21] Through being led out of Egypt, the people Israel becomes YHWH's inheritance; God can dispose of it in sovereign fashion. The concepts *nachalah* and *segullāh* are almost synonymous.

This is not the place to present the Old Testament "people theology" in its entire development; the literature already cited must be consulted. This "people theology" cannot be viewed as belonging to the past and as something finished; it continues to define the self-understanding of the Jewish people. In the entire Rabbinical corpus of writings, Israel and the Jewish people are theologically identical concepts.[22] To be sure, the New Testament also proclaims the Church as the people of God.[23] But the expression "the new people of God" is not found anywhere in the New Testament. The Church is not the people of God which has taken the place of Israel, the Old Testament people of God. Rather, according to Rom. 11:1, the Church is only "the participant in the root" (Israel and its forefathers), the extended people of God who together with Israel form the one people of God. An important text for this is found in the speech of James the brother of the Lord at the Apostolic Council. James based the decision of God to take a people out of the Gentiles for his name (cf. Acts 15:14) in the Scriptures, with citations of Amos 9:11f. and Jer. 12:15: "After this I will return and I will rebuild the dwelling of David, which has fallen; I will rebuild its ruins and I will set it up that the rest of humanity may seek YHWH, and all the Gentiles who are called by my name." This promise by the prophets Amos and Jeremiah, proclaimed for the messianic time of salvation, now finds its fulfillment in the reality that God has built himself a people out of the Jews and Gentiles. For example, it was stated in Zech. 2:15 (LXX), that is, the Septuagint Greek translation of the Hebrew Bible: "There will be many peoples on that day who will seek their refuge in the Lord and they will become his people," which the Targum thus interpreted: "Many peoples will be led to the people of the Lord in that day and they will become one people before me." Thomas C. Kruiff remarks[24]: "Normally the final thought would be expressed in Aramaic as follows: 'they will become one people for my name.' Zech. 2:14–17, however, is the *locus classicus* of the theme which the Septuagint introduced in the text of Amos 9:11–12. If therefore one presumes that Acts 15:14 is playing off of Zech. 2:15, the text gains its full meaning. It is clear that there is not talk here of a substitution of the Gentiles for the Jewish people, but rather of a Christian-Jewish interpretation of the conversion of the Gentiles with help from Zech. 2:14–17 and Amos 9:11: the converted heathen peoples will be inserted into the true Israel." Of course, the New Testament is aware that Israel and the Church, although together the one people of God, temporarily present separated communities which follow different paths, but it nowhere says that after Christ only the Church is the people of God. Paul uses the concept "people" *(laos)* in his epistles almost exclusively in Old Testament citations in Rom. 9:25/Hos. 2:23 ("those who were not my people I will call 'my people' and who was not beloved I will call 'my beloved' "); 9:26/Hos. 2:1 ("and in the very place where it was said to them,

'You are not my people,' they will be called 'sons of the living God' ");
10:21/Isa. 65:2 ("all day long I had held out my hands to a disobedient and
contrary people"); 11:1f. ("I ask, then, *has God rejected his people?* By no
means! I myself am an Israelite, a descendant of Abraham, a member of the
tribe of Benjamin. *God has not rejected his people* whom he foreknew");
15:10/Deut. 32:43 ("and again it is said, 'rejoice, O Gentiles, with his
people!' "); 1 Cor. 10:7/Exod. 32:6 ("The people sat down to eat and drink
and rose to dance"); 14:21/Isa. 28:11f.[25] ("By people of strange tongues and
by the lips of foreigners will I speak to this people, and even then they will
not listen, says the Lord"); 2 Cor. 6:16 ("I will live in them and move among
them, and I will be their God, and they shall be my people"—a combination of Ezek. 37:27 and Lev. 26:12).

In the passages just cited, the concept "people" refers to Israel, but also
to the Church (Christian community), its behavior and its mission. Most
important of all is the passage of Rom. 10:21 ("God stretched out his hands
to the people Israel") and especially 11:1f. ("Has God rejected his people?"); for in this passage it is clear that the people Israel who remain
hardened to the gospel are designated God's people ("his people"), that
God even now has not rejected them! Therefore, Israel, alongside the
Church, still remains God's chosen people. Paul has not written off the
Jewish people, from whom he himself has come forth, because God continues to stretch out his hands toward them. Certainly, "the promise given
to Israel and the present discernible goal of the decree of salvation are split
asunder,"[26] a fact which manifests itself strikingly in the existence of Israel
and the Church living as communities separated from one another. However, if God has not rejected Israel as his people, then Israel exists even
post Christum not as an accidental conglomerate of individuals, but rather
as a people with the characteristics of "peoplehood." That is the way Jews
understand themselves: *We are a people.* And to that extent there is a
distinction between the people of God "Israel" and the people of God "the
Church." The Church is a people of God in a spiritual sense, Israel on the
other hand is also one in an ethnic sense; nevertheless, Israel is more than
and other than the rest of the peoples of the world. It is indeed "a people of
possession" and "heritage" of God. That introduces the obvious tension in
Israel's concrete existence as a people. Israel is an incomparable people set
apart and nevertheless a complete people. Because the Jewish people exist
as a physical people, they are not therefore the people of God in the same
sense as the members of the Church. They are a people and the people of
God at the same time. This is one of the fundamental causes of the inner
tensions which exist in the Jewish people themselves, as well as those

tensions within which the Jewish people live and must live in relationship
to the other peoples and to the Church. These tensions characterize Jewish
existence up to this very day and will also characterize it in the future.
Naturally to be a believer means "something completely other than 'to sit in
the land,' " as M. Görg has correctly remarked;[27] however, for the Jews the
hope for the return of the land springs precisely from their unshakable faith
in the God of their forebears.

ISRAEL AND ITS LAND

No theme "pervades all the areas of the Old Testament in the same
manner [as the theme of the land]; hardly any other would be as suitable as
a structure on which to form an overall outline of the theology of the Old
Testament."[28] Alongside the themes "covenant" and "Torah," the land
belongs to the fundamental themes of Jewish thought and Jewish existence
to this very day.[29]

The "theology of the land" of the Old Testament does not run in a single
line. Rather, it is differentiated. On the one side there are diverse levels of
tradition and their various goals. On the other side there is the concrete
development of the history of the Jewish people in the Old Testament.

According to Gen. 12:1, God says to Abraham: "Go from your country
and your kindred and your father's house *to the land* that I will show you."
This land is the land of Canaan, present-day Palestine (12:5). According to
12:7, God gives to Abraham the promise: "To your descendants I will give
this land." Indeed for the patriarchs the land is at first still a "land of
foreignness" because the Canaanites still live in the land, but this does not
continue: "I will give to you and to your seed after you the land of your
foreignness, the whole land of Canaan, as an eternal possession; and I will
be your God."

The Moses tradition reaches back to this ancient promise: "And I will
bring you into the land which I swore to give to Abraham, Isaac, and to
Jacob; I will give it to you for a possession. I am YHWH" (Exod. 6:8; cf. also
3:8). Later Joshua will be charged to enter the heritage of Moses: "Now
therefore arise, go over this Jordan, you and all this people, into the land
which I am giving to them, to the people of Israel" (Josh. 1:2). In Josh.
21:43f. the taking of the land is expressly approved: "Thus YHWH gave to
Israel all the land which he swore to give to their fathers; and having taken
possession of it, they settled there." Thus is a decisive portion of the early
history of Israel closed. The creedlike summaries of the saving acts of God
for Israel in Deut. 26:5–10 and 6:20–25 find "their decisive goal" (Rolf
Rendtorff) in the giving of the land. As Psalm 105, written prior to the

Chronicler, recalls the ancient saving acts of God for Abraham and his people, so the giving of the land is linked in a significant way with the concept of the "covenant": God "certifies it (the covenant) as valid for Jacob, for Israel, as an eternal covenant: 'the land of Canaan I will give you as your portion for an inheritance!' " (vss. 10f.). According to the conclusion of the psalm, the quid pro quo of the people for the giving of the land is their grateful obedience to the instructions of God ("that they attend to his laws and that they keep his commands"). Covenant, giving of the land, and Torah thus stand in a unique relationship to one another. All three are gifts of God to Israel. Therefore the land is also designated as *nachalah:* Israel receives the land as an "inheritance," but only in the form of a "loan" from God; "he gave their land as a *nachalah,* a *nachalah* to Israel his servant" (Ps. 136:21). Deuteronomy, and especially the Deuteronomic view of history, further developed the theology of the land.[30] "The land of Israel is YHWH's land and the people of Israel is YHWH's people—the two belong indissolubly together" (Rolf Rendtorff). Because the land and the people are totally and entirely YHWH's inheritance, "every false possessor relationship of a nation which thinks in the categories of 'blood and soil' is . . . thereby broken."[31]

However, the giving of the land to Israel is not bound up with a saving guarantee, so the land can be taken away temporarily. This is emphasized above all by the theology of the land as seen in the prophets. The continuing living in the land is bound up with the social structure of the possession of the land and with the loyalty of Israel to the Torah. "Woe to those who join house to house, who add field to field, until there is no more room, and you are made to dwell alone in the midst of the land": Isaiah calls down this woe upon the speculators in land and housing (Isa. 5:8). And Jeremiah proclaimed: "For if you truly amend your ways and your doings, if you truly execute justice with one another, if you do not oppress the alien, the fatherless or the widow, or shed innocent blood in this place, and if you do not go after other gods to your own hurt, then I will let you dwell in this place, *in the land* that I gave of old to your fathers forever" (7:5–7). Particularly through idol worship (the cult of Baal) Israel desecrates the land given to it as a loan: "And I brought you into a plentiful land to enjoy its fruits and its good things. But when you came in you defiled my land, and made my *nachalah* an abomination" (2:7). Therefore must "Israel . . . surely go into exile away from its land" (Amos 7:17). The path into exile is often indicated as the path "away from its land."[32] "Thus he led Israel into exile, away from its land" (2 Kings 17:23; 15:21). "Thus the judgment of YHWH upon Israel in its decisive high points takes the form of the loss of the land."[33] However, the leading away from the land of the fathers is not the last word of YHWH. He will give the land to his people Israel again (cf. Hos. 2:16–25). "For thus says YHWH of hosts, the God of Israel: Houses and fields and vineyards shall again be bought in this land" (Jer. 32:15). The prophet writes to the exiles in Babylon as a "saying of YHWH": "I have . . . for you plans for welfare and not for evil, to give you a future and a hope. . . . I will restore your fortunes and gather you from all the nations and all the places where I have driven you" (29:11, 14; cf. also 30:3). The formula "restore your fortunes" is found eleven times in Jeremiah alone, and elsewhere in the Old Testament it goes together with Israel's return home from its scattering among the nations.[34] In this connection it is important that this promise also continues in the post-exilic prophecy so that one cannot say that it pertains only to the Jews' return home from the Babylonian captivity. Since the Babylonian captivity (586–537 B.C.E.), it is nevertheless true that a large portion of Jewry no longer lives in the land of its fathers, but rather scattered about, in "a Diaspora." "Thereby an essentially new element in addition to the land of Israel enters into the history of Judaism: the *galut*."[35] "Israel remains *one* people in the land and in the *galut*. The tension-filled dialectical relationship between the two characterizes from then on the people's life, thought and belief,"[36] and indeed, so must one add, it continues to do so to this very day. However, the lifting of the *galut*, the returning home of the scattered into the land of the fathers, is predicted for the end of times. According to the Old Testament, not the Messiah, but God himself will lead the scattered back home. The return home precedes the messianic kingdom. "The restitution of the people is the unconditional presupposition of the eschatological lordship of the Messiah, which is included in the lordship of God."[37]

When the Messiah is spoken of, Christian theology thinks of Jesus of Nazareth. What was his relationship to the land of his fathers? First, however, another question: Is the New Testament at all aware of the biblical promise of the land? The promise of the land to Abraham is mentioned in the speech of Stephen (Acts 7:33/Gen. 12:1 LXX) and also in Heb. 11:9: "By faith he [Abraham] sojourned in the land of promise, as in a foreign land, living in tents with Isaac and Jacob, heirs with him of the same promise." Abraham's existence as a foreigner in the promised land is grounded thus in 11:10: "For he looked forward to the city which has foundations, whose builder and maker is God"; that is, the heavenly city. The earthly promised land is thereby eschatologically devalued, which follows the entire theological tendency of the Letter to the Hebrews.[38] Likewise in Matt. 5:5, where the promise of the land from Ps. 37:9, 11 is taken up, the "land" is transformed into a spiritual subject. In the psalm itself the "land" means the land which the "poor received as a pledge of the saving concern and the life-bearing goodness of YHWH" (H. J. Kraus). Concretely the land of the fathers (Palestine) is meant. Early Judaism had related the land to the entire earth and generally interpreted it eschatologically in the sense of the "life to come."[39] Jesus and the gospel tradition probably understood the material handed on in Matt. 5:5 in this same sense. For the rest, however, the promise of the land plays no role in the New Testament, a fact which fits together with the separation of the community of the Church from the community of Israel, which took place in the first century after Christ.

In the period of the primitive Church, the Church had already loosed itself from Israel and thereby also—at least as far as Gentile Christianity is concerned—from the land of Israel. For the Church, according to the New Testament, there is no earthly "promised land" in the sense that there is such for the Jews. However, this should not mislead Christian theology into denying Jews the promised land, the land of their fathers, and into characterizing the Diaspora existence as the only valid existence for Jews, even if there are individual Jewish voices which represent this opinion today.[40] Furthermore, there remains the historical fact that Jesus restricted his mission to Israel and its people, with very few exceptions.[41] Through him the land of Israel has become "the holy land," even if not in the quasi-sacramental sense that the land has in Jewish consciousness. For the Jews the salvation promised them by God is *also* incorporated *in the land;* the land for Israel is a "sensible sign of God's freely working grace and the gracious permission to humanity to make this place itself an effective field of expression of its own obedience."[42] Jewishness, remarks Hans Urs von Balthasar, "is an essential unity of religion and nationhood. In Israel unity is not that cosmic and mystical thing of which the other religions dream in their highest representatives and which is not passed on without a spiritualizing deviation from the concrete individual and particulars; rather, it is grounded much more in that wedding of a particular human being with a particular soil, of an *adam* with an *adamah,* of a personal and people-spirit with this earth: a wedding which is not physical and not chthonic, but rather spiritual and dependent upon the Spirit: through the obedient people which follows the leading of God the land opens itself, it grants rain and fruit; the disobedient people however are driven out of the holy soil into alienation and exile."[43] Among Jewish thinkers none has spoken so profoundly of the connection, specifically the mystical connection, of Israel with its land as has Martin Buber in his little work *Israel and Palestine.*[44]

The biblical promise of the land, which has as its consequence the mystical wedding of Israel with the land of the fathers, is therefore likewise the ultimate source of the so-called *Zionism* which is more than a political movement, even though it is often so interpreted by atheistic Zionists, while "salvation" is seen only in the totally secularized form of the return to Palestine and the exclusively political control of the land. Such a Zionism must be rejected not only by the Christian but also by the Jew. Indeed, the Jew understands himself falsely if he no longer wishes to see the transcendent mystery of his existence, if he understands himself only as one human being among other human beings and only as a member of one people among other peoples. An atheistic Jew is a *contradictio in adiecto*, a self-contradiction. In Zionism the mysterious, unique quality of Jewish existence is again clearly visible, particularly in the unbridgeable tension between Zionism and so-called assimilation Jewry. Paradigmatic for this tension are Jewish figures such as Theodor Herzl and Walter Rathenau and their programs: with Herzl the idea of the "Jewish state," and with Rathenau the idea of "assimilation" *(Anartung)*.[45]

In the meantime the Jewish state has become a reality in the state of Israel and the attempt to achieve *Anartung* has miscarried. The realization as well as the attempt are bound together for the Jewish people in a tragedy of the greatest degree. The fact that the state of Israel became a reality is, in a sense, to be credited to Adolf Hitler; without the persecution of the Jews during the Nazi regime, it may be presumed the Jewish state would not have become a reality. However, the total shipwreck of the *Anartung* is also to be credited to this greatest criminal of German history. For only through the tragedy of their persecution did many of the Jews become clearly aware of their "special existence," as Jews themselves have assured me.

While Rathenau expected the Jewish nation to regain its health from the *Anartung* or assimilation, Herzl and Buber expected it from the return of the people to the land of the fathers, and both were probably right. For it does correspond to the promise of God in the mouth of his prophets, even if no one can say with absolute certainty whether the state of Israel as it currently exists is precisely the fulfillment of the prophetic promise. Nevertheless, the Christian must follow the events in the Near East with the greatest of attention. He can in no case say at the outset that the modern state of Israel has nothing to do with the prophetic promises, however difficult a final pacification in the Near East may appear to be. In any case the Christian cannot avoid the conclusion that without the will of God a return of Israel to the land of its fathers would never have been possible; this does not, however, mean that *all* Israel should return. The principle of representation is valid throughout the Bible. Even at the time of Jesus only one-eighth of the Jews lived in Palestine, the great majority being in the Diaspora. For the rest, it is not the task of this tractate on the Jews to give concrete political instructions. What, however, is the duty of all Christians is this—to pray for a lasting peace in the Near East with regard to Israel as well as with regard to its Arab neighbors. The existence of the state of Israel brings the world and the Church daily into awareness that Jews exist and that God has not excluded them from his guidance. Therefore the state of Israel is a *sign* that cannot be overlooked. B. Klappert gives three models of a theological understanding of the promise of the land of Israel:[47]

1. The *model of christological implication* according to which the land is "placed" in Jesus Christ; the land "is understood as a necessary and concrete implication of the covenant which is fulfilled in Jesus Christ as the Messiah of Israel." This model is too direct.

2. The *model of theological indifference* which speaks of a crisis of the promises to the people and the land which has been caused by Jesus Christ; thus the Christian could, and indeed would have to be, indifferent toward the question of the land, an attitude which is widespread.

3. The *model of symbolic analogy* in which "a christological-theological reflection and meditation see the de facto possessing of the land and statehood of Israel as the fulfillment of the covenant of God with Israel; thus the statehood of Israel should be understood and appreciated as a sign of the loyalty of YHWH to his people, as a sign of the validity of the promises of God to the people Israel, and as a sign of the remaining parallels and not-yet parallels to the covenant fulfilled in the Messiah of Israel."[48] Seen thus, the state of Israel is "a sign of the end of the dispersion and the beginning of the return home" (J. Moltmann) and therewith *a sign of hope* as much for Israel as for the Church.

THE CONTINUING COVENANT OF GOD WITH ISRAEL

God made a covenant with his chosen people Israel. The Old Testament tells of this. The question which concerns us in this tractate on the Jews is this: Has this covenant of God with Israel been terminated because of the "hardening" of Israel toward the gospel, or does it continue? The answer to this cannot be attained through speculation, but only through an inquiry into the New Testament. What does the New Testament say about this? Here are two important texts:

Acts 3:25

"You are the sons of the prophets and of the covenant which God gave to your fathers, saying to Abraham, 'And in your posterity shall all the families of the earth be blessed.'" The promise of blessing to Abraham (cf. Gen. 12:3; 18:18; 22:18) is related in Genesis to all the "nations" *(ethnē)* of the earth. But in the speech of Peter in the Temple square (Acts 3:12–26) it concerns all "generations *(patriai)* of the earth," whereby on the basis of the context, the generations of the people Israel are meant. These will be blessed through the servant of God, Jesus, whom God has "raised up . . . first for you," that is, to the good of Israel, that he might bless the sons of Israel through the forgiveness of sins which they have committed, especially the killing of Jesus (cf. Acts 3:15, 26). The Jews are thereby addressed by the Lukan Peter as "the sons of the prophets and of the covenant." The expression "sons of the covenant," also found in Ezek. 30:5 and the Song of Sol. 17:15, which Peter uses concerning Israel, declares the Jews to be those who belong to the covenant which God once made with the forefather of Israel. They are taken up in connection with the covenant which begins with Abraham. What is important about Peter's formulation is that it is in the present: "You *are* the sons of the prophet and of the covenant"; therefore, they still are, even though they have killed "the author of life [Jesus]" (Acts 3:15). The Jews' belonging to the covenant which God founded with Abraham is not eliminated with the killing of Jesus; it continues to exist— and nowhere in the Acts of the Apostles does it say that one day it will be terminated—for example, when it becomes clear that the great majority of Israel continues to reject the gospel proclaimed in the post-Easter mission. On the contrary, according to Acts 1:6, God will "restore the kingdom to Israel" at the end of days (for further details see below pp. 36ff.).[49]

Rom. 11:26f.

"And so all Israel will be saved [in the end]; as it is written, 'the Deliverer will come from Zion, he will banish ungodliness from Jacob'; *and this [is (will be)] my [established] covenant with them [for their good]* when I take away their sins." Paul here combines Scripture citations from Isa. 59:20f. and 27:9 and adapts them to the final salvation of Israel. This final salvation, the saving of all Israel, is thereby declared a "covenant" by the apostle which God will establish with Israel or already has established. It cannot be determined whether the reference to the covenant is meant in a present or a future sense, since in the scriptural verse 11:27a a verb is missing ("a nominal sentence").[50] Also, there is nothing about a "new" covenant in the text. If one supplies an "is" (present), then the sentence is to be understood thus: This (namely, the coming absolution of the sins of Israel by God) will be the renewal of the covenant once established by God with Israel. If one supplies a "will be" (future), then a final establishment of the covenant of

God with Israel is proclaimed. However, because this covenant will not be made with any individual, but rather with the ancient covenant people Israel, the apostle declares thereby once again that God has not rejected his people Israel (cf. Rom. 11:1), but instead remains the loyal covenant partner of Israel. God does not release Israel from the covenant relationship. This covenant is "for them," for their advantage (Dat. comm. *autois*), and goes forth from God *(par' emou):* The initiative remains as always, and thus also here, completely with God; it comes forth from his boundless mercy which does not let him forget his ancient covenant people Israel. "The promise still always remains over Israel. And if now only a 'remnant' hears it and 'some' trust in it, thus God will in the end fulfill it for 'all Israel' so that every single Jew as a member of his people continues to remain under the promise."[51]

"JOY IN THE TORAH"

If Christians wish to understand Judaism, then they must above all grasp the relationship of the Jew to the Torah. This relationship has a long prehistory reaching back into the Old Testament, which in its details is not very easy to explain, as research indicates.[52]

The term "torah" is found in the Hebraic Old Testament 220 times. Its meaning is "instruction," "law." There are synonymous, or half-synonymous, concepts for torah, such as "wisdom," "word," "way." However, the "wisdom" Torah must be distinguished from the "legal" Torah. In professedly theological connections, one must distinguish between the Torah of God, the Torah of the priests, and the Torah of Moses.[53] The teaching of the Torah originally belonged to the tasks of the priests; they "teach Jacob your *mishpatim* (ordinances) and Israel your Torah" (Deut. 33:10). "2 Chronicles 15:3 (cf. Lamentations 2:9) illuminates the fact that the absence of a 'teaching priest' . . . in Israel is equated with the absence of the true God and with the absence of the Torah."[54] The priestly Torah is the equivalent of the Torah of YHWH; it was published orally and it transmitted to the laity information about the correct distinction between holy and profane, clean and unclean, about Pesach, specific sacrifices, leprosy, discharge, and Nazirites.[55] The priests thereby utilized the *da'at* tradition. The entire priestly teaching tradition had been made known in the time of Ezra.[56]

The prophets Hosea and Jeremiah spoke in opposition to the Torah interpretation of the priests and "stressed the Torah of YHWH," whereby Hosea "understood not individual teachings, but rather the 'entire expression of the will of YHWH' which is already fixed in writing (H. W.

Wolff)."[57] Isaiah complains to the Israelites because they "despised the Torah of YHWH" (Isa. 5:24), that they "are sons who do not listen to the Torah of YHWH" (Isa. 30:9).[58] Also in Jeremiah the formula "Torah of YHWH" is used polemically against priest and people (Jer. 6:19; 8:8). It has been supposed that this pointed speech about the "Torah of YHWH" was connected to the Sinai tradition.[59] The "Torah of YHWH" is likewise the key word in the so-called Torah Psalms, especially in Ps. 119. This psalm expresses above all the *joy* of the just and the pious in the Torah, which until today defines the relationship of the believing Jew to the Torah and which has led to its own festival, "joy in the Torah," which is celebrated in connection with the feast of Succoth. "The torah piety of these psalms is in contrast to the older torah understanding primarily related to individuals, not to the people."[60] Joy in the Torah is manifoldly expressed in the Old Testament and in Judaism,[61] especially as exemplified in Ps. 119: "In the way of thy testimonies I delight as much as in all riches" (119:14). "I will delight in thy statutes; I will not forget thy word" (119:16). "Thy testimonies are my delight, they are my counselors" (119:24). "I find my delight in thy commandments, which I love" (119:47). "Let thy mercy come to me, that I may live; for thy law is my delight" (119:77). "Oh, how I love thy law! It is my meditation all the day" (119:97). "Thy commandment makes me wiser than my enemies, for it is ever with me" (119:98). "Thy word is a lamp to my feet and a light to my path" (119:105). "Thy testimonies are my heritage for ever; yea, they are the joy of my heart" (119:111). "Hold me up, that I may be safe and have regard for thy statutes" (119:117). "Great peace have those who love thy law; nothing can make them stumble" (119:165). "My soul keeps thy testimonies; I love them exceedingly" (119:167). "I long for thy salvation, O Lord, and thy law is my delight" (119:174).

There is a close connection between "torah" and the name of Moses, especially in the Deuteronomic and Chronicler's literature of the Old Testament. Here the concept of "torah" no longer means the individual commandments, but rather the overall revelation of the will of God to Israel. This finds expression in formulas such as the following: "This [entire] Torah" (Deut. 1:5; 4:8; 17:18; 31:9–11; 29:20; 30:10; 31:26); "[All] the words of this Torah" (17:19; 27:3, 8, 26; 28:58; 29:28; 31:12, 24); "The Torah of Moses [which Moses had given]" (1:5; 4:8, 44; 31:9).[62] "Torah" has now gradually become the fixed written will of God, the written Torah. In Chronicles the formulas "Torah of Moses" and "Torah of God" stand next to one another. Now the Torah has become a grand thing of timeless validity and is identical with the entire Pentateuch. However, there also appears a tendency to strongly stress the individual commandments of the Torah and

to explain them casuistically. Indeed, the growing view which had manifested itself in the prophets Hosea and Jeremiah and also in Deuteronomy
of the unit of the "law" now leads to the entire Old Testament being
referred to as "Torah," a development which also found its expression in the
Torah piety of the Psalms.[63] With the frequent use of the Hebrew term
"torah" in the Jewish translation of the Old Testament into Greek, the
Septuagint, as *nomos* (law), it is natural that the legal element of the Torah
should receive strong emphasis. "On the other side, the significant elements in *torah* which expand the legal viewpoint in the direction of
teaching, counsel, and revelation have to a certain degree gone into *nomos*
and at times tend to burst the framework of this word in its Greek setting."[64]

In early Judaism the Torah becomes increasingly the bearing foundation
of the relationship of Israel to God. Oftentimes the term "Law" refers
simply to the Pentateuch, because the legal portions in it are felt to be
central. The entire Scriptures receive the title "The Law and the Prophets"
(2 Macc. 15:9).[65]

The divine binding quality of the Law is strongly emphasized and the
superordination of the Law over all other religious institutions becomes
visible. "Indeed, the Law is more important than the Temple, learnedness
in the Scriptures is more important than priestly activity."[66] The revolt of
the Maccabees takes place under the sign of the "Law" (cf. 1 Macc. 1:41ff.);
the Pharisaic group which gradually arose in connection with it was especially determined "under all circumstances and including all consequences
to hold itself to the Law and to the Law alone."[67] The danger of the cultural
foreignization of the people in the Hellenistic period led to seeing the Law
as a defensive and isolating agent; the Torah became a "fence" around
Israel. Hellenistic civilization was a "secular power" in Palestine with many
dangers for Judaism which had to be defended against.[68] The major help in
this was provided by the Law, which in connection with the Wisdom
literature came to form an entire "Torahogy" ("Torah-ontology"), whereby
Wisdom transferred to Torah its cosmic functions.[69] The statements about it
(Wisdom) were transferred to Torah:

> That Torah is created before the world.
> The Torah was by God.
> The Torah is of divine origin ("my daughter").
> The Torah was God's instrument of creation.
> The Torah brings life.
> The Torah is light.
> The Torah is truth.
> The Torah is a kind of presence of God in the world.
> The Torah represents precisely God himself.

In connection with this process of transfer, the Torah became a cosmic figure: Just as the world is ordered by the Wisdom of God, now the Torah becomes the "Law of the world" and the "order of life"; for it is the expression of the order of Creation.[70] Therefore "every attack on the Torah . . . necessarily had also to be understood as an attack on the order of Creation desired and set out by God."[71] "God does not stand outside of or above these orders, but rather he manifests *himself* in them. That is, the order which is revealed in the Law is a part of the divine work."[72]

Doubtless, in the course of the history of Israel there can also be observed an increasingly strong presentation of Torah as connected with the political fate of Israel. As a consequence of the national catastrophe in the sixth century B.C.E., a new understanding of the Torah came forth from prophetic influence; for the catastrophe was indeed said to be caused precisely by the manifold violation of the divine Law (Jeremiah, Ezekiel). And especially after the national catastrophes of the first and second centuries of the Common Era, which brought with them the definitive loss of the Temple and of the land, the Torah remained to Judaism the only integrating factor, alongside its feasts, which distinguished it from the Gentiles. Thus, for Jewish sensitivity the Torah is no abstract element, no "dead letter," but rather the constitution of the covenant with its God, to which Israel is bound if it does not wish to fall under the curse of God.[73] For Jewish consciousness covenant and Torah cannot be separated from one another: "Under covenant nothing other than Torah is to be understood" (*Mekilta* Exod. 12:6). The Law is "always related to the covenant."[74] Cf. also Ben Sirach 17:11ff.: "He bestowed knowledge upon them, and allotted to them the Law of life. He established with them an eternal covenant, and showed his judgments"; 24:23: "All this is the book of the covenant of the most high God, the Law which Moses commanded us as an inheritance for the congregations of Jacob," whereby under *sefer berit* nothing other than the Pentateuch is meant, the book of the Law clearly and simply: "Moses commanded us a law, as a possession for the assembly of Jacob" (Deut. 33:4). The field of words which belong together—"commandment," "law," "(eternal) covenant"—is found also in Isa. 24:5. The Community Rule of Qumran demands that "the commands of God be fulfilled in the covenant of grace" (1 QS I, 7f.). Torah is a grace, not a burden![75] The fulfilling of the instructions of the Torah is for Jews the consequence of their relationship to God which rests primarily on *emunah* and on obedience to God. The Habakkuk commentary from Qumran understands the sentence from Hab. 2:4 "The righteous shall live by his *emunah*" thus: "This refers to all in Jewry who carry out the Torah. On account of the labor and their faith in

him who expounded the Law aright, God will deliver them from the house
of judgment" (VIII:1).

The Jew's understanding of life according to the Law is therefore often
completely different from that attributed to him by Christians. He understands life according to the Law precisely not as "a collection of earnings" or
as an "accomplishment" leading to his honor before God. Rather, the Jew's
understanding of life according to the Torah which remains valid to this
very day must be grasped on the basis of three fundamental elements
which determine the Jewish understanding of faith: *emunah,* realization in
works, sanctification of the everyday.[76] The Hebrew "concept of faith,"
emunah, means primarily "trust" ("to entrust" something to God).[77] The
Jew however cannot imagine *emunah* without the obedient realization of
the instructions of God according to the Torah. "To believe, in Jewish
understanding, is not an experience or a being grasped by someone or
something, but rather a doing, a making, a completing and a carrying out
. . . an activity, a deed with the accent on realization."[78] For the Jew, faith as
obedience to Torah, which God gave to Israel, is the sanctification of the
everyday. For that is the real meaning of the instructions of the Torah in
Jewish understanding: Whoever daily and in all things submits himself to
the yoke of the Law, de-profanates thereby the everyday and sanctifies the
entire life in all its relationships and expressions. Judaism is a religion of
sanctity! The "timeless" Torah works in time and history.[79]

"The Jewish Law forms a way of life of partial asceticism. No area of
existence, no particle of the universe is excluded, nothing is given unlimited freedom."[80] "Human life is not worthless or banal, but it also
deserves in its most elementary expressions to be consciously directed
toward a goal and pervaded with the divine. The fulfilling of a commandment therefore is not the bending under the whip of the lawgiver, but
rather, when correctly understood, the making happy of the one who walks
in the divine way which can give eternal value."[81] Therein the joy of the Jew
in the Torah is grounded; that is the reason for his desire to fulfill the
instructions of God. This therefore has nothing to do with a mere formal
obedience to the Law, with an ethical formalism, which many Christians
attribute to the Jews. The Jew fulfills the Law *because he loves the God* who
has made an eternal covenant with Israel. Rabbi Jochanan ben Zakkai
classically formulated how the Jew thinks about obedience to the Torah: "If
you have held to the Torah in a rich measure, you have thereby done
nothing in your favor; for you have been created for that" (*Mishnah* Abot II,
8b). "Whereby Hanina, son of Akaschia, said: the Holy One, praised be he,
wished to show his appreciation for Israel, and therefore he multiplied his

instructions and commandments to it, for he said: 'the Lord had the desire to make the instruction great and glorious for the sake of his grace' " (*Mishnah* Makkot III, 16). Rabbi Jehoshua, son of Levi, said: Whoever is traveling and has no accompaniment with him should concern himself with the instruction, for it says: "A lovely accompaniment . . ." (Prov. 1:9a). Whoever has a headache should concern himself with the instruction, for it says: "They are a lovely accompaniment for your head" (Prov. 1:9d). Whoever has a pain in the throat should concern himself with the instruction, for it says: "And a necklace for your throat" (Prov. 1:9c). Whoever has pain in the body should concern himself with the instruction, for it says: "It will be a healing for your body" (Prov. 3:8a). Whoever has pains in his members should concern himself with the instruction, for it says: "A refreshing drink for your members" (Prov. 3:8b). Whoever has pains throughout his whole body should concern himself with the instruction, for it says: "And a healing for all your flesh" (Prov. 4:22).[82] "Do not ask me whether a world without Jews means a world without Torah. However, a world without Torah is a world without Jews."[83]

For Paul, of course, Christ is "the end of the Law unto righteousness for everyone who believes" (Rom. 10:4). This thesis of the apostle is not founded on the notion that he thinks of the Law as something of lesser value which misleads people to a merely formal obedience, but rather on his christological convictions. I shall return to this later.[84]

THE SALVATION HISTORICAL ADVANTAGES
OF ISRAEL ACCORDING TO
ROMANS 9:4f. AND EPHESIANS 2:12[85]

"Then what advantage has the Jew? Or what is the value of circumcision?" asks Paul in Rom. 3:1, and he responds: "Much in every way. To begin with, the Jews are entrusted with the oracles of God" (3:2). "The oracles of God" entrusted to the Jews are "concretely the words of the promise and of the Law."[86] The apostle does not enumerate further gifts to Israel here, but he does so in Rom. 9:4f.: "They are Israelites, and to them belong the sonship, the glory, the covenants, the giving of the law, the worship, and the promises: to them belong the patriarchs, and of their race, according to the flesh, is the Christ." The here-enumerated advantages of Israel are also called its "privileges," which God has granted to it.

The Jews are allowed to call themselves "Israelites" after the honorific name "Israel" which Jacob once received (Gen. 32:38f.) and which was transferred to the people. To them belongs the sonship; for Israel is, according to Exod. 4:22, "the first-born son" of God (cf. also Hos. 11:1). To them belongs the glory, the *kabod YHWH;* it accompanied Israel on its journey through the desert (Exod. 16:10; 24:16; 40:34f.; Lev. 9:6, 23 and elsewhere), and as a sign of the graceful presence of God it filled the Temple as soon as the ark of the covenant was placed there (cf. 3 Kings 8:10f.; 2 Chron. 5:14). And the devout Jew is convinced that the glory of God (the *shekinah*) still dwells to this very day in the Temple square at the place of the most holy and accompanies Israel everywhere that it might dwell. "When one draws to one's attention that in Rom. 3:23 it states: 'since all have sinned and fall short of the *glory* of God,' this statement in Rom. 9:4 becomes only all the more extraordinary."[87] To them belong the covenants in a comprehensive sense.[88] To them belong the giving of the Law—the apostle is thinking here less of the Torah as such than the act of giving of the Law on Sinai, which granted Israel an honor. To them belongs the worship, which indeed at the time of the apostle was still carried out in the Temple at Jerusalem. To them belong the promises, which meant the promises given to the fathers of Israel, especially the promise of the Messiah. To them belong the fathers: Abraham, Isaac, and Jacob (see the following details of the apostle in Rom. 9:7ff.). And from them came the Christ according to the flesh: to be sure, a position stemming from the believing view of the Christian Paul, for whom Jesus is the Messiah, but in his eyes it is nevertheless a special honor for Israel that the Messiah has come from it and from nowhere else in the world.

That the advantages of Israel are not the past gifts to Israel, but rather the continuing ones, is clear from the present tense, "they *are* Israelites," at the beginning of 9:4,[89] and from the fact that for Paul, Christ is not dead. That "however" these advantages and privileges of Israel have "now" been transferred to the Church, as H. Schlier suggests,[90] is precisely not said by Paul. The Church participates in part in these advantages because, according to Rom. 11:17, it has by grace become "a sharer in the root" of Israel. The apostle does not refer to former advantages of Israel which in the meanwhile have been lost to the Church; rather he enumerates them because for him it is all the more astounding that the majority of Israel, despite these advantages, has not been obedient to the gospel, and could therefrom pose the following question: "What if some were unfaithful? Does their faithlessness nullify the faithfulness of God?" (Rom. 3:3). The apostle answers himself: "By no means! Let God be true though every man be false" (Rom. 3:4). And God will show himself true when in the end, despite its partial hardening toward the gospel, he will save all Israel (Rom. 11:26). His loyalty to Israel cannot be nullified. Therefore the Christian must look upon the privileges of Israel with reverence and gratitude because through the kindness and mercy of God he is permitted to participate in them. "Paul then puts forth in detail in Rom. 9—11 the evidence that the Word of God has retained its truth and the people of God their specialness in spite of their disbelief, that God despite the disbelief of Israel remains God."[91]

Likewise in view of Eph. 2:12 one can speak of the privileges of Israel.[92] For the statements made here concerning the theological situation of the Gentiles are made *within the horizon of Israel,* of the "circumcision" (cf.2:11). The fundamental assertion about the Gentiles, to whom the addressees of the epistle once belonged—"you were at that time without Christ"—is subsequently made explicit in detail: You were alienated from the commonwealth of Israel. You were strangers to the covenants of promise. You had no hope.[93] You were without God *(atheoi)* in the world.[94] If one formulates these five statements on the unsaved condition of the Gentiles in a positive way with a view to Israel, then they would sound as follows; Israel possesses the hope of the Messiah. Israel forms a "commonwealth" *(politeia):* the *qehal* YHWH. To Israel belong the covenants of the promise. Israel possesses thereby hope. Israel lives in community with God and in the knowledge of God in the world.

These five sentences signify five privileges which belonged to Israel as opposed to the Gentiles, who lacked them as long as they were Gentiles. "Now" of course they have changed "in Christ Jesus" from being "far" to being "near." The "dividing wall" once erected between Jews and Gentiles represented by the Torah, the "fence" around Israel, has been broken down by Christ and out of the two, Jews and Gentiles, a single community *(hen soma)* has been created in the Church and a spiritual temple erected in which both have the same access to the Father (cf. Eph. 2:13–22).[95] Doubtless the author of the epistle is thinking of the new community in the Church consisting of Jewish Christians and Gentile Christians, but he does not say that Israel had lost its privileges enumerated in 2:12. Of course, he does not leave out the fate of salvation of that Israel which had not found the path to the gospel. The noteworthy thing here, however, is that the ecclesiology is developed entirely within the horizon of Israel, out of the instinctive knowledge that the Church without its "root" Israel would be an ahistorical abstraction. There is no ecclesiology without reference to Israel. "Fundamentally we can no longer speak of Israel as if we were dealing there with a noteworthy, perhaps even interesting, given, which one can observe as an uninvolved onlooker, or one could take note of as an additional enrichment of knowledge."[96] The Gentile Christians, indeed, are in Jesus

Christ only *"fellow* heirs, members of the same body, and partakers of the promises" (Eph. 3:6) which Israel was once granted by God.

"SALVATION IS FROM THE JEWS"
(JOHN 4:22)

This sentence is found in the pericope of John's Gospel in which the encounter of Jesus with the Samaritan woman is related (John 4:1–42) within this context: "Our fathers worshiped on this mountain; and you say that in Jerusalem is the place where men ought to worship. Jesus said to her, 'Woman, believe me, the hour is coming when neither on this mountain nor in Jerusalem will you worship the Father. *You* worship what you do not know; *we* worship what we know, *for salvation is from the Jews*" (4:20–22). This justification at the end of verse 22 is astounding in face of the "anti-Judaism" otherwise found in the Gospel of John. [97] For here we have before us an unambiguously positive statement about the Jews in the fourth Gospel:[98] From the Jews is salvation and not from any other people! The preposition "from" *(ek)* indicates the source of salvation.

In the speech of Jesus the concern is about the coming place of the worship of the Father. His response is as follows: This coming place is identical neither with Gerizim, the sacred mountain of the Samaritan people, of whom today a small remnant exists, nor with Jerusalem, where until the year A.D. 70 the Temple of the Lord with its sacrificial cult was located. The coming place of the worship of the Father is much rather there where God "in spirit and truth" will be worshiped (cf. 4:23).

Within this structure what function does the response of Jesus in verse 22 have? This is a difficult question. It concerns the worship of God of the Samaritans and of the Jews. In it the Samaritans' worship of God is clearly downgraded ("you worship what you do not know"), while the Jews' worship of God is upgraded ("we worship what we do know"). In the "we" Jesus identifies himself with the "Jews," as likewise the Samaritan woman expressly speaks of his being a Jew in 4:9 *(su Ioudaios ōn)*. The positive evaluation of the Jews' worship of God is supported with the sentence: "Because salvation is from the Jews." Within the entire structure of the section 4:21–23, therefore, verse 22 has the function of supporting the salvation historical precedence of the Jews over the Samaritans. For the Jews "know" that the messianic salvation comes from among *their* number, and likewise John the Evangelist and the Christians are convinced that the Messiah, who, according to their faith conviction is none other than Jesus of Nazareth (cf. John 1:41, 49), "is from the Jews," as corresponds to the Christian proclamation according to the witness of the New Testament (cf.

the infancy narrative of Jesus in Matthew and Luke; Rom. 1:3, etc.).[99] C. H. Dodd calls the sentence "Salvation is from the Jews" "a far-reaching equivalence" of the statement of the prologue in John 1:14: "And the word became flesh and dwelled among us and we have seen his glory."[100] It is therefore incorrect to see in John 4:22 a "gloss" of later redaction[101] or "a marginal remark of the reader of the Bible which a copier of the Bible text viewed as the original text and therefore had copied into the text."[102] One could also designate the sentence "Salvation is from the Jews" as a parallel to that in Rom. 9:5 in which Paul mentions among the privileges of Israel the fact that the "Christ according to the flesh" stems from the Jews. We are not here concerned with a gloss[103] which in secondary fashion was inserted into the original text. Rather, the verse specifies within its context the presupposition of why now the Father will no longer be worshiped on the mountain Gerizim or in Jerusalem, but rather "in spirit and in truth," namely, in the *locus cultus* which has become personal in Jesus Christ. However, even with this the sentence "Salvation is from the Jews" has not yet been adequately analyzed.

The abstract sounding term "salvation" *(hē sōtēria)* must still be considered in itself (not "the Savior of the world" as in 4:42 at the end of the pericope; or "the Messiah" as in 4:25). Why this abstract choice of words? Is "salvation" here really only *abstractum pro concreto*, that is, simply identical with the "Savior" (the Messiah), as many commentators assume? In the Nestle edition of the New Testament in the margin alongside John 4:22, a cross-reference to Rom. 11:18 is indicated which seems to be correct. There the talk is of the "root" which bears the Church, and by the "root" Israel is meant.[104] Thus it appears that the term "salvation" in John 4:22 is more than the Messiah, the eschatological bringer of salvation, who for the Church is identical with Jesus. It should be noted that the term "salvation" *(hē sōtēria)* appears here only in the Gospel of John. Thus verse 22b is not a secondary gloss, but rather an ancient statement of conviction (of Jewish-Christian provenance?) which was taken over by the evangelist into his Gospel because it also corresponded to his faith conviction, as it belonged to the faith conviction of the entire Church, that the salvation of the world indeed "is from the Jews"—and the present tense of "is" *(estin)* is to be particularly noted. Indeed, it does not say in the text that salvation "comes" *(erchetai)* from the Jews; rather, it "is" from the Jews. Should verse 22b really be dealing with an ancient sentence from pre-Johannine tradition— for which the apodictic brevity and precision appear to argue—then that community which formulated it for the first time emphasized with him that *the eschatological salvation of the world remains with Judaism;* it "is from the Jews." Although for the rest John the Evangelist may live and write at a distance from the Jews, he has through the positive reception of this sentence confessed to the root of the Church just as Paul did, despite his "un-Jewish" teaching about justification.

Can present-day Christendom ever forget this sentence? Had Christendom never forgotten it, perhaps a theological anti-Semitism with its fearful consequences would never have been possible. Sentences have their consequences!

"ALL ISRAEL WILL BE SAVED"
(ROMANS 11:26)

The sentence of the apostle in Rom. 11:26 "All Israel will be saved" will be analyzed in the following in response to five questions: (1) Who is meant by "all Israel"? (2) In what manner will "all Israel" be saved? (3) Why will "all Israel" be saved? (4) Why does Paul confess "the mystery" of the salvation of "all Israel"?[105] (5) Finally, is the notion of the salvation of Israel at the end of time found anywhere else in the New Testament?

Who Is Meant by "All Israel"?

The Term "Israel" in the Epistle to the Romans

The term "Israel" is found in the Epistle to the Romans eleven times, all within chapters 9—11, which of course is connected with the subject of those chapters: It concerns the ultimate salvific fate of the Jewish people. The term "Jew" or "Jews" also appears eleven times, although only twice in Rom. 9—11. Paul speaks of "Jews" especially in distinction to "Greeks" (cf. for example Rom. 10:12: For there is no distinction between Jew and Greek. What is meant here is that the word of the prophet [Isa. 28:16], "He who puts his faith in it shall not be shaken," is valid for the Jews as well as for the Gentiles; for "the same Lord is Lord of all and bestows his riches upon all who call upon him" [Rom. 10:12b]). By "Israel" is meant the Jewish people which has been adorned with this ancient honorary title, Jewry as the people of God. "Israel is from the beginning a sacral concept; it refers to the entirety of those chosen by Yahweh and who are united in the Yahweh cult"; it is a "spiritual self-designation."[106] Thus it is also with Paul in Rom. 9—11. Nevertheless, in view of his formulation in 9:6 ("for not all who are descended from Israel belong to Israel"), a restriction must be made. The term "Israel" has in both halves of this sentence different meanings. "All who are descended from Israel" means all those who belong to the people Israel, while the formulation "belong to Israel" has a limiting significance ("not all"!); for with this is meant those Jews who have been obedient to the gospel. Here, therefore, the term "Israel" breaks through a purely folkish conception of "Israel," without encompassing the Gentile Christians in "Israel." Rather, it is to be understood as Paul himself interprets in 9:8: "It is not the children of the flesh who are the children of God, but the children of the promise" who are acknowledged, and therefore only the children of the "choice." The limitation in Rom. 9:6 is therefore specified by the notion of the "choice." The "choice" refers to the people Israel: some of which—in 11:5 "a remnant, chosen by grace"—God chose in a free choice and they listened to the gospel; the others from it—in 11:7b "the rest"—God hardened and they did not listen to the gospel. A partial "hardening" came upon Israel (11:25).

Otherwise, however, Paul in Rom. 9—11 uses the terms "Israel" monosemantically. The question also comes up: Is this also true for the formula "all Israel" in 11:26? An exegesis of this passage must deal with this question. The unique semantic differentiation in Rom. 9:6 is connected precisely with the real questions of the apostle in Rom. 9—11: How is it possible for a portion of Israel to remain "hardened" toward the gospel? And: Did God reject this hardened portion of Israel for all time and exclude it from salvation?

Diachronic Use of the Term "Israel"

What results from a diachronic observation of the term "Israel"? The Septuagint often speaks of "all Israel" and means with that the people in its entirety.[107] In the exegesis of Rom. 11:26 *Mishnah* Sanhedrin X, 1a is always referred to: "All Israel has a part in the world to come, for it says [in Isa. 60:21] 'Your people shall all be righteous; they shall possess the land forever,'" that is, eternal life. The Jewish scholar S. Krauss remarked on this in the "Giessener Mishnah" (Giessen [1933], p. 264): "The sentence is framed in view of the criminal in Israel, which the discussion up until now concerned, and the life to come which they will participate in if in the hour of their death they arouse penitence [cf. VI, 2]; this is also the only basis on which this apparently dogmatic sentence would be taken into this tractate." In X, 1b–3h all those are enumerated then who will have no participation in the life to come. Likewise *Mishnah* Rosh Hashana is formulated in III, 1a in reference to the moon: "The court of justice and all Israel have seen it. . . ." A diachronic observation of the linguistic use of "all Israel" allows/permits the formula to be understood as expression for the entirety of Israel.

"All Israel" Seen in the Context of Romans 11:26

We pose the question: In what sense here is "all Israel" used? Perhaps simply as it is in the Septuagint? That is not the case. For here there is very clearly a tension between the attributes "all (Israel)" and "part" *(apo merous)* from the preceding verse: a "hardening" (toward the Christ and the gospel) for a specifically limited time or on a specifically limited portion has come upon Israel, the Jewish people, from God. It lasts "until the full number of the Gentiles (specified by God) come in." The "remnant, chosen by grace" had at that time accepted the gospel—Paul was thinking of the Jewish-Christians of his time—"but the rest were hardened (by God)" (11:5–8), but not for all eternity, but rather only "until the full number of the Gentiles come in."

Who, therefore, is meant by "all Israel" in Rom. 11:26? The attributive "all" before "Israel" both of itself and on the basis of the diachronic linguistic usage does not here permit a limitation of the term "Israel" in the sense of Rom. 9:6, that is, a limitation to that Israel which has accepted the gospel, or indeed to the Church as the (alleged) true Israel.[108] Rather, "all Israel" consists of the "remnant" who by the grace of God have accepted the gospel and the "rest" who were hardened (by God)—cf. 11:5–7. A reference to the entirety of Israel also turns up in 10:16 when the apostle there formulates: "But they have not all [of Israel] heeded the gospel." "Not all" means a portion of Israel, namely, those who remained "hardened." One must therefore describe the formula "all Israel" as the sum of an addition; in this sense Paul modified the handed-on formula.

From the perspective of this insight the much-disputed "and thus" *(kai houtōs)* at the beginning of 11:26 can also be explained. It is often incorrectly understood as an anticipation of the "how" *(kathōs)* in verse 26b, in the sense: All Israel will "thus," that is, in this manner, be saved "as it is written" in Isa. 59:20f. "And thus—as" is understood as a parallel relationship. However, had Paul such a parallel in mind, then he would have placed the "thus" in verse 26a in another position in the sentence and would have begun it without the particle "and" *(kai):* All Israel will *thus,* that is, in this manner, be saved as it is written in Isaiah. Rather, Paul proclaims: "The remnant" of Israel, that part which had accepted the gospel, God had already saved, as corresponds to the prophetic statement of Rom. 9:27 (Isa. 10:20: "The remnant will be saved"). But also "the rest," whom God for incomprehensible reasons "hardened," will be saved by him, namely, when the "full number of the Gentiles come in." "And thus" *in the end*—the apostle states this prophetically—"all Israel will be saved." The emphasis lies on the attributive "all" *(pas): All* Israel will be saved, not just a part of it, for example, that portion which has accepted the gospel. Incidentally, that the "hardened" part of Israel which was not able to obey the gospel will be saved by God is stated by Paul with the help of the Isaiah citation not for the first time in 11:26b; he had announced this earlier with all possible clarity in verse 24: "For if you have been cut from what is by nature a wild olive tree, and grafted, contrary to nature, into a cultivated olive tree, *how much more will these natural branches be grafted back into their own olive tree.*" This is an indicative statement and prediction without limitation: God will re-engraft them.

Did "All Israel" Mean Then or Throughout History?

Concerning the formula "all Israel" in Rom. 11:26 there remains still another problem: Is the apostle thinking only of his generation, or of "all Israel" in its historical-temporal extension? The answer to this question can perhaps be found by an investigation of the diachronic structures and the use of time in Rom. 9—11. What is the result of this? Rom. 9:3f., with the apostle's reference to his Jewish "brothers according to the flesh" of whose privileges he speaks in the present (cf. 9:4a),[109] could at first permit the view that in speaking of the salvation of all Israel Paul was thinking of his Jewish contemporaries, that is, in the sense: I say to you: All Israel will yet convert to the gospel in my lifetime. Did he mean that?

Diachronically seen, the view of the apostle is directed toward the time of the prophetic statement (see the numerous scriptural citations in Rom. 9—11), then to his Jewish comrades in the present and his mission experience with them, which is largely negative (cf. 10:1f., 16–19), and finally to the saving of all Israel at the end of time. The eschatological future, as it is before us in the formulation "will be saved," is repeatedly found in chapter 11: outside of 11:26a also in verse 22 ("otherwise you too will be cut off"); twice in verse 23f. (they "will be grafted in"); in verse 26b ("he will banish ungodliness from Jacob"). These uses of the future, however, are not bound up with a time indication. In the context of these uses of the future in chapter 11 we find only the temporal indication of a goal: "Until the full number of the Gentiles come in"—a goal which apocalyptically remains concealed. From this we may conclude that if the apostle is thinking of his Jewish contemporaries at the beginning of Rom. 9 and in Rom. 10 is addressing the largely negative mission experience with the Jews, then in the decisive section of Rom. 11, which concerns the salvation of Israel at the end of time, he is referring to the temporal indication of a goal only in apocalyptically concealed language. This date, in the sense of an earthly chronology, is set for the salvation of all Israel; for the time when the full number of the Gentiles come in is known to no human being and is not revealed by the apostle. The honorific title "Israel" for the Jewish people, its being called "the seed of Israel" (in 9:6) and "Jacob" (in 11:26b), the reference to the "fathers" in 9:5 and 11:28 who are "the fathers" of all Jews, of all Israel, allows the assumption that the dative "with them" *(autois)* in 11:27a in reality extends to "all Israel" in its diachronic expansion through history and not merely to a part of it (as for example the "Orthodox" among the Jews); otherwise the attribute "all" in the statement of the apostle, *"All Israel will be saved"* ultimately would become a farce. We may, therefore, assume that when Paul spoke of "all Israel," he was really thinking of the entire Jewish people and affirming their salvation at the end of time, and indeed because of the fathers, whose being chosen in fact makes the choosing of Israel irrevocable.

In What Manner Will "All Israel" Be Saved?

There are in exegesis essentially two opinions on this matter: (A) Israel will be saved in that, one day, or shortly before the end of days, naturally stimulated by the grace of God, it will convert to the gospel, that is, come to believe in Jesus Christ. (B) Israel will arrive at eschatological salvation[110] by a "special path."[111]

What is to be said of these divergent exegeses? Only the text of the Epistle to the Romans can give the answer. First of all, nowhere in the text is there talk of a conversion of Israel, but rather of a "hardening" and of a "saving." The partial hardening has come upon Israel on the basis of an incomprehensible decision of God, "until the full number of the Gentiles come in": thereby a temporal indication of a goal is given, but without the specification of a terminus, a fact I have already emphasized. The future passive "will be saved" *(sōthēsetai)* is clearly spoken as a "theological passive": God himself will save Israel. But in what manner? The following text helps. The salvation of all Israel at the end of time is presented as founded in the Scriptures, introduced with the usual formula "as is written," whereby one must, as was already remarked above, take the particle "as" *(kathōs)* as the parallel to the anticipatory "(and) thus" *([kai] houtōs)*. B. Mayer correctly remarks: "The attempt to set up an immediate correspondence between *houtōs* and *kathōs gegraptai* founders on the linguistic usage of Paul."[112] The particle "as" is not related to "and thus," but rather to that portion of the sentence "All Israel will be saved"; that is, in Rom. 11:26b the particle "as" does not have a comparative, but rather a modal function: "Corresponding" to the mode referred to in the Scriptures, the salvation of all Israel follows. Beyond that, it has a foundational function. Thus, at one time it means: all Israel will be saved by God in the manner "as" it is stated in the Scripture; then at another time: all Israel will be saved "because" it is stated in the Scripture.

What is there in the Scripture about this? What is to be read in the Scripture about this is provided by Paul in the style of a combination citation which joins elements from Isa. 59:20, 21 and 29:7 with a reminiscence of Jer. 31:33, 34. Before we concern ourselves more closely with the scriptural passage, however, let us immediately look at the broader context with the question: Does it permit the recognition of the decisive motive of the salvific action of God? The apostle affirms: The Israelites are "the beloved ones for the sake of the fathers in accord with their election"; the added sentence, "for the gracious gifts of God and the call of God are irrevocable," can only have the meaning that Israel's continuing to be beloved is to be grounded in the concept of the irrevocability of the pledges of God, therefore, in his loyalty. The Gentiles have found the mercy of God in the time of salvation which is already present in that they are justified by faith in Christ. Even they were once disobedient (v. 30a) as Israel now is disobedient (v. 31a), for God has consigned *all*, Gentiles and Jews, to disobedience. But why? The answer of the apostle is: "That he may *have mercy* upon all" (v. 32). The final reference of the section is to the mercy of God! From it Israel is not excluded, for God remains true to the promises which he once gave to the fathers of Israel, which he never revoked.

From here let us return to the scriptural citation of 11:26b, 27. The scriptural passage makes concrete *how* the encompassing mercy of God will manifest itself toward all Israel. It will manifest itself according to the statement of the prophets: "The Deliverer will come from Zion, he will banish ungodliness from Jacob; and this will be my covenant with them when I take away their sins." Most commentators correctly presume that the future "will come" *(hēxei)* looks ahead toward something yet to come (thus, not to the first coming of the Messiah in Jesus of Nazareth), because indeed it corresponds to the preceding future "will be saved." All Israel will be saved because the Deliverer comes from Zion. However, who is meant by the "Deliverer" *(ho hruomenos)*? Many commentators think it is God, because Isaiah himself, from whom the scriptural citation comes, also thought of God. But this is not so certain. In Rom. 10:11 the citation is from Isa. 28:16: "No one who believes in him will be put to shame," in which "in him" refers to God. However, in Paul, on the basis of the context, it refers to "the Lord of all," that is, to Jesus Christ (compare 10:9 with 10:12). Add to this that in 1 Thess. 1:10 "savior" ("deliverer") means Jesus the Son of God whom the Christian community should "await from the heavens," a clear reference to the *parousia* Christ. He also appears to be thought of in Rom. 11:26b.[113] The decisive thing remains this: Israel, according to the passage of 11:26b–32, will not attain salvation on the basis of a "mass conversion"[114] preceding the *parousia*, but rather simply and only through the initiative of a God merciful *to all*, completely independent of the attitude of Israel and the rest of humanity, which will consist concretely in the *parousia* of Jesus. The *parousia* Christ saves all Israel without a preceding "conversion" of the Jews to the gospel.[115] God saves Israel by a "special path" which likewise rests upon the principle of grace (*sola gratia*) and thereby maintains the divinity of God, his "choice," his "call," and his promises to the fathers and his "decision" which is independent of all human ways and speculation. It is the victory of the free grace of God which will save all Israel. This also corresponds to the prophetic statement of Jesus himself in Matt. 23:39:[116] "For I tell you, you will not see me again, until you say, 'Blessed be he who comes in the name of the Lord.'" God saves all Israel through Christ (*solus Christus*) and, indeed, "through grace alone" and through "faith alone" without the works of the Law, since Israel's *emunah* turns now totally toward the Christ who comes again. Thus in the "special path" of the saving of all Israel, the Pauline doctrine of justification remains completely effective.

This thesis of the "special path" by which God at one time will save all Israel appears therefore to be the only correct one, because according to Paul it was God himself who "hardened" Israel. To be sure, the apostle affirms in 10:21 with Isa. 65:2 that Israel is a "disobedient and contrary" people, but he affirms in 11:7f., with reference to the "hardening" of the rest and with a scriptural quotation from Deut. 29:3 and Isa. 6:9f., that "God gave them a spirit of stupor, eyes that should not see and ears that should not hear, down to this very day." Why God did this remains a mystery that is not rationally explainable.[117] If, however, God himself has hardened Israel, then logically only he himself, not the Church, can withdraw it from its "hardening." It is not the Gentile peoples who have been converted to the gospel that will save "all Israel"—an absolutely unbiblical thought—but God alone. *The hardening and saving of Israel correspond to one another.* The one who hardens is likewise the one who saves. The saving of all Israel which Paul refers to in Rom. 11:26a is therefore indissolubly linked to his preceding thought that the hardening is done by God himself. And if all Israel will be saved at one time by a special act of God, is not then the "mission to the Jews" really a questionable enterprise?[118] The conversion of individual Jews to Christianity is not to be viewed as the normal case, but rather as an exceptional case, obviously also made possible only through the gracious light of God.

Why Will "All Israel" Be Saved?

The answer to the above question can be given briefly on the basis of Rom. 9—11:

1. Because God has not rejected (11:1) his people Israel whom he once chose, and his word does not "fail" (9:6).

2. Because God is "powerful" enough to graft again the partially hardened "portion" of Israel "back into their own olive tree" (11:23b, 24).

3. Because God's "gifts" and his "call" are irrevocable (11:29).[119]

4. Because the Jews "regarding the (divine) election are the beloved [of God] for the sake of their forefathers."[120]

5. "For God has consigned *all* men to disobedience, that he may have mercy upon *all*" (11:32). Israel does not remain excluded from this mercy.

6. God himself, for reasons which ultimately are not rationally explainable, has "hardened" Israel, as was already mysteriously stated in the Scriptures (cf. 9:18; 10:8f. with Deut. 29:3; Isa. 6:9f.; Ps. 69:23f.). In Jesus Christ God has laid before the feet of Israel "a stone that will make men stumble, a rock that will make them fall" (Rom. 9:33); they stumbled over this stone. Therefore the "disbelief" of Israel is and remains a complete mystery of God.[121] Israel is the best evidence for the fact that God does not allow one to look into the cards, and its continuation through history is the best "proof of God."

7. As God once "raised up" Pharaoh "for the very purpose of showing my power in you, so that my name may be proclaimed in all the earth" (9:17), thus God manifests his irresistible gracious power in the end in that he will save all Israel. "So it depends not upon man's will or exertion, but upon God's mercy" (9:16). In the saving of all Israel the ultimate victory of the free grace of God, the divinity of God, will show itself.

Why Does Paul Confess the "Mystery" of the Saving of "All Israel"?

A first answer to this question is given by the apostle himself in the immediate context of 11:25a: "Lest you be wise in your own conceits" (11:25b), that is, lest we be conceitedly, rationalistically scrambling after our own solutions for problems where only God can provide the solution.[122] Perhaps the addressees of the epistle, the Roman Christian community, had thoughts about the so-called hardening of Israel, perhaps indeed proud, self-righteous thoughts which expressed themselves in boasting against the Jews. The theme of "boasting" turns up expressly in the context of Rom. 11: "Do not boast over the branches. If you do boast, remember that it is not you that support the root, but the root that supports you."[123] Likewise the Gentile Christian desire to be clever toward Israel turned up earlier in 11:20b in the admonition of the apostle to the Gentile Christians: "So do not become proud, but stand in awe!" Paul, therefore, appears to have professed the mystery of the saving of "all Israel" because in the Roman Christian community, largely made up of Gentile Christians, many not only reflected on the so-called hardening of Israel and the final salvation of Israel (which was true throughout the entire primitive Church, as can be seen from the Gospels and the Acts of the Apostles),[124] but also because they believed that they could proudly lift their noses over the "hardening" of Israel. Perhaps an anti-Judaism was widespread among the Gentile Christians of the Roman Christian community, nourished by Gentile anti-Semitism. The apostle decisively rejects this attitude, and in order to end all human speculation, confesses the mystery of the eschatological and ultimate saving of all Israel. His own knowledge of this mystery does not absolutely have to rest on a special revelation to him; rather it could be the fruit of his reflection on the appropriate statement of the Holy Scriptures of Israel in which the saving and reestablishment of Israel by God at the end of time is spoken of, as for example in Isa. 44:22: "Israel, I will never forget you!"; 45:17: "Israel will be saved by God with an eternal salvation"; 45:25: "All the seed of Israel finds salvation and glory in God."

In reference to Judaism, the admonition of the apostle to the churches of today would doubtless be none other than: "Do not become proud, but stand in awe!"

The spelling out of this by the apostle in Rom. 11 holds a hermeneutical key position in the structuring of a tractate on the Jews. "Presumably Rom. 11 first established with definitive certainty that theology has the right and the obligation to develop a *Tractatus de Judaeis*."[125]

Is the Thought of a Saving and Reestablishment of Israel at the End of Time Found Anywhere Else in the New Testament?

It appears that Luke in the Acts of the Apostles, 1:6–8 and 3:20f., is also thinking of a reestablishment of Israel at the end of time.[126]

Acts 1:6–8

"So when they had come together, they asked him, 'Lord, will you at this time restore the kingdom to Israel?' He said to them, 'It is not for you to know times or seasons which the Father has fixed by his own authority. But you shall receive power when the Holy Spirit has come upon you; and you shall be my witnesses in Jerusalem and in all Judea and Samaria and to the end of the earth.'"

"When they had come together" apparently refers only to the apostles, not a larger circle of disciples (as afterwards in 1:14). They asked Jesus: "Will you at this time restore the kingdom to Israel?" How did they come to this unexpected and extraordinary question? Doubtless on the basis of the promise of the Spirit *for the immediate future* (v. 5: "Before many days"!). According to the prophetic statement of the Old Testament, the pouring out of the Spirit indeed introduces the final days (cf. also Acts 2:17: "In the last days").[127] How, however, do the apostles understand their question? Usually it will be responded: in the sense of a "materialistic" eschatology. Thus, for example, A. Wikenhauser remarked in his commentary: "They are thinking, however, of the kingdom of God as a glorious renewal for the benefit of the pious ones of the Jewish people; they are thus still held captive in the earthly-national messianic hopes of the great masses."[128] And E. Stauffer thinks: "The question shows how fruitless all counter explanations of Jesus remained in the face of the contemporary expectations of the end which had been brought into connection with his person, message and effectiveness."[129] This judgment does not do justice to the true sense of the apostles' question. The promise of Jesus of the pouring out of the Spirit predicted for the end of time "before many days" must first of all have awakened in the apostles an "imminent expectation": If the Spirit is already poured out, then the end or the kingdom of God will also come soon. However, on the basis of the prophetic promise the reestablishment of the (Davidic) kingdom of Israel belongs to the Jewish expectation of the end; cf. for example, Jer. 33:7: "I will restore the fortunes of Judah and the fortunes of Israel, and rebuild them as they were at first"; see further Isa. 11:1–12; 49:6; Jer. 12:14–17; Amos 9:11; Ps. 14:7; 85:2; Hos. 6:11; according to Sirach 48:10 Elijah redivivus will "restore the tribes of Jacob."[130] The restoration *(apokatastasis)* of the kingdom for Israel is therefore a sign of the imminently expected arrival of the new aeon, if not already of its beginning. According to Acts 1:6–8, Jesus in no way rejects the question of the apostles about the restoration of the kingdom for Israel,[131] as is often maintained; rather he only corrects the imminent expectation by affirming that the time of the events of the end, to which the restoration of Israel also belongs, lies alone with God, who "by his own authority has fixed the times or seasons" of salvation history.

Acts 3:19–21

"Repent, therefore, and turn again, that [*a "finales" pros*] your sins may be blotted out [through God], that times of refreshing may come from the presence of the Lord, and that he may send the Christ appointed for you, Jesus, whom heaven must receive *until the time for establishing all* that God spoke by the mouth of his holy prophets from of old." In this text Israel is urged by Peter to repentance so that the "times of refreshing" may come for Israel and God may send it its Messiah Jesus. Thus even the coming of Jesus again is primarily for Israel and its "refreshing." For the present he lives in the hiddenness of heaven, not for all eternity, but rather until "the time for establishing all," which, on the basis of the entire context which refers to the salvific fate of Israel (prediction of this "establishing" by the prophets of Israel!), in fact again can only mean the *apokatastasis* of Israel—and it coincides with the return of the Messiah Jesus. How this will look and what its content will be, of course, escape our knowledge; concerning this, the text of the sermon of Peter is silent. However, it is stated clearly enough that God's salvific dealing with Israel has not come to an end with the violent death of Jesus. It continues, and will grow even more intense in connection with the *parousia* of the Messiah.

In any case, it can be said that Luke also knows of the saving of Israel at the end of time, even if he does not speak of it in the same terms as Paul. The Christian must take into consideration this "establishing" of Israel already spoken of by the Old Testament prophets and referred to by Luke. It belongs together with the continuing choosing of Israel by God and the continuing covenant of God with Israel. God has not written off his people. Jesus is and continues to be the previously described Messiah who is "for you," that is, for the Jews, even if Israel in its majority is still not able to see that.[132]

ISRAEL, "THE ROOT" OF THE CHURCH

The New Testament textual foundation for the following reflections is provided by Rom. 11:15–21: "For if their rejection means the reconciliation of the world, what will their acceptance mean but life from the dead? If the dough offered as first fruits is holy, so is the whole lump; and if the root is holy, so are the branches. But if some of the branches were broken off, and you, a wild olive shoot, were grafted in their place to share the richness of the olive tree, do not boast over the branches. If you do boast, remember it is not you that supports the root, but the root that supports you. You will say, 'Branches were broken off so that I might be grafted in.' That is true.

They were broken off because of their unbelief, but you stand fast only through faith. So do not become proud, but stand in awe. For if God did not spare the natural branches, neither will he spare you." The text is difficult.[133] It is borne along by basic words which fit together: Root, olive tree, branches, to break off, to graft in. Its high point doubtless is the sentence "It is not you that support the root, but the root that supports you"—a sentence which prompts the question: Who really is meant by the "root"? Commentators often respond: The fathers of Israel (the patriarchs) is meant by the root, with reference to Rom. 11:28 ("for the sake of the fathers"). This needs to be tested.

There is a whole theology of the "root" in the Old Testament which cannot be presented here.[134] When the Hebrews speak of the "root," they can also be thinking of a "runner" which can be explained "from a specific Hebraic and Semitic viewpoint."[135] The Semite sees the object or the activity "more wholly" than the Westerner. J. Becker provides the following example of this: "Hand" *(jad)* often means "arm"; "foot" *(regel)* often indicates the "leg"; "many" *(rabbim)* is like our "all." "Similarly the Hebrew sees the 'root' pregnant as a pressing force to bring forth runners,"[136] that is, "the root" is not simply the root, but also the runner of the root, indeed the tree ("trunk"). Thus, when Paul in looking at the Jews and the Gentiles speaks of the natural and engrafted "branches," he sees the branches not merely in relationship to the root, but also to the trunk ("olive tree") which comes up from the roots. Therefore when he says: "The root supports you," he thinks therewith of the "trunk," which in reality "supports" the branches. This means, then, that "root" *(hridza)* in Rom. 11:16, 18 is not merely "the root," the fathers of Israel, but also the trunk which has grown up out of the root and is identical with Israel. The fathers of Israel do not alone "support" the Church; Israel as a whole "supports" the Church. Israel alone is the "noble olive tree" *(elaia, kallielaios).* Indeed, it is not the Church but rather the Gentiles that are the "wild olive tree" *(agrielaios).* However, God does not ennoble the "wild shoot" by engrafting it with branches from the noble olive tree. Rather, the branches of the "wild shoot" are grafted onto the "noble olive tree" (Israel) and at any time God can break them off again (11:21). Behind the apostle's metaphor there is, theologically seen, the idea of the one people of God which consists of Israel and the Church. Israel and the Church stand, therefore, not next to one another as two large elements independent of one another; rather the Church of the Gentiles is "engrafted" onto the "root" Israel.

Paul's view appears to be important for the specification of the relationship Israel-Church and vice versa. The Church and Israel stand in an indissoluble salvific historical relationship to one another and, from the perspective of the Pauline metaphor,[137] this does not mean that Israel may have been dissolved by the Church or that God may have planted a second "noble olive tree" in the world next to Israel; rather, there is only *one* noble olive tree, Israel, and the Church is "engrafted" onto this olive tree. The "branches" of Israel that have been temporarily broken off from this noble olive tree will at the end again be "engrafted" (Rom. 11:24). This obviously includes the idea that these branches will endure and not be dried up and burned in the "in between times"; this must be understood. If this olive tree along with its root "supports" the Church (the engrafted branches), then the Church lives on from Israel and cannot dispense with Israel if it does not wish to "wither." It would cut itself off from its root if it would forget Israel. Therefore Karl Barth correctly remarked that there is no true *oikoumene* without relationship to Israel.

Certainly for the rest, Pauline ecclesiology is particularly taken up with the thought of the "body of Christ." However, the idea of the Church made up of Jews and Gentiles, which perhaps came to the apostle through Jewish Christianity, was indispensable to him

> because through the Old Testament, as for example the Creation doctrine, he felt forced to connect the people of the promise with the end of time. . . . The thought of the people of God characterized with him the eschatological phenomenon of the Church according to its historical connection. . . . For Paul there is no Church made up only of Gentile Christians. That would be two worlds cut out and placed next to one another, not the goal of the divine plan of salvation for the world. That would be to abstract from history before Easter, to give up the claim on the entire world which was grounded by and since Creation, and to reduce itself to a religious group. History would be sacrificed for the sake of the spirit and a counterworld would be set up. The thought of the people of God which grows out of the root Israel has therefore an indispensable function in the Pauline ecclesiology, although it puts forth only one of its aspects, and not even its center. There is for the apostle no salvation which could disregard the history of Israel.

These sentences come from the commentary on the Epistle to the Romans by Ernst Käsemann.[138] I quote it at length because it appears to explain the theological depth dimension of the Pauline text. I can, of course, not agree with Käsemann's sentence "Just as there is no Church without Israel, so Israel alone remains the people of God when it becomes the Church,"[139] because that is not found in the text of the apostle. Rather, the apostle understands the continuing special existence of Israel alongside the Church willed by God.

In an ecumenical dialogue between the Church and Judaism, just how far Israel even in its "special existence" alongside the Church is still "the root" of the Church would have to be a matter of consideration. It is to be noted that Paul speaks in the present tense, not the past, when he states; "It is not you that support the root, but the root supports you," even though he himself knew long since that Israel in its majority remained "hardened" against the gospel, as indeed can be seen from the context. Even today "the root" Israel supports the Church, and Israel has not disappeared from history; rather it still stands alongside the Church as its "root." Israel accompanies the Church through history until its end, and the Church should finally recognize Israel as its companion on the way. Then it would grasp more clearly that God is with it, because he is with Israel.[140]

One consequence of this is that the models of the relationship between Israel and the Church customary in Christian theology must be critically tested and better ones must be placed in their stead. B. Klappert has undertaken this task in an outstanding manner in his essay "The Loss and the Recovery of the Israelite Contour of the Passion Story of Jesus (the Cross, the Suffering, the Paschal Meal, the Trial of Jesus)."[141] Klappert mentions five models of relationship between Israel and the Church "which specify the loss of the Israelite contour of one people of God":

1. *The substitution model,* according to which the Church replaced Israel, while for Israel itself there remains only the history of rejection and curse.

2. *The integration model,* according to which the Gentile Christian Church integrates into itself the chosen remnant of Israel (the Jewish Christians).

3. *The typology model,* according to which Israel of the old covenant is the proto-presentation and preliminary stage of the Church and Israel *post Christum* is completely lost from view because it allegedly has lost its salvation historical rank.

4. *The illustration model,* according to which Israel is denigrated "to only an exemplar negative foil of human existence and human history." For Israel there is reserved the curse, for the Church grace."

5. *The subsummation model,* according to which "what is proper to Israel is categorized and subsumed into what is generally valid for all human beings," so that the special status and the special role of Israel in history will no longer be recognized.

Over against these five negative models, which have been extremely influential in the history of Christian theology, Klappert sets up three positive models:

1. *The complementary model* which emphasizes the fact that Israel and

the Church belong together in a salvation historical context under the arch of the covenant (proclaimed for Israel), and which leads Israel and the Church together in a fraternal dialogue.

2. *The representation model* which grows out of the solidarity of the messianic hope through which the world is promised a saving future, which according to Christian conviction of faith already appears in a preliminary way in the resurrection of Jesus from the dead.

3. *The christological-eschatological participation model* which "picks up the fundamental fact of the continuing call of the Gentiles through the history of Jesus Christ to the history of the choosing and hope of Israel," as Paul does in Rom. 11, but in which he has found hardly any successors in Christian theology.

With these three positive models, Christian theology has been presented with important tasks, especially in the new working out of ecclesiology and eschatology. In their solutions Israel will finally again come into the field of view of Christian theology.

ISRAEL AND THE "SERVANT OF GOD"

When the discussion turns to "the servant of God," one immediately thinks of the "hymns of the servant of God" of Deutero-Isaiah (42:1; 49:3, 5, 6, 52:13; 53:11). Every biblical scholar knows with what difficulties the explanation of these hymns remain bound up. The discussion is especially concerned with the question of who is meant by the "servant of God." An individual figure? A "collective figure"? The answers to these questions are divided.[142] The discussion will continue and presumably will never come to an end. C. Westermann, for example, in the *Theological Handbook on the Old Testament II* (Munich, 1976) holds forth this position (p. 195): "A collective explanation of the figure of the servant of God in the hymns cannot in this case [namely, "in speaking of Israel as a servant in the oracle of salvation"] be sustained (despite 49:3, which today is viewed overwhelmingly as a supplementary collective explanation of the servant); however, in this reference to Israel as the servant of YHWH a future task of Israel in the service of YHWH is probably alluded to. The collective explanation is, in a very limited fashion, appropriate in that the word of the servant of God of the hymns, even when they speak of him clearly as an individual figure, at the same time concerns the future task of Israel." Opinions on the explanation of the hymns, especially from Isaiah 53, were likewise divided in early Judaism.[143]

The continuing dispute about the correct interpretation of the figure of the servant of God, the oscillating character of the texts, the knowledge that it also "concerns the future task of Israel" (C. Westermann), appears hermeneutically to be of great significance in our connection. That in the primitive Church a christological narrowing took place in the explanation of Isaiah 53 is no longer surprising: Jesus of Nazareth with his atoning suffering and death is in the view of the primitive Church the "servant of God" seen by the prophets.[144] The Jew is not able to see that. The Church on the other hand is often unable to see that the "future task of Israel," of which C. Westermann speaks in connection with the servant of God hymns, is not definitively fulfilled in Jesus. In any case the Church must ask itself when it reads the sentence of Paul in Col. 1:24: "Now I rejoice in my sufferings for your sake, and in my flesh I complete what is lacking in Christ's afflictions for the sake of his body, that is, the Church," whether Israel, who is seen with the servant of God in Deutero-Isaiah in a mysterious joint view, must not also endure a "supplementary" atoning suffering in the world, not only for its own sins, but also for the sins of the whole world.

There are enough Jewish voices which understand the frightful suffering of Auschwitz and elsewhere as representative atoning suffering for the sins of the Gentiles. Indeed, according to an early rabbinic view, God himself suffers in his *shekinah* when Israel suffers: "Every time the Israelites are enslaved the *shekinah* at the same time is enslaved with them" (*Mekilta* on Exod. 12:41).[145] Can the Christian remain indifferent to such an explanation? If according to the apostle there is a supplementary participation in the afflictions of Jesus, with what right then dare the Christian exclude a participation of Israel in such a "supplement"? The Christian should be filled with reverence when the Jews understand the fearful suffering which has come over Israel in the course of the centuries as "the sufferings of the servant of God" by which they assist in the redemption of the world.

Leo Baeck, one of the most impressive figures of modern Judaism, has written: "One of the prophets . . . has found the great answer for the community of Israel when it proclaimed to it the meaning of life: *your suffering is suffering for the reconciliation of the world.* For him Israel is the servant of the Eternal One."[146] Baeck sees the messianic task of the Jewish people prefigured in the suffering servant of God.

And in reference to Isa. 53, Joseph Klausner remarks in his book *The Messianic Idea in Israel,* "Thus the *whole* people of Israel *in the form of the elect of the nations* gradually became *the Messiah of the world, the redeemer of humankind.* This Messiah must suffer just as the prophet suffers. Here also punishment precedes redemption; but this punishment is unique; it comes as a penalty *for the sin of others.* And it redeems the world. . . . And for this punishment, bringing good to all peoples except

Israel, this people receives a worthy reward in 'the end of days,' in that it becomes 'a light to the Gentiles,' in that it is placed in the center of humankind."[147]

In his Christ images the great painter Marc Chagall has interpreted the crucified Christ as the suffering Jew because, presumably, in Jesus the crucified one he saw the prototype of the suffering Jew; this is especially clear in the *White Crucifixion*.[148] "The manner of portrayal by an artist can disclose an authentic reality without its being theologically reflected and clarified for him."[149] The crucified Christ is not separated by Chagall from the people from whom he comes; rather the suffering of Israel flows together with the suffering of Christ and the suffering of Christ together with the suffering of Israel.[150] Chagall has thereby penetrated deeply into the mystery of the "collective figure" of the "servant of God." It appears to me that the Jew Paul did the same. With the primitive Church he recognized in the crucified Jesus of Nazareth the "servant of God"[151] and wished to supplement with his own suffering the afflictions of Christ. Likewise Shalom Ben-Chorin has remarked: "I cannot see the cross of Golgotha isolated, but rather for me it stands today in the midst of a frightful smoke which comes from the crematoria of Auschwitz and Maidanek, climbing toward heaven, where innocent children were gassed and burned—they all were the servants of God."[152]

Here likewise "Holocaust theology" (total sacrifice theology) must be mentioned, although several of its representatives use it against Christianity because supposedly Christian anti-Semitism reached its catastrophic high point in Auschwitz.[153] I will not pursue the matter; rather I will cite in agreement the sentences of Clemens Thoma:

> For a believing Christian the meaning of the victimization of the Jews under the Nazi terror . . . is not too difficult to establish. The six million Jews who were killed in Auschwitz and elsewhere direct their thoughts first of all to Christ, whom these Jewish masses in their suffering and death are like. Auschwitz is the most monumental modern sign for the most intimate bonding and unity of Jewish martyrs—representing all Judaism—with the crucified Christ, although this could not have been conscious for the Jews concerned. The Holocaust is for believing Christians, therefore, an important sign of the unbreakable unity, grounded in the crucified Christ, of Judaism and Christianity despite all divisions, individual paths, and misunderstandings.[154]

The Christian must, in face of the "total sacrifice" of the Jews in Auschwitz, openly confess his complicity in anti-Semitism. However, he cannot grasp the meaning of this sacrifice without the crucified Christ, who took up the sacrifice of Auschwitz into his glorified crucified body, as Chagall was able to see it.[155]

DOES ISRAEL *POST CHRISTUM*
STILL HAVE A "SALVIFIC FUNCTION"?

An uncommonly difficult question! It concerns not simply whether Judaism still has a function in the world, but rather, whether it *post Christum* still has a *salvific* function or a special salvation historical status. The question is often answered negatively by Jews as well as by Christians. It is in fact not easy to answer. When, for example, the Jews, as many Jews themselves have assured me, *no longer* wish to be anything other than one people among the other peoples of the earth, then the question of a *salvific* function of Israel *post Christum* becomes completely moot. If on the other hand one answers the question with "Yes; the Jews still *do have* a salvific function in the world," there immediately arises the further question: What function? This question is difficult to answer in the extreme, and therefore what I present here is only an attempt—nothing more—naturally an attempt that I hope may be a contribution to the building of a Christian theology of Judaism. One could a priori reject my posing of the question— and many probably will do that. However, in face of the statement of the apostle in Rom. 11:26: "All Israel will be saved" and in face of the continuity of the choice of Israel and of the covenant of God with it as is confirmed in the New Testament, it appears to me that my posing of the question is not merely legitimate but necessary, above all for Christian theology.

I proceed to the answer to my question from a simple reflection: If all Israel at that time, in the time of the primitive Church, had converted to the gospel, the consequence would have been that there would have no longer been a Judaism, and thus also no longer any Jews. The Jew would no longer be there. An anti-Semite and a Nazi would arbitrarily say: "There could be nothing better than this!" The Jew, the "world poisoner of all peoples," as Adolf Hitler called him in his political testament, would finally disappear! Apparently, therefore, the world perceives the existence of the Jew as a continuing thorn in its flesh from which it would wish to be freed, but from which it cannot break free because God does not allow his people to be written off. Why, therefore, does the Jew remain? Why has God himself laid a "spirit of deafness" on his heart? Only so that *post Christum* he is still there and still brings forth "chimera"? One could in answer refer to what the book *Deutschland ohne Juden*[156] shows: what a massive loss in spiritual potency Germany suffered through the annihilation of its Jews. One could point out that the modern world has been significantly shaped by Jews if one, for example, thinks of the names of Karl Marx, Sigmund Freud, Albert Einstein, and Arnold Schönberg. However, a Christian theology of Judaism must doubtless refer to other givens of a theological sort when it searches for an answer to the question of the salvific function of Judaism *post Christum*. Without, however, being able to make absolutely certain statements about the vocation of Israel in the world, I would like to mention the following points:

The Jew Is the Continuing Witness
to God in the World and as Such
a "Proof of God"

This was once perceptively remarked by the physician of Frederick II of Prussia to the king. The continuing existence of the Jewish people, despite its small number, despite the more than two thousand-year Diaspora among the peoples of the world, despite the terrible catastrophes which in the last one hundred years and even before have been visited upon Judaism, probably cannot be otherwise explained except that God himself stands behind this people as its real advocate. Therefore, for Karl Barth the Jew was the only proof of God to which he granted validity.[157]

The Jew Is the Continuing Witness
for the Concreteness of "Salvation History"

What does this mean? With progressing secularization in all areas of the world we observe the tendency to view so-called salvation history as an "idealistic superstructure" which is suspected of being an ideology and supernatural, and therefore as being something really nonexistent. This tendency, however, is thwarted by the existence of the Jew, because the world has the feeling that the existence of the Jew, which is not to be overlooked, today more than ever, somehow disturbs the ability to encompass the whole of history. The German philosopher Hegel, and with him Marxism, believed and believes in the possibility of ultimately getting behind the logic of history; however, Hegel had the distinct feeling that the existence of the Jew shattered his historical philosophical concept, and he spoke therefore of the "dark puzzle of Israel."[158] I would indeed like to put forth this thesis: This conscious or unconscious feeling of not being able to place the Jew in the customary pigeonholes of history is a main root of present anti-Semitism. "Whoever is made the same is physically and morally ruined. Whoever is other, is not the same; that is one of the reasons why the Jews so often come up," Ernst Jünger has remarked.[159] The Jew is perceived as a "disturbing factor" of the first order. Judaism disturbed and disturbs "a general outline of the universal reality in that it does not allow itself either socially or ecclesiastically or spiritually to be subsumed and relativized. Thus only in negation of its independence could it be endured, which at that time, as today, concerned not only its theological significance, but also its political-physical existence."[160] The Jew is the continuing witness to the concreteness of salvation history, and therefore to the fact that salvation history does not take place in an "empty space" but rather in history itself. The existence of the Jew constantly points to the fact that there are other "factors" to be reckoned with than those which are capable of being seen through and being known rationally and reckoned with. Likewise the existence of the state of Israel, I would wish to say, is more than a merely profane historical givenness; rather, it is an indication of the leading of Israel by God who through the Old Testament prophets spoke of the restoration of Israel. Likewise the Church must finally see that alongside itself there is still another supernatural element in the world in which God is present and works in the world: The Jewish people. The existence of the Jew does not allow a merely profane view of history to be cultivated; rather, the Jew is the continuing witness to the concreteness of salvation history, its real relationship to history. One could also say: The Jew bears witness with his continuing existence to the corporeality of salvation history; the so-called salvation history has incarnated itself not merely in the old covenant Israel or in the new covenant Church; it incarnates itself continually and visibly ever more strongly in the Jewish people.

The Jew Is the Witness
of the *Deus Absconditus*,
Whose Ways Are Not Discernible

The Apostle Paul ends his reflections on the hardening and the eschatological saving of Israel in Rom. 9—11, which for him especially in their linkage are not rationally discernible as a "mystery," with the sentences: "O the depth of the riches and wisdom and knowledge of God! How unsearchable are his judgments and how inscrutable his ways" (Rom. 11:33). If Jesus of Nazareth really was and is the promised one, as Christendom believes, why then did not his own people recognize him as such? I have already indicated above that the apostle knows no better answer to this dark question than: "God gave them a spirit of stupor" (11:8). *Why* God did that, however, *why* he brought Israel to the so-called hardening in order, nevertheless, at the end to save "all Israel," *why*, therefore, these extraordinary ways and "detours,"—all that is simply not to be explained rationally. To be sure the apostle also attributes to Israel a certain amount of its own guilt in the "hardening" (cf. Rom. 10:13–21) and he says in 11:12 that from Israel's case "riches for the world" and from Israel's rejection "riches for the

Gentiles" have come forth, because precisely now the gospel has come to them, the Gentiles. However, one clearly has the feeling in the study of Rom. 9—11, especially when one thinks of the closing sentences of Rom. 11, that even the apostle himself is ultimately not able to explain rationally the complicated dealings of God with Israel. Rather in the end he can only refer to *Deus absconditus*, whom Israel always knew: "Truly, thou art a God who hidest thyself, O God of Israel" (Isa. 45:15).[161] Israel's God is a God who does not hold his cards open and into whose cards one cannot look, even if we Christian theologians (and not just Hegel) often try to do so, as if for us all puzzles were solved and all the cards of God lay open.

In view of the frightful tragedies in the Warsaw ghetto, as day by day whole blocks of houses were evacuated with violence by the SS and the Jews were transported into the annihilation camps of Treblinka and elsewhere, Chaim A. Kaplan also posed the bitter question in his shattering Warsaw diary *Book of Agony:* "Does Israel have no God? Why has he withheld from us his help in our need?" And he writes further: "Even if we say with Isaiah: 'for the Lord holds a day of confusion and distress and dismay,' we do not exhaust the essence of this 'day of gruesomeness.' Nothing like it has ever happened in the forty years since I settled in Warsaw. The anger of the victor and the anger of our God pours itself out at one and the same time over us. There was a time when I thought that the words of Isaiah were only rhetorical phrases. Today I know that a gruesome prophecy has been completely fulfilled" (p. 248). But the questions which Kaplan posed are not answered. Neither a Jew nor a Christian can ultimately say why God allowed the tragedy, even if one would make use of the Holocaust idea or refer to the criminal attitude of Hitler and his accomplices. Ultimately there remains only the recourse to the *Deus absconditus*, whose mysterious ways no one knows, neither the Jew nor the Christian— whose witness, however, must be the Jew, on whom God has always laid his hand.

The Jew Does Not Allow the Messianic Idea to Disappear from the World

"The messianic idea" states first of all that God will send an eschatological, definitive bringer of salvation out of the lineage of David. Thus the prophets of Israel state it. Although Christendom is convinced in its faith that this promised one has already come in Jesus of Nazareth, nevertheless, together with Judaism it looks forward to the coming one, even though according to Christian faith the conviction of this coming one is identical with the *parousia* Christ. There are Jews who agree with the Jewish professor of the history of religion from Erlangen, Heinrich J. Schoeps, who says in his book on Paul: "However, it could well be that the one who comes at the end of days, who is the awaited one of the synagogue as well as of the Church, will bear the same countenance"[162] or, as David Flusser has formulated it: "It appears to me that very few Jews would raise an objection if the Messiah, when he comes again, were the Jew Jesus,"[163] or Pinchas Lapide in his radio dialogue with Hans Küng: "When the Messiah comes and if he should then reveal himself as Jesus of Nazareth, then I would say that I know no Jew in this world who would have an objection."[164] In any case, the messianic idea belongs in a special way to the great heritage of Israel which came into the world through Israel and through it and the Church is maintained in the world, even though the opinions within Judaism about who the Messiah is and how he will come might be widely divergent, as we are time and again assured from the Jewish side. The following point is connected with this.

The Jew Holds Up the Vision
of a "Better World"

The Messiah will indeed be the one who brings the world to salvation, or in any case the one who introduces that process. Behind the story of paradise, as it is related in Genesis, there lies the knowledge and experience that the present world is not well, or saved, but rather is often "ill," especially as a result of the presence of death. It appears to me to be no coincidence that two Jewish thinkers have reflected upon the theme of "the future"—Karl Marx, and Ernst Bloch, the philosopher of the "not yet." Their thinking is moved by the visions of the future and the hopes of the future. The prophets of the old covenant speak pressingly of this better future, predict it and describe it in impressive images. They are, of course, convinced that it is *God* who will bring about this future. It must be said that it is through Judaism that the eschatological dimension, which is oriented to the future and toward the end of earthly history, has come into the thought of humanity, even if this dimension today has been widely secularized and is thought of and propagated as a future without God. However, the vision of the future of the Old Testament prophets is primarily a vision related to "this earth" and to "heaven." The *earthly* conditions should be brought into salvation, of course a salvation which bursts the human possibilities and can be brought about only by God. Jesus of Nazareth and the people of the primitive Church to whom the New Testament leads back live here entirely out of the great spiritual heritage of Israel to which the theme of the future essentially belongs, and along with it the theme of the fulfillment of history by the God "before us." The continuing existence of the Jew, I would like to say, of itself points to the future. Paul connects the coming salvation of the Gentiles and the world in Rom. 11:12, 15 expressly with the salvific fate of Israel: "If their failure means riches for the Gentiles, *how much more will their full inclusion mean!* . . . For if their rejection means the reconciliation of the world, what will their acceptance mean but life from the dead?"

"Israel Is the World Historical Witness for the Not-Yet of the Divine Will"[165]

Marquardt spelled this out as follows: "With its 'no' it represents the eschatological reservation of God himself. It resists the Christian pathos of eschatological time, truth, and judgment. It exists as the ferment of the decomposition of false fulfillments."[166] Perhaps the most profound sense of this is to be found in the Jewish "no" to Jesus Christ, who still did not bring the world into definitive salvation, as much as the *praesentia salutis* already broken in in Jesus Christ lies of course on the hearts of Christians. As certain as it is, according to the Christian conviction of faith, that "the end of the ages has come" (1 Cor. 10:11), just so certain is it not yet the *final* time; this will begin only when "all Israel will be saved" (Rom. 11:26), that is, with the *parousia*.[167] The extraordinary formulation of the apostle in Rom. 11:28 must be understood from the perspective of this "eschatological reservation" of God himself as it is expressed in the Jewish "no" to Jesus Christ and the Church; that is, the Jews have become "as regards the gospel the *enemies of God, for your sake.*" They reject the gospel, but their rejection turns out to the advantage of the Gentiles (cf. also 11:15). In this formulation "enemies for your sake," the paradox of the inscrutability of the ways and decisions of God are expressed (cf. 11:33). The God-willed "no" turns into something positive—it is not a real negation; rather, it belongs to the divine logic of salvation history. Thus, one can agree with the definition of Judaism which Thoma has given: "Judaism is a people of provisionality. . . . Judaism possesses nothing in perfection, nothing that is closed off; everything, rather, is provisional in inchoative fashion. Initiatives and foundations are waiting to be transformed and to be taken up into larger unities."[168] Together with the Church, Israel is a *signum prognosticum,* a "pre-indication sign" in the world. The following point is connected with this.

"The History of Humanity Has Become a Holy History through Judaism

I mean a unified, organic process of development which, beginning with family love, will not be completed until the whole of humanity becomes a single family whose members are bound together in such solidarity through the Holy Spirit, the creative genius of history, as are the various organs of a living body by means of a likewise holy creative power of nature."[169] In the primitive Church, Paul above all developed such universal thoughts with his teaching of the Christ as the "final Adam" and the Church as the "body of Christ" embracing all human beings because, as a Jew, he knew that the God of Israel is likewise the God of the Gentiles and of all creation.[170]

Israel, Despite the Christological "Narrow Pass" in the Church Has Not Ceased, Even *Post Christum*, To Be, Through Its Unheard of Sufferings, Together with Christ the Reconciling "Servant of God" for the Sins of the World

In particular, today it is the so-called Holocaust theology which attempts to make us aware of this.[171]

One may, and also must, say in summary: Israel has a significant and comprehensive salvific function in the world even *post Christum*.[172] The Christian needs the Jew to stand behind him.[173] The Jew helps the Christian to retain his identity, for Israel remains the root of the Church: "He [the Christian] knows and sees that Israel is more than an idea. For we live. We are eternal, not as an idea might be eternal, but we are it, when we are it in full reality. And thus we are for the Christian the truly undoubtable."[174]

2

The Great Heritage of
the Faith of Israel

Christian theology has for a long time experienced only the "difference" vis-à-vis Judaism, which has led to a false image of Judaism in the Church, if not in part even to the demonization of Judaism. The following points ought to be presented in theology, catechesis, and preaching not as the discoveries of Christianity, but rather as the great heritage of the faith of Israel which has come into the Gentile world through Jesus and the Church. Through the reception of this heritage, Israel became paradigmatic for the Gentile world. Through this heritage, Israel is also the continuing theological root of the Church.

MONOTHEISM[1]

Theon hena ginōskein tois Hebraiosis hapasin koinon ("To acknowledge God as one is common to all the Hebrews"), remarked the Jewish historian Flavius Josephus (*Antiquities*, V. 1, 27, 112). "There is only one God and no other one," remarked the Jewish Sibylle (*Sib.* III, 629). The Jewish philosopher and contemporary of the Apostle Paul, Philo of Alexandria, numbers among the great teachings of Moses the following: "The second teaching is *that God is one*, because the representatives of polytheism are so shameless that they transplant the worst of the worst constitutions of states, the dominance of the masses, from earth unto heaven."[2]

How did Israel come to monotheism?

The rise of the insight that there is only one God is for Israel bound up with the rise of "Yahwism." However, the history of the rise of "Yahwism" is illuminated only in a beginning way by Old Testament scholars. Because of this there is still today no complete clarity about the semantics of the name of God, YHWH. Is "YHWH" originally a "toponym," that is, a place name, which was transferred to the local god? Is YHWH identical with the "God of the fathers"? When did he become identical with him? One thing appears clear; namely, that after certain onomastic fusions (El, Baal Shamem, YHWH) a monolatry then came about, which means that within its own area polytheism was denied and only a single God was honored ("henotheism"), without questioning the existence of other national deities. The initial Yahwism, therefore, was still not yet identical with a universal monotheism. "For Moses and the following period YHWH alone is the highest personal 'God of Israel' "[3] but his powerful nature already breaks through the limitations of a merely national god. "His unlimited power showed itself in Egypt as well as on Sinai and extended over nature as a whole."[4] Now YHWH gradually comes to be identified with the "God of the Fathers." The Exodus event, however it may have taken place historically, appears to have decisively fostered "Yahwism," in which the founding figure Moses presumably had an important role. And YHWH is now experienced as a covenant God who imparts teachings to his people, and national fortune and misfortune depending on whether such teachings are observed. However, the "taking of the land" brought with it the danger of exchanging YHWH with "Baal" and of relativizing "Yahwism." The Canaanite Baals and Astartes, and the later Phoenician, Assyrian, and Babylonian gods entered into competition with the God of the fathers and his "founders" (cf., for example, Judg. 2:11–13; 3:7; 1 Kings 14:22–24; 16:31–34; 2 Kings 22:2–7, among others). The danger of syncretism grew and lasted until the Babylonian exile, despite the measures of King Hezekiah and Josiah. The ancient prophets of Israel rose up against this development.[5] Thus Elijah demanded a clear decision for YHWH and against Baal (1 Kings 18:21) and proclaimed "that YHWH is God" (18:21, 27, 39), that he alone is God in Israel" (18:36). The prophet Amos emphasized that YHWH is also lord over the foreign peoples (Amos 1:3–15; 9:7), indeed, is lord of heaven and earth (5:8; 7:4; 8:9) and of the underworld (9:2). Hosea designated the worship of other gods as "whoring" (Hos. 2:2–5) and struggled against the worship of Baal and images (3:4; 4:12f., 17; 5:6; 8:4; 11:2). For Isaiah, YHWH is the only one who is raised above all (1:4; 5:19; 6:3; 10:17, and elsewhere), the only one who is the "God and spirit" (31:3), powerful and imperishable. The gods on the other hand are "nothings" (41:24, 29; 44:9) and the work of human beings (2:8, 20). Jeremiah fought along the same line. Thus the prophetic preaching is "inspired by pure monotheism" (P. van Imschoot), however, it rests upon the "time of the founders." The prophets do not call Israel to a new teaching; rather they call it back to the ancient faith, to the "first" love between YHWH and his people Israel (cf. Jer. 2:2; Ezek. 16:3–14; Hos. 2:14–24). However, now YHWH is presented as the universal ruler more strongly than before (for example, Isa. 7:18–20; 8:7–10; 13; Jer. 46f.; Amos 1:2—2:3; 9:7) and as the morally demanding God (Isa. 1:17; 11:9; Hos. 6:6; Amos 5:4f., 24; Mic. 6:8, and elsewhere). In Deutero-Isaiah it is stated (44:6–10):

Thus says YHWH, the king of Israel
and his Redeemer, YHWH of hosts:
"I am the first and I am the last;
besides me there is no god.
Who is like me? Let him proclaim it,
let him declare and set it forth before me.
Who has announced from of old the things to come?
Let them tell us what is yet to be.
Fear not, nor be afraid;
Have I not told you from of old and declared it?
And you are my witnesses!
Is there a God besides me?
There is no Rock; I know not any."

All who make idols are nothing, and the things they delight in do not profit; their witnesses neither see nor know, that they may be put to shame. Who fashions a god and casts an image, that is profitable for nothing?

That is the sum of the prophetic YHWH proclamation in Israel. It is not the result of philosophical speculation.

Now YHWH is proclaimed the universal creator God, the lord of the universe in numerous psalms, for example, and in the Wisdom literature (cf., for example, Job 38; Pss. 8; 104; 93:2; 96:10; Prov. 8:23–30; Sir. 24:3–8; Wis. 9:1–3; Jth. 9:7; 16:15–19). For early Judaism at the time of Jesus, universal monotheism was something indisputably self-evident in Israel, and naturally also for Jesus of Nazareth. To the question of the scribes, "Which commandment is the first of all?" Jesus responded, according to Mark 12:29f.: "The first is, 'Hear, O Israel: the Lord our God, the Lord is one; and you shall love the Lord your God with all your heart, and with all your soul, and with all your mind, and with all your strength.'" Jesus recited the *Shema Israel* (Deut. 6:4f.),[6] the fundamental confession of Israel which every devout Jew recites morning and evening, which every Jew carries on himself and puts on the door frames of his house written down in the prayer capsules. God had revealed himself as the only God in Israel and nowhere else. In pre-Christian times Israel was the only people on the earth that was strictly monotheistic. Therefore one may not overlook the important implications of monotheism for Israel. For YHWH was from the beginning the God who "participated" in the fate of Israel. The God of Israel is the God who lives "with" Israel, and indeed in the following four ways:[7] YHWH is the *trustworthy* God ("I am there with you so that you can firmly reckon on me"); YHWH is the *nonmanipulable* God ("I am there with you so that you have to reckon on me, when and as I wish"); YHWH is the *exclusive* God ("I am there with you, so that you may reckon only with me"); YHWH is the *always-present* God ("I am there with you where I [also] am").

The God of Israel is not a God who was born from the ancient womb, the "deep soul" of Israel. Rather, YHWH is an "Octroy" (taxing agent), a God who "forced himself" on Israel, as the Old Testament reports it, but forced himself as the God of love, who stands in a bridal relationship and a covenant relationship to his people (Jer. 2:2; Exod. 16:8–14; Hos. 2:16; 9:10) and concluded an eternally lasting covenant with it.

THE IDEA OF CREATION

The idea that the world is created by God is given expression in classically pregnant form in the first verse of the Bible: "In the beginning God created the heavens and the earth" (Gen. 1:1). Many commentators view this statement as a kind of heading over the priestly writings of the Creation story.[8] "*Bereshit* does not have in view the beginning of the Creation story with the first work, but rather the beginning which sets forth the events of Creation subsequently reported within the context of the entirety of the course of the history of the divine establishments as described in the priestly writings."[9] The statement from Gen. 1:1, however, is more than just a superscription; it contains a theological program of the greatest significance for all humanity, a program which in any case sets the horizon of the primordial history of Gen. 1—11. The verse programmatically affirms that *creator* and *creature* are not identical, interchangeable, and substitutable. In the first verse of the Bible the ontological difference between God and the world is expressed a priori and for always. Rabbi Ishmael asked Rabbi Akiba, "What do you do with the word *et* which is here?" He responded to him: "If *bereshit bara elohim et shamayim va-aretz* were there alone, then one could say, 'heaven and earth are divine beings.' " At this point he gave the following explanation of Deut. 32:47: "Presume the case that 'the Torah is an empty word for you,' then the cause lies in you because you do not understand the explanation at a time in which you deal with it; the meaning of the words is rather this: 'It is your life' at a time wherein you deal with it. In the same manner the words *et ha-shamayim* also wish to state: sun, moon and stars were included and *et ha-aretz* mean: The earth with the trees, growing things and paradise."[10] With this the *creature* quality of all creation, of the heavens and the earth, are laid out by Rabbi Akiba; it is not a divine being. There exists a qualitative difference between the creator and his creation. Cosmogony is not theogony as in the Babylonian creation myth.[11] "There is not a single word in the cosmogonies of other peoples which is like unto this first word of the Bible."[12]

The Hebrew word for "to create" (*bara*) in Gen. 1:1 is a "reserved word" in the Bible; it is reserved for God in regard to his creation act. There are a large number of investigations into this.[13] C. Westermann remarks: "In the definition of the meaning of the word three peculiarities were recognized early and have been repeated up to the present commentaries: the subject of the verb *bara* is always YHWH, never a human being, never another god. *Bara* never has a preposition with it, nor does it ever use the material accusative, nor is anything ever mentioned from which God creates."[14] However, in the Creation stories of Genesis the concern is not with the *creatio ex nihilo*, but rather with the fact that *God* has created the world and the world is different from him.[15]

It is the creative, bidding word of God which calls the world into existence, as is classically formulated in Ps. 33:9: "For he spoke, and it came to be" (cf. also Ps. 148:5). Indeed, in Gen. 1:16 the stars are also granted a dominating function. However, "it is not a domination which binds the conscience; it consists simply in 'the domination over the day and the night, to distinguish the light and the darkness.' "[16] Everything is subordinated to the command of God.

Despite the easily misunderstood formulation in Gen. 1:26: "Then God said: 'Let us make man in our image, after our likeness;' " which allows humanity to be understood as the likeness of God, we may not overlook that even here the difference between God and humanity comes to expression clearly enough, above all through the immediately following statement: "So God created man in his own image, in the image of God he created him, male and female he created them." "Since the involvement of YHWH in the bipolarity of sexuality is alien to the Old Testament in its entirety, the remark that humanity from the beginning is created in this bipolarity makes it clear from the beginning that humanity is thereby differentiated from the uniqueness of God."[17] Moreover, here "it is not the human form of God, but rather the divine form of humanity that is spoken of. What is meant here is that humanity will only be understood from this 'whence.' "[18]

Among the prophets, Deutero-Isaiah especially belongs to the great Creation theologians of Israel who push forward into new areas, which, however, remain completely along the line of the Creation stories of Genesis. Isa. 45:7: "I form light and create darkness, I make weal and create woe, I am YHWH who do all these things." There is nothing which exists outside the sphere of God's creating activity. Deutero-Isaiah then binds the Creation work of God closely to the historical deeds of God for Israel (51:9–11):

Awake, awake, put on strength,
    O arm of YHWH;
awake, as in days of old,
    the generations of long ago.
Was it not thou that didst cut Rahab in pieces,
    that did pierce the dragon?
Was it not thou that didst dry up the sea,
    the waters of the great deep;
that didst make the depths of the sea a way
    for the redeemed to pass over?
And the ransomed of YHWH shall return,
    and come with singing to Zion;
everlasting joy shall be upon their heads;
    they shall obtain joy and gladness,
    and sorrow and sighing shall flee away.

According to this text, the Creation of the world and the liberation from Egypt guarantee the coming liberation from the Babylonian captivity. Creation and redemption are the work of the same God: "Thus says YHWH, your Redeemer, who formed you from the womb: 'I am YHWH, who made all things, who stretched the heavens alone, who spread out the earth, who spread out the earth by myself. . . . Who confirms the words of his servant, and performs the counsel of his messengers; who says of Jerusalem, 'She shall be inhabited, . . .' " (Isa. 44:24, 26). " 'I made the earth and created man upon it; it was my hands that stretched out the heavens, and I commanded all their host. I have aroused him in righteousness [the King], and I will make straight all his ways; he shall build my city and set my exiles free, not for price or reward,' says YHWH of hosts" (45:12f.). "For thus says YHWH, who created the heavens (he is God!), who formed the earth and made it (he established it; he did not create it a chaos, he formed it to be inhabited!): 'I am YHWH, and there is no other. I did not speak in secret, in a land of darkness; I did not say to the offspring of Jacob, "Seek me in chaos." I YHWH speak the truth, I declare what is right' " (45:18f.). It is therefore the creator God who forms salvation for Israel. "The category of creation is a comprehensive category for the activity of YHWH at the beginning of the world, at the historical beginning of Israel, and in the present which is opened out toward the future in which the message of salvation will be fitted out with eschatological characteristics."[19]

Finally, the Creation thinking likewise plays an important role in the Wisdom literature of Israel.[20] In it an extraordinary connection between Creation and Wisdom is set forth, which, however, is already expressed briefly in Ps. 104:24: "In Wisdom hast thou made them all," and again in

Prov. 3:19f.: "YHWH by Wisdom founded the earth; by understanding he established the heavens; by his knowledge the deeps broke forth, and the clouds drop down the dew." According to Sir. 1:9, God "poured out Wisdom upon all his works." Prov. 8:22–31 goes further in that "Wisdom" presents itself in personified fashion:

> The Lord created me at the beginning of his work, the first of his acts of old. Ages ago I was set up, at the first, before the beginning of the earth. When there were no depths I was brought forth, when there were no springs abounding with water. Before the mountains had been shaped, before the hills, I was brought forth; before he had made the earth with its fields, or the first of the dust of the world. When he established the heavens, I was there, when he drew a circle on the face of the deep, when he made firm the skies above, when he established the fountains of the deep, when he assigned to the sea its limit, so that the waters might not transgress his command, when he marked out the foundations of the earth, then I was beside him, like a master workman; and I was daily his delight, rejoicing before him always, rejoicing in his inhabited world and delighting in the sons of men.

Wisdom here does not have a "divine status, nor is it a hypostatized attribute of YHWH, rather, it is something created by YHWH and something set out to perform its function. Although clearly distinct from the whole of Creation, it is an inner-worldly element, even if it is in fact the first of the works of Creation, the creature above all creatures."[21] Here Gerhard von Rad correctly calls attention to the fact that Wisdom is not an objectified property of God, but rather a property of the world, "Namely, as that mysterious accident by whose power the life of human beings orient themselves." "Israel stood before the same phenomenon which more or less fascinated all antique religions, namely, before a religious provocation of humanity by the world. It did not permit, however, a mythicization and divinization of the ground of the world. Its interpretation was completely other because it grasped this phenomenon within the horizon of its faith in YHWH as the creator."[22] The Wisdom literature of Israel expresses the thought and the experience that the world at hand is an ordered world, that there is a world order in creation. At the same time, however, it does not forget that this world ordered by Wisdom is the creation of God. Even the late Wisdom literature of Israel retains the ontological difference between creator and creation unconditionally. And because Wisdom in regard to its being has to do with thinking and the thought of humanity, the Wisdom teaching of Israel therefore orders this thought process for all times. The maintenance of the ontological difference between creator and creation is a fundamental presupposition for the health of thinking and the thought of humanity. Wisdom itself speaks in Prov. 8, but its "I," which is not identical with the "I" of God, calls humanity to a correct thinking about God and his creation. The addressee of this call is not Israel alone, but humanity in general. "The bearers of these theological presentations must doubtless have been men who, in terms of knowledge, were intensely involved, cosmopolitan Wisdom teachers who in the association with the Wisdom of foreign peoples received strong impulses. But more interesting than their dependence on these stimulations, is indeed their particular theological accomplishment."[23]

Israel too had experienced intensely the provocation and the fascination which exudes from the world; however, it "did not capitulate before the often apparently impenetrable visible side of the world, rather it held to the question about a meaning, about an effective order in the world."[24] The world is not dumb, it speaks; the heavens "tell," the firmament "proclaims" (Ps. 19:2); "All his works praise God" (Ps. 145:10). Israel indeed saw the fascinating primordial order of the world, but it did not therefore fall into a divinization of the world and its pagan representation in divine figures and their cult, but rather held firm to the sentences of the Creation story in which the ontological difference between creator and creation was forever expressed. Precisely that belongs to the great heritage of faith of Israel with which the thinking of Israel became paradigmatic for the thinking of humanity. Through Jesus and the Church this heritage of faith came into the entire world. Precisely the category of creation preserved the thinking of humanity from the Gnostic interpretation of the world and from Hegelian philosophy, according to which world history is the self-explication of God (of the "world spirit"). The world has its own history, but God accompanies this history with his "salvation history" in order to preserve the history of humanity from corruption and in order to save his creation.

HUMANITY, THE "IMAGE OF GOD"

The basic biblical assertion of the idea that the human being is the "image" of God is found in Gen. 1:26f.: "Then God said, 'Let us make ha-adam in our image, after our likeness; and let them have dominion over the fish of the sea, and over the birds of the air, and over the cattle, and over all the earth, and over every creeping thing that creeps upon the earth.' So God created man in his own image, in the image of God he created him; male and female he created them." Much has already been written about these verses of Genesis.[25] In the original Hebrew text of Gen. 1:26f. *tzelem* is used for image, and *demut* is used for likeness. According to the general conviction of commentators, the significance of the two terms is "not far from one another" (H. Wildberger). In the formulations of the two verses two things stand out: one is the plural, "let *us* make *ha-adam* in *our* image, after *our* likeness." The second is that in verse 27 the term used for God in the sentence "In the image of God he created him" is *elohim*. The plural "let us" includes God along with his court (cf. concerning this also Gen. 3:22; 11:7; 3 Kings 22:19; Isa. 6; Job 1; Dan. 7:10); for the creation of *ha-adam* God consults with his heavenly court. The previous "according to our image" is in a certain manner corrected with the plural *elohim:* The human being is not directly an image of God, but rather the image of divine beings" (H. Wildberger), a fact which is confirmed by Ps. 8:6: "He'll have made him a little less than *elohim*," which, according to Wildberger can mean not "God," but merely "divine beings."[26] This means that God created human beings "like *elohim*." The human being is not identifiable with God himself; the ontological difference between creator and creature is maintained even here. The "divine image" of humanity can be seen concretely in the context of the Genesis passage: "Let them have dominion over all the earth, and over every creeping thing that creeps on the earth," which was again confirmed in Ps. 8: "Thou dost crown him with glory and honor. Thou has given him dominion over the works of thy hands; thou has put all things under his feet." The divine image of humanity and its being given dominion over the entire subhuman creation belong, therefore, close together. The two predicates used for humanity in Ps. 8:6, "glory" *(kabod)* and "honor" *(hadar)*, are in the Old Testament often indications of the kingship of God[27] (cf. especially Ps. 145:5, 12: "Of the glorious splendor of thy majesty, and of thy wondrous works, I will mediate. . . . to make known to the sons of men thy mighty deeds, and the glorious splendor of thy kingdom"). According to Ps. 8:6, God grants "to humanity participation in these predicates which for Creation are like a model path of salvation" (H. Gross). Thus the divine image of humanity is grounded in this, "that God has given the human being a share in God's *lord-liness,* in his *being-lord,* in that as God's image he reflects the majestic highness of God and radiates it onto the nonhuman creature."[28] The Creation story of Genesis is likewise taken up again in Sir. 16:26–17:10 and further interpreted in Wis. 2:23: "For God created humanity for incorruption, and made him in the image of his own eternity."

With these statements about Creation from the Old Testament concerning humanity, it is likewise implied that "humanity is placed in creation as the concrete image of God" (H. W. Wolff); humanity carries out the dominion of God over the earth as the steward over the rest of the creatures. "He carries out the task not in self-glorifying arbitrariness, but rather as a responsible business manager."[29] In this regard the text from Gen. 1:26b still needs to be investigated, for it states: "That they may have dominion." It is in the plural, and therefore the previous "ha-adam" is to be understood collectively. It does not refer to the individual "Adam," but rather to the genus "humanity." "Dominion over the world will not be given to the great individuals, but rather to the community of humanity."[30] They should in common feel responsible for the world. "Therefore, the stewardship of the world is entrusted to humanity at large with the multiplicity of its members."[31] This presumes a demythicized world, which indeed is presented clearly enough in the first verse of the Bible with its implication of the ontological difference between creator and creation. The world created by God is itself not divine. Humanity is allowed to carry its office of steward in this world which is different from God. "And you, be fruitful and multiply, bring forth abundantly on the earth and multiply in it" (Gen. 9:7). In the previous verse the prohibition against spilling human blood is grounded with this statement: "For God made man in his own image." The biblical proclamation that humanity is the image of God implies, therefore, the inviolable dignity of humanity and what today are called "human rights."

It may be that the early Judaism-Rabbinic interpretation of Gen. 1:26f. has produced an exegetical bottleneck since in face of the easily misunderstood plural of "let us make 'ha-adam,'" they were concerned about monotheism, and therefore identified "ha-adam" with Israel.[32] Nevertheless, there stood behind this the penetrating insight that only *that* human being is truly "human" who orients himself toward the will of God as he has revealed himself in the Old Testament, especially on Sinai. "The world is indeed an Israelite world and can exist only as such."[33]

The teaching of the divine likeness of humanity is also connected by Judaism with ethics, as already happened in Gen. 9:6.[34] Hence one can understand that it is precisely the fratricidal Cain "who is the prototype of the human being who is not in God's likeness."[35] Whoever murders lessens the likeness of God (*MekEx* 20:17).[36] "You shall not despise your neighbor who is created according to the image of God" (*MekEx* 20:26). "When you despise your neighbor, know whom you despise: according to the image of God he created him" (*GenR* 24:8). "Blessed is he who opens his mouth to praise the Lord! Cursed is he who opens his mouth to insult his neighbor! Cursed is he who makes a creature of the Lord despicable!" (*Slav. Hen.* 52:1, 2, 6). "The Lord created with his own hands a human being and made him like unto his own countenance. . . . whoever despises the countenance of a human being despises the countenance of the Lord!" (44:1). Here too the ethical attitude toward one's fellow human being is grounded in the teaching of the divine likeness of humanity.

The formulation of James 3:9 in the New Testament comes entirely from these traditions: "With it [the tongue] we bless the Lord and Father, and with it we curse men, who are made in the likeness of God" (cf. also 1 John 3:12). The ethics which is bound up with the explanation by the rabbis of Gen. 1:26f. and 9:6 continues in this direction: You shall respect the likeness of God of your fellow human being! Behind this stands the conviction of the dignity of the human being. According to Rabbi Akiba the human being is loved by God because he is created according to the image of God: "Beloved is humanity for he was created in the image [of God]. Extraordinary is the love made known to him that he was created in the image [of God]" (*Mishnah* Abot III, 14). Because a human being *knows* that he is created according to the image of God, he can recognize therein the love of God.

All of these convictions belong to the great heritage of faith of Israel; and, thus seen, Israel has become paradigmatic for the nations, who without observing these convictions make a concentration camp out of the world, as the experience of history shows ever more clearly.

FUNDAMENTAL ATTITUDES BEFORE GOD

Holiness

Israel is the chosen special property of God.[37] This is also expressed in the fact that according to the Old Testament, Israel is a *holy* people, by which first of all not an ethical qualification is meant, "but rather the being chosen out for the special possession of YHWH."[38] "For you are a people holy to YHWH your God. YHWH your God has chosen you to be a people for his own possession, out of all the peoples that are on the face of the earth" (Deut. 7:6—14:2). "Now therefore, if you will obey my voice and keep my covenant, you shall be my own possession among all peoples; for all the earth is mine, and you shall be to me a kingdom of priests and a holy nation" (Exod. 19:5f.). If one compares the two texts, a tension between the indicative and imperative shows up: Israel is a holy people of God and therefore it should also be a holy people of God! Thus it is only logical that in the "holiness code" (Lev. 17—26) God's demand on Israel for holiness should be grounded with God's being holy: "You shall be holy; for I YHWH your God am holy" (Lev. 19:2). Conversely, the prophetic statement of the loss of salvation is grounded in the fact that Israel did not carry out God's demands for holiness: "For they have rejected the law of YHWH of hosts, and have despised the word of the Holy One of Israel" (Isa. 5:24). In these connections one must realize, if one wishes to understand the Jewish conviction of faith according to which in following the "Law" life consists in the making holy of the everyday,[39] that in the fulfilling of the demand of God to be holy, it is because he himself is holy. And therefore it is proper above all to "hallow" the Sabbath (Exod. 20:8/Deut. 6:12). The command to keep holy the sabbath (cf. Ezek. 12:20) intends to lead to the knowledge "that it is I who makes you [the Israelites] holy" (12:12; cf. also Exod. 31:13).

Obedience

God's law is a bidding word which demands obedience from Israel. The obedience of Israel toward God comes to expression linguistically in the three verbs "to hear" (*shama*), "to observe" (*shamar*), "to do" (*asah*).

"Hearing" is a fundamental act of Israel which has been commanded and prepared for obedience ("*Shema Israel!*"). Thus the father demands of the son untiring listening: "Hear my son and be wise!" And the person who "listens" to Wisdom will be praised as blessed (Prov. 8:34). The converse is true: "Cease, my son, to hear instruction only to stray from the words of knowledge" (Prov. 19:27). Humanity is the hearer of the word, that is, the instruction of God.[40] To listen to God or his representative (Moses, Joshua, the prophets) means to do what God says and wants. "Hearing is better than sacrifice" (1 Sam. 15:22). "If you are willing and obedient, you shall eat the good of the land" (Isa. 1:19). And conversely, the prophet Ezekiel: "But the house of Israel will not listen to you; for they are not willing to listen to me" (Ezek. 3:7). Hearing has precedence over seeing. What Israel has "heard" it should "observe," "cherish," "hold to," "follow" (*shamar*). When Israel obediently "hears" the instructions of God, it also "holds to" the covenant. "Now therefore, if you will obey my voice and keep my covenant, you shall be my own possession among all peoples; for all the earth is mine" (Exod. 19:5). In the "Torah Psalm" 119 the term "to observe" occurs twenty-one times. "Thou hast commanded thy precepts to be diligently observed" (119:4). "Give me understanding, that I may keep thy law and observe it with my whole heart" (119:34). "My soul observes thy testimonies; I love them exceedingly" (119:167).

God expects from Israel that it listen to his instructions and that it "do" (*asah*) them. This term "with its 2,627 occurrences is the third most frequently used verb of the Old Testament."[41] The concept becomes a theological utterance then and there where it concerns the "action" of humanity before God. "You shall teach them the statutes and the decisions, and make them know the way in which they must walk and what they must do" (Exod. 18:20). "All that the Lord has spoken we will do" (19:8). "You shall therefore keep my statutes and my ordinances, by doing which a man shall live" (Lev. 18:5; cf. Ezek. 20:13). Consequently Israel is definitely not a people which acts on the basis of the "works principle," as Christian theologians speak of them up to this very day, but rather a people of "realization," to use a favorite expression of Martin Buber, namely, the realization of the will of God as he announced it to Israel in the Torah. The realization, the "doing," is the consequence of the obedience of Israel to the instructions of God. The "doing" of the will of God takes place "on the ground of the covenant" (H. Braun). Israel would be untrue to the covenant if it did not "do" the instructions of God. Israel knows that. It knows that everything depends on that "doing" as far as God is concerned, but that even so it knows that the human being, despite his doing, would be lost if God did not allow his mercy to rule at the judgment. Rabbi Akiba has said: "Everything is foreseen, yet freedom of choice is granted; in mercy is the world judged; and everything is according to the preponderance of works" (*Mishnah* Abot III, 15).

The term "to do" (*poein*) in the sense of realization also plays an extremely significant role in the New Testament. "By far the largest group of New Testament *poieō*-passages concerns the obedient or disobedient action of human beings toward the Law, the will of God, and the proclamation of Jesus, whether it be in fundamental observation or in individual commandments."[42] Indeed "*poiein* is almost the only term with which the Synoptics express the action commended to human beings by God," and "Jesus, as well as the accompanying tradition, give to doing and hearing a clear priority over saying and thereby likewise remain on the ground of official Judaism."[43] In this Jesus remained entirely within the framework of Judaism. One should not overlook this in Christian theology—despite the Pauline doctrine of justification.[44]

Fear of God

Israel knows itself as the beloved people of God and as being near to its God. Nevertheless, it is also taught to fear God without allowing itself to be driven into an anxiety in the face of God. In the fear of God Israel learned that God is not a "comfortable older uncle" (Kierkegaard). It experiences itself time and again as creature before its creator and lord. It learns in the fear of God that God does not allow himself to be played with, that his ways are unfathomable. The fear of God belongs to obedience toward the commandments of God, which are not merely "good advice." And because the commandments of God promise salvation, it is therefore "understandable that talk of the fear of God as the attitude of the human being before YHWH quite surprisingly contains an outspoken accent on trust."[45] "In the fear of YHWH one has strong confidence, and his children will have a refuge. The fear of the lord is a fountain of life, that one may avoid the snares of death" (Prov. 14:26f.). "Thus one might formulate the matter: Whoever fears YHWH need have no anxiety; whoever, on the contrary, does not fear YHWH, must be anxious."[46] The fear of God is the beginning of knowledge" (Prov. 1:7).[47] And with this we are at the next theme.

The Knowledge of God[48]

"To know" belongs to the fundamental verbs of the Old Testament which continue into early Judaism, especially in the Qumran writings and in the New Testament, and in the latter especially with Paul and John. As *vox theologica*, "to know" in the Old Testament does not mean the rational, speculatively won insight of reason (as for example in the sense of the "proofs of God"), but rather a holistic personal act in the sense of acknowledgment, trust, entrusting, giving oneself over, believing. "To know" describes the correct attitude toward God which is born out of the center of existence exactly as is the Johannine "to know."[49] The opposite is "not to know," which depends not on defective talent, but rather describes the voluntary not wishing to take account of, rejection. If Israel does "not know" God, then that often means that it takes no notice of him and his commandments. Thus, "to revolt against" can be a precise contrast to "to know" (cf. Jer. 2:8). The "knowledge" of God in the prophets Hosea and Jeremiah becomes a "key concept of prophetic proclamation,"[50] especially in the application of the "formula of knowledge": Israel should "know that . . . ," God himself is at work in this or that event. It should "know that YHWH is God" and no other (1 Kings 8:60; 18:37; 2 Kings 19:19). Likewise, God's judgment of Israel should let the people "know that I YHWH have spoken in my jealousy, when I spend my fury upon them. Moreover I will make you a desolation and an object of reproach among the nations round about you and in the sight of all that pass by. You shall be a reproach and a taunt, a warning and a horror, to the nations round about you, when I execute judgments on you in anger and fury, and with furious chastisements—I, YHWH, have spoken" (Ezek. 5:13–15; cf. also 6:7, 10, 13, 14 and others; Jer. 16:21; Mal. 2:4). However, even the proofs of God's salvation are sources of the knowledge of God (cf., for example, Isa. 41:20; 45:3). God makes the king into an instrument of his plans of salvation for Israel "that men may know, from the rising of the sun and from the west, that there is none besides me; I am YHWH, and there is no other. I form light and create darkness, I make weal and create woe" (Isa. 45:6f.). When God frees Israel with a strong arm, "then all flesh shall know that I am YHWH your Savior, and your Redeemer, the Mighty One of Jacob" (49:26b).

The knowledge will ultimately be spread out among all the peoples of the world (cf. Ezek. 21:10— "all flesh"; Isa. 45:6—among others). In this connection a text such as that of Isa. 45:1–13 is important: Here the bringing of scattered Israel from all the ends of the earth into the land of the fathers becomes the occasion for the nations to reflect on the mysterious and powerful leading of Israel by God. "Let all the nations gather together, and let the peoples assemble. Who among them can declare this, and show the former things? Let them bring their witnesses to justify them, and let them hear and say, It is true" (43:9). " 'You are my witnesses,' says YHWH, 'and my servant whom I have chosen, that you may know and believe me and understand that I am He. Before me no god was formed, nor shall there be any after me. I, I am YHWH, and besides me there is no savior. I declared and saved and proclaimed, when there was no strange god among you; *and you are my witnesses,*' says YHWH. 'I am God' " (43:10–12). Israel is a witness of God in the world which produces the knowledge of God, is precisely a "proof of God." The nations should "know" this. They will come to this knowledge when God saves "all Israel" in the end (Rom. 11:26).

Love[51]

God loves his people Israel and indeed on the basis of his election: "Because he loved your fathers and chose their descendants after them" (Deut. 4:37); "Not because you were more in number than any other people did YHWH set his love upon you and chose you. . . . but because YHWH loves you . . . " (7:7f.; cf. also 7:13; 10:15); "I have loved you with an everlasting love" (Jer. 31:3). "The basis lies in the love of God as a sovereign decision of the will which is not further derivative."[52]

Therefore, Israel should also love God. This demand belongs especially to the parenesis of Deuteronomy, particularly in the "chief commandment": "Hear, O Israel: YHWH is our God, YHWH alone. And you shall love YHWH your God with all your heart, and with all your soul, and with all your might" (Deut. 6:4f.; cf. also 10:12; 11:1, 13, 22; 13:4; 19:9; 30:6, 16, 20). The love of Israel for God "makes itself concrete as the mutual love responding to the love of YHWH in loyalty and obedience within the covenant of YHWH,"[53] that is, in obedience to the commandments of God. In immediate connection with the "chief commandment" of love there follows in Deut. 6:6 the admonition: "And these words which I command you this day shall be upon your heart." "Know therefore that YHWH your God is God, the faithful God who keeps covenant and steadfast love with those who love him and keep his commandments" (Deut. 7:9). Thus, the love of God in Israel is not a "mystical" love, but rather the expression of obedience toward God and his commandments. However, such love in Israel will nevertheless be the expression of the closest community with God, as it says in Ps. 73:23–28: "Nevertheless I am continually with thee; thou dost hold my right hand. Thou dost guide me with thy counsel, and afterward thou wilt receive me to glory. Whom have I in heaven but thee? And there is nothing upon earth that I desire besides thee. My flesh and my heart may fail, but YHWH is my rock and my portion for ever. For lo, those who are far from thee shall perish; thou dost put an end to those who are false to thee. But for me it is good to be near YHWH; I have made YHWH my refuge, that I may tell of all thy works."

Israel, however, is also urged: "You shall love your neighbor as yourself" (Lev. 19:18).[54] Even if the concept "neighbor" referred primarily to fellow members of the people, already according to Lev. 19:34 the commandment to love the neighbor was expanded to include the "stranger": "The stranger who sojourns with you shall be to you as the native among you, and you shall love him as yourself" (cf. also Deut. 10:19), because God also loves the stranger, "giving him food and clothing" (Deut. 10:18). The charitable instructions, as, for example, in Exod. 22:20–26, are only a logical consequence of the commandment of love which was put together with the commandment of the love of God into the double commandment of love by Jesus, or before him by Judaism.[55] In any case "the commandment of the love of neighbor or stranger is not the simple expression of the morality of kinship . . . rather it is theologically motivated by the love of YHWH for the people and for the stranger and rests, as the other commandments of YHWH, on the covenant relationship."[56] Judaism has never forgotten that. "Because the love of humanity is commanded by God, because love cannot be commanded except by the loving one himself, the love for humanity is immediately traced back to the love for God. Love for God should express itself in the love of neighbor. Therefore the love of neighbor can be commanded. Only by means of a form which has its origin in the form of commandment, the mystery of the directed will, is the presupposition of God's own loving visible, through which it is distinguished from all moralisms."[57]

Emunah

A key word for the life of Israel before God is the substantive *emunah* which in English is rendered "firmness," "loyalty," "trust," "faith." The related verb *he'emin* (Hiphil—form from the stem *aman*) has the meaning: "To hold fast," "to trust," "to believe."[58] The statement in Gen. 15:6 may be viewed as a fundamental text in this regard: "[Abraham] believed the Lord; and he reckoned it to him as righteousness." This sentence deals with a judgment of the narrator—more specifically, the so-called Elohist—on Abraham's attitude as he can only persist in silent listening and looking in view of the promises of God that his descendants will be as numerous as the stars in heaven. "The narrator to a certain extent leaves the man looking up into the starry heavens and turns himself toward the reader in that he communicates to him a theological judgment of great theological intensity whereby the real course of events upon which this judgment bases itself is described neither by Abraham nor by YHWH."[59] Because Gen. 15:6 involves a statement "of great theological intensity," it is not concerned simply with an episode out of the life of Abraham but rather a "fundamental program of the Elohist's narrative which has its beginning with Abraham."[60] The passage here concerns to a certain extent the Law according to which Abraham the patriarch of Israel takes up his office. It concerns a fundamental attitude which determines the relationship of Israel to God forever. The Apostle Paul perceived absolutely correctly that the statement of Gen. 15:6 concerned a "fundamental statement" of the highest theological rank (cf. Gal. 3:6; Rom. 4:3). This likewise refers to Abraham in Rom. 4:11 as "the father of all who believe." In Gen. 15:6 Abraham is placed before the eyes of Israel as the prototype of faith. Abraham "believed God," that is, he trusted in God that he would be able to bring to completion his promises despite all the impossibilities seen from a human point of view. And therefore this faith was also "reckoned to him as righteousness," that is, he was declared to be one who stood in the correct relationship of community with God. He trusted the promises and plans of God, even when it was hidden from him how God would realize and carry out these plans.

"Faith" is likewise for Isaiah a "comprehensive expression of the total relationship between God and humanity,[61] which comes out in him in the striking programmatic play on words of 7:9: "If you will not stand firm [that is, in God's statements], you will not stand at all," which is commonly rendered: "If you will not believe, surely you shall not be established. In Isa. 28:16 it is thus formulated: "He who believes will not be in haste." In 2 Chron. 20:20 the people are urged to trust God and his prophets; Jehoshaphat stepped forward and said: "Hear me, Judah and inhabitants of Jersualem! Believe in YHWH your God and you will be established; believe his prophets, and you will succeed." In Ps. 119:66 good judgment and knowledge are brought into connection with trust in the commandments of God: "Teach me good judgment and knowledge, for I believe in thy commandments." According to Jon. 3:5, faith effected conversion. According to Isa. 43:10, Israel had to be the witness of God "that you may know and believe me and understand that I am he." Faith leads ultimately to the praise of God: "Then they believed his words; they sang his praise" (Ps. 106:12).[62]

Among the great Jewish thinkers Martin Buber in his book *Two Types of Faith*[63] has dealt with the essence of *emunah*, if in part in an inaccurate contrast to the Pauline-Christian *pistis*[64] and in connection with his theses on the hiddenness of God.[65] "*Emunah* is the 'persistence'-relationship . . . of the human being to a leading which is invisible and yet lets itself be seen, which is hidden but also revealing; nevertheless the personal *emunah* of every individual remains embedded in the people and draws its power from the living memory of the generations of the great leadings of their primordial time. In the historical process of individualization the form but not the essence of this being embedded changes itself. And still when an Hassidic Rabbi at a fork in the road sees the *shekinah*, the 'indwelling' of God, going before him, something of the former leading is present. Only in our age is the connection in an increasing measure loosened." However, Buber hopes: "The individuals, reborn in the crisis held in the *emunah*, if it so develops, would have fulfilled the function of hearing the living substance of faith through the darkness."

In the meanwhile Israel has gone through unheard-of darknesses, and the whole world goes through great darknesses. Many Jews, it has been witnessed, went into the gas chambers of Auschwitz and elsewhere singing psalms aloud; they could do so because, even in the darkness of that hell, they had not given up the *emunah* which they had inherited from their fathers. *Emunah* overcomes all crises: This is the moral from the history of Israel, rich in catastrophe. Of the theologians of the primitive Church, the Apostle Paul above all lived from the "concept of faith" of Israel.[66] "Christianity in no way set itself up as a new religion of faith over against the Jewish religion of Law, rather Christian faith is Old Testament-Jewish faith in a new salvation historical situation,"[67] which has come about through the death and resurrection of Jesus. "Christian faith will always be a faith within the structure of Jewish faith."[68] In her attitude of faith the little Jewish girl Miriam, whom Christians recognize under the name "Maria" the mother of Jesus, showed herself completely a daughter of Abraham.[69]

Conversion[70]

Israel often failed before Holy God and his commands, as does every human being who is a sinner. Therefore it is understandable that "conversion" is a central theme of the prophetic preaching of the Old Testament. However, the prophets never speak in the substantive of "conversion" (*teshuvah*), but rather always in the verb form of "converting" (*shuv*); only in Rabbinic literature does the substantive frequently appear as an abstract image.[71] The prophets, therefore, look to the act of conversion.

In his sermon in 4:6–12, Amos confirms the stereotypic six types: "Yet you did not return to me says YHWH." The goal of the conversion was the "return to the original relationship with YHWH."[72] Although according to Hosea (11:1–11) God called Israel his son out of Egypt and drew it to him with the bonds of love, his people "were bent on turning away from me" and disdained "the return"; nevertheless, God does not wish to destroy his people, but rather: "I will return them to their homes, says YHWH." In the need which God allowed to come upon Israel, Israel gave up its whoring with the Baals (cf. 2:4—3:4) and turned back to YHWH: "Afterward the children of Israel shall return and seek YHWH their God" (3:5). "Come, let us return to YHWH; for he has torn, that he may heal us; he has stricken, and he will bind us up" (6:1).

The theme "conversion" plays an especially significant role in Jeremiah. God affirms: "You shall say to them, Thus says YHWH: When men fall, do they not rise again? If one turns away, does he not return? Why then has his people turned away in perpetual backsliding? They hold fast to deceit, they refuse to return" (8:4f.). Indeed, it appears to be impossible for the people to return: "If a man divorces his wife and she goes from him and becomes another man's wife, will he return to her? Would not that land be greatly polluted? You have played the harlot with many lovers; and would you return to me? says YHWH" (3:1). To God's command: "Return, O faithless sons, I will heal your faithlessness," Israel reacted with a forthright confession of sins. "We have sinned against YHWH our God, we and our fathers, from our youth even to this day; and we have not obeyed the voice of YHWH our God," (3:22, 25) to which God said: " 'If you return, O Israel, says YHWH, to me you should return" (4:1), but this pledge is connected with ethical conditions which Israel must fulfill (cf. 4:2–4). When Ephraim pleaded: "Bring me back that I may be restored, for thou art YHWH my God," God responded: "Is Ephraim my dear son? Is he my darling child? For as often as I speak against him, I do remember him still. Therefore my heart yearns for him; I will surely have mercy on him, says YHWH" (31:18, 20). "In this manner, the theme 'conversion' is at home in the eschatological statements of salvation. YHWH makes the impossible possible!"[73] The same is also true for the sermons of conversion of Ezekiel and Deutero-Isaiah:[74] "Remember these things, O Jacob, and Israel, for you are my servant; I formed you, you are my servant; O Israel, you will not be forgotten by me. I have swept away your transgressions like a cloud, and your sins like mist; return to me, for I have redeemed you" (Isa. 44:21f.). "The grace of forgiveness overpowers the unfaithful ones."[75] Likewise in the Deuteronomic historian the theme of conversion is found "in almost all the significant places . . . alongside the warning against falling away and the threat of judgment."[76] 4 Kings 17:13 appeals expressly to the "commandments of the prophets": "Turn from your evil ways and keep my commandments and my statutes, in accordance with all the Law which I commanded your fathers, and which I sent to you by my servants the prophets." Whenever the judgment for falling away from God and his commandments comes up, Israel is urged to conversion: "If they turn again to thee, and acknowledge thy name, and pray and make supplication to thee in this house, then hear thou in heaven, and forgive the sin of thy people Israel" (3 Kings 8:33f.; cf. also 8:46–53; Deut. 30:1–10).

According to the Deuteronomic historian, conversion is a radical turning toward God "to listen to his voice," a returning to the covenant of the fathers to live according to the commandments of God.[77] Conversion is reflecting on that which has served the salvation of Israel. Therefore it is not surprising that the theme "conversion" has continued to play an important role in the religious thought of Israel. For conversion time and again grants a new chance for salvation before God. "Praised be you who were pleased by conversion" (Shemone Esre, fifth petition, Palestinian Recension). "Turn us toward a complete conversion before your countenance" (Babylonian Recension). "If Israel converts, it will be redeemed" (Rabbi Eliezer). In Rabbinic literature the sentence gedolah teshuvah, "great is the conversion," appears often. To see "monergism of human endeavor" as the driving force behind the Jewish conversion theology, as does J. Behm[78] and other Christian theologians, is to do Judaism a bitter injustice. Conversion is not concerned with "achievement," but with the demands of God. It is the divine imperative which drives one to a conversion, behind which the awareness of the mercy of God in judgment was never forgotten. That for the Jews conversion oriented itself to the commandments of the Torah is self-evident: Conversion is a turning away from sins and obedience to the divine commandments to which the promises of life are attached. The ancient prophets and the Deuteronomic historian likewise understood the essence of conversion thus. Therefore the demand for conversion also belongs to the thematic of the preaching of John the Baptist and Jesus. They continue the conversion preaching of the prophets of Israel; the Gospels bring the theme "conversion" into the world of the Gentiles.

The Praise of God[79]

"Israel brought forth the praise of YHWH unceasingly" (G. von Rad). The praise of God by Israel has not ceased. Devout Judaism is a praying and God-praising people. To praise is to live and to live is to praise; for the dead no longer praise God (cf. Pss. 6:6; 30:10; 88:11f.; 115:17; Isa. 38:18f.; Sir. 17:27f.). "Praising is the form of existence most proper to humanity."[80] Praise, linguistically expressed best of all in the two verbs *halal* and *yadah*, "must take place so that God will be acknowledged, affirmed, and confirmed in his being God and indeed in the complete fullness of his being God,"[81] and it must take place in joy.[82] It is not the intellect that loves God, but rather "the breathing, joyful, singing human being."[83] Almost always it is the community that is urged to praise God (more often the plural: "Praise ye!"), a fact which permits the recognition that the authentic locus of the praise of God is the liturgical gathering: "In the midst of the congregation I will praise thee" (Ps. 22:22; cf. also Pss. 35:18; 109:30). Not just humanity, but all creation should participate in the praise of God: "Let everything that breathes praise the Lord!" (Ps. 150:6; cf. 145:10; 89:6). Kings and nations, all the world should participate in the praise of God (Ps. 148:150). However, each individual should also praise God: "My lips will pour forth praise" (Ps. 119:171); "My mouth will speak the praise of the Lord" (145:21, and elsewhere). "His praise shall continually be in my mouth" (Ps. 34:1). For God "recompenses praise" (Ps. 65:2), indeed "Thou art my praise" (Jer. 17:14); "He is your praise; he is your God" (Deut. 10:21); God is "enthroned on the praises of Israel" (Ps. 22:3). In Chronicles the praise of God often took place at the highpoints of the course of events that were presented:[84] "And it was the duty of the trumpeters and singers to make themselves heard in unison in praise and thanksgiving to the Lord" (2 Chron. 5:13). In this early period of pre-Christian Israel, the praise of God was even institutionalized;[85] cf. 2 Chron. 18:4; Ezra. 3:10; Neh. 12:24. "And they shall stand every morning, thanking and praising the Lord, and likewise at evening" (1 Chron. 23:30). In prophecy a future praise of God is predicted. In the time of salvation Israel again will become "praise" (cf. Isa. 60:18; 62:7) and it is urged now to praise God for his coming acts of salvation (Isa. 62:9). Above all, however, God is praised for the works and beauty of Creation, especially in the "Creation psalms" (cf. Pss. 8; 19a; 33:6–9; 89:12f.; 90:2; 100:3; 104; 139; 148), and further for the past acts of salvation for his people Israel, or for both together as in the litanylike Ps. 136 with its constant refrain, "For his mercy endures forever." Likewise, God is praised for his just judgments: "I will give thanks to thee, O Lord, for though thou wast angry with me, thy anger turned away, and thou didst comfort me. Behold, God is my salvation; I will trust, and will not be afraid; for the Lord God is my strength and my song, and he has become my salvation" (Isa. 12:1f.). Therefore the verb *yadah* ("to praise") also has the meaning of "to confess": because Israel "confesses" its sins before God, it honors God and praises him for his forgiving kindness which it time and again is allowed to experience.

An important thought in this connection appears to be that the praise of God is carried out by Israel "before the nations" (cf. Pss. 18:50; 57:10; 108:4). The praise of God, therefore, has a public character. It is carried out before the eyes of the world. With its praise of God, Israel thereby bears a public witness to God who indeed is not merely the God of Israel, but of all creation and all peoples, as the Old Testament proclaims and as Judaism testifies unto today. In the "enthronement psalms," among which certainly Psalms 47, 93, 96, 97, 98, and 99 are to be numbered,[86] God is praised as the king of the whole world and the Gentiles are urged to join their voices with Israel in praise:[87]

> Clap your hands, all peoples!
> Shout to God with loud songs of joy!
> For the Lord, the Most High, is terrible,
>   a great king over all the earth.
> He subdued all peoples under us,
>   and nations under our feet.
> He chose our heritage for us,
>   the pride of Jacob whom he loves.
> God has gone up with a shout,
>   the Lord with the sound of a trumpet.
> Sing praises to God, sing praises!
>   sing praises to our King, sing praises!
> For God is the king of all the earth;
>   sing praises with a psalm!
> God reigns over the nations;
>   God sits on his holy throne.
> The princes of the peoples gather
>   as the people of the God of Abraham.
> For the shields of the earth belong to God;
>   he is highly exalted! (Ps. 47).

In this section I have attempted briefly to sketch out those fundamental attitudes which characterize the life of Israel before God. One could object that that is essentially all "Old Testament theology" and not the "theology of Judaism." However, one would find it difficult to draw sharp lines of division here, for these fundamental attitudes largely drawn from the Old Testament still define the life of the devout Jew. It is the spiritual inheritance which has come to Israel from its fathers, and has also come into the Gentile world over the "bridge" Jesus. These fundamental attitudes are not "discoveries" of the Church; rather they belong to the spiritual dowry of Israel, to the "root." They have been transmitted to the Church in its mission to the Gentiles. Thus, through the mediation of Jesus and the Church, Israel became paradigmatic for the Gentiles, even if Jesus of Nazareth accentuated the life before God in his own manner, without thereby stepping outside the framework of Judaism.[88]

THE COVENANT

In the following section, I am not concerned with briefly presenting the entire Old Testament "covenant theology," but rather with making two points: that according to Old Testament proclamation "the covenant" presents a continuing institution and that in this institution a continuing relationship between God and Israel and between God and the world comes to expression, whatever semantic significance one attributes to the Hebrew term *berit*.[89]

The beginning point of the following reflections is the covenant of Noah (Gen. 9:1–17),[90] especially the fact that Noah is the representative of all humanity. He and his sons form that remnant which after the catastrophe of the deluge should people the earth anew. The blessing which, according to Gen. 1:28, God has spoken over the first human couple, is repeated verbatim in 9:1 over Noah and his sons. The horizon of salvation within which the conclusion of the covenant with Noah moves is unambiguously a universal-cosmic one; it refers to the whole "earth" (9:13), to "all living creatures" (9:10, 12, 15, 16), to "all flesh which is on the earth" (9:16, 17), including the animal world (9:10).[91] The covenant which God concluded with Noah for all humanity, the animal world, and the earth did not indeed make humanity an equal partner with God—God is and remains the sovereign founding lord of the covenant—but what C. Westermann formulated is from now on valid:[92] "The history of nature and the history of humanity presume an unconditioned yes by God to his creation, a yes by God to all life, which can be shaken neither by any sort of catastrophe in the course of history nor by failures, corruption, or outrage of humanity. The pledge of God remains absolutely firm 'as long as the earth exists.'" The rainbow, which after a storm is visible everywhere in the world, in a certain measure binds together heaven and earth. According to 9:12–17 it is the "sign of the covenant" between God and the earth (9:13): "When the bow is in the clouds, I will look upon it and remember the everlasting covenant between God and every living creature of all flesh that is upon the earth" (9:16). This may sound anthropomorphic, but the term "remember" is spoken by God not anthropomorphically but with a higher theological dignity. For the remembering of God is a powerful, effective remembering[93] which intervenes in history and which in the end will lead to the redemption of the world with which God concluded "an eternal covenant" in the pledge to Noah after the deluge. God will save the world even if the earth again "lies polluted under its inhabitants; for they have transgressed the laws . . . broken the everlasting covenant" (Isa. 24:5).

By "the everlasting covenant" the covenant with Noah is intended here.[94] According to the Old Testament, not only did Israel repeatedly break the covenant which God had concluded with it and its patriarch Abraham, but so also did the nations, all humanity, break this covenant of God with the earth.[95]

In this connection the text of Gen. 9:1–7 written by the priestly writer with the threefold threat of God "to demand a reckoning" (cf. 9:5) for all innocent blood shed on earth, especially for the shedding of human blood, is particularly important: "Whoever sheds the blood of man, by man shall his blood be shed; for God made man in his own image." The threefold repetition of the verb "require" in 9:5 gives the threat of God a special weight, and the purpose is clear; "the commandment 'thou shalt not kill!' which stands behind 9:5, 6 is in conscious and stressed fashion reformulated into the statement which expresses God's being the Lord unconditionally over the life of human beings. In this connection—in the blessing of humanity saved from the flood—the unconditioned and unlimited validity of the command 'thou shalt not kill!' pertains, however, to the *whole of humanity*."[96] The brotherly relationship of human beings among one another is destroyed by murder. The sharp word against murder is based herein: "For God made man in his own image" (9:6c). Consequently it follows that every murderer stands against God, whose "image" he has destroyed. God does not conclude a covenant with murderers, but with those who allow their fellow human beings to flourish in their dignity and who are prepared to live in community with them.

It is thereby immediately apparent that Creation is the basis for the salvific actions of God in the world not only with regard to the covenant with Noah, but also with regard to the covenant of God with Abraham, who was to be the patriarch of Israel and at the same time the father of many nations, and to the covenant of God with Israel, and further to the "new covenant" predicted by Jeremiah, which indeed is primarily the renewed covenant with Israel (cf. Jer. 31:31–34; 32:37–41; Ezek. 16:60–63; 34:25–31; 37:15–28). Especially in Deutero-Isaiah are covenant and Creation brought together, since the Creator and the Redeemer are identical: "For your *Maker* is your husband, YHWH of Hosts is his name; and the Holy One Israel is your *Redeemer*, the God of the whole earth he is called" (Isa. 54:5). The "eternal covenant of peace" promised to Israel by God is expressly brought into relationship with the covenant of Noah: "For this is like the days of Noah to me: as I swore that the waters of Noah should no more go over the earth, so I have sworn that I will not be angry with you and will not rebuke you. For the mountains may depart and the hills be removed, but my steadfast love shall not depart from you, and my covenant of peace shall not be removed, says YHWH, who has compassion on you" (Isa. 54:9f.).[97]

The guarantee for this covenant is the servant of God, whom God made in person "a covenant to the people," and at the same time also "a light unto the nations" (Isa. 42:6). Because the Creator of the world is also the Redeemer, it cannot be other than that "the covenant" will constantly be seen in universal salvific dimensions since the peoples are drawn into it. The peoples owe the idea of the covenant, according to which God himself binds himself forever to Israel and the world and therefore will save the world, to the theological thinking of Israel. The Jew Jesus of Nazareth in no way moves outside of this framework when at the Last Supper he designates his blood as "blood of the covenant for many" (thus, Mark 14:24; Matt. 26:28) or the chalice offered by him as "the new covenant in my blood" (thus, Luke 22:20; 1 Cor. 11:25). Salvation shows itself as a covenant through which God has entered into a lasting relationship of loyalty to Israel and to the whole world. "Covenant" says that God will not forget his creation. The world knows this primarily through Israel.

THE MESSIANIC IDEA

The messianic idea in Judaism and in Christianity has its roots in the Old Testament, especially in the prophetic promises of a bringer of salvation for Israel and the peoples at the end of time. The prediction of the prophet Nathan to King David in 2 Sam. 7:12f., 16 is still the classical fundamental text: "When your days are fulfilled and you lie down with your fathers, I will raise up your son after you, who shall come forth from your body, and I will establish his kingdom. He shall build a house for my name, and I will establish the throne of his kingdom for ever. I will be his father, and he shall be my son. . . . And your house and your kingdom shall be made sure for ever before me; your throne shall be established for ever."

It cannot be the purpose of this tractate to lay out once again the history of the understanding of the Messiah; for this reference must be made to the wealth of existing literature.[98] Likewise the history of the messianic idea in postbiblical Judaism cannot be presented here. For this also, reference must be made to the most important literature.[99] In this tractate I attend above all to the significant place which the messianic idea in Judaism, as mediated through Judaism and Christianity, has taken in the world. For through the fact that the Church proclaimed and proclaims Jesus of Nazareth as the promised Messiah, the Old Testament-Jewish messianic idea has come into the thinking of the Gentile world and has become fermentive, not however, merely through the Church, but likewise through Judaism itself.

The best work written on the understanding of the messianic idea in Judaism is probably that by the great Jewish scholar Gershom Scholem (see n. 99). Judaism never developed a unified messianic idea either in its Old Testament era, or at the time of Jesus or in the postbiblical period. There were always various "types" or "powers" in the Jewish idea of the Messiah. Sholem distinguishes three: conservative, restorative, and utopian, and describes these three thus:[100]

> The conservative forces are directed toward the preservation of that which exists and which, in the historical environment of Judaism, was always in danger. They are the most easily visible and immediately obvious forces that operate in this type of Judaism. They have established themselves most effectively in the world of *Halacha,* in the construction and continuing perservation and development of religious law. This law determined the nature of the Jew's life in exile, the only frame in which a life in the light of Sinaitic revelation seemed possible, and it is not surprising that it drew to itself, above all, the conservative forces. The restorative forces are directed to the return and recreation of a past condition which comes to be filled as ideal. More precisely, they are directed to a condition pictured by the historical fantasy and the memory of the nation as circumstances of an ideal past. Here hope is turned backward to the re-establishment of an original state of things and to a "life with the ancestors." But there are, in addition, forces which press forward and renew; they are nourished by a vision of the future and receive utopian inspiration. They aim at a state of things which has never yet existed. The problem of Messianism in historical Judaism appears within the field of influence of these forces. To be sure, the conservative tendencies, great and even crucial as their role and/or their significance were for the existence of the religious community of Judaism, have no part in the development of Messianism within this community. This is not true, however, of the two other tendencies which I characterize as restorative and utopian. Both tendencies are deeply intertwined and yet at the same time of a contradictory nature; the messianic idea crystallizes only out of the two of them together. Neither is

entirely absent in the historical and ideological manifestations of Messianism. Only the proportion between them is subject to the widest fluctuations.

The question which concerns us in this tractate is: What did and does the messianic idea originating in Judaism bring to the impulses in the Gentile world which both interpret and change history? Three answers arise:

1. The messianic idea breaks open the cyclical thinking of humanity; history does not move in a circle, it is not the eternal return of the same; rather, history is goal-oriented, it moves toward a goal, a *telos.*

2. This movement of history understands itself as a movement out of nonsalvation into salvation.

3. The turn toward salvation will be brought about by a definitive bringer of salvation who is called the "Messiah."

Utopian Messianism is often achieved by restorative elements: the primordial should be reestablished (the idea of *apokatastasis!*),[101] that which was lost should be brought back. "However, knowingly or unknowingly, certain elements creep into such a restoratively oriented utopianism which are not in the least restorative and which derive from the vision of a completely new state of the messianic world."[102]

The messianic idea as it is encountered in the Old Testament prophets is, however, by no means merely the declaration of a more beautiful future for humanity, its "redemption" at the end of times, rather it is also born out of the experienced needs of the time, which are mostly political and social in nature. Therefore, it comes fundamentally from the knowledge that the world as it is is not in order. The world shall and should, however, come into salvation, of course often passing through catastrophes which shake it and which signal "the end." "This aeon" will be shuffled off by the "coming aeon." Someday a better world will come about. This conviction stands behind "utopian" Messianism. The Messiah will bring the world to salvation.

However, there are two differing opinions about how the world arrives at salvation: either along the path of evolution, a gradual development of history toward a better future in which justice reigns, or along the path of revolution. While the prophets and apocalyptics of Israel know no evolutionary progress of history itself toward redemption, according to them "it is rather transcendence breaking in upon history, an intrusion in which history itself perishes, transformed in its ruin because it is struck by a beam of light shining into it from an outside source."[103] Other messianic utopians, above all Karl Marx and Ernst Bloch, await the final salvation of the world, which they see as inner worldly in the "classless society," from the revolutionizing of the world. This "Messianism became tied up with the idea of the eternal progress and infinite task of humanity perfecting itself."[104] Scholem even believes that "Jewish Messianism is in its origins and by its nature—this cannot be sufficiently emphasized—a theory of catastrophe. This theory stresses the revolutionary, cataclysmic element in the transition from historical present to the messianic future."[105] However, in the biblical texts themselves "which serve as the basis for the crystallization of the messianic idea it is nowhere made dependent upon human activity."[106] Nevertheless "the enticement to action is inherent"[107] in the messianic idea.

Through the Jews and through the Jew Jesus, the messianic idea has come into the world of the Gentiles. It very strongly characterizes even the secularized thinking of present-day humanity, above all in the area of Marxism. The Jewish people, believes Scholem,[108] had to pay a high price, indeed "out of its substance" for the messianic idea which it gave to the world.

The magnitude of the messianic idea corresponds to the endless powerlessness in Jewish history during all the centuries of exile, when it was unprepared to come forward unto the plain of world history. There is something preliminary, something provisional about Jewish history; hence its inability to give of itself entirely. For the messianic idea is not only consolation and hope. Every attempt to realize it tears open the abysses which lead each of its manifestations *ad absurdum*. There's something grand about living in hope, but at the same time there is something profoundly unreal about it. . . . Thus in Judaism the messianic idea has compelled a *life lived in deferment,* in which nothing can be done definitively, nothing can be irrevocably accomplished. One might say, perhaps, the messianic idea is the real anti-existentialist idea [I would like to add: It is also the real anti-structuralist idea.][109] Precisely understood, there is nothing concrete which can be accomplished by the unredeemed. This makes for the greatness of Messianism, but also for its constitutional weakness. Jewish so-called *Existenz* possesses a tension that never finds true release; it never burns itself out. And when in our history it does discharge, then it is foolishly decried (or, one might say, unmasked) as "pseudo-Messianism." The blazing landscape of redemption (as if it were a point of focus) has concentrated in itself the historical outlook of Judaism. Little wonder overtones of Messianism have accompanied the modern Jewish readiness for irrevocable action in the concrete realm, when it set out in the utopian return to Zion. It is a readiness which no longer allows itself to be fed on hopes. Born out of horror and destruction that was Jewish history in our generation, it is bound to history itself and not to meta-history; it has not given itself up totally to Messianism. Whether or not Jewish history will be able to endure this entry into the concrete realm without perishing in the crisis of the messianic claim which has virtually been conjured up—that is the question which out of his great and dangerous past the Jew of this age poses to his present and to his future.

How did the Jew Jesus, in whom Christians honor the Messiah, understand the messianic idea? Doubtless he saw himself as the promised Messiah of Israel,[110] even if his works appeared to be partly unmessianic in the
eyes of his Jewish contemporaries. Scholem understands the Messianism of
Jesus of Nazareth and Christian Messianism as an interiorization of the God
relationship and thereby as an individualization of the idea of the Messiah.
There is much that is correct in this, but Jesus' conversion preaching
understands itself messianically because it is bound up with the proclamation of the imminent eschatological reign of God (cf., for example, Mark
1:15). And already with the prophets, and especially with John the Baptist,
conversion preaching is understood as preparing the way for the Messiah
(cf. Mark 1:2–8 and parallels), and the wonders of Jesus signify a saved
world in which the blind see, the lame walk, the lepers are cleansed, the
deaf hear, the dead rise, and the poor have the good news preached to them
(cf. Luke 7:22). Jesus predicts his coming again at the end of times as a
public act which pertains to the whole world: "And then they will see the
Son of man coming in clouds with great power and glory. And then he will
send out the angels, and gather his elect from the four winds, from the ends
of the earth to the ends of heaven" (Mark 13:26f. and parallels). However,
the Johannine Apocalypse understands the return of the Lord as a completely political event in which the antichrist, who according to the Apocalypse is the strongest political and economic force of the world, will be
annihilated by Christ the Messiah who comes again and a new heaven and a
new earth will be inaugurated. With this the Messianism of the Johannine
Apocalypse stands totally within the tradition of biblical prophetic Messianism. The restorative and utopian elements of biblical Messianism also
find here a completed synthesis. History finds its catastrophic end and the
new world of God in which all is saved breaks in, inaugurated not by human
activity, but solely by the activity of God and his Messiah. Thus the
biblical-Jewish character continues also in Christian Messianism. It does
not move outside of this framework. Christianity has decisively contributed
to the bringing of the biblical-Jewish Messianism into the thinking of the
world. "Utopian" Messianism is more fermentive today than ever. The
world no longer wishes to turn in circles; it looks into the future and toward
a goal.[111]

THE DISCOVERY OF THE FUTURE

The messianic idea, above all in its utopian form, presses toward the
future. The messianic idea provides hope and binds the awaiting of the
future, that is eschatology, together with the hope in YHWH. The eschato-

logical thinking of Israel and the Bible breaks open cyclical thinking and sees history within a dynamic which is pulled toward a goal. One could say in brief: Israel had discovered the future, but in connection with judgment and salvation, promise and fulfillment.[112] Israel's eschatology is therefore the teaching of the coming salvation of Israel, the Gentiles, and all humanity. Thereby Israel's eschatology is closely bound up with its history, that is, eschatology itself has its history which is indissolubly connected with the history of revelation in Israel. Thus the development of eschatology has nothing to do with evolution or with the "world process" of Hegel and of Marxism. The path to the *eschaton* is much more the path of God, his saving leading,[113] which knows no mutation leaps, but rather only grace and judgment. Eschatology is not the doctrine of the inner-worldly completability and completion of history, but rather the doctrine of the "last things" and of the "ultimate" toward which history orients itself—thus, for example, the world must be "ripe" for the appearance of what the New Testament calls "the antichrist"—which, however, lies beyond it, transcends history, for there is an absolute break which in the Old Testament is sometimes called the "day of YHWH."

Since it cannot be the intention of this tractate to present in extended fashion or even in an abbreviated form the complex history of biblical eschatology, a history which in no way has been fully clarified in research, this eschatology will be demonstrated here paradigmatically with the Old Testament term "the day of YHWH," especially since "day" is a temporal term in which the temporal element in eschatology, which concerns the future, is extraordinarily well expressed.[114]

The earliest text which speaks of the "day of YHWH" is Amos 5:18, 20: "Woe to you who desire the day of YHWH! Why would you have the day of YHWH? It is darkness, and not light. . . . Is not the day of YHWH darkness, and not light, and gloom with no brightness in it?" In this text two things are clear: First, the phrase "the day of YHWH" appears to already be firmly set and known. Secondly, "the day of YHWH" had been seen as an especially happy day. The prophet, on the other hand, proclaims it to be a day of calamity. He dispelled the false expectations which the people had hung on "the day of YHWH."

In Isa. 13:6–13 the judgment on Babel as the "day of YHWH" is described:

Wail, for the day of YHWH is near; as destruction from the Almighty it will come! Therefore all hands will be feeble, and every man's heart will melt, and they will be dismayed. Pangs and agony will seize them; they will be in an anguish like a woman in travail. They will look aghast at one another; their faces will be aflame. Behold, the day of YHWH comes, cruel, with wrath and fierce anger, to make the earth a desolation and to destroy its sinners from it. For the stars of the heavens and their constellations will not give their light; the sun will be dark at its rising and the moon will not shed its light. I will punish the world for its evil, and the wicked for their iniquity; I will put an end to the pride of the arrogant, and lay low the haughtiness of the ruthless. I will make men more rare than fine gold, and mankind than the gold of Ophir. Therefore I will make the heavens tremble, and the earth will be shaken out of its place, at the wrath of YHWH of hosts in the day of his fierce anger.

Likewise in this text "the day of YHWH" is a day of judgment and of calamity, first of all proclaimed against Babylon, but already seen within a cosmic horizon: The whole cosmos and all humanity will be drawn into the judgment event!

Likewise in Ezek. 7 the catastrophe of the "end" and of the "day" pertains first to Judah-Jerusalem. However, even here world-embracing elements flow in; the calamity of the judgment comes over the whole earth.

7:2: "Thus says the Lord YHWH to the land of Israel: An end! The end has come upon the four corners of the Land."

7:5–7: "Thus says the Lord YHWH: Disaster after disaster! Behold, it comes. An end has come, the end has come; it has awakened against you. Behold, it comes. Your doom has come to you, O inhabitant of the land; the time has come, the day is near, a day of tumult, and not of joyful shouting upon the mountains."

7:10–12a: "Behold, the day! Behold, it comes! Your doom has come, injustice has blossomed, pride has budded. Violence has grown up into a rod of wickedness; none of them shall remain, nor their abundance, nor their wealth; neither shall there be pre-eminence among them. The time has come, the day draws near."

The goal of the day of judgment is this: "Then you will know that I am YHWH, who smite" (7:9); cf. 7:27: "And they shall know that I am YHWH." The political calamity which has come upon Israel shall lead to its knowledge of God.

Even so, however, in Ezek. 30:11ff. "the day of YHWH" is proclaimed as a day of calamity for Egypt and other lands; "Thus I will execute acts of judgment upon Egypt. Then they will know that I am YHWH" (30:19). Cf. also Jer. 46:3–12.

It does not stop, however, at the "day" of judgment, for the "day" of salvation for Israel follows (Ezek. 36:33–37):

Thus says the Lord YHWH: On the day that I cleanse you from all your iniquities, I will cause the cities to be inhabited, and the waste places shall be rebuilt. And the land that was desolate shall be tilled, instead of being the desolation that it was in the sight of all who passed by. And they will say, "This land that was desolate has become like the garden of Eden; and the waste and desolate and ruined cities are now inhabited and fortified." Then the nations that are left round about you shall know that I YHWH have rebuilt the ruined places, and replanted that which was desolate; I YHWH have spoken, and I will do it.

Thus says the Lord YHWH: This also I will let the house of Israel ask me to do for them: to increase their men like a flock. Like the flock for sacrifices, like the flock at Jerusalem during her appointed feasts, so shall the waste cities be filled with the flocks of men. Then they will know that I am YHWH.

"The day of YHWH" plays a special role with the prophet Joel. As in the previous prophecies, the day is first of all one of calamity for Israel: "Blow the trumpet in Zion; sound the alarm on my holy mountain! Let all the inhabitants of the land tremble, for the day of YHWH is coming, it is near, a day of darkness and gloom, a day of clouds and thick darkness!" (2:1f.).

The storm on the city is described (2:7–11) and the threatening prophecy concludes with the sentence in 2:11b: "For the day of YHWH is great and very terrible; who can endure it?" However, in the midst of the prophetic announcement of the fearful "day of YHWH" there sounds the announcement of salvation and the promise of rescue; cf. 2:30: "And I will give portents in the heavens and on earth, blood and fire and columns of smoke. The sun shall be turned to darkness, and the moon to blood, before the great and terrible day of YHWH comes. And it shall come to pass that all who call upon the name of YHWH shall be delivered; for in Mt. Zion and in Jerusalem there shall be those who escape, as YHWH has said, and among the survivors shall be those whom YHWH calls."

Immediately following comes the final judgment upon the nations, but the turn of fate for Judah and Jerusalem is announced (3:1f., 12–14):

> For behold, in those days and that at time, when I restore the fortunes of Judah and Jerusalem, I will gather all the nations and bring them down to the valley of Jehoshaphat, and I will enter into judgment with them there, on account of my people and my heritage Israel, because they have scattered them among the nations, and have divided up my land. . . . Let the nations bestir themselves, and come up to the valley of Jehoshaphat; for there I will sit to judge all the nations round about. Put in the sickle, for the harvest is ripe. Go in, tread, for the wine press is full. The vats overflow, for their wickedness is great. Multitudes, multitudes, in the valley of decision! For the day of YHWH is near in the valley of decision.

It is in the "valley of decision" that the "day of decision" takes place, that is, "the day of YHWH." This day is very certainly not just any "day" of judgment in history, but very clearly the end time "day," the "day" of world judgment, not to be understood, however, as the final word of God in history, but rather as the endtime transitional catastrophe for all the world, behind which lasting salvation and continuing redemption shine forth.

Once more the theme of "the day of YHWH" turns up urgently in the prophet Zephaniah. After the judgment on all humanity and on Judah and Jerusalem is announced in 1:2–13, there follows in 1:7, 14–18 a prophetic hymn of praise of the "day of YHWH":

> Be silent before the Lord YHWH! For the day of YHWH is at hand; YHWH has prepared a sacrifice and consecrated his guests. . . . The great day of YHWH is near, near and hastening fast; the sound of the day of YHWH is bitter, the mighty man cries aloud there. A day of wrath is that day, a day of distress and anguish, a day of ruin and devastation, a day of darkness and gloom, a day of clouds and thick darkness, a day of trumpet blast and battle cry against the fortified cities and against the lofty battlements. . . . A sudden end he will make of all the inhabitants of the earth.

And in 3:8 the prophet calls to all the nations: " 'Therefore wait for me,' says YHWH, 'for the day when I arise as a witness. For my decision is to gather nations, to assemble kingdoms, to pour out upon them my indignation, all the heat of my anger; for in the fire of my jealous wrath all the earth shall be consumed.' "

However, "that day" is also the inbreaking "day" of salvation for Israel (cf. 3:16a, 14, 20b): "On that day it shall be said to Jerusalem: '. . . Sing aloud, O daughter of Zion; shout, O Israel! . . . I will make you renowned and praised among all the peoples of the earth, when I restore your fortunes before your eyes, says YHWH.' "

I shall proceed from the thesis that Israel discovered the future; it brought eschatological thinking into the world, which destroyed the cyclical interpretation of history. Thereby Israel also discovered historical consciousness.[115] A prophetic prediction of the "day of YHWH," however, brought the special character of biblical thinking about the future paradigmatically to the level of consciousness. This special character is summarized in the following sentences:

1. Eschatological thinking in Israel did not appear from one day to the next. "The day of Israel" is connected first of all with political events of a catastrophic nature in the history of Israel. "The day of Israel" is a day of war and defeat brought about by God as punishment for the failure of the people before him.

2. However, even early "the day of YHWH" received a universal-cosmic dimension: it emcompassed the whole world within a horizontal and temporal perspective. It looked toward "the end" as such.

3. As the "final day," the "day of YHWH" is not a day which can be reckoned on the calendar. God alone knows it and brings it about.

4. This "day" is therefore not the gradual and final product of the evolution of the world (its omega point), but rather the catastrophic break brought about by God which brings this aeon to an end and distinguishes it from the coming aeon.

5. Nevertheless, this "day" energizes history and drives it on toward its end.

6. This "day" proves that the idea of an inner-worldly completability and completion of history is an unrealizable utopia. History does not of itself move toward a "kingdom of freedom." This "day" contradicts the theses of Hegel, Marx, and others.

7. This "day" is a "day" of transition. With it God definitively brings forth his future, which includes in it a world of salvation and justice. Therefore this "day" gives the world hope.[116]

Israel "infested" the world with thought about the future. It no longer rests quietly within it. There are, of course, in the Old Testament tendencies to attach Israel to "that which exists," as for example in the priestly writings[117] or in what Scholem calls "conservative Messianism." There is in Judaism, however, also the danger of "utopian Messianism" as soon as Messianism understands itself as an attempt at inner-worldly completion of history, as for example in genuine Marxism[118] or with Ernst Bloch who in his life's work *The Principle of Hope* arrived at the thesis: "*Ubi* Lenin, *ibi* Jerusalem."[119] Nevertheless, since the prediction of the "day of YHWH" the attention of the world is directed toward the future; since then it can no longer understand history as "the eternal return of the same." The prophets of Israel had "dynamized" the world. Naturally, Jewish apocalyptic likewise took up the idea of the coming "day" (of the Lord) in its visions of the future. Here the "day" means the time of the great final judgment on the world and is called the "day of judgment," "the day of God," "your day," "the day of the Messiah," "the day of the servant," "the day of the chosen."[120]

Jesus and the primitive Church also took up the theme of the "day of YHWH" in their proclamation, even though it is now appropriately partly in christologized form and, of course, in tension with the first coming of the Messiah Jesus. In any case, the day (of the Lord) is now unambiguously related to the action of God at the end of times. Thus Jesus in Luke 17:24 speaks of the "day of the Son of man" and means thereby the time of his appearing in the glory of the kingdom; likewise in John 8:56 "my day" means the day of the final revelation of the glory of Jesus. In 2 Pet. 3:12 "the

day of God" is the day of the burning of the world and in Apoc. 16:14 it is
the day of battle of the (true) ruler of the world with the atheistic kings of
the earth. In Paul "the day" is the day of the final judgment of the Christian
community (1 Cor. 1:8; Phil. 1:6, 10), but also that of the rest of humanity.
In 1 Thess. 5:2 and 2 Thess. 2:2 "the day" is the day of the *parousia* of
Christ; in 1 Thess. 5:5; 1 Cor. 3:13, and Heb. 10:25 it is the day of final
judgment as is also "that day" (Matt. 7:22; Luke 10:12; 2 Tim. 1:12, 18) the
judgment day at the end of times. In Jude 6; Apoc. 6:17 and 16:14, this day
is called "the great day." Christian eschatology therefore also lives within
this eschatological framework of the Old Testament-Jewish heritage. This
heritage subsequently entered into world thinking, if often in secularized
form, in the utopian dreams of the coming days of great freedom and justice
in all the world. It is the future which inspires new ideas.[121]

THE YEARNING FOR A JUST WORLD

The prophets of Israel were not merely predictors of the coming judgment and coming salvation; at the same time they were critics of the
existing state of affairs, especially in societal and social perspective. They
were social critics, but in an indissoluble linkage with their prediction of
judgment and salvation; for their social criticism immediately depicted a
utopian image of a coming world of justice and of freedom.[122] Thus, what
H. W. Wolff formulated is true: "It is characteristic for the Old Testament
that concrete measures and utopian plans are found alongside one
another."[123]

The Prophetic Critique of Existing Injustice

For this paradigmatic material from the prophetic books will be brought
forth, first of all from Amos, the prophet of the eighth century B.C.E. who
mercilessly pilloried the bending of justice and the social injustice in the
northern kingdom of Israel and predicted its demise. In 5:10 it is said of
those who cast justice to the ground (cf. 5:7): "They hate him who reproves
in the gate, and they abhor who speaks the truth."[124] With this the abuses of
the legal procedures were openly addressed.

5:11: "Therefore because you trample upon the poor and take from him
exactions of wheat, you have built houses of hewn stone, but you shall not
dwell in them; you have planted pleasant vineyards, but you shall not drink
their wine." The possessors have no concern for the helpless and the poor,
who are shamelessly exploited. This exploitation goes so far that—as it is
pilloried in 2:6—"They sell the righteous for silver, and the needy for a pair
of shoes." Human beings are dealt with as wares. Cf. also 2:7: "They . . .

trample the head of the poor into the dust, and turn aside the way of the afflicted." The prophet holds up for criticism those who carry on unfair business (8:4): "[Hear this you who say]: 'When will the new moon be over, that we may sell grain? And the sabbath, that we may offer wheat for sale, that we may make the ephah small and the sheckel great, and deal deceitfully with false balances?' " "Bad wares, false measures, unjust prices—those are the evil consequences of the greed for profit."[125]

Other prophets of the eighth century similarly raise their voices against social injustice. Thus Micah: "Woe to those who devise wickedness and work evil upon their beds! When the morning dawns, they perform it, because it is in the power of their hand. They covet fields, and seize them; and houses, and take them away. They oppress a man and his house, a man and his inheritance" (2:1f.). "But you rise against my people as an enemy; you strip the robe from the peaceful, from those who pass by trustingly with no thought of war. The women of my people you drive out from their pleasant houses; from their young children you take away my glory for ever. Arise and go, for this is no place to rest; because of uncleanness that destroys with a grievous destruction" (2:8–10). "Hear this, you heads of the house of Jacob and rulers of the house of Israel, who abhor justice and pervert all equity, who build Zion with blood and Jerusalem with wrong. Its heads give judgment for a bribe, its priests teach for hire, its prophets divine for money" (3:9–11a). Isaiah warns: "Learn to do good; seek justice, correct oppression; defend the fatherless, plead for the widow" (1:17). In 5:8–10 he calls down a woe upon those who are greedy for land and in 10:1f. he says to unjust judges: "Woe to those who decree iniquitous decrees, and the writers who keep writing oppression, to turn aside the needy from justice and to rob the poor of my people of their right, that widows may be their spoil, and that they make the fatherless their prey!" The successors of these early prophets are in agreement; cf. Jer. 5:1f.; 5:27ff.; 7:9.; 9:1f., and elsewhere; Ezek. 18:6ff.; 22:6–10; Isa. 58:1–12; Zech. 7:7–9; Mal. 2:14–16.

Thus into the fifth century the prophets proclaimed that God acted in favor of the poor and those who suffered injustice and that true belief in God without helping those in need and the disenfranchised poor is not possible. They are thereby simply establishing Israel's ancient order of justice and identifying its violation. It concerns "right" and "justice," two fundamental concepts of the community order of Israel. In the eyes of the prophets of Israel, the violation of this order is, along with the breaking of the covenant, the true sin against God.

In the language of ancient Israel what is really meant by the terms "right" and "justice"? Both concepts are more than purely juridical concepts; they are sociological concepts. They are "relational concepts" related to community, be it the communal relationship between God and humanity (Israel), or between each human being. Both concepts include an "inter," an "area," a "link." When the link between God and the human being and on the other hand between human beings is correct, when it corresponds to the God-willed order, then right (*mishpat*) and justice (*tzedakah, tzedek*) prevail, then is everything "right," in the correct relationship to one another; then there exists a saving world order.[126] The prophetic critique on the existing order is connected with the prediction of a world in which right and justice prevail, the world order based upon right, justice, and peace.

A Prophetic Prediction of a Coming World Order in Right, Justice, and Peace

Justice becomes "a concluding point of a new salvation history," particularly with the prophets Hosea and Isaiah.[127] Cf. Hos. 2:18–19: "And I will make for you a covenant on that day with the beasts of the field, the birds of the air, and the creeping things of the ground; and I will abolish the bow, the sword, and war from the land; and I will make you lie down in safety. And I will betroth you to me for ever; I will betroth you to me in righteousness and in justice, in steadfast love, and in mercy."

And Isaiah sees in a vision the kingdom of freedom and justice of the coming Messiah; cf. 9:2–7:

> The people who walked in darkness have seen a great light; those who dwelt in a land of deep darkness, on them has light shined. Thou has multiplied the nation, thou hast increased its joy; they rejoice before thee as with joy at the harvest, as men rejoice when they divide the spoil. For the yoke of his burden, and the staff for his shoulder, the rod of his oppressor, thou hast broken as on the day of Midian. For every boot of the tramping warrior in battle tumult and every garment rolled in blood will be burned as fuel for the fire. For to us a child is born, to us a son is given; and the government will be upon his shoulder, and his name will be called "Wonderful Counselor, Mighty God, Everlasting Father, Prince of Peace." Of the increase of his government and of peace there will be no end, upon the throne of David, and over his kingdom to establish it, and to uphold it with justice and with righteousness from this time forth and for evermore. The zeal of YHWH of hosts will do this.

Cf. also 11:4–9; 16:9; 32:1: "Behold, a king will reign in justice, and princes will rule in justice." With the "pessimist" Jeremiah the true breakthrough of right and justice on earth "is awaited only in the eschatological future."[128] Cf. Jer. 23:5f.: "Behold, the days are coming, says YHWH, when I will raise up for David a righteous Branch, and he shall reign as king and deal wisely, and shall execute justice and righteousness in the land. In his days Judah will be saved, and Israel will dwell securely. And this is the name by which he will be called: 'YHWH is our righteousness.' "[129]

Out of the rich material of Deutero-Isaiah only a few things will be presented, for example, Isa. 51:4–8:

> Listen to me, my people, and give ear to me, my nation; for a law will go forth from me, and my justice for a light to the peoples. My deliverance draws near speedily, my salvation has gone forth, and my arms will rule the peoples; the coastlands wait for me, and for my arm they hope. Lift up your eyes to the heavens, and look at the earth beneath; for the heavens will vanish like smoke, the earth will wear out like a garment, and they who dwell in it will die like gnats; but my salvation will be for ever, and my deliverance will never be ended. Hearken to me, you who know righteousness, the people in whose heart is my law; fear not the reproach of men and be not dismayed at their revilings. For the moth will eat them up like a garment, and the worm will eat them like wool; but my deliverance will be for ever, and my salvation to all generations.

Cf. also 61:11: "For as the earth brings forth its shoots, and as a garden causes what is sown in it to spring up, so YHWH God will cause righteousness and praise to spring forth before all the nations."

Justice is bound with peace (shalom); cf. 60:17: "I will make your overseers peace and your taskmasters righteousness." An encompassing world peace belongs alongside right and justice through the content of the eschatological expectation of salvation.[130] In early Judaism these expectations of salvation live on. The Messiah is called "the Messiah of justice."[131]

It should cause no wonder that in the utopian Messianism of Judaism time and again the vision of a world of right, of justice, and of peace turns up, often together with the idea of a world free of domination.[132] Such visions are in the blood of Judaism.[133] They fit together with the idea of Messianism and the discovery of the future; they are the fermentative continuing heritage of the prophets of Israel which has subsequently strongly influenced the thinking of the nations.[134]

Christ in the New Testament is also given the honorific term "the Just One" (cf. Acts 3:14; 1 Pet. 3:18; 1 John 2:1; 2:29; 3:7) and is proclaimed as the one who one day will judge the world in justice (Acts 17:31) and the one who came to proclaim peace to the distant and the close, that is, to all human beings (Eph. 2:17), who indeed is peace in person (2:14). Here also the great faith heritage of Israel lives on in the Church.

The prophets of Israel, of course, are convinced that right, justice, and peace are neither the product of world evolution nor the product of world revolution, but the eschatological gift of God which he will provide through his Messiah in the coming aeon of the world; this, of course, does not mean that justice and peace work do not belong now to the tasks of humanity. The prophetic visions must constantly translate into impulses for present-day justice and peace work. The *eschaton* must be effective in the present; indeed, according to Christian conviction the *eschaton* became present in Jesus Christ, if not yet in its final form. Along with the "critical theory" of the prophets there must be the intention actively to engage in building up a world in justice and peace. Our hands may not be placed in our lap in a simple waiting for the future. Theory must be bound to practice, whose ultimate impulse must always be *love*. And salvation is always something more than a simply socially functioning world.[135] The prophets of Israel knew that and neither Jews nor Christians may forget it. The prophets protect us from a historical unawareness. Alongside their predictions of salvation there are their predictions of judgment; but their predictions of judgment always issue again in the predictions of salvation—of course, in the prediction of a salvation that ultimately lies beyond history.

The Church, along with Israel, awaits "new heavens and a new earth *in which righteousness dwells*" (2 Pet. 3:13) and for the day in which God "will judge the world *in righteousness*" (Acts 17:31).

ATONEMENT AND REPRESENTATION[136]

The idea of "atonement" and of "expiation" plays a central role in Judaism in the Old Testament; it is expressed linguistically above all in the verb *kaphar*.[137] Atonement is very often carried out by substitution, especially when blood guilt is concerned. Such substitutions are the lives of human beings, the lives of animals, and expiatory gifts in the form of sacrifices. The atonement, however, is not produced by the human being but by God. The human being performs expiation, God grants atonement. Here only a few classical quotations will be cited in which the idea of atonement is expressed. According to Exod. 32:30–32 Moses offered himself as the representative atoning sacrifice for the sins of his people: "On the morrow Moses said to the people, 'You have sinned a great sin. And now I will go up to YHWH; perhaps I can make atonement for your sin.' So Moses returned to YHWH and said, 'Alas, this people have sinned a great sin; they have made for themselves gods of gold. But now, if thou wilt forgive their sin—and if not, blot me, I pray thee, out of thy book which thou hast written.'"

Num. 35:33: "You shall not thus pollute the land in which you live; for blood pollutes the land, and no expiation can be made for the land, for the blood that is shed in it, except by the blood of him who shed it." Blood, therefore, is atoned by blood; this truth is connected with the conviction expressed in the following text of Lev. 17:11: "For the life of the flesh is in the blood; and I have given it for you upon the altar to make atonement for your souls; for it is the blood that makes atonement, by reason of the life." In the ritual of the great Day of Atonement, the greatest feast day of Judaism to this very day, the idea of atonement, carried out by the animal's "sin offering," plays the greatest role (cf. Lev. 17).

Since the destruction of the Temple, prayer as the means of atonement has taken the place of animal sacrifice. The Old Testament idea of atonement reached a highpoint in the fourth song of the servant of God, Isa. 52:13—53:12, in which for the first time in the Old Testament the thought of representative atoning suffering turns up: "Surely he has borne our sicknesses and carried our sorrows; yet we esteemed him stricken, smitten by God, and afflicted. But he was wounded for our transgressions, he was bruised for our iniquities; upon him was the chastisement that made us whole, and with his stripes we are healed. All we like sheep have gone astray; we have turned every one to his own way; and YHWH has laid on him the iniquity of us all" (Isa. 53:4–6).

"Yet it was the will of YHWH to bruise him; he has put him to grief; when he makes himself an offering for sin, he shall see his offspring, he shall prolong his days; the will of YHWH shall prosper in his hand; he shall see the fruit of the travail of his soul and be satisfied; by his knowledge shall the righteous one, my servant, make many to be accounted righteous; and he shall bear their iniquities. Therefore I will divide him a portion with the great, and he shall divide the spoil with the strong; because he poured out his soul to death, and was numbered with the transgressors; yet he bore the sin of many, and made intercession for the transgressors" (Isa. 53:10–12).

The idea of atonement, of the "guilt sacrifice," and that of representation are bound together here indissolubly. The primitive Church interpreted the figure of "ebed Yahwe" individually and related it to Jesus, but the "collective" interpretation has not disappeared from the world; rather it lives on in the thoughts of the representative suffering of Israel for its own sins and the sins of the nations, to which I have already referred (pp. 42ff.).

Atonement and representation will likewise play an important role in early Judaism.[138] "The question of atonement won . . . in post-exilic times a great importance and in an increasing measure became determinative for the understanding of cult in general."[139] Also, after the destruction of the Temple the rabbis for a long time concerned themselves with the problem of the cultic means of atonement. According to Midrash Shir. r. I, 15 the cultic sacrifice also has an atoning significance for the Gentiles: "As a dove [as a sacrifice] atones for sins, so the Israelites produce atonement for the Gentiles. For the seventy young bulls which the Israelites bring forth on the feast of Succoth correspond to the seventy nations, so that for their sake the world will not be destroyed." Of course, after the destruction of the Temple in the year 70 after Christ the noncultic means of atonement moved into the foreground, that is, suffering, death, the works of love, the study of Torah, fasting and prayer, but especially conversion.[140] Rabbi Ismael taught—and in this he transmits the thoughts from an earlier origin—[141] that there are four kinds of atonement:

1. If someone transgresses a commandment and repents, he must not leave there (namely, the place of the sin) until one has forgiven him. For it says: Repent you traitorous sons, for I will heal the consequences of your apostasy (Jer. 3:22).

2. If someone transgresses a prohibition and repents, the repentance has a postponing effect and the Day of Atonement provides atonement. For it is written: For on this day he will make you atonement (Lev. 16:30).

3. If someone transgresses a commandment for which there is the punishment of annihilation and the death punishment is issued by a court, and repents, the repentance and the Day of Atonement effect a postponement and the sufferings an atonement. For it is written: With the staff I will afflict your going and with blows your guilt (Ps. 89:32).

4. If, however, someone is guilty of the desecration of the divine name and repents, neither the repentance has the power to effect postponement nor does the Day of Atonement have the power to atone, but the repentance and the Day of Atonement atone one-third and the rest of the days of the year atone a third, and death wipes everything away. For it is written: This misdeed shall not be atoned until you die (Isa. 22:14). That teaches that death wipes out (all guilt).

In *Mishnah* Yoma VIII, 8 it says: "Death and the Day of Atonement atone in connection with repentance." There is also an interesting passage in *Midrash* Pesiqt. 158b:[142] "As one asked human wisdom what should happen to the sinner, it answered: 'Misfortunes pursues sinners' (Prov. 13:21). As one asked prophecy what should happen to the sinner, it answered: 'The soul which sins must die' (Ezek. 18:4). As one asked the Torah what should happen to the sinner, it answered: 'He should bring a guilt offering so that he may be forgiven' (Lev. 1:4). As one asked God himself what should happen to the sinner, he said: 'He should repent so that atonement can be provided him.' For it says: 'Merciful and just is the Lord, therefore he teaches the sinner the path (of repentance)' (Ps. 25:8)."

We have already encountered the connection between atonement and representation. In pre-Christian early Jewish writings this connection is especially encountered in the conviction of the representative function of atoning suffering and atoning death—as, for example, in 2 Maccabees. The youngest son of the mother says first of all to King Antiochus: "For we are suffering because of our own sins" (7:32), and later: "For our brothers after enduring a brief suffering have drunk of everflowing life under God's covenant" (7:36), and he then continues: "I, like my brothers, give up body and life for the laws of our fathers, appealing to God to show mercy soon to our nation . . . and through me and my brothers to bring to an end the wrath of the Almighty which has justly fallen on our whole nation" (7:37f.). In these texts the thoughts of atonement and representation are clearly expressed: the Maccabee brothers wished to die representatively for the atonement for the sins of their nation. This comes out still more clearly in the prayer of the dying Eleazar, according to 4 Macc. 6:28f.: "Be merciful to your people, and let our punishment suffice for them [hyper autōn]. Make my blood their purification, and take my life in exchange for theirs." Eleazar viewed his violent death as a representative atoning death for the sins of his people. Then looking back it was written in 4 Macc. 17:20–22: "Because of them our enemies did not rule over our nation, the tyrant was punished, and the homeland purified—they having become, as it were, a ransom for the sin of our nation. And through the blood of those devout ones and their death as an expiation, divine providence preserved Israel that previously had been afflicted." In 4 Macc. 16:21 the Maccabean mother points to the examples of the three young men in the fiery oven, and in the prayer of Azariah (Dan. 3:26–45) the three young men offer their lives as an atoning sacrifice: "As burnt offerings of rams and bulls, and ten thousands of fat lambs, such may our sacrifice be in thy sight this day." This was said after the confession of sins had been proclaimed and the judgment of God acknowledged as just: "Thou hast executed true judgments in all that thou hast brought upon us and upon Jerusalem, the holy city of our fathers, for in truth and justice thou hast brought all this upon us because of our sins. For we have sinfully and lawlessly departed from thee, and have sinned in all things and have not obeyed thy commandments; we have not observed them or done them, as thou hast commanded us that it might go well with us. So all that thou hast brought upon us, and all that thou hast done to us, thou hast done in true judgment. Thou has given us into the hands of lawless enemies, most hateful rebels, and to an injust king, the most wicked in all the world" (3:28–32).

The idea of representative atonement has never died out in Judaism. The Jew Jesus and the primitive Church also lived in these traditions, and the primitive Church interpreted the violent death of Jesus of Nazareth as a representative atoning death "for our sins," as the ancient credo taken over and handed on by Paul confesses (cf. 1 Cor. 15:3). According to the eucharistic interpretive words Jesus poured out his blood "for the forgiveness of sins" (Matt. 26:28).[143]

Likewise, the death of martyrs and just ones has a representative atoning power attributed to it by the ancient rabbis.[144] Thus, *Midrash* Prov. 9, 2 (31b) relates that Rabbi Akiba suffered a martyr's death on the Day of Atonement. "The statement certainly may be understood to mean that an atoning power was attributed to his death as well as to the Day of Atonement."[145] Rabbi Eleazar ben Pedath (around 270 c.e.) taught that the martyrdom of the three young men in the fiery furnace took place on the Sabbath and on the Day of Atonement.[146]

This material should suffice. The idea of atonement and of representation likewise belongs to the great heritage of faith of Israel. It did not first arrive in the world with the Church, even though the Gentiles, according to the evidence of the history of religions, always had an awareness that sins must be atoned through sacrifice. The idea of atonement and of the representative atoning death time and again wrenches the world out toward the holy God; time and again it prevents the world from falling into self-satisfaction and self-righteousness. It helps to keep the conscience awake in the world and it serves to dismantle the lust of aggression.[147]

CONSCIENCE AND THE DECALOGUE

"The Jew invented conscience." This slogan belonged to the arsenal of the Nazi persecution of Judaism. Of course the Jew did not "invent" conscience, nor even the word "conscience," which is not present in the Old Testament. However, the Jew was and is most intensely concerned with the matter commonly expressed by the word "conscience."[148] Or better said: The Jew, Israel, is caught up by this matter, that is, by God himself. Israel was called by God to hear his voice and instruction. The organ in the human being which hears the instruction of God is called in the Old Testament not "conscience," but "heart."[149] Likewise rabbinical early Judaism and Qumran do not know of the word "conscience"; they also speak of "heart," or of "good or evil drive." "As long as the Jew spoke of 'heart' he perceived the interior life with all its willing, feeling and thinking as a unity."[150] Rabbi Jochanan ben Zakkai said to his disciples: "Go out and look: what is a good path that humankind should follow?" Rabbi Eliezer said: "A kindly eye." Rabbi Jehoshua said: "A good companion." Rabbi Jose said: "A good neighbor." Rabbi Shimeon said: "Whoever sees the consequences." Rabbi Eleazar said: "A good heart." Then Rabbi Jochanan said to them: "I give the words of Eleazar ben Arakh the first place among your words because your words are contained by his" (Abot II, 9a).

Therefore, what is called "conscience" ancient Judaism called "heart." In it are made the decisions of the human being, but not his autonomous decisions. Rather, they stand in obedience or disobedience to the instructions of God which Israel "has heard" and should "hear," especially according to the teaching of Deuteronomy. "Live according to your conscience" in the Old Testament and in Judaism means: Listen to the voice of God![151] "From hearing (Hören) there must be an ought (Gehören), from a harkening (Horchen) there must be obedience (Gehorchen)."[152] "The human being of the Old Testament possessed as the exclusive norm of his thinking and behavior the will of his God."[153]

This is especially reflected in the introduction to the "covenantal constitution," that is, in the Decalogue, in Exod. 20:3–17, namely, in the statement of 20:2: "I am YHWH your God who has led you out of Egypt, out of the house of slavery." God himself, therefore, is the indicative who gives the imperative which Israel must fulfill. According to Exod. 34:27, Moses receives the command from God: "Write down these words; on the basis of these words I conclude with you and Israel a covenant!" Indeed, according to 34:28b God himself wrote "on the tablet the words of the covenant, *the ten words*" (cf. also Deut. 4:10–13). These "ten words," the *Decalogue*,[154] have become the fundamental order of life of Israel, indeed of all humanity.

The ancient rabbis reflected on why the Torah was not given in the land of Israel, but in the desert. A first answer is: "In order not to provide the nations of the world with the objection: because it was given in your land, therefore we have not accepted it." Another answer is: "In order not to cause disputes among the tribes so that this might not be said: It was given in my land (tribal area), and another would say: It was given in my land. Therefore it was given in the desert as a common land, openly, in a place without a ruler. The Torah is given in three things: in the desert, in fire, and in water. Just as these are given freely to all inhabitants of the world, so also is it given freely to all inhabitants of the world" (*Mekhilta on Exodus* on Exod. 20:2).[155]

Of course the Decalogue did not fall from heaven. Its individual statements, presumably including the ten commands, are of an ancient age and have their origin in the kinship ethos of the tribes of Israel; they are designed to serve as a protection for the community.[156] "The Decalogue enumerates the crimes which are so grave that they compromise and endanger the community itself."[157] In this the sentences of the Decalogue each point to an entire area; they express brief, guiding "representative commandments . . . for all areas of crimes which damage the community."[158] Because the Decalogue in its final form gradually grew from the developing structure of the kinship ethos of the tribes of Israel, its statements are not strict "statements of revelation," but rather statements of the "natural moral law," which are then declared to be "statements of revelation" and are brought into connection with Mt. Sinai. They form the core of the Torah of Israel, its "covenantal fundamental charter."

The "ten commands" are correctly understood as the essence of moral consciousness not only of Israel but of all humanity. Through them the "natural moral law," which according to Paul "from nature itself . . . is written in the hearts [of all human beings], . . . while their conscience also bears witness and their conflicting thoughts accuse or perhaps excuse them" (Rom. 2:14f.), was formulated in firm statements, without whose observance there is no true community life and also no true relationship to God. The experience of history long since has been that without a conscience following the norms of the "ten commands," "man becomes a wolf to man," the human being is robbed of dignity as the image of God and is degraded to a concentration camp number. The relationships among human beings and nations degenerate. Space is then provided for dictatorships and despotisms which are hostile to freedom and persons. If the "ten commands" were to disappear completely from the consciousness of human beings and the nations, the world would quickly turn into a universal concentration camp. It is no accident that in modern dictatorship, whether of the right or the left, reformulations of the Decalogue born out of an ideology have been time and again transmitted to the people. These are supposed to drive out the Decalogue of Israel, and thereby conscience, this "invention" of Judaism.

Thus through the Decalogue as well Israel has become paradigmatic for the nations.

REMEMBRANCE

It might be surprising that in a tractate on the Jews the theme "remembrance" turns up. However, one does not understand the God of Israel, the cult and the feasts of of Israel, the fate of Israel and the essence of salvation history, if one does not pay attention to the role which "remembrance" plays in biblical and Jewish thought. Therefore it is not surprising that the attention of theologians has turned to "remembrance," to the Hebrew root *zkr.*[159] In the following discussion I shall limit myself to a few essential aspects.

YHWH, the Remembering God

God remembers individuals like Noah (Gen. 8:1), Abraham (Gen. 19:29), Samson (Judg. 16:28), Jeremiah (Jer. 15:15; 18:20), David (Ps. 132:1), etc. God remembers the covenant with Noah, "which exists between me and you as well as all living creatures among all flesh"; he remembers the covenant with the patriarchs (Exod. 2:24; 6:5; Lev. 26:42, 45); he remembers the covenant with his people Israel (for example, Ezek. 16:60: "Yet I will remember my covenant with you in the days of your youth, and I will establish with you an everlasting covenant"; Ps. 105:8–11: "He remembers his covenant for ever, of the word that he commanded, for a thousand generations, the covenant which he made with Abraham, his sworn promise to Isaac, which he confirmed to Jacob as a statute, to Israel as an everlasting covenant, saying, 'To you I will give the land of Canaan as your portion as an inheritance'"; Ps. 106:43–45: "Many times he delivered them, but they were rebellious in their purposes, and were brought low through their iniquity. Nevertheless he regarded their distress, when he heard their cry. He remembered for their sake his covenant, and relented according to the abundance of his steadfast love"). The petitioner calls upon YHWH to remember his community Israel (e.g., Ps. 74:2: "Remember thy congregation, which thou hast gotten of old, which thou hast redeemed to be the tribe of thy heritage! Remember Mt. Zion, where thou hast dwelt"). When God graciously remembers his people Israel that means a blessing for Israel (Ps. 115:12: "YHWH has remembered us; he will bless us; he will bless the house of Israel; he will bless the house of Aaron").

The "history of theology" importance of the word "to remember" can be especially perceived in the context of the above-cited passage from Ezek. 16:60. Twice in that context (16:53–63) there is talk of the "turn of fate," three times of "re-establishment" (of Sodom, Samaria, Jerusalem), five times of "covenant" ("covenant," "my covenant," "your covenant," "eternal covenant"), three times of "remembering." God "remembers" his "covenant" which he once concluded with Israel, and this remembering moves history, drives it forward, leads to the "turn of fate" and to the "re-establishment" and to the setting up of the "eternal covenant" with Israel. "History grows here with such an obvious power from the behavior of a person who directs the whole, of a will which directs the whole, that every individual event of history always comes from this whole . . . and as an event, a given fact, it can have its meaning and be grasped only within this totality."[160] The "remembering" of God is the expression of his loyalty. Therefore, he never forgets his people despite their repeated disloyalty;

rather with his remembering God promises to Israel an "eternal covenant." Paul knows of this and therefore in Rom. 11:26 predicts the eschatological saving of all Israel.[161] That the "remembering" of God is an activity of the highest efficiency can be seen by the history of Israel as the work of God. The Old Testament does not know of a history which is closed in on itself, which is understood from itself, a history without the factor of God, as little as does the New Testament, as can especially be seen in the Apocalypse of John. "Remembering," then, is a term of historical theology of the first rank. As often as God remembers, history is set in motion.

"Remembering" is also a term of prayer by which God is petitioned by the one praying to intervene in history and in the fate of Israel: "Remember this, YHWH, how the enemy scoffs, and an impious people reviles thy name. Do not deliver the soul of thy dove to the wild beasts; do not forget the life of thy poor for ever. Have regard for thy covenant. . . . Arise, O God, plead thy cause; remember how the impious scoff at thee all the day!" (Ps. 74:18–20, 22).

Israel, the "Remembering" People

Not only God remembers, but Israel also remembers. It remembers the saving deeds of God for his people; it "remembers," however, with shame its frequent failures before God. The "remembering" of God and the "remembering" of Israel correspond to one another. The "remembering" of Israel expresses itself especially as "repentance," as "praise," and "thanksgiving," and most especially as "narration." The "praising or glorifying or magnifying narration of the great deeds of God is the fundamental way of making history present in ancient Israel."[162] "Narration" is the way in which Israel remembers the deeds of its God; it is the way in which Israel builds and attains its "consciousness of history." The opposite of remembering is forgetting, which is born out of disloyalty and ingratitude. "They forgot God, their Savior, who had done great things in Egypt, wondrous works in the land of Ham, and terrible things by the Red Sea" (Ps. 106:21–22.). Forgetting leads to the loss of history. "Narration" has a doxological character; it moves over into the idea of "proclaiming," "praising" (cf., for example, Ps. 79:13: "[We] will give thanks to thee for ever; from generation to generation we will recount [proclaim] thy praise"; Ps. 75:1: "We give thanks to thee, YHWH; we give thanks; we call on thy name and recount thy wondrous deeds").

The instructions of the *Mishnah* tractate "Pesachim" state in X, 5b, c: "One is obliged in every period to view oneself as if one himself had flown out of Egypt. For it is written [in Exod. 13:8]: 'And on that day therefore you shall *tell* your son: What YHWH has done to me in my fleeing from Egypt [happens] for their sake.' Therefore, we are obliged to give thanks, to praise, to glorify, to magnify, to lift up, to exhalt the one who has performed all these wonders for us and for our fathers, and he had led us out of slavery into freedom, and we wish to shout before him, hallelujah!" Here in a precise, classical manner we encounter the connection between the "narration" (the wonderful act of God in the Exodus from Egypt, this saving deed of God according to the Old Testament proclamation) and "praising," "magnifying," "thanking," and at the same time the idea that the recalling "narration" is the cultic "making present" of the past saving deed for the present of the narrator and of the cult community. The narration of the past saving deeds in the celebration preserves Israel from the "original sin of forgetting"[163] and allows it to participate in the process of salvation of the past; this latter is made present in the celebrative narration. Narration is a holy command, by which indeed no "cult-dramatic making present" is to be set in motion, but rather "a recollection of his wonder" (Ps. 111:4) is established which produces a consciousness of the continuity and tradition of salvation. "Go in to Pharaoh; for I have hardened his heart and the heart of his servants, that I may show these signs of mine among them, and that you may *tell* in the hearing of your son and of your son's son how I have made sport of the Egyptians and what signs I have done among them; that you may know that I am YHWH" (Exod. 10:1–2). In connection with the celebration of the feast of the Passover and the Exodus from Egypt, it says in Exod. 12:14: "This day shall be for you a *memorial day*, and you shall keep it as a feast to YHWH." Even individual cult objects have a "memorial" function in Judaism; thus, for example, the prayer thongs and prayer boxes which the devout Jew puts on for his morning prayer, and which appear so extraordinary to a non-Jew, are memorial signs in a literal explanation of Exod. 13:9: "And it shall be to you as a sign on your hand and as a memorial between your eyes, that the law of YHWH may be in your mouth; for with a strong hand YHWH has brought you out of Egypt." One could from that point of view say that Judaism is a "memorial religion."

One cannot understand the essence of the feasts of Israel without paying attention to this connection. They are memorial feasts, remembrance feasts, in which the Jew remembers the saving acts of God and thereby is taken into the past saving event and attains assurance of a final salvation and liberation. This eschatological aspect of the feasts of Israel may not be overlooked. In the above-cited specification of the *Mishnah* tract "Pesachim," the attitude of the ones celebrating the Passover is expressed. The feast calls to mind the liberation of Israel from Egyptian servitude and contains at the same time an eschatological component.[164] In all of the great Jewish feasts a saving past, a saving present, and saving future are indissolubly bound together; for they are "remembrance," "recollection," *memoria*.

And without being aware of these connections one also does not understand the great feasts of the Christian church year, and especially the celebration of the Eucharist. In them likewise the three dimensionality of the saving past, the saving present, and the saving future is always involved. They also are *memoria*, "a remembrance of his wonderful deeds." The great Christians feasts of salvation and the celebration of the Eucharist are not thereby feasts *alongside* the feasts of Israel; rather in their salvific significance they stand in a mysterious continuum with the feasts of Israel as, for example, N. Füglister has shown in an outstanding manner in the instance of the feast of Easter.[165] One only half understands the salvific content of the great Christian feasts of the church year if one does not recall their Old Testament-Jewish roots.[166] In the Christian-Jewish dialogue this thematic, therefore, must play an important role. Here the neutral helping toward understanding is particularly proper and to be promoted. The repetition command according to Luke 22:19 and 1 Cor. 11:24f., "Do this in remembrance of me," has its roots in the remembrance theology of Israel. In this point as well Jesus was a Jew.

THE SABBATH[167]

The following section is not concerned with the history of the Sabbath commandment in Israel, but rather with its theology. In this manner the Christian should perceive the deep meaning and significance of the Sabbath in Judaism, which remains largely hidden to many Christians because of the Jewish "Sabbath casuistry."

In a precisely classical manner the meaning and significance of the Sabbath is expressed in the Sabbath pericope of the "Book of Jubilees" (Jub. 2:17–33):[168]

> And He gave us *a great sign*, the Sabbath day, that we should work six days, but keep Sabbath on the seventh day from all work. And all the angels of the presence, and all the angels of sanctification, these two great classes—He hath bidden us to keep the Sabbath with Him in heaven and on earth. And He said unto us: "Behold, I will separate unto Myself a people from among all the peoples, and these shall keep the Sabbath day, and I will sanctify them unto Myself as My people, and will bless them; as I have sanctified the Sabbath day and do sanctify [it] unto Myself, even so will I bless them, and they shall be My people and I will be their God. And I have chosen the seed of Jacob from amongst all that I have seen, and have written him down as My first-born son, and have sanctified him unto Myself for ever and ever; and I will teach them

the Sabbath day, that they may keep Sabbath thereon from all work." And thus
He created therein a sign in accordance with which they should keep Sabbath
with us[169] on the seventh day, to eat and to drink, and to bless Him who has
created all things as He has blessed and sanctified unto Himself a peculiar
people above all peoples, and that they should keep Sabbath together with us.
And He caused His commands to ascend as a sweet savour acceptable before
Him all the days. . . . There [were] two and twenty heads of mankind from
Adam to Jacob, and two and twenty kinds of work were made until the seventh
day; this is blessed and holy; and the former also is blessed and holy; and this
one serves with that one for sanctification and blessing.[170] . . . He created
heaven and earth and everything that He created in six days, and God made
the seventh day holy for all His works; therefore He commanded on its behalf
that, whoever does any work thereon shall die, and that he who defiles it shall
surely die. Wherefore do thou command the children of Israel to observe this
day that they may keep it holy and not do thereon any work, and not to defile
it, *as it is holier than all other days.* And whoever profanes it shall surely die,
and whoever does thereon any work shall surely die eternally, that the children
of Israel may observe this day throughout their generations, *and not be rooted
out of the land;* for it is a holy day and a blessed day. . . . And they shall not
bring in nor take out from house to house on that day; for that day is more holy
and blessed than any jubilee day of the jubilees; on this we kept Sabbath in the
heavens before it was made known to any flesh to keep Sabbath thereon on the
earth. And the Creator of all things blessed it, but he did not sanctify all
peoples and nations to keep Sabbath thereon, *but Israel alone:* them alone he
permitted to eat and drink and to keep Sabbath thereon on the earth. And the
Creator of all things blessed this day which He had created *for blessing and
holiness and glory above all days.* This law and testimony was given to the
children of Israel as a law for ever unto their generations.

The Sabbath according to this important text is "the great sign" which
God himself gave Israel.[171] Before it was made known on earth, God
himself and "the angel of the visage and of the saints," that is, the highest
class of angel, observed it. The Sabbath is "holier than all other days"; it is a
day for rest, consecration, and blessing. It is a special characteristic of Israel
which was not given to the other nations. It is a festive day "for eating and
drinking and blessing." In the keeping of the Sabbath by Israel its specialness among all the nations is shown. If Israel wishes to remain in the
land, it must observe the Sabbath.

Although it may be that the Book of Jubilees also reflects in a special way
the Essene view of the Sabbath, most of the expressions of this text
concerning the Sabbath reflect the general Israelite view. It has a good
grounding in the Scriptures themselves. For according to Exod. 20:10 and
Deut. 5:14, the seventh day is expressly "the Sabbath for YHWH your
God." During it Israel remembers that God himself rested from his work of

creation on the Sabbath day. Therefore a major content of the Sabbath day is the total rest from work for human and animal. The Sabbath, however, is also brought into connection with the liberating deed of God: with the Exodus from the house of slavery of Egypt: "You shall remember that you were a servant in the land of Egypt, and YHWH your God brought you out thence with a mighty hand and an outstretched arm; therefore YHWH your God commanded you to keep the Sabbath day" (Deut. 5:15). "The fundamental meaning of the rest from work on the seventh day according to the Deuteronomic interpretation is therefore the remembrance of the freedom that was given."[172] "The Sabbath illuminates the gift of free time."[173] The Sabbath scans the rhythm of life and work of the human being and prevents a monotony of time. It provides the "catching of one's breath" (cf. Exod. 23:12), as God himself on the seventh day, according to Exod. 31:17, "caught his breath." "The number seven is . . . the light of the number six; for what the sixth allows one to have is shown in complete fullness by the seventh. Therefore [the seventh day] likewise may justly be designated the birthday of the world in which the work of the Father, complete and consisting of complete parts, appeared," remarked the Jewish philosopher Philo from Alexandria.[174] Even the cattle may rest from work on the Sabbath "that they may participate in the celebration of the birthday of the world."[175] It is obvious that being concerned with the Torah is allowed on the Sabbath: "Sabbaths and feast days were given over to concern with the Torah" (jShab. 15a); "The Sabbath is given to the workers who have been busy the whole week for the study of doctrine" (Pesiqt. Rabb. 23). Just as the Sabbath allows the glance of Israel to turn back to the event of the Creation of the world and in so doing reminds Israel of its liberation from Egypt and thus again allows history to be experienced as the deed of God, so also it serves "as an eternal covenant" and as a covenantal sign "forever between me and the people of Israel" (Exod. 31:16f.). With this there is opened up the eschatological dimension of the Sabbath, the coming participation in the eternal "katapausis" of God, concerning which the Epistle to the Hebrews in the New Testament speaks so intensely.[176] The Sabbath makes the life of the human being festive and free and recalls to the human being that God himself desires a festive and free world. The Sabbath points to the saving future: "When [the sons of Adam and Eve] had mourned for four days, Michael the Archangel came to them and said to Seth: Man of God! You shall not mourn your death longer than six days! *The rest on the seventh day is the sign of the resurrection in the coming age;* on the seventh day the Lord also rested from all his works" (*The Life of Adam and Eve*, 51). Christianity underlined this eschatological dimension of the Sabbath by making the resurrection of Jesus into its "Sabbath." In so doing it lived from the "sign" which the Sabbath according to the Scriptures of Israel presented. This leads us to the next point.

THE RAISING OF THE DEAD

Even if the teaching of the raising of the dead at the end of time is a late heritage of the faith of Israel, it nevertheless is no foreign body therein, but rather the final consequence of the Yahweh-faith.[177] Jesus also shared the belief in the raising of the dead and defended it against the Sadducees,[178] and through the proclamation of his own resurrection from the dead in the Christian mission this faith heritage of Israel became the faith heritage of the Christian people. Here also we encounter an essential portion of the spiritual heritage of Israel which binds Jews and Christian together.[179]

It is not the task of this tractate on the Jews to present once again the development of the Old Testament-Jewish hope in the resurrection—for this look to the literature cited in n. 177. Here only a brief indication of the relevance of this hope for anthropological and historical theology—and what is still more important—for the Jewish-Christian image of God, will be given. I shall begin with the latter.

The Resurrection of the Dead and the Image of God

For the Old Testament it is unthinkable that an independent ruler rules in the world of the dead. Even if the dead are cut off from the land of the living and their praise of God is stopped up, God is still present in the world of the dead: "If I make my bed in Sheol, thou art there!" (Ps. 139:8). God is lord over life and death: "YHWH kills and brings to life; he brings down to Sheol and raises up" (1 Sam. 2:6). "See now that I, even I, am he, and there is no god besides me; I kill and I make alive; I wound and I heal" (Deut. 32:39). God gives the human being up to death, but he also saves him from the entanglement of death, whether it be from a dangerous illness or from a threat by evil men which is potentially fatal. Thus one prays who had experienced bitter injustice and to whom then justice was done, according to Ps. 116:3: "The snares of death encompassed me; the pangs of Sheol laid hold on me"; rescue is, then, attributed to God: "For thou hast delivered my soul from death" (Ps. 116:8). True life which deserves the name is for a devout Israelite and Jew only a life with and before God. To live means to stand in relationship to God; therefore, it lies within the logical consequences of the Yahweh-faith that God will raise up the dead again at the end: On the basis of its "concept of God" Israel gradually had to come to this faith conviction; it needed no special stimuli from without, as for example from the Parses. Just as Jesus of Nazareth in his dispute with the Sadducees (Mark 12:18–27, and parallels) taught the resurrection of the dead because for him according to the Scriptures God is "not a God of the dead but of the living," so in similar fashion the Jewish rabbis also prove the resurrection of the dead at the end of times from the Scriptures.[180] "Our masters taught: 'I am the one who kills and who gives life' (Deut. 32:39). One could think that the killing happens to one and the giving life to another, as in the world things pass and are given. However, the text says: 'I wound and I heal' (Deut. 32:39). As with the wounding and the healing so also the enlivening takes place in one and the same person. It is from here then that the answer comes for those who say: The enlivening of the dead cannot be proven from the Torah" (bSanh. 91b). "Rabbi Jehoshua, the son of Levi, said: Where in the Torah is the enlivening of the dead proved? 'Blessed are those who dwell in thy house, they will ever sing thy praise! Selah' (Ps. 84:4). It does not say: They have forever sung thy praise, but rather: They will forever sing thy praise. The enlivening of the dead can be proved from here from the Torah" (bSanh. 91b). According to *Mishnah Sanhedrin* X, 1b, "Those who have no part in the world to come include whoever says that there is no resurrection of the dead in the Torah, and, that there is no Torah from heaven, and the Epicureans." In his thirteenth article of faith, Maimonides confessed: "I believe with complete faith in the resurrection of the dead at the time, since it is the will of the creator, his name be praised and raised up and his remembrance be from eternity to eternity."[181] Three times a day the devout Jew prays in the "Prayer of Eighteen": "You are mighty in eternity, Lord, who enlivens the dead and keeps trust with those who sleep in the dust. . . . He kills and enlivens and allows salvation to spring forth. You are trustworthy in enlivening the dead once again. Praised be you who enlivens the dead." "The death of death . . . is the quintessence of biblical hope."[182] This view is shared by the New Testament (cf. 1 Cor. 15:26–55; Rev. 20:14).

The teaching of the resurrection of the dead brings the dignity of the human being, who is the image of God, to fruition. However, above all it brings the divinity of God to fruition, as the Jew Paul taught with a reference to the father of Israel, Abraham: "[He believed] in the presense of the God . . . who gives life to the dead and calls into existence the things that do not exist" (Rom. 4:17b). Here Paul takes up the already mentioned second Berakah of the Prayer of Eighteen: "God, who enlivens the dead," as also in 2 Cor. 1:9; however, he connects the belief in the God who awakens the dead with the belief in the God who has created the world from nothing. He sees, therefore, in the resurrection of the dead by God "the eschatological repetition of the first creation being presented."[183] Here Paul expresses himself entirely within the Jewish mentality. For the devout Jew, God would not be God if he could not and would not raise up the dead. In the resurrection of the dead the divinity of God, his power over death and over nothingness is manifested. With the teaching of the resurrection of the dead, hope in general is grounded in the world, that hope which is against all earthly hope (Rom. 4:18a) and which directs the vision beyond the horizon of history. With this hope thousands of Jews went into the gas chambers of Auschwitz.

The Resurrection of the Dead and Anthropology

When some in the Christian community of Corinth represented the thesis: "There is no resurrection of the dead!" (1 Cor. 15:12b), they argued from a dualistic anthropology which could see no increase in salvation in the raising of the body. They thought decisively in a Greek[184] but not Hebraic manner, although it is not as if early Judaism had not known any anthropological dualism.[185] However:

> traditional unitary thinking obviously had a decisive influence on Rabbinic speculation. According to this the world is the only theater of the crucial encounter between God and humanity. This idea, along with the strong eschatological expectation that the final goal, whether for salvation or eternal damnation, is the reuniting of body and soul after a period in the intermediate state, sets a limit to the popular dualism rooted in the Hellenistic-Oriental world. In the last judgment the human being receives sentence as a total person according to his or her acts in the life of the body. The body may belong to the lower world and the soul to the upper world. The soul, when embodied in earthly life and put to the test in the body, may in its quality as a pure heavenly being start back in horror from the "drop" which sends forth corruption. Nevertheless, in the last judgment the two will have to render an account in concert. Thus in bSanh., 91b, at the end of a debate between "Antoninus" and the patriarch Jehuda II (circa A.D. 190), we read: "the holy One, blessed be He, will fetch the soul and set it in the body and then judge them both together,"[186]

or, at the resurrection of the dead he will "fetch the soul and put it into the body."[187] The human being for the Old Testament-Jewish sensitivity is a whole, and if it is without a body, it is not a human being. God created not the body or the soul, but "the human being"! Therefore, to the totality of the human being raised from the dead there also belongs the body. A Jew cannot seriously speak of the "resurrection of the dead" without thinking primarily of the resurrection *of the body*. Jewish eschatology is body-oriented. This is implied as a consequence of the biblical Creation faith. Paul here too is consistently Jewish when he speaks up for the resurrection of the body—of course, with the "pneumatic" essential element of the resurrection body very strongly emphasized (cf. 1 Cor. 15:35–44). The Jewish teaching of the resurrection of the dead at the end of times professes the creaturely wholeness of the human being; it suffers no definitive dualism and relates the final salvation of the human being to the body. God will save the entire human being. The resurrection of the dead is completely and only a deed of God.

The Resurrection of the Dead and "Historical Theology"

The Jews discovered the future.[188] In particular, however, with the teaching of the resurrection of the dead at the end of times they discovered that future which lies beyond earthly history. This future turns up with the "day of YHWH," which is proclaimed most of all as a day of judgment, but also as a day of inbreaking salvation which manifests itself above all in the raising of the dead. Therefore the raising of the dead is connected with that great caesura which divides "this aeon" from the "coming aeon." With this a "historical theology" of a special sort is developed which confesses God as the absolute lord of history. History does not move of itself toward a goal; it does not itself determine its end purpose in a dialectical world process. Rather, it runs into a great frustrator and annihilator of everything, death, the overcoming of which is not granted to human beings. Death prevents history from becoming of itself a definitive history of freedom. History will become this only through God, who alone can break the power of death and will definitively break it in the raising of the dead at the end of times. Thus it was above all Judaism which developed an authentic historical *theology* in which God is given honor and which sees the *condition humaine* as it in reality is and which proclaims a future which brings the whole human being into salvation. Here also the eschatology of the Church, precisely in its christological proclamation, lives from the great faith heritage of Israel, which Israel itself has never lost, even if there were and are Jews who believed they had to allow themselves to be taught better by the Jew Karl Marx—as, for example, Ernst Bloch.

SUMMARY

At the end of this chapter on the great faith heritage of Israel, which in no way has been exhaustively expressed, we should once more recall the sentence written at the beginning: "Through the reception of this heritage,

Israel became 'paradigmatic' for the Gentile world." The man above all through whom this heritage entered into the Gentile world is Jesus of Nazareth. The great Jewish philosopher Moses Maimonides (1135–1204 C.E.) remarked: "All these incidents which relate to Jesus of Nazareth . . . served only to prepare the way for the king Messiah and to prepare the entire world for the honoring of God with a unified heart, as it is written: 'Then, however, I will give the nations pure lips, that they all should call upon the name of the Lord in order to serve him with a single heart' (Zeph. 3:9). In this manner the messianic creation, the Torah, and the commandments have become a generally distributed heritage of faith—among the inhabitants of the distant islands and among many nations, uncircumcised in heart and in flesh" (*Mishnah Torah*, Hilchot Melachim XI, 4). Through the Church, Jesus of Nazareth became the bridge between Israel and the nations; he became not merely the great "mediator between God and humanity" (1 Tim. 2:5), but also the great mediator between Israel and the nations. He made humanity, insofar as it became and is Christian, "Jewish"; for through him, "the Jewish categories" (G. Scholem) came into the consciousness of the nations and work there as a leaven which leavens the whole.[189]

I have attempted above all to draw the Jewish categories from the Old Testament, the common Scripture of Israel and the Church. Certainly an expanded onamastic of Jewish categories could be developed which would also have to include the later Jewish writings. However, the Jewish categories drawn from the Bible are the decisive ones for the attainment of the spiritual-intellectual identity of Judaism. These categories determine the consciousness of the devout Jew to this very day, as Jewish writing shows, insofar as Judaism has not succumbed to total secularization. It could also be shown that these categories are of the sort that their neglect would lead not merely to the deterioration of Judaism but to that of humanity in general. These categories interpret human life before God, even if there is a specifically Christian expansion of the same, as, for example, through the Pauline "being in Christ" and the likewise Pauline "body of Christ."

When Karl Marx set up the program: "We transform the theological questions into worldly ones,"[190] he likewise implied the usurping secularizing of the Jewish categories, however, upon a totally atheistic and materialistic basis which in reality eliminates the Jewish categories because they were born out of Israel's dealings with its God. The political experience of modern history shows that the Jewish categories in reality are not subject to transformation into Marxist categories—as little as vice versa, as, for example, the significant Jewish thinker Walter Benjamin tried to do in part. His friend Gershom Scholem, the great Jewish scholar, wrote in a letter to Benjamin on 30 March 1931 that "there has developed in me in a clear and specific way the insight that you in this production are engaging in an unusually intense kind of self-deception . . . ," and in a letter of 6 May 1931 "that one can indeed live in this tension of ambiguity. . . . However, likewise, to express the matter very sharply, that one will collapse with it, because . . . the morality of the insights into this existence must deteriorate and this heritage is indeed important for life and cannot in any case be neutralized. You write [in his responding letter of 17 April 1931] that my letter pertains not only to you but also to some others with whom you are inclined to discuss it. Well, I can only welcome that and that it pertains to Ernst Bloch is likewise evident to me. . . . "[191] One should reflect on these sentences of Scholem before one so cheerfully takes up a "materialistic biblical exegesis," as it is attempted today in certain Christian circles.[192] The Jewish categories such as "revelation," "creation," "atonement," "conscience," "redemption," "Messiah," "remembering" (a favorite term of Benjamin!), which were largely taken over by Christianity, do not allow themselves to be transmitted to Marxism, despite all the messianic yearning of the Jews for a just world. Consistent Marxism knows that clearly, as does the anti-Semitism which is groping about within the Communist arena of domination.

The Jew does not allow himself to be assimilated into the world process because he, alongside the Church, wished or unwished, must be the continuing witness of God in the world. The question which Dostoevski's Grand Inquisitor put to Christ: "Why then have you come, to disturb us? For you have come to disturb us! You know that yourself," could also be put to the Jew. The existence of the Jew disturbs the circles of the world. The Jewish categories stand against the worldly categories, but the world has need of these categories more urgently than ever if it does not wish to become a world of unfreedom and inhumanity. The Jewish categories prevent humanity "from becoming finally a single, one-voiced anthill" (Dostoevski).

What I wish to bring to Christian consciousness in this chapter on the great faith heritage of Israel is this: Among the *notae ecclesiae* in the future *the indissoluble rooting of the Church in Israel* should also be enumerated.[193]

3

The "Jew" Jesus

THE DISCOVERY OF THE "JEW" JESUS IN
JUDAISM AND IN CHRISTIAN THEOLOGY

The increasingly intensive Jewish research into the life of Jesus is discovering the "Jew" Jesus.[1] Judaism recognizes Jesus of Nazareth as its "great brother" (Martin Buber), who has not only gone forth from Judaism, but continues to belong to the great ones of the Jewish people. Gradually Jesus is again receiving a place of honor among his people.

In the following, several Jewish voices concerning Jesus of Nazareth will be presented.

Joseph Klausner, for whom the story of the life of Jesus is "that of one of the most noteworthy Jews of a long epoch," asks what Jesus means for the Jews of our time.[2] He affirms that no Jew can deny the world historical significance of Jesus and of his teaching. "He was indeed himself as far as feeling is concerned doubtless a national Jew and indeed an extreme nationalist: the sharp response to the Canaanite woman shows that, as well as his disdainful stand toward the 'pagans and tax collectors,' and the characterizing expressions, 'son of Abraham' and 'daughter of Abraham,' his strong love for Jerusalem and his sacrificing himself for the 'lost sheep from the house of Israel.' " Klausner, however, adds the interesting remark: "Despite all that, however, there was something in him from which an 'un-Jewishness' developed."[3] I shall return to this later. According to Klausner, Jesus is for the Jewish people "a teacher of high morality and a teller of parables of the first rank. He is precisely *the* teacher of the morality which for him and the religious sphere meant everything," even if his ethics, according to the opinion of Klausner, was, "as a consequence of its extreme stance only an ideal for individuals, an anticipation of the coming world."[4] His moral teaching is "a noble ethical system of a more carefully chosen and original form than all other Hebrew ethical systems. . . . And if the day should ever arrive when this ethic strips off the shell of its mystical and miraculous wrappings, then the book of ethics of Jesus will be one of the most read treasures of Jewish literature of all time."[5] As far as the Law is concerned, however, Jesus always remained a Jew.[6]

A very independent presentation of Jesus and his teaching, quite unre-

lated to the Jesus book of Klausner which has been so influential in
Judaism, is the widely distributed book of David Flusser entitled *Jesus*. "In
order to understand Jesus a knowledge of contemporary Judaism is indispensable."[7] And therefore Flusser illustrates the life and teaching of Jesus
from the perspective of contemporary Judaism, with which Flusser is
thoroughly acquainted. "However, the extraordinariness of his life also
speaks to us today: from his call at the baptism, from the tearing of the
bindings to his alienated family and the discovery of a new, noble childhood, into the pandemonium of the sick and the possessed and still further
to his death on the cross. Therefore the words which according to Matt.
28:20 the risen one is supposed to have spoken receive for us a new, non-
churchly meaning: 'And behold, I am with you all days and unto the end of
the world.' "[8] Jesus was "a Torah true Jew . . . who never faced the necessity
to assimilate his Judaism to the European way of life."[9] Jesus had "lifted up
the moral side of life over against a purely formal side of Torah praxis."[10] Of
the non-Jews, the Gentiles, Jesus had "no high opinion."[11] "The revolutionary starting point in the proclamation of Jesus," according to Flusser, "was
not a critique of the Jewish Law, but proceeded from other premises. Jesus
did not first produce this: his encounter proceeded from positions which
had already been established before him. The breakthrough came at three
points: the radicalized commandment of love, the call for a new morality,
and the idea of the kingdom of heaven."[12] Jesus knows "the social realities;
but it is not the important thing."[13] "He is the only ancient Jew known to us
who not only claimed that they were standing at the edge of the final time,
but also simultaneously that the new time of salvation had already begun,"
namely, with John the Baptist.[14]

Flusser confirms that Jesus had a special consciousness of being the Son
which, however, had led him "not to life, but rather to the death which
some prophets already before him had suffered."[15] "Since the transfigura-
tion his consciousness of being a child of God was bound up with the
presentiment that he would have to die. Already before the entry into
Jerusalem then, he had a presentiment of this tragic end. However, this
awareness of the sonship is with Jesus hardly identical with his messianic
self-consciousness."[16] Flusser asked, Could Jesus have understood himself
as the "Son of man"? He responded: "We must not forget that he had felt
that he was the chosen one of God, his servant, the only Son, before whom
the secrets of his heavenly Father lay open. Precisely this feeling of majesty
could have led him to the point that he obviously at the end felt confident
enough to make himself equal with the Son of man—and the Son of man
was sometimes understood in Judaism as the Messiah."[17] What led to the

"catastrophe" in the life of Jesus was above all his words against the Temple
and his action in the "cleansing of the Temple."[18] These had to bring the
Sadducean priesthood into the situation; however, "Jesus apparently was
delivered to Pilate without a judgment, and nowhere in the sources is a
condemnation to death by Pilate mentioned. In the catalogue of vices of
Pilate which the philosopher Philo of Alexandria has drawn up [*Legatio ad
Gaium*, 302], there is found among others the 'constant executions without
the issuance of a sentence.' It appears, therefore, that the tragic end of
Jesus came about without the sentencing of an earthly judicial authority. It
was the fruit of the gruesome play between naked spheres of influence, in
the shadow of brutal resentments, and, externally seen, without any relationship to the human being Jesus and his concerns."[19] The Jesus book of
Flusser ends with the sentence: "And Jesus departed," but according to
Flusser, "it cannot be doubted that the crucified one appeared to Peter,
'then the twelve, then he appeared to more than 500 brethren at one
time. . . . Then he appeared to James, then to all the apostles and finally to
Paul on the road to Damascus (1 Cor. 15:3–8)."[20] Flusser also makes the
interesting remark: "One could easily put together a whole Gospel from out
of the ancient Jewish writings, without a word of it having come from Jesus.
However, one could do this only because we now in fact possess the
Gospels."[21] Doubtless Flusser's book is one of the most remarkable presentations of the life of Jesus to come from Jewish hands. It does not attempt to
make anything out of Jesus other than what the Gospels bear witness
concerning him.

The small Jesus book of Schalom Ben-Chorin was written "out of the
feeling of a deep relationship with the figure of Jesus and the Jewish world
in which he lived, taught and suffered."[22] Ben-Chorin attempted a "Jewish
view of Jesus from within"[23] and is convinced "that Jesus did not perceive
himself as Messiah, even if here and there a presentiment of messianic
calling as an unsolved question of his own existence may have broken
through."[24] According to Ben-Chorin, Jesus remained "completely in the
line of the scribes of his time," but spoke "out of his own fullness of power
without proclaiming and transmitting the sayings of God,"[25] and is insofar
not a prophetic figure. He stands as a "third authority" alongside the great
rabbis Hillel and Shammai, and in his interpretation of the Law there can
be recognized the clear tendency "toward the *interior relation of the Law*
whereby *love* forms the decisive and moving element."[26] In this "interiorization," the inbreaking of the new aeon takes place in which Jesus
himself overcomes and transforms the expectation of an immediately imminent inbreaking of the kingdom of God—Ben-Chorin speaks of an "inner

development" of Jesus—until he ends "in the freely chosen path of the victim laid out by the Jewish and Roman authorities."[27] "In the Jewish-historical view this was a tragic collapse," a collapse which, however, did not destroy his greatness, because of which Jesus is incorporated into Jewish history: "So Jesus of Nazareth is a tragically mistaken person whose eyes were blinded out of love for Israel."[28] And thus Ben-Chorin confesses:

> Jesus is for me the eternal brother, not only the human brother, but my *Jewish brother.* I feel his brotherly hand which grasps me that I may follow him. It is *not* the hand of the Messiah, this hand marked with wounds. It is definitely *not a divine,* but a *human* hand in whose lines the deepest suffering is engraved. . . . It is the hand of a great witness of faith in Israel. His faith, his unconditioned faith, that complete trust in God the Father, the readiness to humble himself completely under the will of God, that is the attitude which is lived before us in Jesus and which can bind us—Jews and Christians: the faith of Jesus unifies us. . . . But the faith in Jesus divides us.[29]

By 1950 Martin Buber in his book *Two Types of Faith* had confessed similarly: "From my youth onwards I have found in Jesus my great brother. That Christianity has regarded and does regard him as God and savior has always appeared to me a fact of the highest importance. . . . My own fraternally open relationship to him has grown ever stronger and clearer, and today I see him more strongly and clearly than ever before.

"I am more than ever certain that a great place belongs to him in Israel's history of faith and that this place cannot be described by any of the usual categories."[30] That "a great place in the history of the faith of Israel belongs" to Jesus is also the conviction of Leo Baeck.[31]

Jules Isaac's book *Jesus and Israel,*[32] which all Christians should read, briefly summarizes the Jewishness of Jesus thus:

> Jesus was a Jew, a simple Jewish handworker. An historical fact, but also a truth of faith, since it was the will of God. Why then does one attempt to "de-Judaize" him? Jesus, who "was born under the Law" (Gal. 4:4), was circumcised and wished only to be a "servant of circumcision" (Rom. 15:8). Jesus spoke a Semitic language, Aramaic: the word which Christians through various translations have received in mutilated form, was a Semitic word. Jesus was raised with respect for the Law and matured in it, and . . . contrary to certain groundless claims he lived in respect toward the Mosaic law and toward the Jewish cult. Jesus taught in the synagogues and in the Jewish temple. And the first statement of faith of Christians is to acknowledge in Jesus the Christ, that is, the Messiah proclaimed by the Jewish prophets.

It is not possible here to quote all the voices from modern Judaism concerning Jesus. In any case, Judaism is in the process of again recognizing in Jesus of Nazareth its "great brother," of "bringing him home," and of bringing to the consciousness of Christian theology the "Jewishness" of Jesus, which has as a consequence that Jesus will be seen by Christians no longer only as the one who divides them from Israel, but rather much more precisely as the one who in a unique way binds them with Israel. Indeed, Christian theology is in the process of seeing Jesus of Nazareth no longer only in the light of their traditional Christology, but also with the eyes of Jews, with Jewish eyes, and thereby experiencing what Martin Buber thus formulated: "We Jews know Jesus in a manner which is hidden to the pagans." Jules Isaac searches for the reasons which led to the fact that Christians no longer were able to see the Jew in Jesus of Nazareth. I will come back to these reasons later.[33]

Meanwhile Christian theology is also in the process of discovering the "Jew" Jesus, without thereby having to give up their christological convictions.[34] I myself have described the Jewishness of Jesus in my article cited in n. 34 with the following statements which can be documented from the Gospels:

The God of Jesus is the God of Abraham, Isaac, and Jacob, the God of Israel.

Like the prophets of Israel, Jesus calls human beings to submit radically to the will of God.

Jesus represents the Old Testament-Jewish idea of representation and atonement.

Jesus represents the thoughts of the covenant.

Jesus is a decisive representative of the "piety of the poor," as it had developed in Israel.[35]

Jesus came out in favor of a better justice.

Jesus is a foreteller of the future of God.

Jesus is a representative of *emunah.*

Jesus of Nazareth not only knew the great spiritual heritage of Israel, his people, but he himself represented it in a decisive manner. Jesus prayed with his people[36] and celebrated their feasts with them. He thought and spoke in Jewish categories. This, however, had consequences of a world-wide and world historical magnitude: The teaching of Jesus, freighted with this great heritage of Israel, did not remain entrenched in the space of Israel; it expanded by way of the Christian mission into the world of the Gentiles—a process which still continues. The Gentiles are through this entrusted with the great spiritual heritage of Israel. It works among them as a leaven, often even in the secularized consciousness of our time. The Gentiles did and do learn to think and to speak in Jewish categories. Through Jesus of Nazareth the world became Jewish, and it belongs to the work of the antichrist to "de-Judaize" the world again, particularly in the area of language. In the place of the Jewish "lexicon" of Jesus, "the dictionary of inhumanity" steps forth, as the onward-marching experience of history teaches. Schleiermacher remarked in his hermeneutical sketches: "Christianity made language. It was from the beginning and still is a potent language spirit."[37] This is true, but Schleiermacher overlooks the fact that Israel had made that language which then through Jesus and Christianity was transmitted into the Gentile world.[38]

Jesus was a Jew, despite the un-Jewishness in him, concerning which I have yet to speak. In the Jew Jesus is to be found the great "feedback," the great connecting link between the Church and Israel. This has long since disappeared from the consciousness of Christianity, but Christianity is fortunately in the process of again becoming conscious of this fact and thereby once again recognizing more clearly its "root." On the other side, Judaism is also called upon "to grasp its own in order to know its own" in the gospel, as the Jew Leo Baeck has remarked.[39]

If Jesus is again viewed as "Jewish" by the Church as well as by Judaism, then the prophecy contained in the praise of the old man Simeon (Luke 2:29–32) will be fulfilled in a specific way. The light of the Messiah Jesus "will so shine upon the pagan peoples that they will receive the necessary 'disclosure,' 'revelation,' which will save them from their darkness, remove them from their error concerning God and his people Israel. . . . The people Israel is thought of as the locus where the glorious light of God exists, which prepares salvation, where thus the *doxa* of Israel can be become reality effected by God. Thus only through the mediation of Israel is there salvation for the pagans": thus comments H. Schürmann.[40] I would like to add my own reflection to this point: Since at last the Jewishness of Jesus is again perceived by the Church and Judaism, the knowledge of Jesus among the nations is filled with a new light which also serves the glorification of Israel, which makes the glory of Israel in Jesus visible to the nations.

THE "FULFILLING" OF THE LAW BY JESUS

In the following reflections I shall proceed from the words of Jesus in Matt. 5:17f.: "Think not that I have come to abolish the law and the prophets; I have come not to abolish them but to fulfill them. For truly, I say to you, till heaven and earth pass away, not an iota, not a dot, will pass from the law until all is accomplished." The controversy concerning the origin and meaning of these sentences has not to this day come to an end.[41] In a tractate on the Jews these sentences must be dealt with because the loyalty of Jesus to the Torah appears to be expressed here in a completely special way.

According to Rudolph Bultmann,

> Matt. 5:17–19 deals with the dispute between the conservative (Palestinian) community and the (Hellenistic) community, which was liberal in its dealing with the Law. The *mē nomisēte* [do not believe] shows that verse 17 arose from debates and the *ēlthon* [I have come] looks to the working of Jesus. One is already accustomed to perceiving his activity from the viewpoint of teaching; for the *plērōsai* [to fulfill] and *katalysai* [to abolish] is not concerned with practical attitude, as verse 19 clearly shows. Verse 18 can in its principal formulation and in its contradiction of the primary tradition only be a formulation of the community, and verse 19 cannot be a polemic against Jewish teachers of the Law, but only against the [Christian] Hellenists.[42]

With these theses of Bultmann concerning Matt. 5:17–19 it becomes immediately clear how difficult the question of the attitude of Jesus of Nazareth to the Torah is to answer. Indeed, in reference to the words in Matt. 5:17–19, and especially in reference to 5:17f., there are the following problems:

1. Do these words reflect only the disputatious situation in which the Jewish-Christians and the "Paulinists" found themselves? Are they therefore so-called community formulations and not words of Jesus? Does the passage concern the problem of the continuing validity of the Law in the Church?

2. Are these sentences indeed the words of Jesus, but words spoken by him in a situation which had nothing to do with the redactional situation of the "Sermon on the Mount"? Is the word in verse 18, this most Jewish of all Jesus' words, as has been remarked, really formulated by a Jewish-Christian community "at the conclusion of an eschatological speech like Mark 13:30f., and indeed according to the same schema"?[43]

3. How does the final redactor (Matthew) understand these sentences? Pro-Jewish or anti-Jewish? This last question is not easy to answer.

4. Does the final redactor "bring a completely new understanding of the Law," as O. Hanssen thinks?[44]

5. Does this "completely new understanding of the Law" fall completely outside of Judaism and thereby the Sermon on the Mount in general?

Christian theology which is under the influence of the Pauline teaching of justification is inclined ahead of time to reject the sentences of Matt. 5:17f. as being spoken by Jesus and to ascribe them to the community, especially the Jewish-Christian community. Klausner, on the other hand, the greatest of the scholars concerned with the Jewish life of Jesus, does not doubt in the least that in Matt. 5:17–19 the words of Jesus are before us.[45] Likewise for Flusser the sentences in Matt. 5:18–20 are the words of Jesus.[46] For them Jesus was, despite some sharp criticism on the Pharisaic observance of the Law, always a Jew true to the Law.

We ask first: How does the Matthean redactor understand the passage Matt. 5:17, 18 (19, 20) within the framework of the redactional composition of the Sermon on the Mount? He understands it as an opening text for the following corpus of the Sermon on the Mount. Comparatively the opening text has that function which the key has, for example, the violin key in a work of music. The opening text produces a semantic and hermeneutic "isotope" according to which the following text moves and to which understanding can be brought.[47] The opening text says, therefore, how the following text is to be understood and explained. By applying this to Matt. 5:17–20 and the following corpus of the Sermon on the Mount we have: The verses Matt. 5:17–20 state as the opening text how this corpus is to be understood and explained—namely, as that law of the Messiah Jesus, from which "not an iota, not a dot, will pass . . . until all is accomplished" (5:18). Thus as the Torah has an eternal, continuing significance for Judaism, so according to the evangelist Matthew the torah of Jesus, as it is presented in the Sermon on the Mount, has a continuing significance for the disciples of Jesus. The instructions of Jesus as they are presented in the corpus of the Sermon on the Mount are instructions in the sense and rank of the Torah of Israel—to be sure, not the instructions of just any teacher in Israel, but rather of the *messianic* teacher who has become the sole normative teacher for the post-Easter community.[48] Thus in fact does the Matthean redactor appear to understand the instructions of Jesus in the Sermon on the Mount which, as is clear from the opening text in Matt. 5:17–20, present a subsequent composition from individual logia. The instruction of Jesus is for the Christian community a continuing "law."

Is this "law" of the Messiah Jesus of Matthew brought into opposition with the Torah of Israel? This appears not to be the case, even not in the "antitheses" of the Sermon on the Mount (more concerning this below). Probably, however, the "law" of Jesus is understood as "fulfillment" of the Law or of the prophets (5:17), that is, as fulfillment of the instructions of the entire Scriptures. This "fulfillment," according to the indication of the Sermon on the Mount, lies in the direction of a concentration on the law of love. If this is correct, then the Matthean evangelist only makes the sentence of Paul fundamentally explicit with his composition of the Sermon on the Mount: "Love is the fulfilling of the law" (Rom. 13:10; cf. also Gal. 5:14), whereby, however, it should not be forgotten that the law of love stems from the ethical traditions of Israel (cf. Lev. 19:18: "You shall love your neighbor as yourself"—expressly quoted by Paul in Rom. 13:9 and Gal. 5:14!). Of this law of Jesus so understood, according to Matt. 5:18, not an iota or a dot may be lost until everything is accomplished, that is, as long as the time of this rule continues in which the plans of God are carried out.

To come back from the level of the redaction now to Jesus himself: Can the Logia put together in Matt. 5:17–20 be traced back to him? The statement in Matt. 5:18 of the non-passing away of the law has its parallel in Luke 16:17: "It is easier for heaven and earth to pass away, than for one dot of the law to become void." In the contextual connection of the Gospel of Luke this probably says: The rule of God means that although now tax collectors and sinners press into it, that is not a "lawless" situation! Would Luke have taken this Law-logion up into his Gospel written for Gentile Christians if he had not held it to be of Jesus? Presumably not. Therefore it appears improbable that it is a Jewish-Christian creation, although doubtless it was found very convenient by the Jewish Christians living according to the Law.[49] How the logion originally came from the mouth of Jesus can no longer be determined with certitude because of its double form in the tradition. Above all it can no longer be discerned in which situation Jesus spoke it. Whoever does not read the evangelical Jesus tradition a priori in the light of the Pauline justification teaching, which grew out of the reflection on the saving significance of the death and the resurrection of Jesus and, therefore, did not have its origins in the teaching of the pre-Easter Jesus, does not need to hesitate to view such a Law-logion, as in Matt. 5:19 (Luke 16:17) as from Jesus. The Jewishness of Jesus is especially reflected in it. However, whoever views the opening text of Matt. 5:17–20 as a composition from (Jewish-Christian) "community sayings" cannot, therefore, maintain that Jesus of Nazareth fell out of the framework of Judaism with his demands presented in the Sermon on the Mount. Fundamentally he does not do so, not even with the antitheses of the Sermon on the Mount,[50] as is often maintained. This will be illustrated first of all in exemplary fashion by the first antithesis (Matt 5:21f.).

"You have heard that is was said to the men of old, 'You shall not kill (Exod. 20:15; Deut. 5:18); and whoever kills shall be liable to judgment.' But I say to you every one who is angry with his brother shall be liable to judgment; whoever insults his brother shall be liable to the council, and whoever says, 'You fool!' shall be liable to the hell of fire."

The introduction of the logion ("You have heard") sounds a bit strange. Why does Jesus not begin immediately with "It was said to the men of old"? Probably because he did not wish to speak in general, but immediately directed himself to his Jewish listeners: "You have heard," with which he takes up a *terminus technicus* of rabbinic language.[51] The beginning of verse 22 can thus be expanded in meaning: "But listen now to what *I* have to say to you concerning this. . . ." Who really had said to the "men of old," to the elders,[52] to the fathers: "You shall not kill"? Not just any human being, but God himself! Thus, hidden behind the passive "it was said" God is the true subject. This is important to note if one wishes correctly to translate and interpret the Greek particle *de* (which usually is rendered "but") after the "I" (*egō*) of verse 22. For it is impossible that Jesus would declare a commandment *of God* as invalid (cf. 5:17: "I have come not *to abolish* . . ."). This means that the particle *de* may not be understood here adversatively, in the sense of an excluding contradiction to "it was said" (*errethē*); that is, not in the sense of an antithesis, but rather in the sense of a fulfillment: I say to you not merely: You shall not kill (as of old had been said by God), rather, I say *beyond that:* Everyone who is angry with his brother. . . . From the grammatical evidence, there is a double use for the Greek particle *de*, an adversative and a copulative use.[53] In the copulative use *de* has the meaning of "clarifying, expanding, grounding"; in the adversative it has the meaning of "but" (in the oppositional sense). Therefore, in the first antithesis of the Sermon on the Mount we are in reality dealing not at all with an antithesis to the ancient commandment, but rather with its "fulfillment" (*plērōsai*) in the sense that Jesus here brings out the hidden, the final, and the real intention of the instruction of the Torah. With this Jesus does not fall outside the framework of Judaism. Rather the ethic of the Old Testament is completed by the Jew Jesus in that he expands the ethical demands of the Torah into the innermost soul of the human being, into his "heart." In the first antithesis Jesus condemns not only killing, but beyond that every kind of anger exhibited in words. In this he moves toward a climax from an angry word to an insult, to a grave insult, and likewise in a corresponding climax from the customary court (*krisis*) to the regional court (consisting of twenty-three), to the council (with seventy-one members) and to *Gehenna* (hell).

Naturally all the antitheses of the Sermon on the Mount are subject to the historical-critical question of just how far they are to be viewed as genuinely stemming from Jesus. In addition there is the further problem of how far these antitheses in their final formulation in Matthew are Matthean or even pre-Matthean. In any case, it is rather certain that antitheses I (concerning killing), II (concerning adultery), and IV (concerning swearing) should be viewed as pre-Matthean (with small Matthean interventions), while antitheses III (concerning divorce), V (concerning retribution), and

VI (concerning the love of enemies), are Matthean formations. However, in content all six antitheses can be traced back to Jesus, although of course in all of them specific transformations have taken place which are connected with their being taken out of their historical situation in the preaching of Jesus and placed in the context of the post-Easter tradition of the primitive Church. Within the framework of this tractate I cannot enter into further detail in this matter.[54]

"In their core the antitheses reach back to very ancient traditions (Q^{Pal}, the historical Jesus). . . . Therefore it is valid to ask how the primitive tradition of the antitheses of the proclamation of the historical Jesus is to be ordered."[55] G. Strecker thinks: "Despite the intensification of the Torah the Rabbinic and Qumran teaching of the Law is not set in opposition over against the Old Testament commandment of Moses. It is other with the speaker of the original antitheses: his instruction stands fundamentally over against the tradition of the 'old'; it *de facto* leads to the lifting of individual commandments of the Torah. This is shown above all by the absolute prohibition of swearing . . . and fits in with the oldest tradition of the divorce prohibition (1 Cor. 7:10f.; Mark 10:2ff.), and also the criticism by Jesus of the Jewish observance evidenced in the synoptic Gospels (above all of the Sabbath: Mark 2:23ff.; 3:1ff.; Luke 13:10ff.; 14:1ff.; cf. John 5:9ff.; 7:22f.; 9:14ff.)."[56] I cannot completely agree with this. The antitheses of the Sermon on the Mount in any case indicate an "extraordinary *exousia*-consciousness in Jesus . . . without its thereby having to be designated 'messianic.' "[57] With this Jesus in no way disputes the salvific necessity of the Law. "He stands within Judaism"; to be sure: "He however has not yet taken the path to Jamnia."[58] But what he is concerned with is that something "more" (*perisson*) be done (Matt. 5:47) and that the perfection of the heavenly Father should be made the measure of one's own perfection (5:48).

The Jew Ben-Chorin remarks in his book *Bruder Jesus. Der Nazarener in jüdischer Sicht:*

> First a Christian theology which was alienated from its Jewish roots interpreted into the Sermon on the Mount an antagonism: "Jesus placed the demands of justice over against the demand of God" (R. Bultmann). No: He placed the casuistic flattening out of the Law by certain schools of the Pharisees over against the original purpose of the Law. The radicalness of Jesus, which here always interprets "*lechumra*," more intensively, separates him again also from Hillel, with whom so much binds him in regard to the love of peace. Beyond this there is to be discerned in Jesus a certain introversion of the Law. It is not only the carried out action, but the intention, *kavanah*, which decides. That again, is by no means a special characteristic of Jesus.[59]

One could describe Jesus of Nazareth, precisely in what concerns his understanding of the fulfilling of the Law, as a "Reform Jew," but of course as the most significant and most radical Reform Jew Judaism has ever produced. There has, however, always been a place for a Reform Judaism within Judaism. With his criticism concerning the concrete realization of the life according to the Law Jesus has not fallen outside the framework of Judaism, as precisely the Jewish life-of-Jesus scholars emphasize. In the question of the fulfilling of the Torah Jesus was concerned above all with what in Matt. 23:23 is called "the weightier matters of the Law" (*ta barytera tou nomou*): justice, mercy, and faith (*krisis, eleos, pistis*).[60] Naturally this means a shift of the center of gravity in the fulfilling of the Torah. However, on this account Jesus is still far from falling outside the framework of Judaism; for with this Jesus stands completely within the succession of the prophets of Israel.[61] To be sure, the fact that after Easter a decisive limitation to a single teacher, namely, Jesus of Nazareth, took place in the primitive Church[62] and that the gradual collection of the "Jesus material" also found its *Sitz im Leben* in the ongoing process of the Church's separating itself from Israel[63]—and the influence of the Pauline justification teaching—led, and misled, Christian theology to look for the un-Jewishness of Jesus precisely in the Law question, whereas in reality it is to be found in completely different areas, concerning which we are yet to speak. Thus, Jesus is incorrectly placed in opposition to Judaism and his violent death is incorrectly brought into connection with the question of the Law. "The alleged sovereign transgressor of the Law Jesus does not exist at all!"[64]

THE DOUBLE COMMANDMENT OF LOVE

The so-called double commandment of love is present in all three of the Synoptics: Mark 12:30f.; Matt. 22:37–39; Luke 10:27. It is found within the pericope which usually bears the superscription: The Question Concerning the Greatest Commandment (Mark 12:28–34; Matt. 22:34–40; Luke 10:25–28, with a continuation in the parable of the merciful Samaritan: 10:28–37). The most important distinction in the threefold tradition of the pericope is this: that in Luke it is the Jewish teacher of the Law—who poses the question "Master, what must I do to gain eternal life?"—who responds to his own question with the double commandment of love, formulated according to Deut. 6:5 and Lev. 19:18, with the two commandments being bound to one another by an "and," while in Mark and Matthew Jesus gives the answer to the question concerning the greatest commandment in the Law. With this there arise for us two questions: If Jesus himself gave the answer, did he thereby fall outside the framework of Judaism? If the Jewish teacher of the Law, however, gave the answer, as is the case in Luke, we must ask: Was there in Judaism itself, independent of Jesus, already something like a summary of the Torah in the double commandment of love?

Concerning both questions the opinions are divided.[65] According to C. H. R. Burchard, the double commandment of love is "probably a part of the heritage of Hellenistic Judaism."[66] K. Berger also comes to this conclusion.[67] In any case, the Lukan tradition shows that "the Christian community . . . obviously did not everywhere . . . consider the summary of the Law in these two commandments as a special deed of Jesus, but rather presumed it to have been carried out before him—and probably correctly. It will be a Jewish tradition which the Mark composition puts in the mouth of Jesus."[68] It is certainly correct that the Christian community did not everywhere consider the summary of the Torah in the double commandment of love as a specific deed of Jesus, otherwise Luke would have followed his Markan model. This also means, however, that in the Lukan community the double commandment of love was not understood as anti-Jewish, but as the teaching of Judaism, represented by the teacher of the Law. Jesus himself is in Luke 10:28 presented as one who agrees with the representative of Judaism: "You have answered correctly." To be sure, Luke (together with Matthew) remarks that the teacher of the Law wanted "to tempt" Jesus with his question (10:25); to a certain extent he was probing the Jewish mentality of Jesus, and with the praising acknowledgment of the answer of the teacher of the Law Jesus confesses to agree with the response of his Jewish discussion partner. Thus, in the matter of the double commandment of love, Luke does not see Jesus as one who has fallen outside the framework of Judaism. In Mark (Matthew) Jesus himself gives the answer to the question about the "first"or "greatest" of all the commandments; and the scribe confirms that he has spoken "rightly" and "according to the truth" (Mark 12:32). R. Pesch also believes that the Markan form of the pericope of the greatest commandment "as the posing of the question, the individual motive, and the dependence on the Septuagint show, cannot in the form that we have be traced back to the Palestinian horizon of Jesus and the first community."[69] Pesch looks for the source of the Markan composition in Hellenistic Jewish-Christianity.[70] Thus, in none of the evangelists do we have a historical reportage; this, however, makes the question about the origin of the double commandment of love more difficult. Is it to be sought in Jesus or in Judaism?

There was in Jewish circles a parenesis in which the love of God and the love of neighbor were demanded in a single breath, without of course the scripture being thereby expressly cited. Compare, for example, *Test. Iss.*

5:2: "Love the Lord and the neighbor"; 7:6: "I loved the Lord and every human being with my whole heart"; *Test. Dan.* 5:3: "Love the Lord in your whole life and one another with a true heart"; *Test. Benj.* 3:3: "Fear the Lord and love the neighbor"; *Jub.* 20:2: "And he commanded them that they should keep to way of the Lord, that they should practice justice and everyone should love his neighbor"; 20:9: "Honor God almighty . . . and practice right and justice before him!"; 36:4, 6: "Love one another, my sons, as brothers, as one loves one's self, and seek to do good to one another and to act in common on earth! You should love one another as yourselves! . . . Be mindful, my sons, of the Lord, of the God of your father Abraham." The parenetic passages of the Testaments of the Twelve Patriarchs can be considered as special admonitions to fulfill the double commandment of love. There, as with Jesus, the commandment of the love of God is placed before the commandment of the love of neighbor. In the Jewish context this was a foregone conclusion. Even if the original formulation of the double commandment of love really could be traced back to Jesus himself,[71] he himself does not transgress this context. Likewise the famous Rabbi Hillel (around 20 B.C.E.) formulated the commandment of Lev. 19:18 into the negative form of the "golden rule": "What you hate, do not do to your neighbor!" He declared this to be the very essence of the Torah: "That is the whole Torah; the rest is commentary."[72] And the likewise famous Rabbi Akiba (died about 135 C.E.) said: "You should love your neighbor as yourself (Lev. 19:18); that is a great general fundamental statement in the Torah."[73] No devout Jew would ever have hesitated to understand the command of the love of God as the core of the religion of Israel. Bar Qappara said (c. 220 C.E.): "What is the smallest section of the Scripture on which all essential determinations of the Torah hang? In all your ways know him, thus, will he make your paths smooth (Sir. 3:6)."[74]

It appears to be just as certain, however, that the post-Easter tradition and the redactors of the Gospels partly exploited the double commandment of love as anti-Jewish. This is to be connected with the gradual process of the separation of the Church from Israel in which Jesus became the single normative teacher; the Jesus tradition had to deliver the material within the context of the attainment of a new, that is, Christian self-understanding. Understandably then, the material was correspondingly transformed and expanded. One sees this, for example, in the "commentary" with its critical jab at cult (the double commandment of love is "much more than all whole burnt offerings and sacrifices") which according to Mark 12:32f. the "scribe" makes on the answer of Jesus. Here Pesch sees that "a missionary-oriented reworking and expansion, which clearly points to the Hellenistic Jewish-

Christian milieu is evidenced. . . . That in the second half the 'scribe' is placed in close proximity to the kingdom of God betrays a recruiting purpose of missionary activity in the Jewish-Hellenistic milieu; Judaism is . . . declared to be the preliminary stage to Christianity."[75] In Jesus himself we do not see this tendency.

Christian exegesis would do well to ask itself more frequently: Which "anti-Jewish" accents did the post-Easter tradition and the final redaction of the Jesus materials place upon the latter, and for what reasons did they do it? I shall return to this question. In Christian exegesis the anti-Jewish accents were frequently intensified, sometimes to the point of being unbearable, as, for example, the history of the explanation of the pericope of the double commandment of love can show. Judaism was widely seen merely as the adversary of Jesus and the gospel. Thus a distorted image of Judaism arose which has its effect to this very day. In reality Jesus did not fall outside of the framework of Judaism with the double commandment of love—if it is to be traced back to him. The pericope does not say in any of its traditional forms that the rest of the instructions of the Torah are to be made invalid by the double commandment of love; in Mark Jesus says only: "There is no other commandment greater than these" (Mark 12:31b); in Matthew: "On these two commandments depend all the law and the prophets" (Matt. 22:40). This is something other than the lifting of the Torah. At most one can say: Here also the "Reform Jew" Jesus, with his goal of concentrating a life according to the Torah on the double commandment of love and in this way "fulfilling" the Law and the prophets, encounters us in an outstanding manner.

THE OUR FATHER AS THE PRAYER OF THE JEW JESUS[76]

The Our Father, which is presented in a longer form in Matthew (6:9b–13) and in a shorter form in Luke (11:2c–4), is doubtless in its still only hypothetically reconstructable original form to be traced back to Jesus himself. It presents an instruction for prayer (a prayer norm) which perhaps had the following form when it came from Jesus' mouth:

> Father!
> Hallowed be your name,
> May your reign come!
> Our bread, of which we have need,[77] give us today
> and forgive our debts
> and do not let us fall into temptation!

The Our Father had its first *Sitz im Leben* in the pre-Easter circle of disciples. Luke builds the Our Father into the great "journey report" (Luke 9:51—18:14). Of course this is a secondary situating of the Our Father, exactly as is its location within the "Sermon on the Mount" in Matthew. However, the work of Jesus in his homeland Galilee was not characterized by a *stabilitas loci,* but rather by a constant wandering: "He went on through cities and villages, preaching and bringing the good news of the kingdom of God" (Luke 8:1); in this he was accompanied by his closer circle of disciples. The disciples thus participated in the "wander radicalism" (G. Theissen) of Jesus. In this the disciples did not live as individuals, but rather within the we-circle of the band of disciples of Jesus. This wandering situation of the circle of disciples in their following of Jesus brought with it the problems addressed in the "we-petitions" of the Our Father. They are based on the daily experiences of the wandering, of the close fellowship with Jesus in the wandering: One always needed a new daily bread because in such a situation no "planned economy" could be carried on. One needed the mutual forgiveness and the forgiveness of the father. One needed protection from the many different attacks. In the prayer Jesus proclaims in his homeland Galilee the imminent closeness of the reign of God and thus no petition is more urgent than the "you-petitions" of the Our Father: "Hallowed be your name, may your reign come!" Thus these petitions as well as the following "we-petitions" fit extraordinarily well into the wandering situation in which Jesus and his accompanying band of disciples found themselves. They were spoken and formulated from the unrepeatable, unique Galilean situation of the life of Jesus. Thus, seen from the perspective of this situation, these petitions are not strictly eschatological petitions, and yet on the other hand they are, insofar as the fellow wanderer is no one other than the Messiah Jesus and God in the Our Father is approached for the ultimate carrying out of his fatherhood.

The address "Father" is understood as an "opening text" which produces a semantic-hermeneutic "isotope" that is extremely important for the interpretation of the Our Father. It concerns the leading of the circle of disciples to the experience of the unconditioned fatherhood of God, which was by no means unknown to Israel (concerning this see below). Everything is related to the address "Father": *Your* name, *your* reign (*your* will), and likewise the following petitionary imperatives, "give," "forgive," "lead not." On the other side all the petitions of the Our Father cast a light upon "Father," that is, on the "concept of God" of the Our Father. God is the father, and indeed the father who listens to precisely these petitions: He manifests himself as the father who gives bread, who forgives sins, and who protects the disciples from attacks. One could, from the perspective of everything that has been seen, perhaps suggest the following definition of the Our Father: The Our Father is the prayerful expression of the eschatological wandering radicalism of the band of disciples in the following of the Messiah Jesus, in whom the disciples daily experience God anew as the father.

Now, however, to the question: Has Jesus, with the prayer instructions for his disciples which are called the Our Father, fallen outside the framework of Judaism? In Christian exegesis it is often so presented, without, however, sufficient consideration of the already-mentioned post-Easter process of separation of the Church from Israel and the connected limitation to a single normative teacher (Jesus). This separation brings with it the isolation of the Jesus materials from the Jewish-Rabbinic tradition, *including the Jewish tradition of prayer*—except for the prayers of the Old Testament tradition (Psalms!). The prayers of Israel as they were customary at the time of Jesus in Palestinian Judaism were, in the wake of this development in the Church, replaced by others, in whose center understandably stood the Our Father, which had inextinguishably impressed itself on the tradition recollection of the band of disciples. The prayer instructions as they are present in the Our Father became *the* central prayer of the Church which, according to Didache 8:3, one should recite three times a day. The Our Father became the "Lord's Prayer." However, to this very day there are frequent attempts to interpret this Lord's Prayer anti-Jewishly, above all with a reference to the address of the prayer "Father!" as it is found in Luke. One says that this "attributeless" address, corresponding to the Aramaic *abbā*, is a certain sign of the *ipsissima vox Jesu*[78] and an expression of the special image of God of Jesus, which is allegedly contradictory to that of Judaism.[79] Indeed, according to J. Becker, it was the image of God "with which [Jesus] stood and fell," and which "was the real, most deeply inherent in all details, cause of death." "In his works Jesus stood forth for a specific image of God, and as a consequence of this his death, which was related to it in a causative way, was also put into play. If Jesus was unacceptable to Judaism because of his objectionable interpretation of God, then one hoped that by his death this unacceptable message of God would become silent. The death of Jesus, then, guaranteed the stabilization of that understanding of God on the basis of which one rejected the God of Jesus."[80] Concerning this there are still the further sentences: "Jesus maneuvered himself with his interpretation of God into the out of bounds situation of prophetic isolation in the face of the predominating Jewish consciousness."[81] "The coming reign of God became present in Jesus in such a concrete reality that all Israel, which had after Jesus gambled away its life in the sense of a saving relationship to its God, was for the last time placed before a new beginning provided by the extra measure of divine kindness."[82] Above all Becker remarked concerning the Our Father: "The first petitions are directed to the coming God, the rest ask for humanity those things which are necessary in view of the eschatological situation. Because the future is thought of here, all relation to the history of Israel is lacking. The coming God is not spoken of in salvation historical terms, but rather addressed in unholy-everyday fashion with the trusted language of children [father equals *abbā!*]. Thus Jesus, who taught his disciples to pray, gathered, with a disdain for the current borders between the upright and the sinners, precisely those whom official Judaism, thinking in the terms of salvation history, excluded."[83] It was for official Judaism impossible "to rediscover in the statements about God by Jesus the God of the fathers."[84] The result was this: "The image of God of Jesus was contrary to that of Judaism and collided with the rooting of Judaism in Israel's salvation history because the constitutive function of the future in the proclamation of Jesus displaced Jewish salvation history. Thus the salvation historical image of God of the Jewish covenant and Law was criticized and in practice suspended with the help of an image of God which lives by the dimension of the future and is set upon a collision course with the old."[85] Therefore: salvation history (of Israel) versus the future (of Jesus) and vice versa! As if it were not precisely Judaism which had discovered the future!

Thank God other Christian theologians think differently. They see in the God whom Jesus of Nazareth proclaimed *precisely* the "salvation historical" God of Israel, the God of Abraham, the God of Isaac, and the God of Jacob to whom Jesus obviously confessed (cf. Mark 12:26). They see also in the Our Father of Jesus the heritage of Israel working further. See, for example, the Old Testament scholar A. Deissler's essay "The Spirit of the Our Father in Old Testament Belief and Prayer."[86] Deissler finds "surprisingly many lines of connection between the belief in prayer of Israel on the one side and the 'Lord's Prayer' on the other." Indeed, "there are few direct dependencies—according to the latter!—among them. However, constantly encompassing perspectives are opened which in their manner make visible or underline the close connection of the two testaments. The individual petitions of the Our Father receive thereby a new explanation for many who pray."[87]

Certainly, many of the fundamental concerns of the preaching of Jesus are expressed in the Our Father,[88] but Jesus did not fall outside the framework of Judaism with either the address of God as "Father!" or with the you- or we-petitions of the Our Father. Obviously we do not deny that when he spoke of God, Jesus often spoke of the "Father"[89] and that in general he more strongly emphasized the fatherhood of God than did the Old Testament and early Judaism.[90] However, Israel did and does know God as its father. Here are some examples:

"Is he not your father, who created you?" (Deut. 32:6).

"Have we not all one father? Has not one God created us?" (Mal. 2:10).

"As a father pities his children, so YHWH pities those who fear him. For he knows our frame; he remembers that we are dust" (Ps. 103:13f.).

"You are the sons of YHWH" (Deut. 14:1f.).

"I am a father to Israel, and Ephraim is my first-born" (Jer. 31:9).

"Have you not just now called me, 'My father, thou art the friend of my youth—will he be angry for ever, will he be indignant to the end?' Behold, you have spoken, but you have done all the evil that you could" (Jer. 3:4f.).

"I thought, how I would set you among my sons, and give you a pleasant land. . . . And I thought you would call me, My Father, and would not turn from following me" (Jer. 3:19f.).

"A son honors his father, and a servant his master. If then I am a father, where is my honor? And if I am a master, where is my fear?" (Mal. 1:6).

"You nevertheless are my father!" (Jer. 3:4; Ps. 89:27).

"Look down from heaven and see, from thy holy and glorious habitation. Where are thy zeal and thy might? The yearning of thy heart and thy compassion are withheld from me. For thou art our Father, though Abraham does not know us and Israel does not acknowledge us; thou, O YHWH, art our Father, our Redeemer from of old is thy name" (Isa. 63:15f.).

"Yet, O Lord, thou art our Father; we are the clay, and thou art our potter; we are all the work of thy hand. Be not exceedingly angry, O Lord, and remember not iniquity for ever" (Isa. 64:8f.).

"Is Ephraim my dear son? Is he my darling child? For as often as I speak against him, I do remember him still. Therefore my heart yearns for him; I will surely have mercy on him, says the Lord" (Jer. 31:20).

"Because he is our Lord and our God, he is our Father forever" (Tob. 13:4).

"I praise YHWH: You are my Father!" (Sir. 51:10 Hebrew).

"For my [earthly] father hath renounced me, and my mother hath abandoned me to Thee; if thou art a father to all that know thy truth, and thou will rejoice over them like a mother who pitieth her babe and thou will feed all thy works as a nurse feeds her charge at the bosom" (1 QH IX, 35; cf. also Ps. 22:11; Jer. 49:15; Hos. 11:1–4).

"And your souls follow me and all my commandments and they fulfill my commandments; I will then be your father and you my children. And you all are called the children of the living God" (Jub. 1:24f.).

"For the Lord will appear before all eyes, and then all will recognize that I am Israel's God, the father of all the children of Jacob and the king on Mt. Zion for all eternity" (Jub. 1:28).

(Abraham to Jacob): "May God the Lord be a father to you and you the first-born son to him, may you become his people for eternity" (Jub. 19.:29).

From Hellenistic Judaism: "They all called upon the almighty Lord and ruler of all power, their merciful God and father" (3 Macc. 5:7a).

"Look upon the descendants of Abraham, O Father, upon the children of the sainted Jacob, a people of your consecrated portion who are perishing as foreigners in a foreign land, O Father" (3 Macc. 6:3).

"And Jonah, wasting away in the belly of a huge, sea-born monster, you, Father, watched over and restored unharmed to all his family" (3 Macc. 6:8).

"But we very severely threatened them for these acts, and in accordance with the clemency which we have toward all men we barely spared their lives. Since we have come to realize that the God of heaven surely defends the Jews, always taking their part as a father does for his children" (3 Macc. 7:6).

"For thou didst test them [the Israelites] as a father does in warning, but thou didst examine the ungodly [Egyptians] as a stern king does in condemnation" (Wis. 11:10).

"But it is thy providence, O Father, that steers its course, because thou hast given it a path in the sea, and a safe way through the waters, showing that thou canst save from every danger" (Wis. 14:3f.).

Since the time of Jochanan ben Zakkai (50–80 C.E.), Rabbinic, Palestinian Judaism spoke, although not all too often, of God as the "Father in heaven" ("Our father in heaven" "Israel's father in heaven").[91] The second of the two *berakot* which introduces the morning Shema says: "Our father, our king, for the sake of our fathers who trusted in you and whom you taught the instructions of life, be merciful to us and teach us." The same address to God is found in the litany of the new year: "Our Father, our King, we have no other King beside you; our Father, our King, for thy sake have mercy upon us!" "Both quotations are liturgical pieces; it is the community which calls upon God as 'Our Father.'"[92]

Therefore throughout its Old Testament period and likewise at the time of Jesus Israel knew of the fatherhood of God.[93] Jesus could continue in this line. In this regard the statistical table concerning the number of references of Jesus' use of the name of father for God which Jeremias drew up is interesting:[94] Mark, 4 times; Luke, 15 times; Matthew, 42 times (31 times in his special material); John, 109 times.

"Father" as a prayer address is found in the mouth of Jesus in Mark once, in the common material of Matthew and Luke 3 times, in the special material of Luke 2 times, in the special material of Matthew once, and in John 9 times.[95] According to the penetrating investigations of Jeremias, a "growing tendency . . . to insert the designation of God as father into the words of Jesus shows itself,"[96] and indeed so strongly "that in all the thirty-one cases in which Matthew as the sole witness carries the word father, the assumption of a secondary structuring carries fundamentally in itself by far the greater probability."[97] "In the Gospel of John 'the Father' is in the mouth of Jesus the predominating term for God (100 passages, and in addition 9 addresses in prayer),"[98] a fact which is naturally connected with the Johannine Christology in which the relationship God-Jesus is seen entirely as a father-son relationship. There are, therefore, relatively few genuine Jesus texts in which the name of God as "Father" appears, and this is especially true for the addresses of prayer. One should bear this in mind before one exploits the image of Jesus' God as anti-Jewish. Likewise, it is by no means so certain as is assumed in Christian exegesis that in the address of God of the Our Father, the "children's word"[99] *aba*—not simply *av* (*pater*)—was found on the lips of the Aramaic-speaking Jesus. Matthew and his communities, in any case, had no hesitations about associating themselves in the designation of God and in the addressing of God with the manner of speaking of Palestinian Judaism, and thereby with speaking of the "Father in heaven."[100] And by no means did they intend this to shove God off at a distance from humanity any more than the prohibition to utter the tetragrammaton. No people knew its God to be so close as did Israel: "For what great nation is there that has a god so near to it as YHWH our God is to us, whenever we call upon him?" (Deut. 4:7). Cf. also Ps. 4:7f.: "Thou has put more joy in my heart than they have when their grain and wine abound. In peace I will both lie down and sleep; for thou alone, O Lord, makest me dwell in safety": what knowledge of the personal nearness of God speaks in this prayer! God in the presence of his "glory" and his *shekinah* is the one who dwells in the midst of his people, in the Temple at Jerusalem, and indeed as devout Judaism is convinced, continues to do so to this very day. It was not the notion of Jesus about the fatherhood of God that divided him from Israel and Israel from him—even though Jesus may have also emphasized God as the kind and merciful father and even though his famous prayer, the Our Father, earns the wonder of all humanity particularly in its brevity and its substantiveness. With it he in no way falls outside the framework of Judaism, despite the failure of every Christology.[101] It is the prayer of the *Jew* Jesus with which every Jew without inner reservation can pray, as fortunately happens today in joint Jewish-Christian worship services. The Our Father is the great "bridge prayer" between the Jewish and the Christian communities. And in the Our Father "the Jewish categories" live on to this very day.

JESUS AS ISRAEL

The thesis which lies hidden behind the formula "Jesus as Israel" is in fact this: Jesus is the real "fruit" of Israel, the spiritual "extract," the spiritual "quintessence" of Israel, its "peak," its "sum." The proper Greek word for this unusual thesis would be *anakephalaioutai:* thus, as according to Paul (Rom. 13:9) the second tablet of the Decalogue "is summarized" (*anakephalaioutai*) in the word of the Torah: 'You shall love your neighbor as yourself.' so also in Jesus is the Jewish existence before God "summarized" in a focal point. He is not merely a true, authentic Israelite (cf. John 1:47), *but rather represents Israel.* I fear of course that with this thesis I will be well received by neither the Jews nor by Christian theologians. Nevertheless, no less a person than Karl Barth has here previously thought out some decisive points.[102] His service is to have rediscovered Israel for Christian theology,[103] and in connection with this discovery Jesus as Israel also became visible as a Jew such as Marc Chagall instinctively could view him. However, even those Jewish life-of-Jesus scholars who are able to recognize in Jesus of Nazareth their great brother are in the process of bringing Jesus home into Judaism. *What becomes of Jesus in this?* Is he lost to the Church? Christian theologians might fear this, and therefore vigorously resist speaking of the Jew Jesus. If, however, the Jewishness of Jesus is taken radically, then Jesus as Israel becomes visible, and in this moment the specification of Israel itself. The servant of God Jesus and the servant of God Israel reveal their identity. In what could this consist? In the following correspondences:

1. Israel is the chosen one of God—Jesus is the chosen one of God.
2. Israel is the "crucified one"—Jesus is the crucified one.
3. Israel "will be saved"—Jesus is the one already saved.

The third correspondence is, of course, no longer a complete one. It stands under the tension of the "already" related to Jesus, and the "not yet," this time related to Israel. As a consequence in this third correspondence Israel is no longer looked back at, as usually happens in Christian theology—Israel is the "merely," whereas in Jesus and in the Church there is the fulfilled "promise"; in this correspondence it is much more a case of looking forward to Israel, as Paul does in Rom. 11:15: "For if their rejection means the reconciliation of the world, what will their acceptance mean *but life from the dead?*" Then the crucified and killed Israel, like Jesus of Nazareth, will be raised from the dead along with the rest of the dead. Then Israel is the ultimately accepted people of God. However, Jesus' being Israel shows itself not only in the parallel fate which his identity with Israel and the identity of Israel with Jesus allows us to perceive, but rather beyond that in the absolute obedience of Jesus to the will of God: "My food is to do the will of him who sent me" (John 4:34); "He became obedient unto death, even death on a cross" (Phil. 2:8); "Although he was a Son, he learned obedience through what he suffered" (Heb. 5:8). The existence of Jesus was an existence of obedience, as the existence of Israel before God should be an existence of obedience, although according to the witness of the Bible it often was not, a fact which no Jew will dispute. Here, however, there was one in Israel who carried out total obedience to God. And to this extent Jesus is in the special sense "Israel," the obedient "son," and thereby the Jew *kat exochēn* (par excellence). We may well say this, even if we do not speak of Israel and Jesus with an unlimited comparability. Jesus' natural milieu was Israel, and in this environment he learned to harken to the will of God.[104] His followers were pious Jews, as can be seen from the narrations of the Gospels.

At the center of Christology there is the two-nature doctrine: *vere Deus—vere homo.* However, the *vere homo* is frequently interpreted in a very limited way, related only to incarnation and the death of Jesus. That to the *vere homo* the Jewishness of Jesus also belongs, his "hidden life" in Nazareth, his public actions in Israel from the baptism on, is often not sufficiently taken into the consciousness of Christian theology. The result is that the *vere homo* is not sufficiently developed because the Jewishness of Jesus is "docetically" suppressed. This in turn has the result that the earthly life of Jesus is isolated from his environment and that Jesus is a priori seen as in opposition to Judaism. It is high time that the Jewishness of Jesus, indeed—in a deep sense—that the identity of Jesus "as Israel" be recognized by Christian theology as well as by Judaism itself. Only then can Jesus of Nazareth exercise that "bridge function" which belongs to him in his human nature. Only then will Jews and Christians truly enter into a fruitful dialogue on Jesus of Nazareth. The "recognition" of Jesus of Nazareth will become the "recognition" of Israel[105]—and in both cases the "objective" genitive is meant—and Israel will be recognized in a deep sense as "formal Christology."[106]

Here I shall add that which Karl Barth has written concerning Rom. 11:17 ("Do not boast over the branches!"):[107]

> In no circumstance was the Gentile Christian to allow his membership of the Church to make him presumptuous in relation to even one of those who belong to Israel: no matter who may be that past or future member of the people of Israel, not even if his name is Judas Iscariot; and no matter what may have happened or may yet happen among the people of Israel. For it is incontestable that this people as such is the holy people of God: the people with whom God has dealt in His grace and in His wrath; in the midst of whom He has blessed and judged, enlightened and hardened, accepted and rejected; *whose cause either way He has made His own, and has not ceased to make His own, and will not cease to make His own.* They are *all* of them by nature sanctified by Him, sanctified as ancestors and kinsmen of the one Holy One in Israel, in a sense that Gentiles are not by nature, not even the best of Gentiles, not even the Gentile Christians, not even the best of the Gentile Christians, in spite of their membership of the Church, in spite of the fact that they too are now sanctified by the Holy One of Israel and have become Israel. Each member of the people of Israel as such still continues to participate in the holiness which can be that of no other people, in the holiness of the natural root who because He is the Last and therefore also the First is called Jesus. This holiness the Gentile Christian has to respect in *every* Jew as such without exception.

I ask: Do Christians do that?

When we say that Jesus is "Israel," we do not make the claim in our mind that the Church likewise is Israel. The Church remains forever the "wild shoot" grafted onto the noble olive tree of Israel, as Paul has taught. God can again dispose of it at any time (cf. Rom. 11:21). And if we have described Jesus "as Israel," we do not thereby tear him out of Israel, but rather give him back to Israel so that in this manner he may belong to everyone: the Church as well as Israel.

4

Paul and Israel

IS PAUL GUILTY OF ANTI-JUDAISM
IN THE CHURCH AND THEOLOGY?

Since this question has already been repeatedly answered in the affirmative, it must be discussed in a tractate on the Jews. The apostle indeed appears, especially with his teaching concerning the Law and justification, to have prepared the theological ground for Christian anti-Judaism. If the human being is justified only by grace and faith in Christ before God, an iron consequence of this appears to be that Judaism is forever and finally done away with, at least theologically; alongside of the Church it leads only a sad shadow existence, despite all its accomplishments and contributions to the knowledge and culture of humanity. Even if the Church today partly embraces the Jews with love (which it did not do for centuries), this by no means indicates that the Church attributes to the Jews a "theological existence." Paul is supposed to have made this impossible once and for all. If one, nevertheless, attempts to do this, it should only be possible because Christianity was built up upon Jesus alone—if one allows the Pauline interpretation of the "Jesus phenomenon" to fall or at least to conduct a "substantive critique" of Paul and his theology.

What can be said about this? In the following I shall attempt to say a few things concerning this, even though I am completely aware of the difficulty of the problem and know that the theme "Paul and Israel" must be fundamentally thought through.[1]

THE ALTERNATIVE BEFORE WHICH
PAUL SAW HIMSELF PLACED

Paul formulated this alternative briefly and pregnantly in Gal. 2:21: "For if righteousness were through the law, then Christ died to no purpose."[2] It concerns "righteousness," that is, the eschatological salvation of the human being. Whence comes this righteousness? From the Law, as the Jew teaches still today, or from Christ, the crucified and risen Messiah and Son? Why, however, did Paul see himself placed before this alternative? This is clear from the previous text (Gal. 2:19f.): "For I through the law died to the law, that I might live to God. I have been crucified with Christ; it is no longer I who live, but Christ who lives *in me*; and the life I now live in the flesh I live by faith in the son of God, who loved me and gave himself *for me."*

According to these sentences, Christian existence is "preposition existence": "In me" (*en emoi*), "for me" (*hyper emou*). It is especially in the last prepositional phrase ("for me") in the sentence "Who gave himself for me," that the answer can be found to the question: Why did Paul see the above-named alternative put before him? This sentence is not something constructed by Paul; rather, it was taken over by him from the soteriological, linguistic, and proclamatory tradition of the primitive Church, similar to that portion of the "primitive credo" which the apostle took over and handed on to his communities as expressed in 1 Cor. 15:3–5: "Christ died *for our sins* in accordance with the scriptures." This "for" (*hyper*), which expresses the representative and atoning thoughts coming from the Old Testament and from Judaism and which belongs to the "primordial words" of Christian proclamation according to the witness of the New Testament,[3] placed the apostle before the alternative: salvation from the Law or from faith in the crucified and resurrected Christ. The opposition Law/Christ in the salvation question, however, allows one also to clearly recognize—and this recognition is of the greatest significance for the Jewish-Christian dialogue—that the key to the Pauline understanding of the Law lies in the Christ faith of the apostle alone and nowhere else. Although the Jewish scholar H.-J. Schoeps in his book on Paul holds that the apostle's understanding of the Law was the true "misunderstanding" which trapped Paul,[4] he nevertheless correctly recognizes that the key to his "misunderstanding" is the apostle's faith that Jesus Christ is the awaited Messiah with whom the coming, the new aeon has already broken in—we will come to these "historical theological" problems further on. According to Schoeps, Paul is a thinker "of the post-messianic situation"[5] in which a new principle dominates: "The old possibility of relationship of the Law which placed the Jew *before* God and was realized in the carrying out of the commandments, is [according to Paul] with it *in Christo* . . . 'taken up,' namely, replaced by a new, closer relationship which God gives to humanity a share in God through his Son who appeared in the flesh. The new principle of this participation is faith, which for the Christian has suspended the old principle of the Law which had bound the Jew to God."[6] Gal. 2:19–21 affirms this view. Through the representative atoning death of Christ, according to Paul, the Law as a way of salvation is surpassed.[7] Otherwise Christ would have died "to no purpose." Law remains further the only agency of salvation, or at least a "co-agency." The path to eschatological salvation is—as the apostle recognizes—in an exclusive way faith in Christ, "who was put to death for our trespasses and raised for our justification" (Rom. 4:25). By declaring (in Rom. 4 and Gal. 3) Abraham to be the primordial model of faith and by no longer seeing in him the exemplary "Torah Jew," Paul appeared to have torn Abraham from his people Israel forever. Similarly in his condemnations of the Law, which according to the harsh statement of Gal. 3:12 "does not rest on faith," he appeared to have torn away theologically from Israel that which to this very day is the most precious possession of the Jew, namely, the Torah. For even if the Torah is still given the greatest respect by the Jews, and even if it is still seen as that instruction which leads to salvation, in the light of the Pauline justification teaching, the Jews seem to honor something and to search for their salvation in something which appears to be de facto obsolete though worthy of respect, something in which the seeking of salvation is a vain labor of love. In reality Paul with his theology is supposed to have "radically desacrilized and paganized" the history of Israel.[8] Has Israel been forever transferred to a "profane" status by the theology of Paul? Is Israel only one people like other peoples? Did Paul become an "anti-Semite"? Did he indeed suffer from "Jewish self-hate"? The following reflections are intended to provide help for these questions. They may be understood as a contribution to the theme "Paul and Israel."

REFLECTIONS ON THE THEME
"PAUL AND ISRAEL"

Salvation Through the Law of Jesus Christ

That Paul facing the previously mentioned alternative—salvation through the Law or through Jesus Christ—decided for the second is connected above all with the fact that for him Jesus was not just anyone, but rather the Messiah promised by the prophets.[9] Why did Paul come to this conviction? Not because the Christian missionary preaching had convinced him, but rather because he himself had "seen our Lord Jesus" (thus, according to his self-witness in 1 Cor. 9:1), because the crucified and risen Christ had "appeared" to him (thus, according to 1 Cor. 15:8), or because it pleased God "to reveal his son" in him (thus, according to Gal. 1:15f.). With this Paul alludes to the "Damascus experience," which is reported three times in the Acts of the Apostles. One cannot doubt the genuineness of this experience. The Jew Leo Baeck remarked on this:[10]

The first thing which we see is a central experience around which everything turns. The point from which everything hangs, to which everything in the life of Paul returns, in which his faith became his life, is the vision which overwhelmed him when one day he saw the Messiah and heard his voice. This vision immediately became and remained the central fact in the life of Paul. Concerning such an experience there can be no discussion. One must begin with it in order to understand Paul, his personality as well as his confession.

A vision had gripped him, and for the Jew which he was and never ceased to be, whose spiritual, intellectual and moral world was the Bible, his vision had to mean a call to a new path; never again might he follow the old one.

Baeck then remarked further:

One usually speaks of the conversion of Paul. However, this expression is insufficient. What took place in the life of Paul was no conversion in the usual sense of the word, but rather a revolution, a transformation. What Paul tells us of the change in his inner life shows clearly the suddenness of the thing. It was a crisis of the moment. No one had influenced or taught him; there was no helper, no mediator there. Paul stood there by himself in this event of the vision.

In this event lies the origin of his proclamation and of his mission. "I proclaim to you, brethren, the gospel which was proclaimed to me: it is not according to the taste of human beings; likewise, I have not received it from a human being nor was I instructed [that is, by human beings], but by the revelation of Jesus Christ" (Gal. 1:11f.). These words, writes Baeck, "are not mere introductory formulations, they are the foundation of his faith."[12] "The vision had said everything to him."[13]

From this moment on Paul knew that Jesus of Nazareth was the promised Messiah, the "hope of Israel." He grounded his christological conviction in the Damascus experience. Then he expanded it by connecting it to the already-developed Christology and soteriology of the early Church. The result was that he saw himself placed by God himself (!) before the alternative that I spoke of above. One must first be aware of this if one wishes to understand Paul. However, with this underivable fundamental experience of his life Paul now saw himself placed over against the phenomenon of "Israel" in a way which forced him to think it through anew: If Jesus in fact is the promised Messiah, what then is to be done with Israel, which according to the mission experience of the apostle was not prepared in its majority to share the new faith conviction of Paul? Above all the new faith of Paul had the following consequence: The apostle suddenly saw himself in the "post-messianic" situation, while on the contrary Israel, now as before, saw itself in the "pre-messianic" situation; it waited and still waits for the coming of the Messiah. This led to an extraordinary split in the consciousness of Paul, to which Peter von der Osten-Sacken has called attention.[14] Because the Messiah is already there in Jesus and this Jesus moreover is risen from the dead and next will come in his *parousia*, Paul was convinced that "the appointed time [still at the disposal of the world] has grown very short" (1 Cor. 7:29), "the form of this world is [already] passing away" (7:31b) and he belonged to that generation "upon whom the end of the ages has come" (10:11b) This all means: The time available is not only brief, the end of history is at hand. The Lord comes quickly. The time in which we live is eschatologically qualified. This time thus qualified is no longer the usual historical time, for the *eschaton* in the form of the Messiah and the "Son" broke into the time of this world so that the *eschaton* now stands over against history. Time has come to fulfillment, for the Son is there (cf. Gal. 4:4). Indeed, he himself was still "born under the law," but at the same time he was "the end of the law for all those who believe" (Rom. 10:4), for he took the curse which the Law placed on all those who did not follow its instructions upon himself in representative fashion "for" everyone (Gal. 3:12f.). This happened, the apostle continues in an interesting fashion in Gal. 3:14: "That in Christ Jesus the blessing of Abraham might come *upon the Gentiles.*" Why not also upon Israel? It lived and continues to live "under the Law." It appears, therefore, to live outside that eschatologically qualified time which, according to the conviction of Paul, had broken in with Christ. It lives still in the "old," not in the "new" which broke in with Christ. It lives still in that time which was qualified by the Law and not by the coming of the Son. Time, so to speak, stands against time, the new against the old, and the old against the new. In this conviction that the *eschaton*, the new, is already there and that the old is past, or is condemned to pass, cannot merely ground that salvation egoism which reckons itself to the new creation" (cf. 2 Cor. 5:17: "When one is in Christ he is a new creation"!), but beyond that can ground the temptation to vilify the other, the Jew, to see in him the "enemy," and the "blind one," who unconditionally holds on to the old and will have no knowledge of the new.[15] To this extent, in fact, anti-Judaism has one of its theological roots in the opposition of history (old time)/*eschaton* (Christ time). Life according to the Law of the Jew appears to be an anachronism, the Jew appears to live in opposition to the eschatologically qualified time in Christ; he appears to be no real "contemporary," but rather a relic from a past time. However, Israel was not "rolled over" by the *eschaton*; it did not disappear from history, despite all pressures which were visited upon it by churchly and unchurchly powers. It was harassed and decimated, but the Jew lives and will continue to live until the end of days. And when the Messiah comes, "all Israel will be saved," proclaims none other than Paul (Rom. 11:26b).[16] This leads to further reflections.

Israel Remains the People of the Law

Israel took and takes no notice of the "turn of the aeon" in Jesus Christ, "but their minds were hardened; for to this day, when they read the old covenant, that same view remains unlifted, because only through Christ is it taken away. Yes, to this day whenever Moses is read [in the worship services of the Jews] a veil lies over their minds; but when a man turns to the Lord the veil is removed" (2 Cor. 3:14–16). These words of the apostle ring harshly; they sound as if Israel guiltily would not allow the veil, which according to Paul lies upon their minds, be taken away. However, if one observes the apostle's sequence of thought carefully, one notes that first of all Paul affirms the "hardening" of Israel, and only then names the observed phenomenon in which the "hardening" is grounded, that is, that "a veil" lies on the minds of the Jews as they read the Scriptures in their worship service. But the apostle does not say who laid this "veil" on the minds of the Jews with the result that they are not able to "convert to the Lord" and have the "veil" in this manner taken away so that they might read the Scripture as the witness of Christ. The passive mood which here is in the Greek text (*epōrōthē mē anakalyptomenon katargeitai*) appears to be the *passiva theologica*, which conceals the true originator of the "hardening," namely, God. In contrast in Rom. 11:8, Paul openly says with a scriptural word from Deut. 29:3, that "*God* gave them a spirit of stupor, eyes that should not see and ears that should not hear, down to this very day." But Paul says neither here nor anywhere else in his letters *why* God did that. He returns only at the end of his discussions concerning the final salvation of Israel in Rom. 11:33 to the unsearchable decisions of God and his unfathomable ways, clearly related to the mysterious leading to salvation by God in the relationship of the Gentiles to Israel. Does God himself, therefore, order that Israel remain "hardened" toward the gospel? It appears so. This leads us back to the Jewish existence *post Christum* in general, but as further reflected on by Paul here.

Israel's "Peoplehood" Not Lost

Although Israel was not able to turn toward the gospel, its peoplehood was not lost; indeed, the circumstance of its "hardening" contributed decisively to the fact that Israel remains standing as a "special people" of God. It is not very probable that an Israel which had become totally Jewish-Christian would still exist today as "Israel." That Judaism would have been taken up into the Church and into the Gentile world. God himself prevented that in order to reveal his power and his grace to Israel before the

Gentiles. The power and grace of God are shown therein that he did not allow Israel to be suppressed in the course of history *post Christum*, despite all the frightful catastrophes which have come upon Judaism.

What, however, holds Judaism together, since it is not held together, as the Church, by the gospel? Here I shall relate a conversation which I had with a Jewish tour leader during a journey in Israel. The tour leader had declared himself "religionless" in front of the entire travel group. In a private conversation with him I asked the following question: In your opinion what would hold Judaism together if the bitter situation were to come about whereby the Arabs would "throw you into the sea," as Nasser constantly threatened? The answer promptly came: "The Law," and this out of the mouth of a "religionless" Jew! It is above all the Torah which guarantees Jewish identity and Jewish peoplehood. Judaism and Torah belong together, even if there are many shadings and nuances within the ways to live according to the Law, when one, for example, thinks of "Reform Judaism" or of the people from Mea Shearim in Jerusalem. Life according to the Law offers a great breadth of variation, but Judaism without the Law is de facto no Judaism, even if atheistic Jews might dispute this. Paul indeed declared Christ as "the end of the Law," but only "for all those who believed [in Christ]," not however for the Jews who never come to the gospel. "I testify again to every man who receives circumcision that he is bound to keep the whole law" (Gal. 5:3). Paul, therefore, does not exempt the Jew, whoever remains a Jew or becomes a Jew, from the Law! Likewise in Rom. 2:25 he remarks that the circumcision "indeed is of value if you obey the law," and this although he as one overcome by the grace of Christ is convinced that "by works of the law shall no one be justified" (Gal. 2:16b). Of course Paul had the hope and the wish that even Israel would find the way to the gospel (cf. Rom. 9:1–3). Paul is also convinced that Jesus Christ, because "according to the flesh he came forth from the seed of David" (Rom. 1:3), is the messianic son of David and as such also the Messiah of Israel; he does not, however, acquit Israel from guilt which pertains to its "hardening" toward the gospel (cf. Rom. 10:2f., 18f.). He takes note, even if painfully, that a partial hardening has come over Israel (Rom. 11:25), but he nevertheless sees this hardening of Israel always in relationship to the salvation of the Gentiles (cf. Rom. 11:15, 25), a fact which is very important. For in this it is shown, indeed precisely in this, that Paul did not write off Israel because God did not write off Israel; indeed, he recognizes that the Jews "as regards the Gospel they are enemies of God *for your sake*," that therefore the hardening of the Jews who really are the first aspirants to messianic salvation ("first to the Jews"!),

and turned to the Gentiles for salvation. He proclaims that the hardening of
Israel lasts only so long "until the full number of the Gentiles come in"
(Rom. 11:25) and that in the end "all Israel will be saved" (11:26b). Paul,
therefore, is not able to view the salvation of the Gentiles in isolated
fashion, but only in connection with the hardening and the final salvation of
Israel. He therefore never loses sight of his people, from whom he has gone
forth. Doubtless this is connected with the fact that according to his
conviction, Jesus is and remains also the Messiah of Israel. "The incarnation of the son of God is for Paul no abstract becoming human, but a coming
'from the seed of David,' under the Law."[17]

With this the following theses can be tentatively summarized:

1. Paul never wrote off his people from messianic salvation.

2. Paul confesses his people and their "privileges."

3. Paul sees the Gentiles and their salvation always in relationship to
Israel, which Christian theology almost to this very day no longer does, or
at most only by way of a demonization of Judaism, completely contrary to
the proclamation of the apostle.

4. Paul did not exempt the Jews from the Law.

Paul Open to a "Substantive Critique"

Paul was able to resolve certain paradoxes of his theology relating to the
Law only dialectically, a fact which could provide the basis for a substantive
critique of Paul. However, these paradoxes are closely connected with what
was spelled out above about the tension between eschaton and history. On
the one side Paul (with the rest of the primitive Church) was convinced that
Jesus the Messiah had already come and that consequently the end of times
had already come (1 Cor. 10:11), and on the other side he had to see that
Israel did not harken to the gospel, that it apparently moved outside of the
eschatologically qualified time brought about by the coming of the Messiah
in Jesus and continued to seek its identity in the Law. This means that
Israel lives its history beginning with Abraham even *post Christum* as if the
Messiah were not yet come, because it was not able to recognize him in
Jesus the crucified one; it does not live in the "post-messianic age" (H.-J.
Schoeps). It continues to understand its history as a continuum—even if it
is a continuum marked by fearful catastrophes—that is identifiable by
loyalty to the Law. Now indeed its history has gone on further, for the
parousia has not yet come—almost two thousand years since the death of
Jesus have gone by. Paul (and the rest of the primitive Church) had not
reckoned with this. Even if, as his letters show, the "*parousia* piety" was
not completely replaced by an "Easter piety," it nevertheless was forced

into the background,[18]—which again had the consequence that the "vertical" vigorously pushed the "horizontal" into the background of Christian consciousness in the sense: Seek not "the God before you," but rather "seek the things that are above, where Christ is, seated at the right hand of God. Set your mind on things that *are above*, not on things that are on earth" (Col. 3:1f.); "But our commonwealth [*politeuma*] is in heaven, and from it we await a Savior, the Lord Jesus Christ" (Phil. 3:20). The look of the Christian community shifted with this largely toward the heavenly, the "upper" spheres, where they knew their *ontōs on*, the glorified Lord, to be at the right hand of the Father. Israel, in contrast, continued to look toward the future and in its prayers called for the coming of the Messiah, for whom it still waits. This produced another image of history and another consciousness of history, one different from the divided consciousness of history of the Christian community.[19] For Jewish consciousness "the coming aeon," of which Judaism at the time of Jesus spoke, did not yet invade "this aeon," as according to Christian eschatology. History followed its course further just as before Christ, even if around the turning of the times there had been strong apocalyptic circles in Judaism that reckoned with an end to history coming soon. History continued even after the destruction of Jerusalem and the Temple in the year 70, and after the catastrophe Judaism gathered itself spiritually above all under the decisive leadership of Rabbi Jochanan Ben Zakkai (1–80 C.E.) in Jamnia (Jabne), who presented obedience to the Torah as the most important commandment for Israel. He did so from the knowledge won from historical events that after the destruction of the Temple the Torah would be the instrument with which Judaism would be held together. History has judged him correct.[20] It is essentially the Torah which holds Judaism together and gives it its identity.

Paul, of course, on the basis of his christological and soteriological convictions, held forth the thesis that the human being will not be justified by the works of the Law, but rather exclusively by faith in Jesus Christ. This naturally led to a strong devaluation of the Law; in Jewish opinion Paul appears to have misunderstood the Law because he was no longer able to think together Law and covenant.[21] Paul, who before his Damascus experience was "as to the law a Pharisee" (Phil. 3:5), in fact denied all salvific value to living according to the Law ("no flesh will be justified by the works of the law"). However, on the other side, he continued to hold that "the law is holy, and the commandment is holy and just and good" (Rom. 7:12), that the Law is "spiritual" (*pneumatikos*) (7:14); he energetically rejected (*mē genoito*) the notion that the Law is "sin" (7:7) and "working death in me" (7:13). What led Paul into death was "sin that sin might be shown to be sin";

it was sin which "[brought] death in me through what is good [the Law], in order that sin might be shown to be sin, and through the commandment might become sinful beyond measure" (7:13). "In its truth the Law does not belong together with sin and death. . . . It is precisely in the Law and through it that it becomes clear what sin is."[22]

From what is in Rom. 5:12ff. it is clear that death is indissolubly connected with sin, whereby Paul is thinking of sin as the sin of the first human being, Adam. Indeed, the apostle says that before the giving of the Law, sin was not reckoned (Rom. 5:13). However, he then speaks of the disobedience of Adam (cf. 5:19), which of course can relate only to the commandment of prohibition given to Adam by God in paradise. This leads to an important clue which should be followed if one wishes to correctly understand the Pauline theology of the Law.

The Law Not Just Judaic but Also Cosmic

With the Law the apostle thinks by no means only of the Jews, but of humanity in general, of the cosmos. This is shown with great clarity in the first chapter of the Epistle to the Romans. Paul does not deny that the Law really would and should bring life, that is, eschatological salvation. However, he remarks in Gal. 3:21b: "For if a law had been given which could make alive (*ho dynamenos zōopoiēsai*), then righteousness would indeed be by the law"; in 3:12 he cites expressly Lev. 18:5: "He who does them [the commandments and the instructions of the Torah] shall live by them," and remarks in Rom. 2:13: "For it is not the hearers of the law who are righteous before God, but the doers of the law who will be justified." The "unreal" formulations in Gal. 3:21b, however, allow one to recognize clearly enough the apostle's conviction that in reality the Law did not and does not bring salvation for the simple reason: because the human being on the basis of the weakness of his flesh was and is not in a position to completely fulfill the Law—and thus he falls under the threatened curse of death in the Law itself. And in the eyes of the apostle this is valid not merely for the Jews, *but likewise for the Gentiles*. This conviction results for him from the Scriptures as well as from the experience made possible by the gospel, and again in reference to the Gentiles (cf. Rom. 2:1–32) as well as to the Jews (cf. Rom. 1:18–32; 2:17–24).[23] Because both the Jew and the Gentile knew the Law—the Jew from the positive revelation of the Law by God to Israel, the Gentile from the voice of conscience in his heart[24]—and still did not fulfill it (the majority of them), "Jews and Greeks, are under the power of sin" (Rom. 3:9) and thus "the whole world may be held accountable to God" (3:19). Therefore "*all* fall short of the glory of God" (3:23), whether Jew or

Gentile, and "so death spread to *all* men because *all* men sinned" (5:12b), whether Jew or Gentile. Thus Paul thinks in his theology of the Law (and therefore also in his theology of justification) within the horizon of all humanity and not just within the horizon of Israel. This is true though the Torah of Israel plays a major role because the Law for Israel was not merely written in the heart "by nature," as with the Gentiles, but because Israel had received the Law on Sinai through Moses as an express revelation of God, and because Paul, coming from Judaism, was a Jew, a Pharisee who "advanced in Judaism beyond many of my own age among my people, so extremely zealous was I for the traditions of my fathers" (Gal. 1:14). With this expansion of the horizon to the whole world there is connected the fact that Paul in Rom. 5:12ff. is able to introduce Adam, the first human being, as the prototype of all sinners. With this, according to Paul, the greatness of the Law is indeed no inner-Jewish greatness, but a greatness pertaining to the whole world. If one notes this, then it is immediately clear that it is nonsense to view the Pauline teaching of the Law and justification as an expression of the apostle's "anti-Judaism." It was, in fact, the post-Pauline Christian theology which made the teaching into an anti-Jewish and anti-Semitic instrument. Paul could and had to think within the world horizon, because for him the Messiah Jesus is *the world savior*, the "second Adam" (1 Cor. 15:47), the *concretum universale*.

Paul's Opponents in His Teaching about the Law

The following question should also be considered: Against whom had Paul really developed primarily his Law and justification teaching? The often-heard answer of Christian theologians, which sounds reasonable enough, states: against Judaism. In reality this is not so, as can be seen in the letter in which Paul for the first time developed literarily the "fundamental statements" of his justification teaching, namely, the Letter to the Galatians, written either in the year 55 or in the year 57.

When Paul wrote this letter he had already worked more than twenty years as a Christian missionary. Only then—which is something many Christian theologians are not conscious of—did he write down the statements of his justification teaching. The occasion for doing so was provided by "some" who had come into the Gentile-Christian community in Galatia which had been founded by Paul and perverted the gospel of Christ (cf. Gal. 1:7). The "some" were very definitely not Jews, but most likely Jewish Christians who proclaimed a gospel other than that which Paul proclaimed, in that they taught that the Gentile Christians also had to have themselves circumcised and live a life according to the Law, despite baptism and belief in Jesus Christ. Against this "other gospel," which for Paul was no real gospel because for him there was no "other gospel" (Gal. 1:6f.), Paul wrote the fundamental sentence of his justification teaching, namely, that no one is justified by the works of the Law, but rather only by faith in Jesus Christ (Gal. 2:16). Therefore, Paul developed his Law and justification teaching *not against Jews, but against fellow Christians!* For the most part this is not attended to in the Christian explanation of the Epistle to the Galatians, even though awareness of this becomes a hermeneutical key to the understanding of this epistle.[25]

If one keeps a careful eye on the text of Gal. 2:11–22, one would indeed have to say that Paul addressed the fundamental sentences of his justification teaching to Peter, the "first pope"![26] For the one immediately addressed in 2:14ff. is indeed Peter who, contrary to his own conviction, conformed to the line of the opponents of Paul in a hypocritical way (cf. 2:12b). Naturally one can say "that Paul in his dispute with his Jewish-Christian opponents arrives at formulations which in their final effect also hit Judaism itself."[27] However, neither in the Epistle to the Galatians nor in that to the Romans, in which the theme of "justification" from faith is further developed, is the apostle concerned about *this* "final effect." He does not intend to lay low Judaism with his formulations. What he wishes to lay low is a Christian pseudo-gospel to which, according to external appearances, even Peter had confessed as he gave up table fellowship in Antioch with the Gentile Christians under the pressure of the people of James. In the Epistle to the Galatians Paul absolutely does not enter into dispute with the Jews, and fundamentally he does not either in the Epistle to the Romans. In the Epistle to the Romans he only indicates that Jews and Gentiles have become guilty in the same way before God because they do not observe their Law (Rom 1—3) and that the Jews, although "partly" hardened toward the gospel, nevertheless in the end will be saved by God (11:26). The term "Jews" ("Jew") appears only four times in the Epistle to the Galatians: 2:13 (referring to the Jewish Christians); 2:14 (referring to Peter); 2:15 (referring to the Christians who have come from Judaism, including Paul); 3:28 (because of baptism *in the Church* "there is neither Jew nor Greek, there is neither slave nor free, there is neither male nor female"). The term "Jew" is never encountered in the Epistle to the Galatians in an anti-Jewish sense!

In the Epistle to the Romans, the term "Jews" ("Jew") is found eleven times: 1:16 (the gospel "is the power of God for salvation to every one who has faith, the Jew first and also to the Greek"); 2:9 ("there will be tribulation and distress for every human being who does evil, the Jew first [because he knows the will of God from the Torah better than does the Gentile] and also the Greek"); 2:17 (here the one who is consciously called "Jew" by the apostle is rebuked by him because he, like the Gentiles, has often transgressed the commandments of God [which no Jew would deny]); 2:28, 29 ("For he is not a real Jew who is one outwardly, nor is true circumcision something external and physical. He is a Jew who is one inwardly, and real circumcision is a matter of the heart, spiritual and not literal." Behind this there clearly stands the idea of the "true Jew," in which of course the physical-national Judaism is extended and in spiritualizing fashion the Gentile Christian, insofar as he fulfills the command of God, is declared the "Jew who is one inwardly");[28] 3:1 ("Then what advantage has the Jew? Or what is the value of circumcision? Much in every way," namely, "to begin with," because of the "word of God" entrusted to the Jews, therefore, because of a "privilege" of Israel. What the apostle says immediately following this is important: "What if some [Jews] were unfaithful? Does their faithlessness nullify the faithfulness of God? By no means!" Here the theme of Rom. 9—11 is clearly announced: The God who is "faithful" to his promises will, despite the faithlessness to the covenant by "some," in the end save all Israel); 3:9 (the apostle accused all human beings, "Jews as well as Greeks," of standing "under sin"); 3:29 (here Paul asks: "Or is God the God of Jews only? Is he not the God of Gentiles also? Yes, of Gentiles also," which no Jew will deny; therefore God wishes also to save the Gentiles because he justifies them by faith); 9:24 (God has called in the Church a people "not from the Jews only but also from the Gentiles"); 10:11–12 (in regard to the sentence of the Scriptures: "'No one who believes in him will be put to shame.' For there is no distinction between Jew and Greek; the same Lord is Lord of all and bestows his riches upon all who call upon him").

When looking at these passages on the Jews in the Epistle to the Romans, one can in no way speak of an "anti-Judaism" of Paul. Especially noteworthy here is the fact that it is particularly in those portions of the epistle in which the apostle presents his justification teaching that the term "Jew" does not appear, with the possible exception of 3:29. In the Epistle to the Romans Paul does not develop his theology in opposition to the Jews. The addressees of his theology are rather "the whole world," "everyone"! It is precisely in this Epistle to the Romans that Paul brings out the "privileges" of Israel and proclaims the eschatological saving of all Israel, even though he is not silent about there being a partial "hardening" that has come over Israel insofar as it does not listen to the gospel because God

himself has laid a "spirit of stupor" upon it. And no Jew will refuse his
agreement to the affirmation of the apostle that not every Jew is "a true
Jew." For the rest, indeed, he does not utter a single syllable to indicate that
there are not also in Israel "true Jews," "inward Jews," and "circumcision of
the heart."[29] The addressee of the Pauline justification teaching is "the
whole world" (Rom. 3:20), to which the Jew also belongs, and to that extent
the next sentence of the apostle in Rom. 3:21 is also valid for him: "But *now*
the righteousness of God has been manifested *apart from law*, although the
law and the prophets bear witness to it, the righteousness of God *through*
faith in Jesus Christ for all who believe. For there is no distinction" (as for
example, between Jews and Gentiles). But it is likewise a fact that Paul
would by no means write off from salvation those Jews who cannot accept
this statement, as Christian theology time and again has done. God,
indeed, has "consigned *all* men to disobedience [the Jews as well as the
Gentiles] that he may have mercy upon all" (Rom. 11:32). God also saves
that Israel which continues *post Christum* to hold fast to the Law! He saves
Israel by a "special path" which apparently bypasses the gospel.[30] It is only
out of an understanding of this that the sentences of the apostle about the
Torah which ring so paradoxically are to be grasped: that on the one hand it
is a holy and spiritual being, and on the other hand it is "not from faith" and
is not able to produce life. One almost has the impression that Paul is not
completely finished with the problem of the Law; the "hardening" of Israel,
the continuing loyalty of its people to the Torah, and its rejection of the
gospel prevent him in this. Israel's faithfulness to the Law does not destroy
the logic of his justification teaching, but it did and does disturb it. It was
not completely clarified even when Paul, according to Rom. 3:31, thought
that with his justification teaching he "upheld the Law," namely, in its true
validity and significance in salvation history. He succeeded in this only in
part. The Epistle to the Romans shows this quite clearly, and this must be
stated in all openness.

Abraham and the Scriptures
Taken from the Jews?

Does not Paul, however, tear Abraham and the Scriptures away from the
Jews and claim them for the Church?[31] Those, indeed, who believe in
Christ are, according to Gal. 3:7, "the sons of Abraham." Are the Jews then
no longer "sons of Abraham"? At first this seems to be true. However, the
following must be kept in mind:

Abraham Taken from Christian Opponents

One presumed that the Jewish-Christian opponents of the apostle went about with the slogan: *"We* are the true sons of Abraham" because we join together the belief in the Messiah Jesus with the Jewish manner of living, especially with circumcision. Because of this conviction the opponents of the apostle demanded circumcision of Gentile Christians (cf. Gal. 5:2; 6:12, 13; Acts 15:1, 5). Perhaps in this the opponents called upon the story of Abraham in Gen. 15 and Gen. 17 (especially 17:9–14: the circumcision of Abraham), avoiding the statement of Gen. 15:6 ("And he [Abraham] believed the Lord; and he reckoned it to him as righteousness"), which Paul therefore raised up to a fundamental statement of his counterargument because there reference is made to justification by faith. Paul thereby tears Abraham away *from his Christian opponents,* not from the Jews, concerning whom in Gal. 3 there is absolutely no discussion whatsoever.

Salvation for the Gentiles

Rather, the concern is much more with the justification of the *Gentiles.* Said more clearly: The concern is with the question of how the scriptural promise to Abraham *that in him all Gentiles will be blessed* (cf. Gen. 12:3; 18:18) can be fulfilled (cf. Gal. 3:8). For Paul's opponents, the only way to achieve this blessing would be for the Gentile to take over the life of the Jew according to the Law, because the Gentile would thereby become a "proselyte," even though in connection with Jesus as the Messiah. Paul, however, taught: Not so, but rather by the way of faith according to the manner of Abraham, as it is witnessed in Gen. 15:6. He argued that the reason why it was to be along the way of faith was that the way through the Law, on account of the weakness of the "flesh," did not lead to the goal, but rather to the curse of death, which was *also* threatened in the Law, namely, in Deut. 27:26 (cf. Gal 3:10). In Gal. 3 Paul develops his line of argument *to the Gentiles:* the term "Gentiles" (*ethnē*) appears three times in Gal. 3, while the term "Jews" does not appear at all. The concern is consistently about the salvation and the way of salvation of the Gentile. This was required by the situation in the Christian community of Galatia.[32]

Jew and Gentile Share in the Faith of Abraham

In contrast, in the Epistle to the Romans the apostle also includes the "circumcised" in the theme of "justification." "God is one; and he will justify the circumcised on the ground of their faith and the uncircumcised because of their faith" (3:30). And Abraham "received circumcision as a sign or seal of the righteousness which he had by faith while he was still uncircumcised [cf. Gen. 17:10f.]. The purpose was to make him the father of all who believed without being circumcised [the Gentiles] and who thus have righteousness reckoned to them, and likewise the father of the circumcised who are not merely circumcised but also follow the example of the faith which our father Abraham had before he was circumcised [the Jewish Christians]" (4:11f.). The promise of God to Abraham that he would be the father of many nations and the "heir of the world" (cf. Gen. 15:5; 17:5; 18:18; 22:17f.) does not follow the way of the Law, but rather the way of faith into fulfillment. "The promise to Abraham and his descendants, that they should inherit the world, did not come through the law but through the righteousness of faith. If it is the adherents of the law who are to be the heirs, faith is null and the promise is void. For the law brings wrath [because of the *de facto* weakness of human beings who are sinners], but where there is no law there is no transgression. That is why it depends on faith, in order that the promise may rest on grace and be guaranteed to all his descendants—*not only to the adherents of the law* [the Jews] *but also to those who share the faith of Abraham* [the Gentile and Jewish Christians]" (4:13–16).

The apostle's line of thought is at first difficult. What, nevertheless, clearly emerges from it is this: that the universal content of the promise of salvation to Abraham, in which the Gentiles are included, could not be attained by the Law, but by faith. For the rest this is clear: that the promise to Abraham (and this emerges especially from 4:16) relates to his "entire" offspring—the emphasis is on *panti* (entire)—to the Jews who live according to the Law as well as to those who live "from faith" (in Christ) in the manner of Abraham, namely, the Jews and the Jewish Christians and the Gentile Christians. Jews, Jewish Christians, and Gentile Christians together form the "entire offspring" of Abraham, and thus in this manner Abraham will become "the inheritor of the cosmos" (not in a political, but in a spiritual sense)[33] and "the father of us all" (Rom. 4:16) so that the promise in the Scriptures in the end is fulfilled in him: "I have made you the father of many nations" (Gen. 17:5; Rom. 4:17).[34]

In retrospect this means that Paul tears neither Abraham nor the Scriptures away from the Jews to claim them for the Church. The Jews are and remain a portion of the "total offspring" of Abraham, although they continue to live "from the Law." Paul clearly distinguishes between his predication of Abraham as the "father of all believers" (Rom. 4:12: related to Gentile Christians and Jewish Christians), and Abraham as "the father of us all" (4:16: related to Jews, Jewish Christians, and Gentile Christians), and as the "father of many nations" (4:16, 18: related again to everyone). Because the Jews belong to the totality of the descendants of Abraham, it is only logical that the apostle in the Epistle to the Romans predicts the saving of "all Israel." Otherwise, an essential portion of the descendants of Abraham would be lost, which would result in God being unfaithful to the promises given to Abraham. God, however, remains faithful to all his promises: It is precisely this fundamental conviction of the Jew Paul which he shares with the other Jews. God is not satisfied with a partial fulfillment, even if his ways for attaining this goal appear indiscernible and paradoxical to human thinking. However, it is precisely here that the divinity of God reveals itself.

Paul, a "Jewish" Theologian

Why, however, does Paul develop his theology against the background of Israel and the "Old Testament" rather than in a speculative manner, as for example a Stoic philosopher? To this question the following brief answers can be given:

1. Paul comes from Judaism and never forgets it (cf. only Phil. 3:5: "Circumcised on the eighth day, of the people of Israel, of the tribe of Benjamin, a Hebrew born of Hebrews; as to the Law a Pharisee").

2. "The Scripture," with which Paul operates is the Scripture of Israel.[35] He is, in addition, rabbinically schooled, as his manner of argumentation shows.[36]

3. The God of Paul is, like the God of Jesus, the God of Abraham, the God of Isaac, and the God of Jacob; therefore, the God of Israel.

4. The Messiah is for him a Jew, namely, the Jew Jesus from Nazareth who was crucified in Jerusalem and was raised from the dead.

5. The God of Israel, according to the conviction of the apostle as well as to the entire primitive Church, had acted in Jesus of Nazareth, and had indeed acted eschatologically.

That Paul had "Hellenized" Christianity must be regarded as absolute nonsense. Paul thinks in "Jewish categories." The fact that in his upbringing Paul was a Diaspora Jew, born in Tarsus, who possessed from his father Roman citizenship, may have marked him in some things; however, this would be difficult to show in individual matters. In any case, thanks to this circumstance he had complete command of the Greek language.

Paul, a Great Ethicist of Judaism
and Christianity

Paul had indeed rejected the way of the Law as an effective way to salvation, but in his ethics he brought the Law in again "through the back door." Indeed, Paul, like Jesus and James, belonged very much to the great ethicists of Judaism and Christianity.

This is proved not only by the comprehensive ethical portions in his epistles. It is proved in detail especially by Rom. 13:8–10, concerning which Ernst Käsemann remarked:[37] "The real problem of the text was precisely that there is no polemic against the *nomos*, let alone another law." Moreover, Paul deviates here "from his usual view of the indivisibility of the Torah."[38] The text states: "Owe no one anything, except to love one another; for he who loves his neighbor has fulfilled the Law. The commandments, 'you shall not commit adultery, you shall not kill, you shall not steal, you shall not covet,' and any other commandment, are summed up (*anakephalaioutai*) in this sentence, "you shall love your neighbor as yourself' (Lev. 19:18). Love does no wrong to a neighbor; therefore love is the fulfilling of the Law." The significant thing in this text for our theme (Paul and Israel) is above all this, that the apostle speaks here of a "fulfilling" of the Torah, not of a "driving out," or a "substitution." How he understands this term "fulfilling" (*plērōma*) can be seen from the verb *anakephalaiousthai* which has the significance of "summing up," "summarizing." Therefore Paul sees in the commandment of love which comes from the "Scripture" of Israel, Lev. 19:18, the highpoint of the Law, following here the Jewish as well as the Jesus tradition. This "reaching a highpoint" in no way implies the abrogation of the "second table," as the context indeed shows, but limits itself, as can be seen from the text, to the so-called moral law of the Old Testament. Paul indeed does not connect with this the question of salvation—whether the fulfilling of the commandment of love would be a viable way along the way of salvation of faith—anymore than he does in Gal. 5:14. However, justifying faith and the fulfillment of the moral law summarized in the commandment of love, as Israel once put it forth in the second table of the Decalogue, are in no way brought into opposition with one another, which appears to belong to the paradoxes of Pauline justification theology—but is a paradox really only for those who have forgotten the sentence from Gal. 5:6 according to which faith must be "effective through love."[39]

This paradox could force itself into our consciousness if we think of the term taken over from Judaism by Paul in Gal. 6:2, "the law of Christ."[40] H. Lietzmann believed that here there existed "an intended antithesis against the Judaistic *nomos* concept."[41] It is precisely not that; the antithesis lies rather in the immediate context with its reference to an attitude which does not correspond to the will of Christ because it injures love. The antithesis lies in the unchristian attitude of Christians, as, for example, in what the apostle formulated before in his admonition: "Let us have no self-conceit, no provoking of one another, no envy of one another" (Gal. 5:26).

The expression "the law of Christ" points to the fact that Paul is very much aware of a lawgiver for the Christian community, namely, Christ himself. In Rom. 7:1–4 he writes: "Do you not know, brethren—for I am speaking to those who know the law—that the law is binding on a person only during his life? Thus a married woman is bound by law to her husband as long as he lives; but if her husband dies she is discharged from the law concerning the husband. Accordingly, she will be called an adulteress if she lives with another man while her husband is alive. But if her husband dies she is free from that law, and if she marries another man she is not an adulteress. Likewise, my brethren, you have died to the law through the body of Christ, so that you may belong to another, to him who has been raised from the dead in order that we may bear fruit for God." Here Paul is clearly operating with analogies from the law of marriage. Of course he does not carry it out consistently insofar as he avoids the term "law" on the side of Christ (consciously?). However, belonging to the Risen One does not give the Christian permission for lawlessness. "Unlike the woman depicted, the Christian does not become his own master, but receives a new lord who replaces the old."[42] The express reference to the Risen One to whom the Christian belongs as the woman belongs to her husband lets us see clearly the christological foundation of the Pauline teaching of the "freedom of the Christian human being." The freedom of the Christian from the Jewish Torah does not mean in any way freedom from obligation. Freedom from the Law can only be spoken of with reference to the new being in Christ, which immediately signifies a new order. "Freedom from the Law" is a term which is only possible and understandable within new structures which include in themselves the "being in Christ." The baptized one, according to the teaching of Paul, is, as he formulates it with classical pertinence, an *ennomos Christou* (1 Cor. 9:21). Almost untranslatable. One can translate it only in paraphrasing fashion: "The baptized one is placed under the Law of Christ," which for the Christian is as obligatory as the Torah of Moses is for the Jew.

Paul's Criticism of Jews

To be sure, Paul experienced some injustice from Jews. In the "*peristasis* catalogue" of 2 Cor. 11:23–33 the apostle remarks: "Five times I have received at the hands of the Jews the forty lashes minus one" (11:24).[43] But no complaint against his compatriots is forthcoming. Matters appear different in 1 Thess. 2:14–16, as the apostle here formulates: "For you, brethren,

became imitators of the churches of God in Christ Jesus which are in Judea;
for you suffered the same things from your own countrymen as they did
from the Jews, who killed both the Lord Jesus and the prophets, and drove
us out, and displease God and oppose all men by hindering us from
speaking to the Gentiles that they may be saved—so as always to fill up the
measure of their sins. But God's wrath has come upon them at last!" This is
a very bitter, precisely "anti-Jewish," text, and presumably the "sting" of
this text cannot be removed by declaring it to be a later insertion by an
"anti-Judaist," as has been attempted. Otto Michel has written outstand-
ingly on this text,[44] and E. Bammel[45] has also contributed importantly to it,
and finally, the work of W. D. Davies[46] has been extremely helpful. According to Davies, Paul combines the typical Christian criticism of the Jews
(reference to the killing of Jesus and the prophets; cf. Matt. 5:12; 23:29–31;
Luke 11:47–51) with the typical Gentile polemic against the Jews ("They
displease God and oppose all men"). With reference to the final coming of
the wrath of God on the Jews there appears for them to be no more hope.
They are lost. In this Paul works with traditional material and traditional
topoi. Thus, one reads, for example, in 2 Chron. 36:15f. the following:
"YHWH, the God of their fathers, sent persistently to them by his messengers, because he had compassion on his people and on his dwelling
place; but they kept mocking the messengers of God, despising his words,
and scoffing at his prophets, till the wrath of YHWH rose against his
people, till there was no remedy."[47] The apostle's remark that the wrath of
God has come upon the Jews "at last" (*eis telos*) must not be related to a
specific historical event; this sentence belongs to the "style." Naturally for
Paul the difficulties the Jews made for the spread of the gospel were a
hindrance to the purposes of God, and thus those Jews who cause difficulties for the Christian mission in Thessalonica and elsewhere do not please
God. However, in no way does the apostle include all Jews or all Israel in
this. "Paul is thinking not of the Jewish people as a whole but of unbelieving Jews who have violently hindered the gospel,"[48] and above all: as Paul
wrote the First Epistle to the Thessalonians (around the year 51), he had
not yet thought through the matter of the final salvation of Israel, as he had
in Rom. 9–11 (written about 57). 1 Thess. 2:14–16 is the reaction "of an
early Paul."[49] At this early period Paul apparently had reflected only little
about the "theological existence" of Israel, perhaps because the problem of
the "Law and gospel" at this time had not yet moved into the center of his
theology. Later, as he wrote the Epistle to the Galatians, it was no longer
the Jews who were the opponents of the gospel, but rather Jewish Christians. One must therefore read the harsh-sounding statements of the apos-

tle in 1 Thess. 2:14–16 in connection with his wandering mission experiences and realize in addition that in this he worked with the conventional handed-on *topoi*. One can draw the conclusion that Paul was an "anti-Semite" as little from 1 Thess. 2:14–16 as from his later statements.[50] None of the men of the primitive Church had so loved Israel as the apostle Paul. This is clear from Rom. 9:1–3: "I am speaking the truth in Christ, I am not lying; my conscience bears me witness in the Holy Spirit, that I have great sorrow and unceasing anguish in my heart. For I could wish that I myself were accursed and cut off from Christ for the sake of my brethren, my kinsmen by race."

What Christian theologian has thus spoken? Paul did not "paganize" Israel, and he did not dispossess them of the characteristic of being a holy people of God. For to Paul, Israel remained the people of Abraham, and God will in the end save "all Israel." Christian theology must learn to think and speak of Israel as did the apostle and Jew Paul.

5

Theological "Reparation"

ISRAEL AND THE ORIGIN OF
THE GOSPELS

Perhaps it will be surprising to find a chapter on the theological "reparation" beginning with a reflection on Israel and the origin of the Gospels introduced with the question: Why were Gospels, that is, reports and narrations about Jesus of Nazareth, written at the time of the primitive Church? Various reasons can be mentioned; for example, people wished to know more details about the founder, and the evangelists responded to this need. Or with the dying out of the first generation, especially the generation of the ear- and eyewitnesses of the life of Jesus ("apostles"), there was the danger of the falsification of authentic Jesus materials by the insinuation of apocryphal materials—and therefore the fixing of the authentic materials in the Gospels.[1] Or the christological homology of the primitive Church which responded to the question "Who is this?" (cf. Mark 4:41; 8:27; John 4:10; 5:12; 8:25; 9:36; 12:34) needed them for their historical verification and correct interpretation of the narrative references to the life of Jesus; the Gospels were narrative "accompanying texts" of homology, of the christological confession.[2] Is the question of why it was particularly in the primitive Church that the Gospels were written thereby exhaustively answered? Especially when one connects this question with the other: Where did the writing of the Gospels really find its *Sitz im Leben* in the primitive Church? In responding to it, one comes upon the theme: Israel and the origin of the Gospels.

In the following reflections I shall proceed from texts written by the Jew Jules Isaac in his book *Jesus and Israel:*[3]

> Now, from the standpoint of historical criticism, we know, and it is necessary to know, that the Gospels were written in a time when a breach was tending to form between Jews faithful to the Law of Moses and adherents to the new faith, in a time when the latter, reacting to the intense hostility of official Judaism, were seeking support from the Gentile world, when the recruiting of Christian communities among the Jews seemed to be flagging. . . .
>
> Intentionally or not, the accusers have started from a point of confusion. Fundamental confusion. Which has been sustained from century to century. Which is still sustained and reigns over minds.

Confusion of two historical problems, two historical facts, which are entirely distinct.

The first of these problems is one we have examined: Jesus and Israel, Jesus and his people. In the apparently rather narrow Jewish sphere in which he lived, preached, and spread the Gospel, Jesus found adversaries, enemies, disciples, the sympathies of the masses. These are the facts. There was neither a rejection of the Jewish people by Jesus nor a rejection of Jesus by the Jewish people.

The second problem is quite other: Judaism and Christianity. We have not broached it but have only alluded to it. It is also a fact, but later and quite other, that at a given moment, after a strong surge of conversions, the Jewish people, regrouped behind their doctors, became resistant to Christian preaching. What the Jewish people rejected at that moment was not Jesus, not even the Christ; it was the Christian faith and rule as they were defined by the new Church. Moreover, there was a parallel and mutual rebuff, of Christianity by Judaism and of Judaism by Christianity, the two rebuffs closely related to one another. Which was cause, which effect? Let us not forget, primitive Christianity was Judeo-Christianity.[4] From the day when it ceased to be so, when Judeo-Christianity saw itself relegated to the rank of an inferior sect, then a heresy,[5] a breach opened between the two confessions: to ask the Jewish people to cast off a Law they venerated as dictated by God Himself, to ask them that, which Jesus had never asked, was truly to ask the impossible. The growing mutual hostility of the doctors (Christian and Jewish) and the development of Christian dogmatics did the rest: the breach became an abyss.

It was easy and it was tempting to Christian doctors to let themselves confuse these two series of facts, distant and distinct though they were from each other. And they have done so. Since the era when it can be established that the canonical Gospels were written. More so thereafter. From this arose certain stylistic practices in the Gospels, certain equivocal, tendentious formulations which we have discussed. From this, and in connection with the incessant Judeo-Christian disputes, was born an even more tendentious tradition, which emptied the Gospels as it were of their historic substance and substituted the myth of rejection, of reprobation, of deicide for an entirely different reality. . . . Thus defensive weapons were sought in the arsenal of reprobation quite as often as offensive. Then when Judaism, outcast, reviled, hunted, seemed definitively out of the battle, the habit had taken hold, the tradition was set. The myth of Crime had engendered the myth of Punishment: together they explained, covered, if not justified Israel's martyrdom. Enough to reassure and lull Christian consciences.

These appear to be important remarks which can cast a new light on the history of the origin of the Gospels: The collection of the evangelical Jesus materials had one of its *Sitz im Leben* in the gradual, troubled process of the separation of the Church from the community of Israel, in their gradual living apart.[6] This process essentially ended with the destruction of Jerusalem and the Temple in the year 70.[7] Now the Church and Israel exist alongside each other.

It is certain that "the gospel is an original creation of early Christianity."[8] What driving powers stood behind this original creation? Jesus was a Jew and lived his life in the social structure of Israel with its religious-cultic customs and institutions. He predicted the imminence of the eschatological reign of God and called Israel to repentance (cf. Mark 1:14f.). He gathered a circle of disciples around him who functioned as "multipliers" of his message, as can be seen from the "missionary pericope" (Mark 6:7–13; Matt. 10:1–42; Luke 9:1–8; 10:1–16). He intended with their help to gather all Israel and mediate to it the salvation of the reign of God. He understood himself "to be sent only to the lost sheep of the house of Israel" (Matt. 15:24).[9] He did not turn merely to the "ones who were cast out," "the religiously déclassé," as is often maintained, but to all levels of his people. His concern was with the establishment of the totality of Israel.[10] However, Jesus had only a partial success with his efforts. The "Galilean crisis" arose which resulted in Jesus withdrawing more and more to the narrower circle of disciples. Nevertheless, he never gave up his work in the public life of his people until the very end. It cannot be denied that in his mission in Israel, Jesus suffered ultimate failure.[11]

After Easter his followers gathered themselves quickly in his name on the basis of the appearances of the Risen One and gradually formed their own cult community in Jerusalem, which remained in close connection with the Temple (cf. Acts 2:46: "And day by day, attending the temple together and breaking bread in their homes, they partook of food with glad and generous hearts, praising God and having favor with all the people"). Again the apostles offered "the whole house" of Israel salvation, which they connected with the name of Jesus (cf., for example, Acts 2:36, 3:26). Their mission did not remain without success: "And more than ever believers were added to the Lord, multitudes both of men and women" (Acts 5:14). "And every day in the temple and at home they did not cease teaching and preaching Jesus as the Christ" (Acts 5:42). Of course strenuous clashes with the spiritual authorities of Judaism arose, and inner disputes in the community of Jesus also developed. Gradually the mission expanded beyond Jerusalem, also beyond Palestine; the missionaries proclaimed "the word" to Jews and Greeks (cf. Acts 11:19f.). "And the hand of the Lord was with them, and a great number that believed turned to the Lord" (Acts 11:21). Then Paul founded his Christian communities in Asia Minor and in Greece. A Christian community also arose in Rome.

Two historical facts, however, must be affirmed in this: (1) One large portion of Judaism did not wish to accept the gospel at all; in fact, a part of it took up sharp opposition to the Christian community. (2) The Gentile-

Christian portion of the Christian community became constantly larger; the Church gradually lost its Jewish-Christian portion, which broke off from the "Universal Church." The process of division of the Christian community from Israel began, and the result was finally the separation of the Church from Israel. The origin of the Gospels seems to be connected with this process of division, as was briefly alluded to above. For this process was above all connected with an important previous event, to which I will later return in more detail: with the restriction to a single teacher, namely, Jesus of Nazareth.[12] This restriction, it would seem, was initiated in its first beginnings with the collapse of the "Galilean spring," the great "time of offering" in the public life of Jesus. If the circle of disciples of Jesus had the important function of "multipliers" during the "time of offering," after the rejection of the offering they received a new function, or more precisely, double functions,[13] which were, however, connected to one another. First of all the disciples' new function consisted in forming the core of the coming salvation community of the Messiah Jesus from which the Church proceeded after Easter. Their second function consisted in their becoming the first bearers of the Jesus tradition, which then after Easter they brought into the Church—and this led to the beginnings of the tradition of the Gospels.[14]

The gradual separation of the Jesus group from the structure of Israel, the connected restriction to a single authoritative teacher, and the gradual transfer from the Jewish mission to the mission to the Gentiles led, necessarily, to the fact *that the Christian community, assembled around the name of Jesus, strove to discover its own self-understanding alongside that of Israel.* Such efforts toward a new self-understanding at the same time served the group's gaining of its own identity. Of decisive, theological help in this was the apostle Paul, who likewise converted from Judaism to the Christian community, and his teaching that the human being is not justified by the works of the Law, but only by faith in Jesus Christ. In this way, naturally the life of the Jew according to the Law, including circumcision, was devalued, if indeed not often despised. Of course one held on to the "Scripture" of Israel—precisely also Paul—but the Jewish teaching authorities were excluded; there was a restriction to Jesus of Nazareth as the sole normative "rabbi." His teaching was no longer seen as one voice among the many voices of the great teachers of Israel, as they are to be found for example in the *Mishnah* and *Talmud* in great number. Naturally this restriction to Jesus was also connected with his fate, by which he appeared to be "catapulted outside" of Israel. Conversely, on the side of Judaism the name of Jesus was not taken up into the role of names of the great teachers of Israel, but rather was treated almost as taboo.[15] Jesus belonged no more to Judaism, but to the Church. It came to an "exodus" of Jesus out of Israel. His teaching was collected by the Church for itself, based firmly on the conviction that Jesus, the crucified and raised from the dead, the Messiah promised by the prophets, is indeed the Son of God. Judaism could not and cannot to this very day accept this faith. This faith conviction of the Christian community that Jesus is Messiah would not unconditionally have excluded him from Judaism; the exclusion was necessitated rather by the belief that he is the Son of God: the true faith objection of the Jew to the present day.[16]

The exclusive restriction to a single teacher in whom the Messiah and the Son of God was honored led "of itself" to the fact that even after Easter Jesus' "teaching" was handed on and finally "fixed" in the Gospels, because with the help of this teaching one could now at best build up one's own self-understanding, since one was no longer able to participate in the self-understanding of Israel, especially no longer within the Gentile-Christian area of the Church. Naturally in the collection of the Jesus materials the concern was not merely with the attainment of self-understanding and identity, but also with the response to the fundamental christological question: "Who is this?" However, because the collection and redaction of the Jesus materials *also* stood in the service of attaining the Christian community's own self-understanding in its separation from Israel, that led—and that is the meaning of this "prolegomenon" to chapter 5 in this tractate—almost by nature to the fact that *this material would be more and more accented in an anti-Jewish manner and that "hostile images" would be built up* (as especially that of the "Pharisees"). These are processes which modern sociology understands. Naturally the new self-understanding was also attained through separation from the surrounding paganism, but it came more from the separation of Israel.[17] Thus the limitation vis-à-vis Israel became the *Sitz im Leben* in the forming of the Gospels' tradition which, however, consistently led to the fact that the Church did not merely forget its "root" Israel, but was often hostile toward it. It is from this limitation which the anti-Judaism, especially marked in the Gospel of John, comes. The division from Israel led to the grave consequence of the "forgetting of Israel" in the Church, which only today gradually and against a great deal of resistance is being rolled back.

Was this development in the mind of Jesus? Would he himself have wished the "exodus" out of Israel? Did he himself develop into an "anti-Judaist?" Jesus wished to gather all Israel around him and mediate to it the salvation of the reign of God. "How often would I have gathered your children together as a hen gathers her brood under her wings, and you would not!" (Luke 13:34b). There follows the judicial sentence, formulated by Jesus in connection with Jer. 22:5: "Behold, your house is forsaken" (Luke 13:35a). Three things are involved in this statement: (1) Jesus wishes to gather the children of Israel around him; (2) Jesus is filled with pain because of the rejection of Israel; (3) Jesus threatens a harsh judgment. With this Jesus remains entirely within the framework of the preaching of the prophets of Israel witnessed to by the Old Testament: The prophets proclaim to Israel the salvation of YHWH; they are filled with pain because of the rejection of Israel (the lamentations of Jeremiah!); they threaten Israel with the judgment of God.[18] No one ever suggested that the prophets, because of their style of preaching, are "anti-Judaists," or indeed enemies of Israel. Just as infrequently was Jesus an "anti-Judaist." He loved his people more than all others on earth. And even threatening speeches of Jesus like these: "I tell you, many will come from east and west and sit at table with Abraham, Isaac, and Jacob in the kingdom of heaven, while the sons of the kingdom will be thrown into the outer darkness; there men will weep and gnash their teeth" (Matt. 8:11f.), or: "Therefore I tell you, the kingdom of God will be taken away from you and given to a nation producing the fruits of it" (Matt. 21:43), do not exceed the manner and style of prophetic teaching.

The latter text is found within the parable of the wicked vineyard tenants (Matt. 21:33–46); it is missing from Mark and Luke. Matthew remarks in the end: "When the chief priests and the Pharisees heard his parables, they perceived that he was speaking about them" (Matt. 21:45). Matthew, therefore, in no way refers the threatening speech of Jesus to the entire people of Israel, but to its spiritual leaders whom he makes responsible for the rejection of his message. Likewise, it is in no way said that the word "people," to whom now the kingdom will be given, means "the Church" (as many Christian exegetes thus argue); and this is equally the case with the "other *farmers*" to whom now the vineyard is rented by the owner. Just who is meant by the "people" and by the "other farmers" remains concealed. The prophetic style often corresponds to this. Likewise, the evangelist Matthew is thinking not of the Church, but of that "people" who, greedy for salvation, took up the message of Jesus. This is clear from the context of our parable: Just before it is the parable of the two sons (Matt. 21:18–32), according to which "the tax collectors and prostitutes" enter into the kingdom of God, and not the expressly addressed opponents of Jesus of 21:45. Following it is the parable of the great banquet (Matt. 22:1–14), according to which in the place of those who were first invited, who rejected the invitation, "whoever you find" will be invited, "the evil and the good." With this the members of the Church are not meant, even though Christian exegesis in its self-righteousness has time and again read this in. Matthew is concerned with the "fruits" (21:41, 43); that is, he is concerned with the realization of the will of God as it has been proclaimed by the prophets of Israel and by the prophet Jesus.[19]

The really anti-Jewish accents were gradually placed upon the Jesus material only after Easter, and indeed in connection with the forming of a self-understanding of one's own, with which of course was connected a change in the historical image. The post-Easter collection of the Jesus materials and its final fixing in the written Gospels which we now have thus also took over "the function of founding a life community in an independent manner,"[20] which likewise created for itself a new historical image. W. Feneberg formulates the situation thus:

> The transition of Christianity in the circles of evangelical tradition from a gathering which had set itself apart as a cult to a church-forming life community produced the forming of the Gospels. On the other hand the forming of the Gospels is the transition of the special Christian traditions existing up to that time (as they had been gradually formed in the period of the "gospel before the Gospels") to their own pre-history. Thus the gospel became necessary to the community as the only legitimate continuation of the history of the people of Israel. The gospel contained in kernel an image of history in which "the Son" was presented in his salvation-founding function. Thus the gospel is that literary genre which the community founded and which grows out of the founding community.[21]

This whole process, which one might perceive as tragic, produced in the end two facts: (1) Israel and the Church completely separated from one another in the time of the primitive Church, and in this each developed its own special self-understanding and its own image of history.[22] (2) The Jew Jesus became the exclusive property of the Church and only today is gradually being recognized by the Jews as one of their own; he is becoming a bridge between the Church and Judaism. This can be brought to the level of awareness by the diagram below. Only with an awareness of these life processes will that "anti-Judaism" which can, in fact, be encountered in the Gospels and in the entire New Testament become understandable.

These processes, of course, can no longer be undone—the Church can indeed self-critically revise its image of history by taking a positive view of Israel, but because of its christological faith convictions it can no longer move back into Judaism. However, reflection on these life processes which led to the separation of the Church from Israel will make possible what I

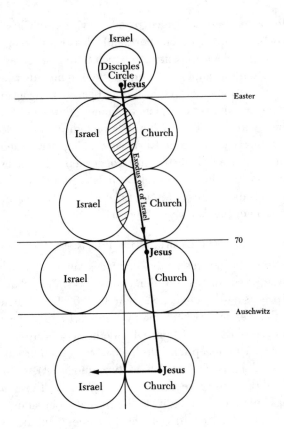

refer to here as theological "reparation," that is, that those distortions of Judaism which have led to its demonization and those hostile images which were developed in the time of the primitive Church and which are largely retained to this very day will finally be dismantled, and thus Israel will again be given its just due, and Christianity's view of its older brother will again be set free. The "Vatican Guidelines" of 3 January 1975 for the implementation of *Nostra aetate* demand this reparation, for example, expressly in reference to the expression "the Jews" in the Johannine Gospel or "the Pharisees." The following discussions illustrate this reparation.

THE PHARISEES

In the Gospels the Pharisees, stylized in a hostile image to an extraordinary degree, are burdened with very negative accents. Scholarly research has already revised this hostile image to a large extent in that it has better illumined the history of Pharisaism and allowed the genuine desires of the

Pharisees to be more clearly recognized. Jewish and Christian scholars have participated in this research effort, and Christian theology is gradually carrying out the theological restitution which here is so necessary.[23]

In this tractate no attempt can be undertaken to provide a new presentation of the extremely complicated history of Pharisaism, concerning which, in any case, there is not yet complete agreement in the research. Rather, I am concerned with providing a number of indications of the authentic desires of the Pharisees, which in Christian theology have been and still are so manifoldly distorted. I am further concerned with investigating the image of the Pharisees in the several Gospels, with groping back to Jesus, and with asking about the continuing significance of Pharisaism for the further formation of Judaism after the year 70 C.E.

The Desires of the Pharisees

Briefly stated, the desires of the Pharisees aimed at the holiness and purity of Israel according to the demand of God: "You shall be to me a kingdom of priests and a holy nation" (Exod. 19:6). The Pharisees believed in attaining this demand of God chiefly through the additional, voluntary fulfillment of the purity regulations which otherwise were mandatory only for the priests. With reception into a Pharisaic "brotherhood," the new member obliged himself above all to two things: (1) to the particular observation of the purity regulations, in particular those of the ritual handwashings before mealtimes; (2) to the special observation of the tithing prescriptions. Josephus remarks on the Pharisees that they "explain the prescriptions of the Law with exactitude."[24] For their piety was in a characteristic way a "Torah piety." They thereby continued those tendencies which had made progress in Judaism after the return from the Babylonian exile under Ezra the scribe. Therefore the *Halacha*, the explanation of the Law, played a decisive role in their thought and teaching. The goal was twofold: (1) the sanctification of the everyday; and (2) the protection of Israel from assimilation into the Gentiles. Thus the oral *Halacha*, also called the "tradition of the fathers," became a "fence around the Torah" (*Mishnah Abot* 1, 1b; 3, 13b) which had the function of "preventative prescriptions" with whose assistance the violation of the biblical Torah was to be hindered. Thereby the teaching decisions of the *Halacha* won a rank almost equal to that of the Torah.[25] In this manner Israel was to be "separated" from the Gentiles—"Pharisees" indeed means nothing other than "the separated ones," in Hebrew, *perushim,* and in Aramaic, *perishajja.* It is disputed, however, whether "Pharisees" was a self-designation, or whether it was conferred on the Pharisees by their surroundings as their designation and distinction from other groups in the Judaism of that time. In any case, "Pharisees" has nothing to do with "hypocrite." The Pharisees were, alongside the Essenes, the most devout people in the Judaism of that time. However, one must not portray the Pharisees as a uniform mass. There were various schools among them, the best known of which are those of Hillel and Shammai. Likewise, the Pharisees had not only political opponents—for example, Herod the Great—but also religious opponents, especially among the Essenes. Thus according to the Damascus Document I, 18 and according to Hodajot II, 15.32, those who bring forth "smooth doctrines" appears to refer to the Pharisees, just as the Damascus Document in general appears to take a stand against the Pharisees.[26] Judaism before the destruction of the Temple presented in general "a manifold and brightly colored appearance in the history of religions,"[27] just as today there are also many groups and directions in Judaism (e.g., "Reform Judaism" alongside the strict "Orthodox" Judaism). According to Josephus, the Pharisees numbered "more than 6,000."[28] Josephus expressed their theological views in the following fashion:[29]

> The Pharisees live continently and know no creature comforts. Whatever reasonable reflection shows to be good they follow and they hold it in general to be their duty to pursue the prescriptions of reason. They honor the elderly and do not direct themselves to contradict their instructions. When they maintain that everything happens according to a definite fate, they thereby do not wish to deny the ability of the human will to determine itself, but rather to teach that it has pleased God to allow the power of fate and human reason to work together so that everyone according to his preference could hold fast to vice or to virtue. They also believe that souls are immortal and that depending on whether a human being was vicious or virtuous that these souls receive under the earth reward or punishment so that the vicious must languish in eternal imprisonment while the virtuous receive the power to return to life. Because of this doctrine they possess among the people such a large influence that all of the worship regulations, prayers as well as sacrifices, are carried out only according to their instruction. The communities gave them such a glorious testimony of fulfillment because it was believed that in word and deed they wished only the best.

Thus the Pharisees at the time of Jesus appeared to have a large religious influence among the people. They were concerned "to prepare a province of God on earth since the comprehensive final rule of God was obviously still to be looked forward to. That meant a life according to the biblical Law and the Law deduced from the Bible, that is, an explanation of and forming of all the areas of life according to wisdom in the greatest conformity with the will of God."[30] That a sharp dispute developed between the Pharisees

and Jesus is always cause for reflection. In the recollection of these disputes
there arose that hostile image of the Pharisees which is encountered in the
Gospels in an increasing measure and which has continued to work until
today in Christian theology and proclamation.

The "Hostile Image" of the Pharisees
in the Gospels

In the following I am not concerned with the historical state of affairs—
why, for example, the clash between Jesus and the Pharisees came
about[31]—but rather with redaction critical observations which flow from
the questions: What do the individual evangelists make of the Pharisees?
Do they consciously build a hostile image which has led to the distortion of
the Pharisees and their genuine desires?

Mark[32]

In the Gospel of Mark the Pharisees are encountered twelve times.
According to 2:16, "the scribes of the Pharisees" take offense at Jesus'
"eating with the tax collectors"; in fact, at the time of Jesus many scribes
were Pharisaically oriented, but "scribe" and "Pharisee" were not simply
identical. According to 2:18, "John's disciples and the Pharisees" asked
Jesus: "Why do John's disciples and the disciples of the Pharisees fast, but
your disciples do not fast?" There is in this no question of a hostile reaction
by the Pharisees to the response of Jesus. According to 2:24, the Pharisees
question Jesus because of the plucking of the ears of corn by his disciples on
the Sabbath; likewise nothing of a hostile reaction by the Pharisees is
reported here at the end of the pericope; nevertheless, the Pharisees
appear here as the special opponents of Jesus. According to 3:6, "the
Pharisees [after the healing of the man with the withered hand on the
Sabbath] went out, and immediately held counsel with the Herodians
against him, how to destroy him." The historical problem here is how the
Pharisees could be collaborators with the party and Herod Antipas, with
whom otherwise they were certainly not in agreement. Possibly the "Herodians" was first introduced by Mark.[33]

According to 7:1, "the Pharisees and several scribes" found themselves
outside of Jerusalem by Jesus; they saw that "some of his disciples ate with
hands defiled, that is, unwashed," the opposite of which Mark in the
following passage declares to be the custom of the Pharisees and "all the
Jews," "thereby observing the tradition of the elders" (7:3b). According to
7:5, "the Pharisees and the scribes" ask Jesus why his disciples do not live
"according to the tradition of the elders," but rather eat with defiled hands.

Jesus thereupon calls them "hypocrites" (7:6) and accuses them of "leaving" the commandment of God in favor of the "tradition of men" (7:8) and "rejecting" (7:9) and "making void the word of God" (7:13). "And many such things you do" (7:13b).

According to Rudolph Pesch,[34] there is in Mark 7:1–13 "historically trustworthy information about the attitude of Jesus toward *Halacha*," but the "primitive Christian tradition [to which the evangelist reaches back] expands the difference between Jesus and Pharisaism to an opposition between the Church and Judaism since 'all Jews' (7:3) are understood as followers of the 'traditions of the elders' as such," a fact which does not correspond to the historical state of affairs. However, "it would not be safe to judge this reference to 'all Jews' as a sign of a special Markan anti-Judaism," Pesch believes.[35] Mark understands the traditions summarized in 7:1–23 in "the sense of the lifting of the barrier between Jews and pagans" in the Christian community; thus the pagan-Christian standpoint of Mark comes to clear expression, as Pesch remarks.[36] This means, however, that the tradition material of Mark is placed at the service of the documentation of the process of dissolution between the Church and Israel which is gradually completed after Easter. This is especially clear in the example of Mark 7.

According to Mark 8:10f., Jesus landed in a boat along with the disciples in the "district of Dalmanutha." "The Pharisees came and began to argue with him, seeking from him a sign from heaven, to test him." With this test they wish "to prove the claim, and its validity, of Jesus. That they do this with a hostile intent is not said; it can be thus interpreted only within the bias of the New Testament Pharisee polemic, and perhaps also from the response of Jesus,"[37] who speaks of "this generation," to whom a designation is never given (8:12). Thus the New Testament Pharisee polemic builds up a hostile image even where no enmity is shown in the historical situations of the life of Jesus.

According to 8:15, Jesus warns his disciples "of the leaven of the Pharisees and the leaven of Herod"; with "leaven" Jesus apparently refers to a specific manner of thinking, but in what this consists according to him can only be surmised. According to Pesch, the following conjecture is "most likely": "Jesus warned against the Pharisaic-Davidic political projection of the Messiah as well as against the political ambitions of Herod."[38] What Jesus really meant can no longer be discerned. Mark, in any case, already thinks "typologically; he sees in the disciples the representatives of the Christian community who are in need of the warning and admonition: The *only loaf* (8:14b) which is their sole need, and which is sufficient for Jews

and Gentiles, is Jesus himself, the son of man, who goes to death for all. . . .
This bread should suffice for the disciples' [Kertelge]."39

The Christian community has no further need of the "leaven" of the
Pharisees. This is what Mark wishes to say to the communities he is
addressing with the puzzling words of Jesus. According to 10:2, "the
Pharisees came up [to Jesus] and in order to test him asked, 'Is it lawful for
a man to divorce his wife?' " The verse belongs in the debate about divorce
in Mark 10:2–12 which is laid out according to the structure of the "school
discussions." "The shaping by the primitive Church is easily recognized
first of all by the question of the Pharisees (10:2), which presumes the
prohibition of divorce by Jesus, that is, it is formulated not on Jewish-
Pharisaic premises, but on Christian premises; and secondly, because it is
based on the scriptural proof of the Septuagint (10:6–8); and thirdly, the
orientation of the line of argument (10:6–9) within the horizon of the
prohibition of divorce *for the man and the woman* (which thereby presumes
not the Jewish but rather the Hellenistic legal relationships)."40

"Christian tradents have their opponents [here introduced as the Phar-
isees] lay before Jesus the question which was controverted between Jews
and Christians."41 12:13: "And they sent to him some of the Pharisees and
some of the Herodians, to again trap him in his talk." The senders are the
Sanhedrin (cf. 11:27). In the pericope to which 12:13 belongs, tax paid to
Caesar is the concern ("Is it lawful to pay taxes to Caesar, or not?"—12:14b).
It ends with the remark about those who are sent: "And they were amazed
at him" (12:17b). Pesch believes that "the story can be considered trustworthy in its relating the efforts of the opponents of Jesus to catch him so as to
be able to deliver him to the Romans with a political accusation."42 However, since the pericope is again laid out according to the typical structure
of the "school discussions," we need to ask further whether in 12:13 the
Pharisees and Herodians were not also introduced in secondary fashion by
Mark according to a specific scheme of presentation.

A review of the Markan Pharisee material shows that, except for 10:2,
Mark pointedly speaks of *the* Pharisees, as if in each case the entire group
of Pharisees were involved in the disputes with Jesus—which, historically
seen, is absolutely improbable. This means that there is in Mark a post-
Easter tendency to speak of *the* Pharisees when an opponent from Pharisaism is thought of (this does not change the observation that in 12:13 there
is reference to "several" Pharisees and Herodians); this is similar to the
situation in the Gospel of John where often *the* Jews are spoken of as the
opponents of Jesus.43 This raises the suspicion that "the Pharisees" have
been secondarily inserted into the material either by the tradents or by

Mark himself. The anti-Pharisaic tendency is especially clear in Mark 7. For the rest, however, the negative judgments about the Pharisees are really few in number. The last expression of Mark about the Pharisees is: "And they were amazed at him" (12:17b).

Logia Source (Q)

Looking at the Logia source, it is difficult to decide whether the Pharisees turned up in its primary traditional material before it was taken into the Gospel of Matthew and into the Gospel of Luke. In Matt. 3:7 (Luke 3:7) in any case "the Pharisees and the Sadducees" appear to have been secondarily inserted by Matthew, for Luke has here "the multitudes." According to Matt. 12:38, "some of the scribes and Pharisees" wanted to see a sign by Jesus, whereas in Luke (11:16) it is only "others" (without a more specific designation), while in Matthew Jesus responds to "some of the scribes and Pharisees": "An evil and adulterous generation seeks for a sign" (12:39). According to Luke Jesus says to the assembled "crowds": "This generation is an evil generation; it seeks a sign . . ." (11:29). The addressees, therefore, appear in each case to have been inserted redactionally; who the original addressees were we do not know. In Matt. 23:13 (within the great woe speech against the "scribes and Pharisees") these are designated as "hypocrites," whereas in the Luke parallel (11:52) the "woe" is directed only toward the "scribes." Similarly in Matt. 23:23, 25, 27, 29 the scribes and Pharisees are designated "hypocrites," whereas in the Luke parallels the reference is to the "Pharisees" (11:39, 42), or to "you" (referring to the Pharisees) (11:44, 47), without their being designated "hypocrites."

If one does not read the specifically Lukan anti-Pharisaic polemic into the Logia source, as A. Polag does,[44] such a polemic is hardly to be found there. This can probably be explained from the circumstance that the material of the Logia source had probably been assembled very early and specifically within the circles of the ("Jewish-Christian-oriented") primitive community which still lived in close connection with Palestinian Judaism and therefore avoided polemic against the Pharisees and the scribes, even when the collection of the materials was bound up with the restriction to a single normative teacher, Jesus of Nazareth. Anti-Pharisaic accents appear to have been inserted only later, especially by the Matthew evangelist.

Matthew[45]

Here the Matthean development of the Markan Pharisee materials is to be focused on, and also the particular materials of Matthew.

1. When Mark in 2:16 speaks of the "scribes of the Pharisees," therefore, of a specific group of the Pharisees, Matthew in the parallel 9:11
speaks simply of "the Pharisees." In Matt. 9:14b there appear "the Pharisees," whereas in the Mark parallel 2:18b it is "the disciples of the
Pharisees." In Matt. 12:14 the Herodians of the Mark parallel (3:6) are left
out, presumably not because of better historical knowledge but rather out
of the inclination to focus on the main opponent. Instead of "the Pharisees
and some of the scribes" as in Mark 7:1, Matthew has "the Pharisees and
scribes" (15:1). In 16:1 Matthew adds, in comparison to Mark (8:11), the
Sadducees; similarly in 16:6 reference is made to the leaven of the Pharisees and the Sadducees, whereas in Mark it is the leaven of the Pharisees
and of Herod. While in Mark 12:13 reference is made to "some" of the
Pharisees and the Herodians, in Matt. 22:15 at first only "the Pharisees"
appear; these then according to 22:16 send "their disciples along with the
Herodians" to Jesus. In 12:24 Matthew writes "The Pharisees," whereas
Mark 3:22 speaks of the "scribes who came down from Jerusalem." In the
parable of the evil wine grower (Mark 12:1–12, parr.), which in Mark is
addressed to the high priests, scribes, and elders (cf. Mark 11:27), there
appear in Matt. 21:45, differing from Mark, "the chief priests and the
Pharisees (by Luke 20:19 "the scribes and the chief priests"). Instead of
"one of the scribes," as in Mark 12:28, one reads in Matt. 22:34, "the
Pharisees." In the debate about the Messiah as the son of David (Mark
12:35–37, parr.), Matthew adds as a secondary redactional introduction
(22:41): "Now while the Pharisees were gathered together, Jesus asked
them a question."

2. In the special material of Matthew the Pharisees appear (together
with the scribes) in 5:20 in the statement of Jesus: "Unless your righteousness exceeds that of the scribes and Pharisees, you will never enter the
kingdom of heaven." Here Jesus in no way denies to the Pharisees (and
scribes) righteousness, but he demands from *his own* disciples something
more. For the rest of Pharisees do not turn up in the Sermon on the Mount.
"The Pharisees" appear again in the special material in 9:34, likewise in
15:12 (in the special material of 15:12–14, which was inserted into the Mark
pericope 7:1–23): Here "the Pharisees" according to the opinion of the
disciples take offense at the word of Jesus. According to 27:62, "the chief
priests and the Pharisees gathered before Pilate" and requested of him a
guard for the grave of Jesus.

Matthew, therefore, strengthens the anti-Pharisaic polemic beyond Mark
and the Logia source, most of all in the great "woes" against the Pharisees
and scribes (23:1–39 with its seven woes, which is "a composition from the

material in common with Luke . . . and the Matthean special material."[46]
For Matthew "the Pharisees . . . are the real opponents of Jesus," and the
repeated introduction of the addressees, the scribes and Pharisees, makes
"the woe speech into an attack against the Judaism led by the Pharisees,"[47]
which, as such, was supposed to be hit. Matthew no longer distinguishes
between the various groups of Judaism. One can only agree with the
concluding judgment of W. G. Kümmel,[48] according to which one may not
dismiss the question of "whether in the Matthean polemic there has not
been forfeited the readiness to see even in the leaders of Jesus and in the
Judaism which the Church had given up on an authentic obedience to God
in the sense of Rom. 10:2: 'I bear them witness that they have a zeal for
God, but it is not enlightened,' and whether there has not been a 'demonization' of the opponent (cf. 23:15, 32!), which not only arrogates the
judgment of God upon the opponent to oneself, but even maliciously
distorts his attitude (23:28)." It is an "erroneous distortion of reality."[49]

Luke (Gospel)[50]

1. Instead of "the Pharisees" of Mark 2:24, Luke 6:2 refers to "some of
the Pharisees." Where Mark 3:6 speaks of the "Pharisees together with the
Herodians," Luke 6:11 refers to the scribes and Pharisees (cf. 6:7) as "they."
It is similar in the comparison between Mark 12:13 and Luke 20:19f.: While
Mark speaks of some of the Pharisees and the Herodians, Luke has the
"scribes and the chief priests" as the ones who "watched him, and sent
spies" to trap him in a statement. The brief Lukan woe statement is
directed, as in Matthew, against the Pharisees (cf. 11:39, 42, 44, 47). In 5:17
Luke redactionally inserts "the Pharisees and teachers of the law," and in
5:21, different from Mark ("some of the scribes"), he adds "the Pharisees" to
the scribes.

2. In distinction to the "people," including the "tax collectors," according to 7:29f., "the Pharisees and the lawyers rejected the purpose of God for
themselves, not having been baptized by him [John]." According to H.
Schürmann, in Luke 7:29f. we are dealing with an element from the Logia
source which shows only "traces of the pre-Lukan redaction";[51] a hypothesis. It might just as well be from the Lukan special material which is to be
addressed as a Lukan image building which fits completely in the modified
anti-Pharisaism of Luke. In the large pericope 7:36–50 (Jesus and the sinful
woman) it is "one of the Pharisees" by the name of Simon who invites Jesus
to a meal at his house and who thereby entertains critical thoughts concerning the attitude of Jesus toward the sinful woman (7:39), whom Jesus with
the help of a brief parable rejects. In Luke 11:37f. it is again "a Pharisee"

who invited Jesus to table and wondered "that [Jesus] did not first wash [his hands] before dinner." Thereupon follows the Lukan woe speech against the Pharisees (11:39–54) with the three woes directed against the Pharisaic way of life. Since Luke has a predilection for guest meal scenes (cf. 5:29; 7:36; 10:38; 14:1), one must reckon with the possibility that the introduction to his woe speech against the Pharisees is to be placed on the account of Lukan redaction. After the woe speech itself, Luke remarks that "the scribes and the Pharisees began to press him hard, and to provoke him to speak of many things, lying in wait for him, to catch him at something he might say" (11:53f.); this development of the pericope is likewise Lukan special material, and one must question whether it has not been inserted by Luke purely redactionally. The conclusion does not fit together with the introduction of 11:37f., in which only one Pharisee is spoken of who had invited Jesus. The consequence sounds generalizing ("the scribes and the Pharisees") and was gained from a judgment of the evangelist who was looking back from a distance. According to 13:31, it was "some Pharisees" who warned Jesus of Herod Antipas. According to 14:1, Jesus was invited to dine "at the house of a ruler who belonged to the Pharisees," and "they were watching him"; in 14:3 these "they" were concretized as "the lawyers and Pharisees" who, according to 14:6, were able to say nothing to the question of Jesus about whether it was allowed to heal the man with dropsy on the Sabbath.

One has the impression that in the structure of the Gospel of Luke from the woe speech onward, the critical distance of the evangelist to the Pharisees grows. This is shown in the introduction of Luke to the three parables of the lost sheep, the lost drachma, and the lost son (15:1–32): "Now the tax collectors and sinners were all drawing near to hear him. And the Pharisees and scribes murmured,[52] saying, 'This man receives sinners and eats with them.'" With their "murmuring" the Pharisees and scribes level criticism at the attitude of Jesus. In Luke 15:1f. we are doubtless dealing with the redactional work of the evangelist, even if behind it there might lie the "hard, historical facts" from the life of Jesus [53] (cf. Mark 2:15–17); with this the Pharisees and scribes, without any kind of differentiation, are put forward as a conspiring group who stand over against Jesus with criticism and hostility. The addressee community of Luke is immediately told with the three parables that their own attitude toward the tax collectors and sinners[54] in their own ranks should be different from that held by the Pharisees and the scribes toward the tax collectors and sinners in Israel, namely, one like Jesus had toward them.[55] The building up of the hostile image, therefore, simultaneously serves the community parenesis.

The three parables in chapter 15 of Luke are immediately followed by the parable of the unjust steward (16:1–13), which likewise is from the Lukan special material, and as a closing remark, which again comes from the special material of the evangelist, we hear: "The Pharisees, who were lovers of money, heard all this, and they scoffed at him. But he said to them, 'You are those who justify yourselves before men, but God knows your hearts; for what is exalted among men is an abomination in the sight of God'" (16:14f.). Again "the Pharisees" appear as a closed, greedy group scorned by Jesus. That Jesus severely criticized the Pharisaic piety is without doubt true. However, what happens in the redaction of the evangelist is a generalization, as if all Pharisees were greedy for money and Jesus had scorned them all.[56] This does not correspond to the historical facts.[57] According to 17:20f., Jesus is asked "by the Pharisees" when the kingdom will come. According to the answer of Jesus, the kingdom of God is already "in your midst," but his opponents do not realize this.[58] This claim, that the kingdom of God is already in the midst of Jesus' contemporaries, namely, in his person, is important because it belongs to the reasons which led to the clash between Jesus and his opponents; I shall come back to this below, pp. 118ff.

The parable of the Pharisee and the tax collector (18:9–14: special material of Luke), with the two unforgettable figures of the Pharisee and the tax collector, has especially misled many Christian readers and hearers into identifying ahead of time with the tax collector in the parable and thus becoming victims of a false consciousness. The true interaction between the reader and the text does not properly develop,[59] of course, completely against the will of the evangelist.

As Jesus came into Jerusalem the "whole multitude of the disciples" called out in a loud voice: "Blessed is the King who comes in the name of the Lord! Peace in heaven and glory in the highest" (Luke 19:37f.). Then "some of the Pharisees in the multitude" said to Jesus: "Teacher, rebuke your disciples" (19:39). The formulation "some of the Pharisees in the multitude" sounds awkward; "possibly the genitive *tōn Pharisaiōn* [the Pharisees] is an addition of Luke to *tinas apo tou ochlou* ["some in the multitude"] from the material before him."[60] Then an anti-Pharisaic tendency of Luke would be present here.

Looking back over the Lukan Pharisee material, one must confirm that in his first work, in distinction to his second work, the Acts of the Apostles,[61] Luke had participated in the building up of the hostile image of the Pharisees, even though it is without the sharpness with which this is done in Matthew. His Gentile Christian addressees, who no longer stand in a

living connection with Israel, thus win by opposition their own self-understanding; or perhaps better said, they should win it by the parenetic
intentions of the evangelist. Thereby the Pharisees fall under a false light.
Perhaps, however, the evangelist was not sufficiently conscious of this.

John

According to John 1:19, "the Jews" send from Jerusalem a delegation of
priests and Levites to John the Baptist to ask him who he is and why he
baptizes. In 1:24 there is the strange remark that the delegates were "from
the Pharisees." The pericope 1:19–34 "has no original unity,"[62] rather it is
the redactional work of the evangelist who thereby inserts traditional
elements—thus especially verses 22 and 23—which introduce a synoptic
characteristic of the Baptist according to Isa. 40:3, and "through the insertion of verse 24 brings it about that alongside of the priests the Pharisees,
the typical opponents, are likewise immediately named." However, this
verse does not thereby intend to say, "that the delegates belong to the
Pharisees . . . but rather that the message which was reported by them was
sent by the Pharisees, so that the latter consequently are behind the
Ioudaioi of verse 19."[63] We have here, therefore, in no way a historical
reportage, but rather a historical image from the time in which the Church
and Israel had completely separated and stood over against one another
with hostility. The highly stylized opponents are thereby cast in the form of
"the Jews" and "the Pharisees."

According to 3:1, Nicodemus is "one of the Pharisees," a formula which
repeatedly appears in John (1:24; 3:1; 7:48; 9:16, 40; 18:3) and gives expression "to the usual designation of membership."[64] This Nicodemus is
also described in 3:1 as "a ruler of the Jews," which is probably intended to
mark him as a member of the Sanhedrin. He has a favorable attitude toward
Jesus (cf. also 7:50f.) and remains loyal to him even beyond death (cf.
19:39f.), which allows one to see that even among the Pharisees there were
followers of Jesus (cf. also Acts 5:34: Gamaliel). In 7:32 "the Pharisees
heard" what the people muttered about Jesus, and thereupon "the chief
priests and the Pharisees" sent police officers to arrest Jesus. Here a vulgar
interpretation breaks through in which the Pharisees are connected with
the chief priests and indeed take up that function which the scribes have in
the Synoptics, although in John the scribes never appear as such. In John,
therefore, the Pharisees are united in action with the Sadducean chief
priests (cf. also 7:32, 45, 48; 11:47, 57; 18:3),[65] which fact can be described
as a "biased account of events." This goes together with the intense styliza-

tion of the Pharisees into *the* opponents of Jesus (alongside the chief priests).

In John the Pharisees are depicted as the very ones who are the Jewish authorities having jurisdiction over the police (cf. 7:32; 18:3), a fact which does not correspond to the historical reality; they put to Jesus questions concerning criminal activity (cf. 8:13). In contrast to the "people," the opponents of Jesus in John are called without distinction "the Jews" (5:15; 7:13; 9:22) or "the Pharisees" (7:32, 47; 8:13; 9:13; 12:19, and elsewhere);[66] that is, in John "the Jews" (with a negative accent) and "the Pharisees" are almost interchangeable terms. This, however, does not correspond to the historical facts; rather it is conditioned by a specific historical image in which "the Pharisees" largely identified with "the Jews"[67] are depicted as acting officially and therefore also claiming the right of interrogation (cf. 9:13, 15, 16, 40; 11:46, 57). According to 12:10 compared with 12:19, "the Pharisees" appear to be identical with the "chief priests," as also according to 11:57 the chief priests and the Pharisees together issue a "warrant of arrest" against Jesus.

According to 12:42, "many even of the authorities [*archonton*] (of the Jewish people) believed in him, but for fear of the Pharisees they did not confess it, lest they should be put out of the synagogue";[68] this is reminiscent of a remark of the evangelist in 9:22: "His parents [of the man born blind who had been healed] said this because they feared the Jews, for the Jews had already agreed if anyone should confess him to be the Christ, he was to be put out of the synagogue." Here likewise belongs the statement of the Johannine Christ in 16:2: "They will put you out of the synagogues; indeed, the hour is coming when whoever kills you will think he is offering service to God." When in 9:34 it is remarked that they (the Jews) "cast out" the healed man, this means in light of 9:22 that he was put out of the synagogue community, that he was "excommunicated." It is "clear that here John writes within the horizon of his own time,"[69] that is, this is the "hard historical fact" (Rudolph Schnackenburg, in an oral remark) from the time of the composition of the Gospel (not from the time of Jesus!) which lies behind these remarks about the casting of those who believe in Christ out of the Jewish religious community, and which is reflected likewise in the twelfth benediction of "the Prayer of the Eighteen Benedictions (*birkat ha-minim*), which benediction was first introduced into the Prayer under Rabbi Gamliel II around the year 90 C.E.[70] "Since the cursing of the Nazarene had become an integral part of synagogue worship and of the daily prayer of every Jew . . . attendance at the synagogue and participation in synagogue worship was impossible for Christians and the complete separation was

accomplished. . . . It is in this time period also that the Johannine statements belong"—so believes W. Schrage.[71]

One must reflect on these things if one wants to understand completely
the harsh image of the Pharisees of the Johannine Gospel. Behind them lies
the knowledge of the tradition that there had been a severe dispute
between Jesus and the Pharisees. However, there also lies the observation
which is valid for the Johannine Gospel that around the years 90–100 after
Christ the Church and the Synagogue were already totally separate communities and that the Church was seeking its own genuine self-understanding and historical image. This led to the building up of the hostile images,
especially in reference to the Pharisees, and beyond that to the hard
historical facts that the Christians who acknowledged Jesus as the Messiah
and the Son of God would be *aposunagōgoi*, that is, they would be
excluded from the community of the Synagogue.[72] All this expanded the
gulf between the Christian and Jewish communities in the extreme, so that
a space was provided for hostility and, on the Christian side, for the anti-
Judaism which has still not been completely eliminated.

Summary

The gradual development of a hostile image of the Pharisees is thus
clearly discernible in an ever-growing measure. This begins with the Logia
source and continues through Mark, Matthew, and Luke to John, in whom
this hostile image shows the sharpest contours and bears within it irrecon-
cilable features. From Pharisees who in their time were involved in disputes with Jesus "*the* Pharisees" developed as the true opponents of Jesus,
the gospel, and the Church.[73] The Gospels, their traditions and their
redactions, have a *Sitz im Leben* of their own in these "life processes" which
we must reckon with and which must lead to a historical understanding if,
in the Jewish-Christian dialogue, we finally are to arrive at the dismantling
of this hostile image and the Pharisees are to be done justice as a historical
reality of Judaism. Of course the rich Pharisee material in the Gospels may
even have been put forth by the evangelists with the parenetic intention of
showing the disciples of Jesus, and that means the Church, *how things
should not be.*

Perhaps what has also contributed to the building up of the hostile image
is the historical circumstance that the Pharisees and Pharisaism constituted
that group and movement of Judaism in the age of the primitive Church
which survived relatively well the catastrophe of the year 70, a fact which
led to the Pharisaic observance, under the leadership of energetic men like
Rabbi Jochanan ben Zakkai, becoming the widely normative Judaism and

thereby led to a certain "narrowing" within Judaism after the other groups (Temple hierarchy, Sadducees, Essenes, Zealots) had disappeared from this stage of history. One could say the Pharisees triumphed; their *Halacha* in its Hillel orientation strongly determined the face of Judaism.[74] "The great period of Pharisaism came only after the destruction of the Temple and the crushing of the Jerusalem hierarchy; however, about this time Pharisaism also fought and attained a victory so thoroughgoing that even the catastrophe under Hadrian (Bar Cochba Revolt, 132–135 C.E.) could change nothing in it."[75]

What role in the new ordering of the Jewish communal essence Rabbi Jochanan ben Zakkai and the gathering of Jabne (Jamnia) played is disputed.[76] In any case the remark of R. T. Herford is correct: "The entire system of the [Pharisaic] *Halacha* served [after the year 70] to hold the Jewish community together as an outer protective wall, within which the spirit of Judaism could conserve its strength and power of life. Without the *Halacha* it is hardly imaginable that Judaism could have survived all of the oppressions and sufferings of the persecutions which filled the centuries of its history in the Christian period. The *Halacha* was an irreplaceable part of the armor of Judaism in the fulfillment of its task, 'the armor of God which should make it capable of withstanding the evil times; and after everything was done, to survive'; and that in fact was its effect."[77] Thus Pharisaism performed the service of protecting Judaism in the storms of its history after Christ against the ups and downs in the Gentile world. One must, however, be aware that the "Rabbinic" Judaism of the period after 70 C.E. was not simply identical with the Pharisaism before that period. Likewise, Pharisaism, which carried out transformations through and in Judaism, did not pass through the catastrophe of the year 70 untouched. There were new givens now, connected especially with the nonexistence of the Temple with its sacrifice services and its feasts. The victory of Pharisaism after the destruction of the Temple led to certain transformations of an essential sort in Judaism, transformations which had already been prepared for before the year 70. One could perhaps formulate them in sloganlike fashion thus:[78]

In the place of the priest there appeared definitively the "rabbi," the one learned in Scripture.[79]

In the place of the Temple there now appeared definitively the Synagogue and the Torah school.

In the place of a political-zealot Messianism there now appeared the sober, nonpolitical sanctification of the everyday through the "realization" of the commandments[80] (although the messianic hope as such, of course, was never completely given up).

In the place of prophecy there appeared the wisdom of the knowledge of the Scriptures.[81]

In the place of the land there appeared the community ("the *Schul* community"), even though the yearning for *erez Israel* in Judaism was never extinguished and is stronger than ever today.

One cannot, however, say that through these transformations Judaism after the year 70 lost its identity and became alienated from itself. For since the days of Moses Israel became and remained "the people of the Torah," and the rest of the spiritual heritage of Israel was time and again infected by this in the history of Judaism. One can with Martin Noth maintain the thesis that around the turn of the century from the first to the second of the Common Era, "Judaism" came forth from "Israel."[82] "Israel remains Israel" (Friedlander).

Jesus and the Pharisees

I shall begin this section with the remark of R. T. Herford:[83] "What the Pharisees said and did during the time of the public appearance of Jesus provides us with only a weak foundation for a judgment of their true essence and character." Ancient Judaism, and with it the Pharisees, had reckoned with the coming of the Messiah, not, however, with the coming of Jesus of Nazareth. Indeed, the Jews saw themselves "suddenly placed over against Jesus";[84] they were not prepared for him.

Historically the following can be affirmed:

Jesus of Nazareth was not a Pharisee; he did not come from a Pharisaic *Havurah*, but more likely from the *am-ha-aretz*,[85] who, however, before the year 70 in no way stood in absolute opposition to the Pharisees, as E. Oppenheimer was able to show.

Jesus of Nazareth conducted disputes and school discussions with Pharisees (not with "*the* Pharisees").

Jesus' *Halacha* was strongly anti-Pharisaic (more about this below), thus a tragic collision between Jesus and the Pharisees occurred.

Jesus of Nazareth had quiet supporters even among Pharisees and allowed himself to be invited to meals by Pharisees.

In the trial of Jesus the Pharisees as such played no role.

According to the evidence of the concordance, the expression "the Pharisees" does not appear in the narrations of the synoptic Gospels about the trial of Jesus—only in the special material of Matthew concerning the guards at the grave of Jesus did they turn up along with the chief priests (cf. Matt. 27:62).

As a "redaction critical" review of the "Pharisee materials" in the Gospels allows us to recognize, in the course of the post-Easter process of tradition and in the wake of the disengagement of the Church from Israel, "the Pharisees" were stylized into the special opponents of Jesus; they became the "type" of the opponent of Jesus. This fact makes the inquiry back to Jesus and his true relationship to the Pharisees difficult, not, however, unattainable. Even Jewish researchers into the life of Jesus do not doubt that there were severe encounters between Jesus and members of the Pharisee community, that, therefore, there are hard historical facts in this area. Thus above all this question must be posed: How, historically seen, did the clash between Jesus and the Pharisees come about?[86] In the following I shall attempt to give an answer in thesislike fashion; in reality this answer would need to be worked out in a monograph with the help of strict historical-critical methods.

Jesus had doubtless predicted the imminent nearness, indeed already the inbreaking, of the eschatological reign of God (the "kingdom of God"). This means that now something new was breaking in, indeed not in the sense of a concept, but rather in the sense of a reality through which the situation changed and humanity was placed under a new claim which surpassed the commandments of the Torah;[87] cf. the demands of Jesus in the "Sermon on the Mount" which one could describe as "kingdom ethics." Since opponents were not able to see this, Jesus accused them of being incapable of recognizing the *kairos* (cf. Luke 12:54–56; 7:31–35). The Pharisees were more concerned with the continuous, calm, further development of that which they already possessed—concretely: with the expansion of the "fence around the Torah" in order to make of Israel a pure and holy community before God. Jesus appears to have been perceived by them as a "troublemaker." They were incapable of "grasping a new action of God which was like the work of God through the prophets."[88] Thus, the new which Jesus proclaimed and wished to bring stood in opposition to the old, that which was handed down and which in itself was capable of development and was pregnant with development, which the Pharisees represented (cf. for example Mark 2:21f.; see n. 22). Of course the new which Jesus represented was not the zealot-revolutionary, but rather that which God now wished: God wished to act anew on Israel through him. This necessarily led to a new evaluation of the Torah. God's lordship is more than the lordship of the Torah. It is the lordship of salvation. This meant a break: "The law and the prophets were until John [the Baptist]; since then the good news of the kingdom of God is preached and every one enters it violently" (Luke 16:16). Something new is there![89]

This new action of God according to Jesus was directed to everyone in

Israel, including the members of the *am-ha-aretz* and including the "tax
collectors and sinners" with whom Jesus openly and ostentatiously had
meals (cf. Mark 2:13–17, and parr.; Luke 15:1f.).[90] This, however, implies
Jesus' "kingdom theory," namely, that for him this new action of God for
Israel announced and implemented by Jesus himself, is primarily a time of
fulfillment, mercy, and salvation, and not a time of judgment, which then
distinguished him from John the Baptist. Jesus did not present the purity
and holiness of Israel as coming from an attitude which was "according to
the Torah," as the Pharisees wished, but from the forgiveness of sins which
he proclaimed in full power.[91]

The following is connected: Jesus apparently placed no value on "Levitical" purity, for example, on the handwashing before meals practiced by the
Pharisees. In the eyes of the Pharisees, however, this was not a minor
matter.[92] It concerned an essential element, especially in questions of pure
food for pious Judaism to this very day, which is especially reflected in
kosher eating.[93] Even if Mark 7, where this theme is treated, represents a
secondary composition of the evangelist, there exists no doubt that material
from Jesus is being worked over.[94] The critical position of Jesus toward the
theme of "clean and unclean," which plays such a central role in the
Pharisaic *Halacha*, had to lead to a conflict between Jesus and the Pharisees. Martin Hengel even believes that "here we run into a fundamental
break of Jesus with the Palestinian Judaism of his time."[95] This struggle was
later continued by the former Pharisee Paul in regard to the "clean and
unclean"-connected *synesthiein* ("eating together") in his own way and in a
totally new situation, not with Jews, but rather with his Jewish-Christian
opponents.[96]

Jesus showed an attitude which could be interpreted as a criticism of the
strict law of the Sabbath, the holiest law of Judaism; cf. the so-called
Sabbath conflict of which all the Gospels speak. To declare this a "product
of the community" is a nonsensical undertaking.[97] even if it is difficult to
say precisely whether for Jewish sensitivities Jesus had thereby stepped
outside the framework of Judaism. Here the intention of Jesus was that the
true will of God not be set aside through a commandment. In any case,
here Jesus did not step outside the framework of the old prophetic preaching in Israel, but his attitude and his "Sabbath critical" words appear to
have gotten on the nerves of the Pharisees.[98] The words of Jesus about the
Sabbath are the "expression of his *exousia*," the full power which he
likewise elsewhere claimed. This leads to the next and last point which I
wish to briefly introduce.

It appears that in general Jesus had made a claim in Israel which had not before been heard, a claim which drove his enemies to plot. I shall say more about this on pp. 234ff. It cannot be denied that the teaching and activity of Jesus in Israel encountered resistance, especially from the Pharisees. It is difficult to decide from whom the attack really originated. It appears that Jesus was the aggressor.[99] This conflict between Jesus and the Pharisees was, indeed, tragic, since for both Jesus and the Pharisees God was the most important thing, and Jesus did not wish to do away with the Law or the prophets but rather intended to carry them out. The Gospels relate that Pharisees were among those who worked for the liquidation of Jesus (cf., for example, Mark 3:6). The historical fact is that he was excluded from the community of Israel and for a long time was almost completely taboo for Judaism, until the Judaism of our day recalled him to its memory. How much shared guilt, or indeed chief guilt, the Pharisees bear for this exclusion of Jesus from Israel is difficult to say. For it was not just the violent death of Jesus, for which one can attribute a special guilt to the Romans (Pontius Pilate),[100] that definitively divided the Church from Israel, but rather a whole series of factors which began with the appearance of Jesus in Galilee and reached far into the period of the primitive Church. One of the divisive factors was certainly the Pharisees, with whom Jesus was not at one and vice versa.[101] How far one can and may judge the reaction of the Pharisees to Jesus as guilt is an almost insoluble question. Even if this guilt actually existed, to consider it today would be completely wrongheaded. In any case, the primitive Church saw in the Pharisees the particular opponents of Jesus, as the Gospels indicate. However, the development of this hostile image played an important role in the Church's gaining of its own self-understanding and historical image, which could not have been much different in any case in the splitting off of one group from the mother group.[102]

"THE JEWS" IN THE GOSPEL OF JOHN

The Reference in the "Vatican Guidelines"

The expression "the Jews" in the Gospel of John is a special sign of an outspoken "anti-Judaism" of this Gospel. In the "Vatican Guidelines" for the implementation of Nostra Aetate of 5 January 1975, reference is made in the second footnote expressly to the term "the Jews" in the Gospel of John, and it is urged that the belief be avoided that the term meant "the Jewish people as such." In the following I shall attempt to respond to this urging.

Comparative Word Statistics

The statistics in reference to the four Gospels show the following results: "(the) Jews" (*[hoi] Ioudaioi*) appears five times in Matthew, six times in Mark, five times in Luke, and seventy-one times in John. When one recalls the negative accent this term "the Jews" often has in John,[103] then in fact the suspicion immediately arises that the "Johannine anti-Judaism" manifests itself especially in this term: In the Christian reading of the Gospel of John "the Jews" often without hesitation is identified with the Jewish people of the time of Jesus (and often, indeed, with the Jewish people as such), and the Jewish people are stamped as the "enemy" of Jesus and of the gospel. Indeed, they are declared guilty of the "murder of God" in the sense that the Jews have killed Jesus the Son of God; they are the "murderers of God" and therefore the murder of Jews is their just punishment.[104]

Concerning the Semantics of the Term "the Jews" in the Gospel of John[105]

It would be helpful for the following discussion to view the term "the Jews" in connection with the geography of the Gospel of John. Thus we see that a large number of the occurrences are limited to Jerusalem and Judea. This is true above all for those "Jews" passages with a negative accent, and this means that a large number of these passages experience a semantic limitation which prohibits the identification of "the Jews" with the Jewish people. Since for semantic judgments above all the position of the lexeme within its context is of decisive significance, this position must be determined for all the "Jews" passages which have a negative accent. In this we follow the list of R. Leistner.[106]

According to John 1:19 "the Jews sent priests and Levites from Jerusalem" that they might question John the Baptist about his baptizing activities; the so-called Sanhedrin. Thus the term "the Jews" in the first passage in which it is encountered in the Fourth Gospel carries an enormous limitation. According to 1:24 there were also Pharisees among those sent. According to R. Schnackenburg with this reference to the Pharisees the evangelist wishes "probably consciously to direct the view toward this party;" for in the Gospel of John "the Pharisees are the opponents of Jesus who observe everything, stir things up, control the people and influence propaganda" (cf. 4:1; 7:32a, 47f.; 11:46; 12:19, 42).[107]

In 2:18, 20 "the Jews" again turn up, specifically, on the occasion of the so-called Temple cleansing (2:13–22); they engage Jesus in discussion with the words: "What sign have you to show us for doing this?" They demand of Jesus a sign of legitimation. "The Jews" in this whole situation deals with "'Temple overseers,' who hold the key and the power of order within the Temple and to whom also the Levitical Temple police (cf. 7:32, 45f.) are responsible."[108]

In 5:10, 15, 16, 18 it remains unclear who "the Jews" really are who engage in discussion the man who was healed by the pool of Bethesda and concerning whom it was then said that they persecuted Jesus and plotted against his life "because he not only broke the sabbath but also called God his Father, making himself equal with God" (5:18). Since the narration appears to take place from 5:14 onward within the Temple precincts,[109] there need be no doubt that "the Jews" here again means the representatives of the Jewish central authorities, and possibly (in view of what is related in John) of Pharisaic provenance. In no case does it refer to the Jewish people as such.

According to 6:41 "the Jews murmured" about Jesus "because he said: 'I am the bread which came down from heaven,'" and they reject his claim with: "Is not this Jesus, the son of Joseph, whose father and mother we know?" According to 6:52, "the Jews then disputed among themselves, saying, 'How can this man give us his flesh to eat?'" This time the scene according to the narration of the Gospel takes place in Galilee (in Capernaum). Who here are "the Jews?" From the perspective of the geographical situation one could say that Galileans are thought of.[110] Here, however, a historicizing perspective seems to be lacking. Rather, the passage deals more with a "theological situation" which reflects the inner Church disputes during the composition time of the Gospel, namely, the disputes concerning the correct Christology and understanding of the Eucharist: For the evangelist, Christ is the Son of man come down from heaven and become flesh, and his eucharistic gift is true food and true drink, his flesh and his blood for the life of the world. "The Jews" here represents, certainly in remembrance of the unbelief of Israel toward Jesus and toward the gospel, the "opposing party," who in Christology and eucharistic doctrine deviate in a docetic-spiritualizing direction. The opponents are masked as "the Jews."

The semantic judgments in chapter 7, in which "the Jews" turns up five times (7:1, 11, 13, 15, 35), are difficult. Because in 7:1 the countryside of Judea is referred to and with that it is again mentioned that "the Jews sought to kill him" (cf. already 5:18), it is the opponents of Jesus in Jerusalem that are meant. "The Jews" at first seek him in vain at the feast of Succoth (7:11). The evangelist remarks that the opinions among the people

about Jesus were divided (7:12), but nevertheless no one dared speak
openly about him "for fear of the Jews." Of which "Jews"? Then as Jesus
unexpectedly came to the Temple during the feast, "the Jews" marveled at
his knowledge of the Scriptures "when he has never studied" (7:15). Jesus
himself then asks the question: "Why do you seek to kill me?" (7:19)
whereupon "the people" answer. Since he again is teaching in the Temple,
"they sought to arrest him; but no one laid hands on him, because his hour
had not yet come" (7:28–30). Moreover the evangelist remarks that "many
of the people believed in him," and since "the Pharisees" learned of
whispering among the people about Jesus, "the chief priests and Pharisees
sent officers to arrest him" (7:32), an arrest which however did not come to
pass. In the end, "the Jews said to one another, 'Where does this man
intend to go that we shall not find him?' " (7:35). Here the semantic value of
the term "the Jews" vacillates back and forth. At one point it is clearly the
opponents of Jesus, then again it can hardly be distinguished from "the
people." However, from 7:32 it is clear that hostile-minded "Jews," especially "the Pharisees and chief priests," are meant (cf. also 7:45, 48; 11:47,
57; 18:3). Therefore, *they* are those "Jews" who sought to kill Jesus. In this
the "anti-Pharisaic polemic" clearly plays a role similar to that in
Matthew.[111]

Likewise in chapter 8 the use of language is not unified. Who in 8:22 are
"the Jews" who say "Will he kill himself?" and to whom Jesus then answers,
"You are from below, I am from above; you are of this world, I am not of this
world"? Here, "the Jews" are obviously meant to be those who reject Jesus
and who therefore are reckoned by him as belonging to "the world."
According to 8:30, many of the Jews believed in him, who Jesus then
instructed. According to 8:48, however, again "the Jews" accuse Jesus of
being a Samaritan and of having a demon, that is, of being possessed (cf.
also 8:52; 10:20). Finally, "the Jews" say to him, "You are not yet fifty years
old, and you have seen Abraham?" whereupon Jesus responds, "Truly,
truly, I say to you, before Abraham was, I am;" thereupon they take up
stones to throw at him (8:58f.). Who are these hostilely oriented "Jews?" In
any case, they are not the entire Jewish people of the time of Jesus.[112]

"The Jews" of 9:18 are "the Pharisees" of 9:13, 15, 16, to whom was led
the man born blind who was healed. Obviously with the word "Pharisees"
here "those learned in the law are meant, who are capable of authoritative
decisions. But John never refers to the *grammateis* [learned in the law, or
scribes] separately. . . . At his time [at the time of the composition of the
Gospel] all teachers of the Law were Pharisees, and they were representative of the entire nomistic and official Judaism."[113] The same is true for

"the Jews" whom the parents of the healed man feared, and also for "the Jews" who "had already agreed that if any one should confess him to be Christ, he was to be put out of the Synagogue" (9:22). A comparison with 12:42 shows that the "Jews" here means the Pharisees, and that with this the evangelist "writes within the horizon of his own time."[114] He wishes to strike at the Pharisaic leaders of the period of composition (that is, after the year 90) "and with the entire concluding reflection of 12:37–42 he aims an annihilating judgment theologically laden with the citation of the hardening of hearts at the Jewish community leaders . . . who struggled against the believers in Christ, especially those who came from Judaism."[115] With this we can already see clearly that the demonization of "the Jews" and of "the Pharisees" in the Fourth Gospel is connected with the relationships of the time of composition. I shall return to this later.

Likewise in 10:24, 31, 33 "the Jews" show themselves as sharp opponents of Jesus; this again results in an attempt to stone Jesus (10:31) and to arrest him (10:39). The scene is played in the Hall of Solomon during the Hanukkah festival (cf. 10:22f.)—again an indication that "the Jews" here do not define just any group of people from among the Jewish people, but rather those who possess police power within the Temple precincts. These can only be members of the Jewish central authorities.

Especially valuable for our thematic is the report of John on the passion of Jesus. According to 18:3, Judas came with "a band of soldiers and some officers from the chief priests and the Pharisees and went there [Mount of Olives] with lanterns and torches and weapons." In exegesis it is argued whether the "band" is of Roman soldiers or a detachment of the Jewish Temple police.[116] Because in 18:12 this "band" with their commanders (*chiliarchos*) is expressly distinguished from the officers of "the Jews," Schnackenburg argues that "the evangelist had certainly connected this *speira* [band] with the Romans." Nevertheless one could "surmise that the underlying source referred to the Jewish police."[117] However that may be, "the Jews," whose officers arrested and bound Jesus, are in any case in the meaning of the evangelist the chief priests and Pharisees mentioned in 18:3. In the report on the trial before Pilate (18:28—19:16) "the Jews" are encountered six times, apart from the designation of Jesus as "the King of the Jews" (18:33, 39; 19:3). As the Jewish partners of Pilate in the trial, in the middle of the report "the chief priests and the officers" are mentioned (19:6), who at that point shout aloud "Crucify him, crucify him!" While according to 19:15 the same demand is raised by "the Jews," immediately thereafter these again are identified with the chief priests (19:15). And even when according to 18:35 Pilate states: "Your own nation and the chief priests have handed you over to me," then what here is meant with "people" (*ethnos*) "cannot mean the entire Jewish people, who indeed did not hand Jesus over to Pilate, but rather their representation in the Sanhedrin, probably the elders . . . who nowhere else are mentioned by John. These Sadducees, who were influential through their heritage and wealth, are for him great figures of the past."[118] Therefore, there can be no talk of "the Jewish people" having striven against Jesus in the trial. Only an outspoken anti-Judaism could maintain such a thing. "The Jews" in the Johannine report of the trial are much rather the chief priests and the circles about them; cf. also 19:21 ("the chief priests of the Jews" complain here about the formulation of the writing on the cross by Pilate). The same is also true for "the Jews" in 19:31 who request of Pilate that out of concern for the Sabbath one should "break the bones of those crucified that they might be taken away." "The Jews" whom Joseph of Arimathea (19:38) and likewise the disciples (20:19) fear are obviously the powerful trial opponents of Jesus (cf. also 7:13).

Conclusions

One point which is now apparent is that in the expression "the Jews," so often weighted in the Gospel of John with a negative accent, it is the opponents of Jesus from the leading class, especially from the chief priests, who are thought of. In this the evangelist, acting out of the anti-Pharisaic polemic which had become a "style" with him, also numbers the Pharisees without the necessary differentiation. For the rest, the linguistic use of the term "the Jews" in the Gospel of John is a neutral one. This is likewise true for the allegedly distancing designation of the feasts, which in the Fourth Gospel are referred to as the "feasts of the Jews" (cf. 2:13; 5:1; 6:4; 7:2; 11:55; 19:42). Since at the time of the composition of the Gospel the Church and Israel were already communities completely divided from one another, the genitive of attribution "of the Jews" is necessary for the reader so that the feasts which are referred to are recognizable as the "feasts of the Jews."

Rudolph Bultmann would like to formulate the situation thus: "The term *hoi Ioudaioi* ["the Jews"] which is characteristic of the evangelist, pulls the Jews in their totality together because they are seen as representatives of unbelief (and thereby . . . the unbelieving 'world' in general) by Christian faith. . . . The *Ioudaioi* are then not the Jewish people in an empirical existence, but in their essence." In reality, however, it does not concern the essence of Judaism, but rather that of "the world."[119] The Johannine linguistic usage in reference to the expression "the Jews" is a differentiated one, and it must be paid attention to. "The Jews" of whom the Johannine Christ says they are "from this world" (8:22f.) are according to 8:13 "the Pharisees." Even this unjust generalization nevertheless is limited to those "Jews" who have the mind of the "world" because they have sharply rejected the revealer sent by God. With this it is also important to keep in mind that "the world" in John to a large extent belongs to his dualistic language world, a fact which gives the impression of "black and white painting." The harshest formulations of this come in the section 8:37–44 in which the Jews are designated sons of the devil: "You are of your father the devil, and your will is to do your father's desires. He was a murderer from the beginning, and has nothing to do with the truth, because there is no truth in him" (8:44).[120] Beforehand in verses 37 and 40, the intention of Jesus' opponents to kill him turns up, which lets one see that these refer to the "devil's sons" and they, according to the presentation of the Fourth Gospel, do in fact later pursue the killing of Jesus. And they, according to John, as was shown above, are the chief priests and Pharisees. Nevertheless, the sharpness of the Johannine diction remains striking; it has its parallels in the Qumran documents,[121] where, for example, in 4 Q Fl 1, 8 there is reference to the "sons of Belial," whereby the Essenes refer to their opponents. This is typical of the style of "heresy-polemics," expressed in John in the linguistic clothing of dualism, similar to that in Qumran. Leistner points out[122] that in the Essene "Damascus Document" "Jew," "the land of Juda," or "the house of Juda" are designations of the enemy party of Qumran. According to the Damascus Document IV, 2f. (cf. also VI, 5), the "converted of Israel" on the other hand are those who "have withdrawn from the land of Juda." From this it can be affirmed "that the polemic against 'Juda' in the Qumran documents is pointed toward a *part* of the Jewish people,"[123] above all toward the Temple aristocracy which was held to be illegitimate by the Essenes. Here in regard to the Johannine Gospel analogous models show up, which perhaps can be thus formulated:

At the time that the Gospel of John was being written the Church had already definitively separated itself from the Jews. It stood in tension with the Synagogue, and the Synagogue with the Church, which fact is clearly reflected in the Fourth Gospel.

Like the Essenes of Qumran, the Church developed in connection with this breaking away from Israel an oppositional self-understanding, which gave rise to hostile images like "the Pharisees" and "the Jews."

Of course, the recollection of the fate of Jesus of Nazareth, his violent death in Jerusalem which was carried out by Pontius Pilate under the urging of the Temple aristocracy, played an important role in this. One did not forget that there had been intense disputes between Jesus and certain circles of his Jewish compatriots, which with the help of the Romans ultimately led to his liquidation.

Nevertheless it must also be openly stated that in the "rereading" of the Gospel of John in the Church "the Jews" (with a negative accent)—in the Gospel itself still identifiable with the leading classes of the Jewish people, especially with the Temple aristocracy—were simply identified with the entire Jewish people. Through the apparent legitimization of this identification, the "Johannine anti-Judaism" had its catastrophic effects which have persisted throughout history up to Auschwitz and beyond: The Jew became "the enemy" and the Jewish people became "the people of the murderers of God."

Christian theology must clearly recognize these connections today without taking away anything of the greatness of the Gospel of John. In its in-depth vision the appearance of Christ in the world leads to the opening up of the true meaning of "the world" and to the struggle between the "light" and "darkness," "life" and "death." Faith stands against unbelief, "the savior of the world" against the "leaders of this world." The Gospel of John remains a *hermeneutica universalis* of the "world."[124] The revealer sent by God brings the definitive "crisis" into the world, which indeed even Jewish researchers have seen.[125] For the rest, however, it is true to say that even John has not forgotten Israel.

Jesus Dies for His People[126]

Christ saves the world (John 3:17), and therefore he is called in 4:42 "the savior of the world." Through his being raised up, he draws all to himself (12:32). Although with this "being raised up" his being raised up on the cross is at first thought of (3:14; 8:28; 12:33), and therefore his violent death which his opponents prepared for him, this nevertheless is perceived as a universal ("all") saving event. Jesus gives his life for the sheep (10:15), and indeed not merely for those "from this fold" (from Israel),[127] but also for those "others" who do not belong to "this fold:" for the Gentile peoples, so that in the end there will be *one* flock and *one* shepherd (10:16). The sheep "from this fold" are the Jews, not the Jewish Christians—where does it say in the text that they are Jewish Christians? "If this exegesis of 10:16 is valid, then we have here the opposite of anti-Judaism."[128]

Here also belongs the extraordinary prophecy of the chief priest Caiaphas and its exegesis by the evangelist in John 11:39–52. Jesus dies "for the people" (*hyper tou laou*): In the mouth of the chief priest the preposition *hyper* means "instead of"; in the understanding of the evangelist it means "for the sake of."[129] The commentary of the evangelist says that Jesus died "not for the nation [Israel] only, but to gather into one [into unity: *eis hen*] the children of God who are scattered abroad." This indication of purpose is to legitimate the mission to the Gentiles.[130] The goal, however, remains the bringing together of the Jews and the Gentiles "into unity," indeed into the one flock under the one shepherd. That eschatological Israel will "not be without the empirical Israel."[131]

Despite the "anti-Judaism" of the Gospel of John, as it above all appears to be expressed in the term "the Jews," and despite the fact that it contributed to the anti-Judaism in Christian theology, the Johannine evangelist did not write the Jewish people out of salvation.[132]

WHO BEARS THE GUILT FOR THE VIOLENT DEATH OF JESUS?

The Council decree *Nostra aetate* expressly declares: "Even though the Jewish authorities and those who followed their lead pressed for the death of Christ, neither all Jews indiscriminately at that time, nor Jews today, can be charged with the crimes committed during his passion," as is often done by Christians to the present day.[133]

Why Jesus Was Killed

The preceding analysis of the "Jews passages" loaded with a negative accent in the Gospel of John has shown that in fact "the Jewish authorities and those who followed their lead" did play a part in the trial of Jesus which led to his liquidation. Why precisely they, is not a question to be easily answered. Was it the dispute about the meaning of the Law in which Jesus and the Pharisees were involved? Was it the "cleansing of the Temple" with its clear claim of a special full power? Was it Jesus' claim to be the Messiah? Was it indeed his claim to be the Son of God, whom the Father had sent into the world? Or did Jesus fall into a fatal conflict with the Roman occupying authorities? As is known, the answers have not yet been clarified in research. Opinions are widely divided. That the Roman Pontius Pilate had Jesus crucified is without doubt, even if according to the New Testament reports no formal death sentence was pronounced by him. In like fashion one cannot doubt that a kind of previous examination by the members of the Jewish Sanhedrin took place against Jesus. Even Jewish scholars of the life of Jesus do not dispute this.[134] The thesis that the initiative for the condemnation of Jesus came from the Romans, is represented above all by the Jewish scholar Paul Winter[135] while the Christian scholar J. Blinzer comes to the conclusion that the chief responsibility for the condemnation of Jesus falls on the Jewish side.[136] Since no court minutes are available, but only the post-Easter narrations, the historical events can no longer be reconstructed exactly. The evangelists agree that something like a "religious trial" took place before members of the Sanhedrin, which was then transformed before Pilate into a political trial in order to attain the goal: the condemnation of Jesus to death.[137]

It appears that the immediate occasion for the authorities to proceed against Jesus was the "cleansing of the Temple" (cf. Mark 11:15–17);[138] for in the eyes of the Jewish authorities, Jesus showed himself with this to be a dangerous troublemaker who could threaten the delicate coexistence with the Roman occupation force. Moreover, the alleged threatening prophecy of Jesus against the Temple, to which several witnesses according to Mark 14:57f. referred, and his actions in the "cleansing of the Temple" appeared to imply a messianic claim which could bring with it dangerous political consequences. In their statements before the Sanhedrin, witnesses were not sufficiently united to come to a juridical conclusion against Jesus, but the reference to the word of Jesus threatening the Temple apparently prompted the high priests to put to Jesus the question: "Are you the Christ, the Son of the Blessed?" (Mark 14:61), to which Jesus responded affirmatively: "I am," whereby he immediately continued: "And you will see the Son of man sitting at the right hand of Power, and coming with the clouds of heaven" (14:62). This response was perceived by the high priest as "blasphemy" (14:64), and with his question to the members of the Sanhedrin: "What do you think?" "they all condemned him as deserving death" (14:64).[139] With this the High Council issued "a statement of guilt which included the measure of the penalty, but no judgment about carrying out the sentence."[140] Wherein, however, did the "blasphemy" of Jesus really lie which prompted the Sanhedrin to find him guilty of death? About this opinions are divided.[141] According to R. Pesch, Jesus' statement in Mark 14:62 "is to be judged as blasphemy in manifold regards." "It can be reflected whether Jesus in his reference to the Son of man intrinsically claimed a vision of God . . . and therefore would be designated blasphemy. Further, it is to be pondered that Jesus in his prophetic threatening statement . . . claimed in an exclusive manner a divine-pneumatic authority which also could justify the accusation of blasphemy. Finally, it should be highlighted that Jesus claimed in a unique manner the full power of God's judgment against his judges, and predicted his being raised up as the Son of man to an unsurpassable nearness to God and his 'coming with the clouds.'"

However, this is only half-satisfying. Perhaps for the members of the

Sanhedrin the "religious trial" which was set in motion by them against Jesus was only an appropriate help "in order to get rid of this dangerous opponent. In reality the appearance of Jesus was in fact fraught with political danger. Popular movements in stormy and agitated times sometimes lead to popular rebellions, and quite unintentionally this could have happened with the popular movement loosed by Jesus."[142] Perhaps it was, therefore, genuine political concern which prompted the members of the Sanhedrin to proceed with force against Jesus, even though the activity of Jesus was unpolitical. The movement which he loosed was much stronger and larger than is generally recognized. Therefore it could have awakened the irritation of the Jewish authorities because in their opinion it might have ended politically.[143]

These reflections are still not satisfying. It appears much more likely to have been an unacceptable and unheard-of claim of Jesus which stimulated the Pharisees as well as the Sadducees to their plan. I shall return later to the claim of Jesus.[144] This claim might have had something to do with the Messiah.[145] It certainly went in the direction of the Son of man as judge, but it went much further than the one or the other. In my opinion this claim moved in the direction of what is expressed in the title "Son of God." Certainly there is now a Qumran reference, to which J. A. Fitzmyer has referred (1 Qps Dan A[a]), according to which the Messiah is designated as the "Son of God" and the "Son of the Most High."[146] But this sole and remote reference in no way means that the high priest had understood his question to Jesus according to Mark 14:61 only "messianically." As the apposition "the Son of the Blessed" in the mouth of the high priest shows, it appears rather that he understood it as the previously referred to "exaggeration."[147] In Matthew (26:63) the apposition is, "the Son of God"; it appears then that Matthew "introduces into the question of the high priest the formula for swearing with the calling upon the living God. Apparently for him the decision comes with the question concerning the worthiness of Jesus as the Christ and the Son of God."[148] In Mark Jesus answered the *whole* question of the high priest with "I am," that is, with "Yes," and the continuation of his answer raised *beyond that* the claim to be as the Son of man the coming judge of his enemies. As is known, in the parallel to Mark 14:61f. Luke has a double question for Jesus; one is the demand of the high priest: "If you are the Christ, tell us" (Luke 22:67), which Jesus does not answer. Following is the question of "all" to him: "Are you the Son of God, then?" which Jesus answers: "You say that I am" (22:70).

R. Pesch would indeed like to see all deviations of Luke from the Markan account as redactional undertakings by Luke.[149] However, that he is definitively correct in this is to be doubted.[150] Likewise G. Schneider, who comes to the conclusion that Luke used, alongside Mark, a pre-Lukan source in his presentation of the three pericopes examined by him in the Lukan passion story, nevertheless believes that in the use of the title "the Son of God" without a messianic addition in Luke 22:70 (the second question to Jesus), this title "could obviously only be explained by Luke's having gotten the question about the Son of God out of the question in Mark 14:61."[151] In the rest, however, the conclusions of Schneider concerning Luke 22:67–70 tend for the most part to affirm the taking over, or the redaction, of non-Markan material. In any case, of the fifty-nine morphemes in Luke 22:67–70 only fifteen are found in the Mark parallels. Thus it could be possible that behind these verses there lies a pre-Markan tradition which Luke had utilized and from which also the double question stems.[152] That the Son of God claim of Jesus played a decisive role in his trial can be seen in Matt. 27:40–43 as well as in Luke 22:70. (The mockers under the cross of Jesus call out: "You who would destroy the temple and build it in three days, save yourself! If you are the Son of God, come down from the cross." In like manner the chief priests together with the scribes and elders jeer when they say: "He saved others; he cannot save himself. He is the King of Israel; let him come down now from the cross, and we will believe in him. He trusts in God; let God deliver him now, if he desires him; for he said, 'I am the Son of God.' ") And further in John 19:7 it says: "The Jews answered him, 'We have a law, and by that law he ought to die, *because he has made himself the Son of God.*' "[153] For the rest John transfers "the 'trial' of Jesus before the 'Jews' to the public disputes in chapters 7—11 and also anticipates in substance Mark 14:55–65: the discussion about the messiahship of Jesus and his sonship of God;"[154] cf. above all John 10:31–36: "The Jews took up stones again to stone him. Jesus answered them, 'I have shown you many good works from the Father; for which of these do you stone me?' The Jews answered him, 'We stone you for no good work *but for blasphemy*; because you, being a man, *make yourself God.*' Jesus answered them, 'Is it not written in your law, "I said you are gods?" ' If he called them gods to whom the word of God came (and Scripture cannot be broken), do you say of him whom the Father consecrated and sent into the world, "you are blaspheming," because I said, "I am the Son of God?" ' " Therefore John also does not need to produce his own report of the trial before the Sanhedrin (cf. John 18:12–27); that was de facto already anticipated.[155] Finally, reference is also to be made to Mark 15:39: "And when the centurion, who stood facing him, saw that he thus breathed his last, he said, 'Truly *this man was the son of God!*' "

This "crowd of witnesses" is so large one can hardly dispute that the Son of God claim of Jesus must have played an important role in his interrogation before the Sanhedrin, as is, in my opinion, also clear from Mark 14:61 ("the Son of the Blessed"). Without the assumption of a claim by Jesus reaching far beyond the claim of a Messiah, the "religious trial" before the Sanhedrin would not be historically understandable. That before the Roman Pilate as representative of the Roman emperor the "religious trial" had to be transformed into a "political trial" is obvious if the Jewish opponents in the trial wished to attain their goal, the liquidation of Jesus; the connecting points for this transformation were of course given with the Messiah question put to Jesus, because this question indeed carried monarchical claims which could be and were used politically against Jesus before Pilate.[156] For the Messiah is the king of the Jews! However, if in the "religious trial" before the Sanhedrin the Son of God claim played a role, then one would be able to say: The high priests and the members of the Sanhedrin gathered with them could come to no other conclusion but that Jesus of Nazareth was a blasphemer of God; they had to view him on this ground as being guilty of death. In this they ultimately followed their religious conviction. This was a consequence of the *Shema Israel*. In their opinion it concerned nothing less than the existence of Judaism, its being or nonbeing![157] A human being, an ordinary carpenter from Nazareth yet, who declared himself in Israel as the Son of God appeared thereby not merely to have stepped completely outside the framework of Judaism, but to have been a flagrant, public blasphemer of God who had to be punished with death. Presumably political considerations also played a role with the members of the Sanhedrin, but ultimately the matter was theological.

One should never forget in this what, according to Matt. 16:17, Jesus said to Peter as Peter confessed him to be the Messiah, *the Son of the Living God*: "For flesh and blood has not revealed this to you, but my Father who is in heaven." How, therefore, should the members of the Sanhedrin recognize in Jesus of Nazareth the Son of God if God had not given them such a revealed knowledge?! This question may be raised. That Jesus was viewed guilty of death only for his claim of messiahship cannot be proven. At this same time there were several in Israel who claimed to be the promised Messiah; none of these were brought to trial before the Jewish Sanhedrin. The great rabbi Akiba had even expressly declared Bar Cochba as the Messiah: "This one is the king, the Messiah" (jTaan 68d, 49). No offense was taken at this.

Guilt for Jesus' Death

Thus one can indeed say with Rudolph Pesch: "The chief responsibility for the execution of Jesus is born by the Jewish authorities who had Jesus seized, declared him guilty of death in an extraordinary session, and delivered him to Pilate as one guilty of high treason,"[158] but with this the "question of guilt" is by no means solved, a fact of which Pesch is also aware.[159] For further reflections I shall proceed from several texts of the Acts of the Apostles:

Acts 2:23 (from the Pentecost sermon of Peter): "This Jesus, *delivered up according to the definite plan and foreknowledge of God,* you crucified and killed by the hands of lawless men [the pagan Romans]."

Acts 3:17f. (from the Temple speech of Peter): "And now, brethren, I know that *you acted in ignorance,* as did also your rulers. But what God foretold by the mouth of all the prophets, that his Christ should suffer, *he thus [houtōs] fulfilled.*"

Acts 13:27–30 (from a sermon of Paul in Antioch in Pisidia): "*For those who live in Jerusalem and their rulers, because they did not recognize him* nor understand the utterances of the prophets which are read every Sabbath, fulfilled these by condemning him. Though they could charge him with nothing deserving death, yet they asked Pilate to have him killed. And when they had *fulfilled all that was written of him,* they took him down from the tree, and laid him in a tomb. But God raised him from the dead."

These texts allow us to see that the primitive Christian proclamation had two answers to the pressing question: How could it have come to the frightful death on the cross of the one that we honor and proclaim as Messiah and Son of God? First of all they mention a "foreground" historical reason: namely, the deed of the Jewish and Roman trial opponents of Jesus that killed him (cf. Acts 2:23b; 3:15; 4:27; 5:30; 10:39b; 13:28); second, a "background" transhistorical reason: the will of God revealed in the Scriptures (Acts 22:23a; 3:18; 4:28; 3:27b; cf. also 1 Cor. 15:3: "Christ died . . . *according to the Scriptures*").[160] The above-cited texts of the Acts of the Apostles show clearly that the real cause of the violent death of Jesus is the inscrutable decision of God who "gave over" his Son and Messiah to death, while the human beings acted "out of ignorance" because they were not able to see the divine mystery of Jesus. *God himself decreed that his Messiah must suffer.* Who, however, would wish to judge God in this matter? It must be said: The violent death on the cross does not admit of a definitive historical explanation. Ultimately it leads to the impenetrable and indecipherable mystery of God and his decisions which are not open to rational clarification.[161] Paul in 1 Cor. 2:6–8 confirms this: "Yet among the mature we do impart wisdom, although it is not a wisdom of this age or of the rulers of this age, who are doomed to pass away. But we impart a secret and hidden wisdom of God, which God *decreed before* the ages for our glorification. None of the rulers of this age understood this; *for if they had, they would not have crucified the Lord of glory.*"

Here historically determinable bearers of guilt are no longer spoken of, but rather the entire "aeon" of this world, which did not recognize the Lord of glory, but rather crucified him. Only in 1 Thess. 2:4 does Paul remark that the Jews killed the Lord Jesus and the prophets.[162] For the rest, however, the apostle is concerned with the theology of the death by crucifixion of Jesus, which with the help of the "Jewish categories" and together with the rest of the primitive Church he interprets as the reconciling death for the sins of all. God had put Jesus "forward as an expiation" (Rom. 3:25), namely, for the sins of all who believe (cf. the context of the passage). God "did not spare his own Son but gave him up for us all" (Rom. 8:32).[163] Christ died "for us" (Rom. 5:8); "for our sins" (Gal. 1:4; 1 Cor. 15:3). This is the conviction of the entire primitive Christian proclamation. "He is the expiation for our sins, and not for ours only but also for the sins of the whole world" (1 John 2:2). Jesus' death possesses the power of reconciliation; it is a saving death for all. "For God so loved the world that he gave his only Son, that whoever believes in him should not perish but have eternal life" (John 3:16).[164] And therefore it is quite problematic to search for those who are historically "guilty" for the violent death of Jesus. The *Roman Catechism*[165] teaches that individuals are not guilty of the cross of Jesus, but rather all human beings "because all have sinned" (Rom. 5:12). Likewise the Second Vatican Council teaches: "The Church always held and continues to hold that Christ out of infinite love freely underwent suffering and death because of the sins of all men, *so that all might attain salvation.* It is the duty of the Church, therefore, in her preaching to proclaim the cross of Christ as the sign of God's universal love and the source of all grace."[166] Because the Christians have largely forgotten this, the historically undeniable violent death of Jesus became for them the fatally illusory legitimation of their anti-Judaism, which beyond that, with predilection called upon and calls upon the Jewish peoples' alleged self-cursing.[167] "The Church's hostility toward Jews used the story of the passion as its arsenal of words."[168]

"HIS BLOOD BE ON US AND ON OUR CHILDREN!" (Matt. 27:25)

In Matt. 27:24f. we read the following: "So when Pilate saw that he was gaining nothing, but rather that a riot was beginning, he took water and washed his hands before the crowd, saying, 'I am innocent of this man's blood;[169] see to it yourselves.' And all the people *[pas ho laos]* answered, 'His blood be on us and on our children!' " That is the famous-infamous special material from the Gospel of Matthew in which a "self-cursing" seems to be expressed by the Jewish people. All catastrophes which have come upon the Jewish people since then are—many Christians even today still claim—nothing other than the working out of this "self-cursing" which "the entire people" call down upon themselves during the trial of Jesus before Pilate![170]

What is to be said concerning this?[171]

In the entire pericope of Matt. 27:11–26 (the condemnation of Jesus by Pilate) there is in comparison with the Mark parallel (Mark 15:2–15) a growing anti-Jewish tendency which moves toward ascribing the guilt for the violent death of Jesus almost exclusively to the Jews. There is, for example, the special material in Matt. 27:19 (the wife of Pilate sends a message to him: "Have nothing to do with that righteous man!"), and then the official claim of innocence by Pilate connected with the ceremony of the washing of the hands, and the shout of the "entire people", "His blood be upon us and on our children!" in 27:24f. This represents an enormous unburdening of Pilate, assuming that his declaration of innocence is not put forward by the evangelist as hypocrisy. Indeed, the guilt for the violent death of Jesus is shoved entirely upon the Jews. Matthew has Pilate saying: "See to it yourselves!"; he thus allows the responsibility for the violent death of Jesus to be attributed to the Jews by Pilate himself.

This tendency intensified later, as the passion narrative of the Gospel of Peter shows:[172] it is King Herod who has Jesus led off to crucifixion (v. 2); he hands Jesus over to "the people" (v. 5b). "They however took the Lord and shoved him and said: 'Let us cut down the Son of God since we have gained power over him.' And they placed a purple cloth around him and sat him on a judge's stool and said: 'Judge rightly O King of Israel!' And one of them brought a crown of thorns and placed it upon the head of the Lord. And others who were standing around spit in his face and others struck him on the cheek and others jabbed him with a rod while several others scourged him and said: 'With such honor do we wish to honor the Son of God' " (vv. 6–9). They commanded that the thighs of Jesus on the cross not be broken, "so that he would die in torment" (v. 14). "And they fulfilled everything and made the measure of sins full over their heads" (v. 17). The Roman military guards hurried after the resurrection of Jesus while it was "still in the night to Pilate . . . and related everything that they had seen, full of unrest saying: 'Truly he was the Son of God.' Pilate answered and said: 'I am innocent of the blood of the Son of God; you made the decision' " (vv. 45f.). Thus, Pilate is completely acquitted and is made into a witness of the divinity of Jesus. The anti-Jewish tendency is completely clear.

The special material of Matthew in 27:24f. is brought together under the key word "blood." It has a completely Old Testament-Jewish coloring, beginning in connection with Pilate with the custom of the washing of the hands. Its roots are to be found in Deut. 21:1–9. If one comes across a person who has been struck down and whose murderer is unknown, the elders of the city should bring a young cow to the stream and there cut its throat. The elders should wash their hands over the cow slaughtered in the river while calling aloud: "Our hands did not shed this blood, neither did our eyes shed it." In this way one hopes that God will drive out from the midst of Israel the guilt for the innocently shed blood. In Pss. 26:6 and 73:13 the formula "to wash the hands in innocence" is symbolic language for the innocence of which the one praying is conscious. Therefore, with the ceremony of the handwashing Pilate underlines the innocence concerning the blood of Jesus claimed by him: "I am innocent of this blood"; this participation of Pilate is found almost verbatim in Sus 46 (Theodotion). "Then the whole people responded: 'His blood be upon us and on our children!' " This shout of the people also has its prototype in the Old Testament; cf. 2 Sam. 3:28f.: "I and my kingdom are for ever guiltless before the Lord for the blood of Abner the son of Ner. May it fall upon the head of Joab, and upon all his father's house"; Jer. 26:15: "If you put me to death, you will bring innocent blood upon yourselves and upon this city and its inhabitants." And if Matthew allows "the entire people" to shout this statement, he himself in this is thinking "by no means of an accidental coming together of a riotous mob,"[173] but rather of the entire Jewish people whom he burdens with collective guilt for the violent death of Jesus. For the formal term "the *entire* people"[174] as well as the similarly formal term "on our children" "refers to the entire population of Israel."[175]

Whether this special material of Matthew stems from an already existing pre-Matthean tradition or is formed by the evangelist himself, with it we are dealing "not with a propensity for legend, but rather with a dogmatic theologumenon,"[176] by which clearly the Roman Pilate is to be acquitted and the Jewish people condemned. This again is connected with the building up of a hostile image to which I have earlier referred. In connection with the separation of the Church from Israel the Jewish people ("the Jew") clearly and simply becomes the enemy.[177] Historically-critically seen, it is also quite unlikely that Pilate as the representative of the Roman state power would himself, in front of the Jewish trial opponents of Jesus, declare the condemnation to death on the cross that was carried out by him to be "judicial murder," which he nevertheless did de facto with the ceremony of the washing of the hands and the protestation connected with it.[178] Moreover, it is simply impossible that "the entire people" of the Jews were gathered along with the chief priests and the elders before Pilate. The place in question—according to a tradition that is undisputed today—"is an inner court paved with limestone slabs within the fortress Antonia—about 2,500 square meters (cf. John 19:13). Within the area of the courtyard at most between 4,000 and 4,500 people could have found room. According to careful reckoning, it is judged that at the time of Jesus Jerusalem numbered about 25,000 to 30,000 inhabitants; however, at the time of the Easter festival, because of the stream of pilgrims from the entire Jewish Diaspora, around 180,000 people were present in Jerusalem. The crowd of people in front of Pilate, of which Matthew reports, could, therefore, be only 2 to 3 percent of all the people present in Jerusalem at that time. Further, qualitatively it was not a representative Jewish group."[179] For these reasons it must be said that the special material of Matt. 27:24f. very certainly does not deal with historical reportage; rather it is a secondary development of tradition, whose tendencies are all too transparent.

Nevertheless, this material is now present in the Gospel, and Christian theology must deal with it. From the perspective of the time of the composition of the Gospel, it is probable that the evangelist saw the cry of the people "His blood be upon us and on our children" fulfilled in the catastrophe of the year 70.[180] The "self-curse" of the Jewish people was supposedly fulfilled here in a fearful manner. Then, however, the blood of the cross of Jesus would not be seen as the blood of a savior but rather the blood of an avenger, and this contradicts the soteriology of the New Testament as it is particularly impressively formulated in Heb. 12:24: The blood of Christ "speaks more graciously than the blood of Abel." It demands not punishment, but forgiveness. "The blood of Christ is not unsaving, but rather grace and blessing."[181] Beyond that one may never forget that on the cross, according to Luke 23:34, Jesus prayed for his enemies: "Father, forgive them; for they know not what they do." Did God not hear the plea of his Son? Israel remains standing under the cross, and the blood of Jesus reconciles its guilt, however great it may be. Jesus died not only for the Gentiles, but for all human beings. He is the "ransom for all" (1 Tim. 2:6), whether Jews or Gentiles. Christian theology must take its proclamations seriously, even toward Israel. No Christian can with a good conscience call upon Matt. 27:25 as a justification of his anti-Judaism. If the blood of

Jesus comes upon the children of Israel, it comes upon them as a savior's blood.

WAS JESUS OF NAZARETH RECOGNIZABLE
FOR ISRAEL?

With this a question is taken up which, as far as I can see, has never really been reflected on thoroughly by Christian theology. Nevertheless, it is of fundamental significance for the Jewish-Christian dialogue, and in a tractate on the Jews it may not be left undealt with—even if the answer, because of the difficulty of the subject, ultimately does not move beyond hypothesis—for the question deals with the inscrutable mystery of the divine direction of salvation. However, an attempt at an answer must be made. Our question of course is: Was Jesus recognizable to Israel in his messianic-divine mystery?

Jesus' Self-revelation in Nazareth

We proceed in our reflections from the so-called Nazareth pericope (Mark 6:1–6a; Matt. 13:53–58; Luke 4:16–30),[182] which often in translations and commentaries bears the heading: "The rejection of Jesus in his hometown."[183] H. Schürmann, however, speaks of "the self-revelation of Jesus in Nazareth."[184] According to Schürmann, Luke moves the Nazareth pericope "deliberately toward the beginning of his report on the activity of Jesus because in a certain manner it contains the entirety of the gospel, and because something typical is illuminated in it in a particularly clear manner."[185] "The first section, 4:16–22, speaks of the *archē* ["the beginning"] of Jesus ... through which the 'fulfilled' *sēmeron* ["today"] is constituted (v. 21); in its second section (4:23–30) there is the exit of Jesus: the rejection in his hometown and in Israel and the coming salvation for the Gentiles."[186] There arises for us thereby the question: If in the pericope the related events of the direction of Jesus and of the gospel are reflected in exemplary fashion—and according to R. Pesch the pericope provides "important historical material"[187]—can then the reasons be discerned from it which led to Israel's rejecting Jesus and his message and to the turning of the gospel to the Gentiles? According to Mark 6:3b (Matt. 13:57a) the compatriots of Jesus "are scandalized in him," while Luke dramatizes this being scandalized in Jesus at the end of his narrative in the following manner: "When they heard this [what Jesus had just said in his 'homily'], all in the synagogue were filled with wrath. And they rose up and put him out of the city, and led him to the brow of the hill on which the city was built, that they might throw him down headlong" (4:28f.). Wherein lie the grounds for this "scandal" and this "wrath" of the Nazarenes, who here represent Israel? The ground for this is not as clearly recognizable in Mark as it is in Luke. In Mark it is the incapacity of the fellow townsmen of Jesus to bring the "wisdom and mighty deeds," or more precisely stated, the "whence" of them, together with the fact that this Jesus, the son of the (known to them, even if perhaps also already dead) carpenter Joseph, lived, along with the rest of his relatives (his mother, his brothers and sisters), among them. They are obviously thinking: He cannot have gotten the wisdom and the power of mighty works with which he speaks and acts from these simple people, from his parents' house. In Luke on the other hand it very clearly concerns the "today" (4:21) which Jesus in his "homily" designated as that "today" in which the prediction of the prophet Isaiah is fulfilled in his own arrival: "The Spirit of the Lord God is upon me, because the Lord has annointed me to bring good tidings to the afflicted; he has sent me to bind up the broken-hearted, to proclaim liberty to the captives, and the opening of the eyes of the blind; to proclaim the year of the Lord's favor" (Isa. 61:1f.; 58:6). Indeed, according to Luke the Nazarenes at first applaud him and are astonished at his "gracious words," but then there also comes in Luke the critical-sounding question: "Is not this Joseph's son?" (4:22b). "The year of the Lord's favor" becomes in the "today" which Jesus proclaimed the "actual present."[188] According to Pesch, the fellow townsmen of Jesus with their question about the "whence" of his wisdom and his power of wonderful deeds "referred back to the messianic claim which came out of the teaching of Jesus. If Jesus had the wisdom from himself, then he is a pseudo-Christ."[189] A similar claim is in the "today" which according to Jesus was now fulfilled in him.[190] Now, "today," is the time of fulfillment, now is the time of salvation![191] Against this claim, however, there is for the sensitivity of the Nazarenes the "common" and "known" derivation of Jesus. In 3:23 Luke remarks that as Jesus appeared in public, one took him "for a son of Joseph" (cf. also John 1:45; 6:42). How then could he all at once claim that he is the one predicted by the prophet of Israel in whom the messianic promises are fulfilled? This was not clear to them, and thus it came to their being scandalized in him, and to his rejection by the Nazarenes, which Luke relates in detailed fashion, whereby in the second section of the pericope "the gospel already becomes the story of the passion"[192]—indeed, the turning of the gospel away from Israel to the Gentile world is already announced. "The opposition in Luke 4:23, Nazareth-Capernaum, becomes in vv. 25ff. Israel-Gentile world."[193]

Naturally everything in Luke, despite various historical elements in his narrative, is *post eventum* interpreted thus. However, the question about his origin, that is, the question of "whence," doubtless played a decisive role in Israel's rejection of Jesus as the Messiah. For this "whence" could "be responded to variously (cf. Mark 11:27–33 and par. in Matt.): from heaven or from humanity (11:30), or from Satan (3:22, 30). The use of the demonstrative pronouns (*toutō-toutō-houtos*, Mark 6:2f.; cf. 4:41!), repeated three times in Mark, is also from the perspective of v. 3 cast into the obscurity of unbelieving (v. 6) wonder and strengthens the skeptical character of the question which they put to 'this man' (cf. 2:7)."[194]

The obscure origin of Jesus from Nazareth also appears to have played an important role in the dispute about him, and indeed far beyond Easter, as the Gospels, especially the Gospel of John, let us see. Here Nathanael asks: "Can anything good come out of Nazareth?" (John 1:46). According to John 6:42 "the Jews" ask: "Is not this Jesus, the son of Joseph, whose father and mother we know? How does he now say, 'I have come down from heaven'?" Likewise the people from Jerusalem, according to John 7:25–27, raised this problem about the origin of Jesus. Of Jesus they believe they know "whence he is" (that is, from Nazareth). "When the Christ appears, no one will know where he comes from" (7:27). Several think that Jesus is perhaps the Messiah. "But some said, 'Is the Christ to come from Galilee? Has not the scripture said that the Christ descended from David, and comes from Bethlehem, the village where David was?' " (John 7:41f. and cf. also 8:14; 9:29f.). From the perspective of the composition time of the Fourth Gospel, this question concerning the "whence" of Jesus appears to have played an important role in the disputes between Jews and Christians. Among other things, the infancy narratives of Matthew and Luke appear to serve the purpose of demonstrating the origin of Jesus from the "city of David," Bethlehem. In any case, the question of the origin of Jesus from Nazareth in Galilee played an important role in the disputes before as well as after Easter.

Nonunderstanding of Jesus' Parents

"And he said to them, 'How is it that you sought me? Did you not know that I must be in my Father's house?' And they [Joseph and Mary] did not understand the saying which he spoke to them" (Luke 2:49f.). Precisely the "must" which Jesus uses here in his response "separates Jesus himself from his parents—precisely from his parents."[195] The mysterious-sounding question of Jesus hints at the "radicalness of his filial obedience toward the Father," which Joseph and Mary do not understand. The extraordinary distance which he takes in relationship to them with these words is puzzling to them. Here we come upon the extraordinary experience which shows up more scandalously in Mark 3:21, 31–35 than is expressed in the Synoptics in other ways in the "motive of nonunderstanding" (concerning this, see below, pp. 202ff.).

Nonunderstanding of Jesus' Relatives

When according to Mark 3:21 "his family" heard of his actions "they went out to seize him, for people were saying, 'He is beside himself.' "[196] In 3:31–35 the following is related by Mark: "And his mother and his brothers came; and standing outside they said to him and called him. And a crowd was sitting about him; and they said to him, 'Your mother and your brothers are outside, asking for you.' And he replied, 'Who are my mother and my brothers?' And looking around on those who sat about him, he said, 'Here are my mother and my brothers! Whoever does the will of God is my brother, and sister, and mother.' " Doubtless this is one of the harshest scenes which Mark knew of from the oldest material about Jesus and which he took up into his *vita Jesu*—Luke took away much of its harshness (cf. Luke 8:19–21),[197] a fact which indicates that Luke understood the scene related by Mark historically, even though it is supposed to be understood "spiritually" in the material available to Mark: The hearers of Jesus who are prepared to obey the will of God form the true, the "spiritual" family. That however this new "spiritual" relationship is so strongly and dramatically disengaged from the natural kinship of Jesus belongs to one of the puzzles of the life of Jesus in which, however, somehow the "un-Jewishness" of Jesus is shown.[198] The pericope in any case shows that Jesus was "unknown" even to his closest relations, that his messianic-divine mystery remained hidden from them.[199] How then a fortiori should all Israel recognize him?

Nonunderstanding of Jesus' People

Just how ambiguous the appearances and claims of Jesus were for Israel can be seen clearly in two other narratives of the Gospel of Mark.[200] In 6:14f. opinions of people about Jesus are reported. One says of him—and this view appears, according to 6:14, 16, to have also reached the ears of the ruler of Jesus' land, Herod Antipas, and to have been shared by him— " 'John the baptizer has been raised from the dead; that is why these powers are at work in him.' But others said, 'It is a prophet, like one of the prophets of old.' "[201] According to Mark 8:27f. Jesus himself one day asked the disciples: "Who do men say that I am?" They answered him: "John the Baptist; the others say, Elijah; and others one of the prophets." These views, partially superstitious (Jesus, the Baptist risen again!), partially connected with the early Jewish expectation of the end of times (Jesus, Elijah redivivus), allow us to perceive two things: (1) The people were not united in their opinions about who Jesus of Nazareth really was. (2) No one among the people held Jesus to be the Messiah.[202] This second finding is especially important.[203]

According to the translation of the Logia source, one day John the Baptist from prison sent some disciples to Jesus with the question: "Are you he who is to come, or shall we look for another?" (Matt. 11:2f., and parr.). For such a tradition to be the product of the community seems impossible, since it there casts such an extraordinary light on the figure of the Baptist, which does not fit well with his image otherwise projected in the Gospels.[204] How did the Baptist come to this action and this question? Apparently on the basis of a genuine crisis of faith concerning Jesus of Nazareth due to the apparent "unmessianic character" of his actions. I shall return to the inquiry of the Baptist later on.

The question of whether the actions of Jesus of Nazareth were "messianic" must first of all be answered with a no, in any case from the perspective of the expectations of his people. Had his actions been unambiguously messianic, his people would have had to recognize him as the promised one. However, the Jews say to this very day: He was not it! Peter, indeed, according to Mark 8:29, bore a clear witness: "You are the Christ." However, here the title of Christ is understood in the sense that it was understood in the Christian communities after Easter. *Their* understanding, however, depends upon the self-exegesis of Jesus which he gave to his actions, not on a pre-given understanding of Messiah specified by Judaism, "which was a polysemy par excellence, as its application for example by the Pharisees, Sadducees, apocalyptics, and in Qumran shows," even if the contents of the Jewish expectations were by no means completely eliminated from the Christian confession of Christ.[205] The Christian dogma, that the *crucified* Jesus of Nazareth is the promised Messiah, was and remains for Jews a "scandal" (cf. 1 Cor. 1:24). The Christian must understand this.

Nonunderstanding of Jesus' Disciples

"The modus for the nonunderstanding of the disciples" likewise cannot go undiscussed here. It plays a persistent role, especially in the Gospel of Mark (cf. Mark 4:40; 7:18; 8:17, 21; 8:31—in reference to Peter; 9:6—again in reference to Peter; 9:10; 9:19; 9:32).[206] Concerning the second prediction of suffering by Jesus (9:31), the evangelist remarks: "But they did not understand the saying, and they were afraid to ask him" (9:32). After the second multiplication of the loaves and the subsequent demand for a sign

by the Pharisees, the disciples were traveling with Jesus over the lake and
had only a single loaf of bread in the boat when Jesus warned them against
the leaven of the Pharisees and of Herod (8:1–15). The evangelist relates
further: "And they discussed it with one another, saying, 'We have no
bread.' And being aware of it, Jesus said to them, 'Why do you discuss the
fact that you have no bread? Do you not yet perceive or understand? Are
your hearts hardened? Having eyes do you not see, and having ears do you
not hear? And do you not remember?' "(Mark 8:16–18). Now precisely the
last question ("Do you not remember?") could confirm what Rudolph Pesch
thinks about the "nonunderstanding of the disciples" in Mark:[207] "The
image of nonunderstanding of that which was given along with the secret of
the reign of God (4:11), which arose from various kinds of motives, is in the
composition a 'sermon against the unbelief of the community' [Wendling]":
The Christian community should remember what Jesus said and did and
thus come to an understanding of the reign of God and of the mysteries of
Jesus. The recollection aims "at *the overcoming* of the nonunderstanding."[208] Doubtless here the recollection can act out this function for the
Christian community. Nevertheless, it appears that the "motive of the
nonunderstanding of the disciples" points back to the pre-Easter reactions
of the circle of disciples to the word and work of Jesus, and was not
introduced after Easter as a warning to the community against unbelief.
Indeed, the disciples committed themselves to Jesus of Nazareth and
followed him, even worked as "multipliers" of his messages of the kingdom,
but one may never forget from what milieu and traditions they stem,
namely, from the milieu and traditions of the Jewish people at the time of
Jesus. One may, indeed, also not overlook the fact that the "motive of
nonunderstanding by the disciples" in the synoptic colleagues of Mark, that
is, Matthew and Luke, is largely suppressed, presumably because of the
contrary notion: The motive of nonunderstanding could make the community uncertain in its faith in Christ.

In this connection a reference must also be made to the "parable theory"
which, like the "motive of nonunderstanding by the disciples," Jesus'
command of silence to the demons, and the command of secrecy to the
ones healed and to the disciples, is often connected with the "messianic
secret" of the synoptic Gospels concerning which, since W. Wrede,[209] a
whole library has been written.[210] In any case the "parable theory" has to
do with the "hardening" problem, as Mark 4:10–12 and parallels evidence.[211] In this Mark may have introduced the hardening logion (4:11f.),
as, for example, Rudolph Pesch assumes.[212] But why has he introduced it at
all, and why precisely in a connection which deals with the understanding

of the parables of Jesus? The parable belongs to a genre of metaphorical speaking,[213] and the metaphor as such is polysemantic and, therefore, "encoded." Thus it allows space for various interpretations and for various decisions both as far as the author of the parable is concerned as well as for the content of what was said. If the eyes and ears of the hearers are not opened by God, the speaker and his word remain puzzling, the connection with the whole (*ta panta*: Mark 4:11!) cannot be discerned, and therefore cannot be believed. The "hardening theory," which is found not only in the Synoptics (Mark 4:10–12; Matt. 13:10–15; Luke 8:9f.; Acts 28:25–28), but also in John (cf. John 12:37–41) and Paul (cf. Rom. 11:8), was presumably the response which the primitive Church gave to this problem which concerned it: Why is it that Israel did not recognize him, and why has it rejected the gospel? The "hardening theory" clearly contains two components: one is the accusation of a guilty attitude on the part of Israel, the other an element of predestination: "To you has been given the secret of the kingdom of God [that is, by God!], but for those outside" it has not been given! In Rom. 9–11 Paul has further worked out[214] the rationally and ultimately insoluble tension between guilt and the "hardening" decreed by God. Luke, in contrast to Mark, "has understood the hardening as a limited thing."[215] According to H. Schürmann, the hardening logion cannot be denied "every foundation in the proclamation of Jesus." It is, Schürmann[216] believes, "thinkable as an encouragement to the circle of disciples themselves, to whom the unsuccessful proclamation of Jesus was a pressing question." Perhaps it had its *Sitz im Leben* in the bitter experience of Jesus that the great mass of Israel rejected him and his message for reasons already discussed above in dealing with the Nazareth pericope: Israel could not reconcile his origin and his claim. Had God so willed it? Why did he not "give the secret of the kingdom of God" to Israel, as according to Mark 4:11a, he did to the disciples? This is the question. Who can answer it? In any case, it is important that the question concerning the "hardening" of Israel in the New Testament be theologically and not psychologically resolved. This must be kept before our eyes.

Recognition of Jesus Only Through Revelation

As Peter, according to Matt. 16:16, bore witness: "You are the Christ, the Son of the living God," Jesus answered him: "Blessed are you, Simon Bar-Jona! For flesh and blood has not revealed this to you, *but my Father who is in heaven*" (16:17). With the adding of "the Son of the living God"[217] upon which special emphasis is laid, "the self-revelation of Jesus as the Son (11:27) is taken up,"[218] and Peter is praised as blessed by Jesus for his confession. However, with that Jesus immediately declares that the recognition that "he is the Son of the living God" could not have been won through human insight and reflection ("flesh and blood has not revealed this"), but only through a revelation of God himself. However the origin of the Matthean special material in Matt. 16:16b–19 may be interpreted,[219] it clearly expresses that no one can confess Jesus of Nazareth as a "Son of God" if God does not expressly "reveal" it to him. Paul says nothing other with his sentence in 1 Cor. 12:3: "No one can say 'Jesus is Lord' except by the Holy Spirit," that is, only by the graceful intervention of the Spirit of God is the "christological" mystery of Jesus discernible in faith. Otherwise not. Paul knew that from his own conversion experience, which he interpreted in Gal. 1:15f. as a genuine revelation event: "But when he who had set me apart before I was born, and had called me through his grace, was pleased *to reveal his Son to me.* . . ."[220] For our theme, however, the question again rises: How should Israel recognize him if Israel was not given this grace of revelation and faith by God? What Christian theologian can with certitude say that God had given Israel this grace! Could not the "Son of God" called Jesus of Nazareth and veiled as a carpenter, as a consequence of his "incarnational form," more readily make nonseers out of seers if God himself had not lifted the veil?

Ignorance of the Jews

Did the Jews act unknowingly when their leaders deemed Jesus worthy of death and demanded his execution from Pontius Pilate? According to Luke 23:34a, Jesus himself while on the cross prayed for his enemies: "Father, forgive them, *for they know not what they do.*" This portion of the verse is, indeed, lacking in a number of textual witnesses;[221] the reasons for this include, for example, the fact that this plea of Jesus stands "in contradiction to the first words of verses 28–31," or, that it is secondary, having arisen out of the testimony of Scripture (Isa. 53:12).[222] However, the lack of this portion of the verse in the text witnesses named below is best explained "for reasons of the current polemic,"[223] namely, that of the Christian communities against the Jews, whom they could not and dared not ever forgive for the "murder of God."[224] The forgiveness plea of Jesus in Luke 23:34a, therefore, may be reckoned as part of the original text. However, this plea is not simply about forgiveness, but is explicitly based on what follows: "*For* they know not what they do." Thereby the guilt, despite Jesus' clear statement of the guilt of his enemies (cf. Luke 21:22–24; 23:28–31), is immensely lessened; for the "action" of the enemy is laid to "ignorance." This goes much further than the law of the love of one's enemy demanded by Jesus, to which reference is eagerly made in the commentaries. Why do the enemies not know what they are doing in their execution of Jesus? To this there is in my opinion only one answer: The messianic-divine mystery of Jesus remains hidden to them. They did not recognize it! And therefore they do not know *whom* they are in reality crucifying.

Luke once again takes up the motive of "ignorance" in connection with the violent death of Jesus in the Acts of the Apostles. Indeed, in Acts 3:13–15 he has Peter say to the Jews in his sermon at the Temple square: "The God of Abraham and of Isaac and of Jacob, the God of our fathers, glorified his servant Jesus, whom you delivered up and denied in the presence of Pilate, when he had decided to release him. But you denied the Holy and Righteous One, and asked for a murderer to be granted to you, and killed the Author of life, whom God raised from the dead. To this we are witnesses." But then he has Peter say to his Jewish listeners the following: "And now, brethren, I know that *you acted in ignorance, as did also your rulers. But what God foretold* by the mouth of all the prophets, that his Christ should suffer, *he thus fulfilled*" (3:17f.). How can Peter now speak of "ignorance" after the guilt of the Jews for killing Jesus has been clearly determined by him? E. Haenchen provides information on this:[225] "In response to this one would have to point out that Luke had taken up traditions of various sorts which were not always without tension; however, he was not aware of it." This would sound plausible if what is said in v. 18 had not followed; in it God himself is presented as the true *causa* of this fearsome event ("thus"!),[226] whereby the sentence is introduced by an intensifying "rather, much more" (*de*).[227] The reference of Peter to the "ignorance" (even of the "leaders" of the Jewish people!) may sound irritating to Christian pious ears and is eagerly declared to be a benevolent quibbling (*captatio benevolentiae*) by Peter in order to more easily win Jewish listeners for the gospel. By referring the fearsome event back to God, who had already announced his mysterious salvific will "through the mouth of all prophets," "the *skandalon tou staurou* [the scandal of the cross] threatens to disappear";[228] in reality with this the scandal of the cross is transformed into an ultimately impenetrable *mysterium Dei*.

And again the question arises: Wherein does "the ignorance" of the Jews and their leaders lie? The answer again can only be: in the impossibility of recognizing Jesus of Nazareth in his messianic-divine mystery. It is not disputed by Peter, as we saw above, that the Jews, especially their "leaders," had participated in the liquidation of Jesus. However, they are acquitted of the guilt with which they appear to have burdened themselves. God has used them as "unknowing" instruments of his mysterious decision[229]—

and the decision of God in the Bible is essentially more than a "permission" or a "dispensation"; it is a decree. God has decreed that his Messiah must suffer.[230] E. Haenchen believes: "In truth the real guilt . . . lies precisely in the [ignorance]: if one had not closed oneself off against God, then one would have recognized Jesus."[231] In reality one must formulate the matter thus: Had one recognized Jesus, then one would have closed oneself against God.

John: Recognition of Jesus Only Through Grace

What is the objective content in the Gospel of John? At the end of the pericope of the healing of the man born blind Jesus says: "For judgment I came into this world, that those who do not see may see, and that those who see may become blind. Some of the Pharisees near him heard this, and they said to him, 'Are we also blind?' Jesus said to them, 'If you were blind, you would have no guilt; but now that you say, "We see," your guilt remains' " (John 9:39–41). Here sin (*hamartia*) is explicitly spoken of in relationship to the unbelief of the Pharisees toward Jesus. Just as clearly this sin of unbelief is spoken of by the Johannine Christ in 15:22, 24: "If I had not come and spoken to them, they would not have sin; but now they have no excuse for their sin. . . . If I had not done among them the works which no one else did, they would not have sin; but now they have seen and hated both me and my Father." With this the guilt is clearly stated. Nevertheless, there are contrasting statements from the same Gospel which are connected with the Johannine thoughts about predestination.[232] Above all the texts from John 6:28–44 are important here. The Jews say to Jesus: " 'What must we do, to be doing the works of God?' Jesus answered them, 'This is the work of God, that you believe in him whom he has sent' " (6:28f.). The Jews indeed have "seen" (namely, "the signs" which Jesus performed), but do not believe (6:36). The Jews "murmur" about Jesus because he said: "I am the bread which came down from heaven" (6:41); according to verse 42, their objection against the claim of Jesus is expressed as follows: "Is not this Jesus, *the son of Joseph, whose father and mother we know?* How does he now say, 'I have come down from heaven?' " Jesus answered them, 'Do not murmur among yourself. No one can come to me *unless the Father who sent me draws him'* " (6:42f.). These texts are very enlightening: The "unbelief" of the Jews is clearly spoken of as guilt (especially in v. 36). The Jews' inability to see in Jesus the one sent down from heaven by God is again revealingly based on the knowing of Jesus' origin: They know his father, Joseph, and his mother (v. 42)—this is precisely the same reason why the townspeople of Jesus of Nazareth came to be scandalized at his unheard-of claim. In contrast to this the Johannine Christ decreed that no one can "come" to him, that is, can believe in him as the one sent by God, "unless the Father draw him" (6:44; cf. also 6:65); this means however that *the unbelief is determined by God*. This paradoxical-sounding dialectic between guilty unbelief and the blindness to Jesus decreed by God simply cannot be resolved psychologically.[233] What is expressed in the verse quoted from John 6 is rather a general phenomenon which Rudolph Bultmann in reference to 6:42 formulated thus: "The claim of revelation calls forth the contradiction of the world; it takes offense precisely in that it encounters revelation in history, in the sphere in which it is at ease and at home, that *it*, the world, wished to be the revealer, concerning whose 'whence' it is informed."[234] With this Bultmann has clearly seen that in the dispute in John 6, the concern is essentially about more than disputations held at one time in Capernaum, where they were localized (cf. 6:24, 59). Of course, it does not concern simply a world phenomenon either that has been projected back onto the historical level of Capernaum, but most probably also very concrete disputes between Jews and Christians about the christological mystery of Jesus at the time of the composition of the Gospel, that is, disputes concerning the fundamental question of all Christology: "Who is this one?"—a question which also appears in the Gospel of John expressly as such (cf. 8:25). According to Schnackenburg, in view of the "predestination" statements "the historical background and occasion are apparent";[235] "the group of the faithful chosen by God know themselves to be in the midst of an unbelieving world and under the pressure of attacks and persecutions join together more intensely and develop thereby their own self-understanding."[236] With this the Johannine community, as the rest of the primitive Church, also concerns itself with the problem of the "hardening" of Israel toward Jesus and the gospel, as is clearly expressed in John 12:37–40: "Though he had done so many signs before them, yet they did not believe in him; it was that the word spoken by the prophet Isaiah might be fulfilled: 'Lord, who has believed our report, and to whom has the arm of the Lord been revealed?' *Therefore they could not believe*. For Isaiah again said, 'He has blinded their eyes and hardened their heart, lest they should see with their eyes and perceive with their heart, and turn for me to heal them.' "[237]

Only the Easter Proclamation Can Lead to the Recognition of Jesus

Certainly the disciples who followed Jesus before Easter had certain experiences with Jesus, and doubtless the question as to who he really was also moved them. From their experience, from their act of seeing, there developed a reflection about Jesus.[238] However, one can say absolutely that their pre-Easter experience and their pre-Easter act of seeing would not have led them to the knowledge of the christological mystery of Jesus if the Easter experience had not intervened, that is, if the crucified and risen Jesus had not appeared to them. The appearances made Jesus "proclaimable," opened up the christological dimensions of the Scriptures, made the pre-Easter life of Jesus transparent to faith, and transmitted a new consciousness of history.[239] Jules Isaac has remarked: How then should all Israel have recognized him as the one whom the disciples, and with them the Church, after Easter confess and proclaim since he did not appear to all Israel, but rather "only to those who were chosen by God as witnesses," as can be read in the New Testament itself (cf. Acts 10:41)? Indeed, the crucified and risen Christ is proclaimed after Easter to "the whole house" and the "whole people" of Israel (cf. Acts 2:36; 4:10), and many Jews do convert to the Messiah Jesus, having been struck by the original apostolic mission preaching—according to the narratives of the Acts of the Apostles—but the great bulk remained unaccepting. The proclamation led to the "hardening" of Israel, which for the primitive Church, as the New Testament shows, became a great problem. Why did it happen thus? I have already dealt with this.[240] However, I now return to it once again in regard to Paul. In any case, the protest of Jules Isaac appears worth considering. For if Jesus after his resurrection from the dead had appeared to all Israel, then all Israel probably would have been overpowered by him, as were the apostles and the rest of the appearance witnesses, among them the Jew and Pharisee Paul. I know of no example in the New Testament of an appearance witness not coming to believe in Jesus. Why the Gentiles believed the kerygma without Jesus having appeared to them, while a large portion of the Jews did not, was and remains a mystery, a subject which the Apostle Paul dealt with in particular.

Paul's Epistle to the Romans, 9–11

Paul devoted himself to this question in Rom. 9–11; therefore we must once again return to these chapters of the Epistle to the Romans, and now from the following specific viewpoint: Guilty unbelief—hardening decreed by God. This problem is indissolubly bound up for Paul with the question: Why are the Gentiles obedient to the gospel, but the Jews not? The lines of the apostle's thought are difficult and, as exegetical experience shows, can at most be only approximately understood. Even a complete commentary on Rom. 9–11 is unable to do more.[241]

Of the statements about God, the very first is of great significance because it lifts up the sovereignty of the graceful choice of God, and indeed on the basis of an example from the Scriptures, namely, from the story of Esau and Jacob: God had loved Jacob the younger one and had hated Esau the older one (Gen. 25:23); the apostle develops this in Rom. 9:6–13. From the perspective of the "concept of God" he prepares on the one side for the calling of the Gentiles to the gospel and, on the other side, for the hardening of Israel toward it: God brings both about, *"in order that God's purpose of election might continue"* (9:11). He chooses whom he will, "not because of works," therefore, not on the basis of one's own righteousness.[242] "From that come the statements in the following verses about the divine election which in their harshness greatly surpass all other utterances on the matter" (Ernst Käsemann). To call in psychology or a salvation historical "development of thought" here as a help for understanding would be a vain effort. Indeed Paul recognizes the privileges of Israel in Rom. 9:4f.[243] Nevertheless, he rejects every claim which Israel could derive from them vis-à-vis God. The heritage from the fathers implies no ongoing continuity of salvation. What alone provides continuity is God's promising word. Therefore salvation history "can always again legitimately break off and even precisely within the area of earthly things and the history of the promise coming from Israel—as well as the Church (!), according to 1 Cor. 10:1–13—be transformed into an unsalvation history."[244]

This "predestination teaching," which is connected with the justification of the apostle and is not deduced from abstract premises but rather from Scripture itself, forms the key to understanding the apostle's further statements about Israel and the Gentiles in their different relationships toward the gospel, wherein Israel's attitude toward the pre-Easter Jesus plays no role. The question of Paul was not: How did the fatal clash between Israel and Jesus of Nazareth come about? Rather, it was: Why do the Gentiles heed the gospel which is proclaimed by missionaries, whereas the great bulk of Israel does not? However, the action of God according to his free choice is not some sort of sphinxlike action with demonic arbitrariness, as the apostle explains in Rom. 9:14–23. Paul understands thoroughly what objections might be brought against his theology here: If God acts thus, then he acts unjustly toward his people Israel! God shows here a demonic visage! Therefore Paul asks: "Is there injustice on God's part?" And he answers immediately: "By no means!" (9:15a). There is no injustice in God because God's driving motive for his action is mercy, which God stated to Moses according to Exod. 33:19: "I will have mercy on whom I have mercy, and I will have compassion on whom I have compassion" (Rom. 9:15b). Of course he not only has mercy on whom he will, but he also hardens whom he will (9:18). He allows "the vessels of anger," the majority of Jews, to remain hardened against the gospel, but not so as to deliver them to final corruption in the end, as once with Pharaoh. Rather, "he has endured them with much patience," which will definitively show itself in their ultimate saving (cf. 11:26), in order in the meanwhile "to make known the riches of his glory for the vessels of mercy" (9:23), that is, the Gentiles and that part of Israel which harkens to the gospel.[245]

The motif of the merciful God, which is met four times in 9:14–23, is again taken up at the end of Paul's developments in 11:32, but now in reference to the "hardened" Israel: "For God has consigned all men [Jews and Gentiles] to disobedience, *that he may have mercy upon all.*" First of all, however, God in his sovereign saving action makes "the people that was not my people," the Gentiles, into his people and into his beloved (9:25), while the majority of Israel remains hardened against the gospel. The apostle indicates why Israel deals so harshly with the gospel: It is zealously concerned about righteousness which comes from the Torah. However, in this it does not submit itself to that righteousness of God which comes from belief in Christ who "is the end of the law, that every one who has faith may be justified" (10:4; cf. 9:31—10:11).[246] In this Israel runs up against "the stumbling block" which God had put in Zion for Israel; it stumbles over it (9:32f.). "The stumbling block" is indeed no one other than Jesus Christ, the crucified and risen. However, the "emphasis in this by no means lies primarily on the death of Jesus or on the historical Jesus, but rather on the fact that Israel stumbles on, and according to God's plan must stumble on, the Messiah given to it by God consequent on the fulfilling of the promise. That stone was set up in Zion by God himself which ahead of time was determined to effect an offense and irritation."[247]

Why did and does Israel stumble on Christ, even if Jews say that they do not stumble on Jesus? From the context of Rom. 9:33 the answer is: Israel stumbles on Christ "insofar as the demand for faith requires a break with its religious past" (Ernst Käsemann), a break with the legal life according to the Torah (cf. 10:2–5), which Israel cannot carry out because it believes it would then be disobedient to God. The explanations of the apostle in Rom. 10 are clear about the tension of Law and gospel (cf. 10:4f. with 10:16). However, because the gospel (understood in Pauline fashion) proclaims Jesus Christ as the foundation of salvation, the initial question of whether Jesus was recognizable for Israel is continued with the post-Easter question: Was the gospel recognizable and acceptable for Easter? Indeed, even Israel heard the preaching of the gospel from which faith goes forth

(10:17f.), but it indeed could be—thus Paul asks further—that Israel had not understood (10:19a). The question itself, however, when looked at carefully, is not answered by the apostle. Rather, he comes back again to the Scriptures which predicted the obedience of the Gentiles to the preaching of the gospel (Deut. 32:21/Rom. 10:19b), but also the disobedience and contradiction of Israel toward whom God had reached out his hands the whole day long (Isa. 65:1/Rom. 10:20). If one looks still more closely, one will see that the apostle confirms the disobedience of Israel to the gospel, but there is no talk of a true indication of guilt by Israel which would demand punishment by God. Rather, Paul makes the affirmation: Gentiles harken to the gospel, while Israel on the other hand does not.

The question which logically arises from the hardening of the Jews toward the gospel can only be the one which the apostle immediately poses in 11:1: "Has God rejected his people?" Has he rejected his people Israel because it is not able to harken to the gospel? Perhaps rejected forever, as Christian theologians maintain to today? The apostle responded again: "By no means!" That God did not reject Israel is shown in the mission experience that a chosen "remnant" (the Jewish Christians) found the way to the gospel. For the rest, it is shown that God will at sometime save "the others" through the savior from Zion so that in the end "all Israel will be saved" (11:26b). These "others" were "hardened" toward the gospel; for according to the prediction of the Scripture (Deut. 29:3), God himself gave them "a spirit of stupor" so that "until this very day" they cannot see and hear (Rom. 11:8). The passive formulization "they were hardened," as well as the active formulation with the subject God as the one who lays upon Israel "a spirit of stupor," leaves no doubt that the apostle attributes the hardening of Israel toward the gospel ultimately to God as the real actor; that is, Paul remains true to his predestination theology developed in Rom. 9. It is God who hardens whom he will![248] "You will say to me then, 'Why does he [God] still find fault? For who can resist his will?' But, who are you, a man, to answer back to God?" (9:19f.).

The hardening of Israel by God is concretely discernible in the disobedience of Israel toward the gospel. Therefore, the hardening of Israel after Easter has its locus in the gospel; the gospel separates Israel—the Israel which remains true to the Torah—from the nations. With this, however, Paul is not satisfied. He asks further: "Have they stumbled so as to fall?" (11:11), namely, forever. Again comes the answer: "By no means!" Rather, says the apostle, "their failure means riches for the Gentiles" (11:12). In this sentence the apostle's own missionary experience is reflected. Nevertheless the question remains: What will happen to "fallen" Israel? The apostle does not avoid this question, rather he announces "the acceptance" of Israel, which for Israel will mean "life from death" (11:15), even for the dead of Auschwitz, for all the victims of the Holocaust. The Church is thereby admonished by the apostle not to raise itself above Israel, but to stand in fear before God who will not spare the Church as he did not spare Israel (11:20f.). Thus in Rom. 11 Paul binds the fate of the nations with Israel in an extraordinarily striking manner which remains hidden to the secular historians. Salvation for the nations has come precisely from the hardening of Israel, and when its "full number" is attained "all Israel will be saved." Thus in the end the power and the mercy of God triumph in that he brings the Jew and the Gentile into salvation—to be sure along paths which for the thinking and speculation of humankind are "unsearchable" (11:33).

What is attained with these extraordinary "paths" of the salvific leading of God? In any case this: *With it the Jew remains until the end of times a witness to the concreteness of salvation history, as well as to the impenetrability of the divine salvific leading.* The Torah helps the Jew remain the Jew. According to Exod. 9:16 (Rom. 9:17), God once hardened Pharaoh "for the purpose of showing my power in you [Pharaoh], so that my name may be proclaimed in all the earth." He also hardened Israel that in the end his power which is merciful to all and his divinity will be revealed to all the world.

Promises Still Unfulfilled by Jesus

What makes it difficult for the Jew to recognize Jesus of Nazareth as the promised one is above all the fact that there is a large "excess of promises" which Jesus has not yet fulfilled.[249] The Christian must take note of this objection because it is grounded: There are many still-unfulfilled promises. The Jew, however, must note that according to the conviction of Christians, a partial fulfillment has taken place in Jesus of Nazareth the crucified and risen one, and indeed to no small degree. Jesus himself speaks of this "fulfillment": according to the Nazareth pericope what was predicted by the prophet is fulfilled "today" in his word and in his actions. The waiting period is "fulfilled" and "the kingdom of God is at hand" (Mark 1:15): It breaks in with his teaching put forth in full power and in his mighty deeds. "But if it is by the Spirit of God that I cast out demons, then [*ara*] the kingdom of God has come upon you" (Matt. 12:28/Luke 11:20). To the inquiry of the Baptist: "Are you he who is to come, or shall we look for another?" Jesus responds: "Go and tell John *what you hear and see*: the blind receive their sight and the lame walk, lepers are cleansed and the deaf hear, and the dead are raised up, and the poor have good news preached to them" (Matt. 11:2–5; cf. Isa. 29:18f.; 35:5f.; 65:1). Likewise, Jesus did not come to do away with the Law or the prophets, but rather "to fulfill them" (Matt. 5:17). Thus Jesus of Nazareth himself possessed a "consciousness of fulfillment."

The post-Easter Church which reflected on Jesus, his word and work, his violent death and his resurrection from the dead, was convinced in its faith that the Scriptures were "fulfilled" in Jesus, his work and his fate (cf., for example, the so-called reflection citations in the Gospels: "This took place that the Scriptures might be fulfilled. . . . " "Here the word of the Scripture was fulfilled"). Even if one can (correctly) point out that in this regard the enlightening "Easter grace" (in Johannine language, "the paraclete") was at work, it nevertheless cannot be denied that the pre-Easter Jesus already possessed a "consciousness of fulfillment" and that his works were open to the naturally largely post-Easter recognition that in him the promises of the Old Testament were fulfilled so that the Church could and can proclaim him as the Promised One. With this was and is assured for the Church the continuity of the old, as it was expressed in the Old Testament, with the new, as it was revealed in Jesus: The God who acted in Israel also acted in Jesus. It is in this revealing action of God in Jesus of Nazareth, especially in the death and resurrection of Jesus, that the Church has its legitimate place alongside Israel, even though the Jew sees the continuation of salvation and the saving action of God other than does the Christian. However, the Christian may not break his staff over the Jew on this. For God alone ultimately knows why the Jew sees things other than does the Christian, and why for him Jesus of Nazareth was and is not recognizable and therefore also unacceptable. Jesus' offer to Israel of the reign of God was doubtless meant seriously, and Jesus spoke his "woe" to Chorazin, Bethsaida, and Capernaum (Matt. 11:20–24/Luke 10:13–15) and thereby affirmed that there was guilt. Nevertheless, there remains the fact that the majority of Israel did not recognize him for various reasons, of which I have named several important ones. For if one looks at what I attempted to say to the initial question of whether Jesus of Nazareth was recognizable to Israel—and it was in fact only an attempt—it must therefore be answered, in careful formulation: It was difficult for Israel to recognize Jesus and the gospel. The unveiling of the word in the incarnate Christ was at the same time a veiling. The seeing of the glory of the only begotten of the Father in Jesus is possible only for the believer enlightened by the Holy Spirit. Søren Kierkegaard was completely right in his demand: Whoever wishes to test his faith should practice "contemporaneity." He should make himself in spirit a compatriot and fellow townsman of Jesus of Nazareth; he should

transport himself in spirit to the synagogue of Nazareth and there hear from
the mouth of the carpenter Jesus the "today" spoken with such claims
("today this scripture has been fulfilled in your hearing" [Luke 4:21]). If he
then can say: "Of course I would have recognized him as the Promised One
and would have greeted him as the Messiah"—only then can he likewise
say with an honest conscience: "I believe." However, which of us Christians
can say this "of course"? Presumably none. Therefore, no one should cast
stones at the "hardened" Israel, but rather praise the inscrutable ways of
God, as Paul does in Rom. 11:33–36 at the end of his difficult discussion of
the hardening and the final salvation of Israel. For likewise no Christian
was the "counselor" of God.

"The 'riches,' the wisdom and the knowledge of God appear to Paul to be
'unsearchably deep.' From all eternity they have thought and wisely directed and ordered all things, and against all expectations lead everything
to a good end. 'God's judgments are unsearchable,' that is, his work in
salvation history, especially his mysterious work in Israel. Impenetrable
darkness surrounds the eternal decisions of God. . . . 'For who has known
the mind of the Lord,' for no one ever has sat in his council as his
'counselor.' There is no access for human beings to the ultimate thoughts of
God. They were and remain out of our reach. Is God obliged to report
something in this regard where no one has given him something
beforehand?"[250]

6

That Which Distinguishes
and Divides

CHRISTOLOGY

The "Un-Jewish" in Jesus?

Whoever in ecumenical work loves intellectual honesty can and may not be silent about that which divides and distinguishes. This is especially true for those Christian theologians who write a tractate on the Jews. Of course, the converse would be equally true for Jews who would put forth a tractate on Christians. Every knowledgeable person realizes that the things which divide and distinguish concern Christology. As much as we today again recognize Jesus of Nazareth as a Jew, we also know that it is the Christian teaching about Jesus, which usually is called Christology, which divides Christians and Jews from one another, and presumably will always divide them.[1] In Christian faith it is above all the Son of God Christology which is the great stumbling block for the Jews. The Jewish scholar H.-J. Schoeps wrote in his book on Paul: "Paul raised the Messiah [Jesus] above all human measure to the status of a real divinity—that is the radically *un-Jewish element* in the thinking of the apostle. Here there are no further possibilities of the Jewish derivations, but rather—if a derivation at all—the assumption of a connection with the pagan-mythological presentations, filtered through the Hellenistic syncretism time, is unavoidable."[2] Further: "This myth of the stepping down, the atoning death and rising up of the heavenly human being is radically un-Jewish."[3]

"We see in the *huios theou* belief—and only in it—the sole, although indeed decisive, pagan premise of Pauline thought. Everything which is connected with it or results from it . . . is un-Jewish and leads near to the pagan presentations of the time."[4] Likewise J. Klausner remarked in his book on Jesus: "For the Jewish people naturally [Jesus] can be neither a God nor God's Son in the sense of the dogma of the Trinity: both for Jews are not only blasphemous, but also incomprehensible."[5] Indeed, Klausner reflects in the same book: "The teaching of Jesus is far from the dogma of the Trinity, but it contains it in a kernel, from which the Gentile Christians could develop the late-Christian doctrine on the tri-unity."[6]

The question for us is whether this "radically un-Jewish" element, especially the Son Christology, is mistakenly connected with what Klausner has designated as that "something" from which the "un-Jewish element developed."[7] In what does it consist, according to Klausner? Essentially in the following things:[8]

1. In the all-too-extreme demands of the ethics of Jesus.

2. In the radical reduction of the Torah to the law of love, which neglects the sanctification of the everyday through legal specifications.

3. In the anational character of the preaching of Jesus: Jesus no longer saw the connection between religion and people.

4. In the concept of God of Jesus, who told his disciples "to love your enemies as well as your friends, 'since your Father in heaven lets his sun shine upon the evil and the good, and lets his rain fall upon the unjust and the just,' for here Jesus goes beyond that justification of the Pharisees who had attacked him because of his association with tax collectors and sinners and to whom he had responded: 'The sick need the physician, not the healthy.' Here it is not at all a question of sick: In the view of God tax collectors and sinners are 'healthy'; sinner and non-sinner, good and wicked, just and unjust, they are all equal 'before God.' " However, according to Klausner "the Jewish concept of God" is this: "The evil are not worthy that the sun should shine on them."[9] For "the sinners who do not repent destroy the world, disrupt the moral and thereby also the natural ordering of the world. If there is no justice in this world, then there is no point in its continuing with its sun and its moon, its stars and its firm laws of nature . . . as noble as the concept of God of Jesus might be for the individual moral consciousness—for the general, social, national and universal consciousness, for whom 'world history is the world judge,' it means ruin and chaos. Judaism could make such a concept its own under no circumstances."[10]

Today's Jewish scholars of the life of Jesus will indeed think differently than Klausner of what Jesus' "concept of God" concerns. However, they also seem to be aware that somehow an "un-Jewish" element in Jesus of Nazareth was at work by which, for Jewish sensitivities, he seemed to fall outside the framework of Judaism. However, the "un-Jewish" element is to be looked for much less in the matters to which Klausner pointed, than in the unheard-of claim which Jesus raised in Israel.

The Claim of Jesus

Wherein above all did Jesus make an unusual claim? I would like to mention the following points:

1. In the spontaneous knowledge of the manner of God's thinking which was revealed in Jesus' own concrete actions. Thus Jesus justifies his ostentatious taking of meals with "tax collectors and sinners," according to Luke 15, with the theory put forth in the three subsequent parables: He must act thus with sinners because God is pleased when those who are lost find their way home. Jesus acts thus as, according to his teaching, God himself acts. "The attitude of Jesus declares the will of God with a parable which is deducible from the attitude of Jesus."[11] For the rest, in the three parables in Luke 15 the concern is not merely with that which is lost, but with the integration of *all*, whether lost or not lost, into a unity and wholeness. Jesus wanted to gather *all* Israel about him.[12] Behind this spontaneous knowledge concerning the manner of God's thinking, there is, however, Jesus' claim, namely, of knowing God better than his opponents, and indeed not merely better than his opponents, but also better than the official theologians of Israel, the scribes. Behind the spontaneous knowledge of Jesus concerning the manner of God's thinking and the essence of God's lordship, there lies a "primordial disclosure" which is connected with his sonship mystery.[13]

2. In the teaching of Jesus which takes place in "full power," and not "in the manner of the scribes" (Mark 1:21), and which is given not as "the saying of YHWH," as with the prophets, but rather as his own authoritative word.

3. In the full power claimed by Jesus to forgive sins (cf. especially Mark 2:1–12;[14] Luke 7:36–50[15]). For Judaism the forgiveness of sins is a prerogative of God, "which according to Jewish interpretation is likewise not given to the Messiah or to the Son of man.[16] Whoever speaks like Jesus . . . blasphemes . . . . According to Lev. 24:11ff. and Num. 15:30, the punishment for blaspheming God is death."[17]

4. In the claim to be something "greater," as is expressed in certain short Logia of Jesus: "Something greater than Jonah is here" (Matt. 12:41/Luke 11:32), that is, "greater" than a prophet of the Old Covenant; "something greater than Solomon is here" (Matt. 12:42/Luke 11:31), that is, "greater" than one of the great and highly honored kings of the early time of Israel; "something greater than the temple is here" (Matt. 12:6), that is, "greater" than the holy place which, according to the believing conviction of Judaism, is the dwelling place of God on earth and as such possesses a completely extraordinary rank in the consciousness of Judaism,[18] of which one must take note if one wishes to understand the claim which Jesus raised precisely with the Temple Logion. Indeed, the claim which he raised with these Logia is hidden first of all in the puzzling "here" (*hōde*) and in the

comparative of the neuter ("greater"—*meizon*—"more"—*pleion*), but there is no doubt that with it he was referring to himself: *He* is the "greater" and the "more."[19] Has another Jew ever spoken thus? Here the "un-Jewishness" in the self-awareness of Jesus shows itself in a special degree.

5. In the claim that the Son of man is to be identified with Jesus, as is clear from the statements of the "confessors and deniers" (Luke 12:8f. and par.),[20] indeed, that he himself is that "Son of man" whom his opponents in the trial will see "sitting at the right hand of Power, and coming with the clouds of heaven" (Mark 14:62). The chief priest judged Jesus' statements to be blasphemy and asked his fellow members of the Sanhedrin: "What is your decision? And they all condemned him as deserving death" (Mark 14:63f.). They considered him guilty of death because "especially . . . of the blasphemy of God of Jesus who gave himself out to be the 'Son of man' who 'would come with the clouds of heaven and sit at the right hand of God.' "[21] With this the following points are connected.

6. I attempted to show (above, pp. 188ff.) that it was ultimately the claim of Jesus expressed in the title "Son of God" which made Jesus guilty of death in the eyes of the Sanhedrin, whether or not Jesus had applied this title expressly as a self-designation. In any case, his claim transcended every claim made until that time by a human being in Israel, even the claim of Messiah; it is in this clear and unavoidable transcendence that the real "un-Jewishness" of Jesus lies which for Jewish sensitivities placed him outside of Judaism.

It was, therefore, not, for example, the question of the Law on the basis of which the action of Jesus in Israel was felt to be "un-Jewish," as is maintained now and again by Christian theologians. Naturally, the sovereign explanation of the Law by Jesus is connected with his claim, and therefore, it is often felt as something which apparently falls outside the framework of Judaism, as for example, his explanation of the law of the Sabbath ("the Son of man is lord even of the Sabbath" [Mark 2:28]). "The words of Jesus concerning the Sabbath are . . . an expression of his *exousia* [power], with which he proclaimed."[22]

7. With this unique claim of Jesus there is also connected his own "consciousness of the time" and his "consciousness of fulfillment": The reign of God breaks in now because *he* is there. "But if it is by the Spirit of God that *I* cast out demons, *then the kingdom of God has come upon you*" (Matt. 12:28/Luke 11:20). "Heal the sick in it and say to them [the inhabitants of the city], 'The kingdom of God has come near to you'" (Luke 10:9; cf. Matt. 10:7f.). "Blessed are the eyes which see what you see! For I tell you that many prophets and kings desired to see what you see, and did not

see it, and to hear what you hear, and did not hear it" (Luke 10:23f./Matt. 13:16f.). "And he began to say to them [his neighbors in Nazareth], 'Today this scripture has been fulfilled in your hearing' " (Luke 4:21). "The law and the prophets were until John; since then the good news of the kingdom of God is preached" (Luke 16:16).[23] "The kingdom of God is not coming with signs to be observed; nor will they say, 'Lo, here it is!' or 'There!' for behold, the kingdom of God is in the midst of you" (Luke 17:20f.).[24] "The time is fulfilled, and the kingdom of God is at hand" (Mark 1:15).[25]

Though one or other of these Logia of Jesus were reworked after Easter, there can be no doubt that Jesus had an especial "consciousness of a break": The time of expectation and promise was coming to an end, and a new time, the final time, the time of the eschatological reign of God, the time of fulfillment, is breaking in now *with him.*[26] With this Jesus "is the only ancient Jew known to us who not only proclaimed that he was standing at the break of the end of time, but also simultaneously that the new time of salvation had already begun."[27] How did Jesus know that the time of salvation began with him? With what right did he bind the eschatological events of that reign of God so indissolubly to his person and to his claim if he had not been filled with an exclusive "self-consciousness" and "con-sciousness of being sent"? Christology attempts to give an answer to the puzzling elements of the person of Jesus which are reflected in these questions.[28] To cite Flusser here once again: "Not only historians but theologians should meditate more deeply on the extent of the historical Jesus' own ideas of authority, and whether there exists a bridge between his self-perception and the 'post-Easter' faith in Christ. If it were true, as certain pulpit Christians maintain with masochistic, self-destructive rage, that Jesus did not think of himself as someone special or even as rather significant, and that his claims to sovereignty belonged to the period after history and that of the Church, then, I think, the Christian faith loses all claim to credibility."[29]

8. Connected with this is the fact that the message of Jesus concerning which the breaking in of the reign of God has already begun is primarily a message of grace.[30] Indeed, Jesus has not eliminated the thoughts of judgment from his message of the reign, but the saving aspects predomi-nate by far in his preaching of the reign and in his actions concerning the reign of God. His driving out of demons; his healings of the sick; his taking meals with "tax collectors and sinners"; his parables of kindly owners of vineyards, of the lost sheep, of the lost drachma, and of the lost son are proof enough that for him the reign of God is above all a reign of kindness, of grace, and of forgiveness. In and of itself, the message of grace would not

necessarily have to place him outside the framework of Judaism—Judaism also knows and indeed proclaims God as the kind one, as the merciful one. However, in indissoluble connection with his claim which shines through everywhere, an "un-Jewishness" shows itself in much of what Jesus of Nazareth said and did, an "un-Jewishness" which in connection with his fate led him in the end out of Judaism.[31] This means also, however, that it is not only by the Christology which was developed after Easter by the Christian community that Jesus and Israel are divided. Further, this does not mean that Christology is only a product of the reception of pagan Hellenism by the Christian community, especially by the Gentile-Christian Church, as is often claimed by Jewish scholars of the life of Jesus—in which of course they could and can base themselves on Christian "historians of religion." Pehaps Jews like Klausner sense a certain "un-Jewishness" in Jesus even more strongly than do Christians; in any case they perceive the Son of God Christology as something plainly pagan. The problem, however, is this: whether something genuinely Jewish stands in the background of this Christology. That will be shown in the following.

From the "Prophet" Jesus to the "Son" Jesus[32]

Jesus was at home in Nazareth of Galilee. After he had begun to appear publicly in Israel he came one day, according to the Gospel of Mark, "to his own country; and his disciples followed him. And on the Sabbath he began to teach in the synagogue; and many who heard him were astonished, saying, 'Where did this man get all this? What is the wisdom given to him? What mighty works are wrought by his hands! Is not this the carpenter, the son of Mary and brother of James and Joses and Judas and Simon, and are not his sisters here with us?' And they took offense at him. And Jesus said to them, 'A prophet is not without honor, except in his own country, and among his own kin, and in his own house' " (Mark 6:1–4).

From this narrative we learn that Jesus lived in Nazareth, that he was a carpenter by trade, and that his kin also lived in Nazareth. To the "offense" which his fellow townsmen took in him after his public appearance, Jesus remarked: "No prophet is honored in his own country, and among his own kin, and in his own house." With this Jesus of Nazareth clearly makes the claim to be something like a prophet himself. The opinions among the people of Israel concerning the question of who this man of Nazareth really is appear to have also gone in this direction. Two further reports from the Gospel of Mark point to this. In 6:14f. Mark relates the following: "King Herod heard of it; for Jesus' name had become known. Some said, 'John the baptizer has been raised from the dead; that is why these powers are at work in him.' But others said, 'It is Elijah.' And others said, 'It is a prophet, like one of the prophets of old.' "

According to Mark 8:27f. Jesus himself one day asked his disciples: "Who do people say that I am?" They however said to him: "John the Baptist; and others say, Elijah; and others one of the prophets." At the raising up of the young man from Nain by Jesus Luke remarked: "Fear seized them all; and they glorified God, saying, 'A great prophet has arisen among us!' and 'God has visited his people!' " (Luke 7:16). The two disciples who were walking toward Emmaus on Easter Sunday described the experience which they had had with Jesus of Nazareth thus: "Concerning Jesus of Nazareth, who was a prophet mighty in deed and word before God and all the people" (Luke 4:19). According to John 6:14 the people who were witnesses of the miracle of the bread said: "This is indeed the prophet who is to come into the world!" According to John 7:40 the people who were the witnesses of the speeches of Jesus said the same thing: "This is really the prophet." The healed blind man answered the question: "What do you say about him, since he has opened your eyes" with: "He is a prophet" (John 9:17). According to Luke 13:13, Jesus said: "It cannot be that a prophet should perish away from Jerusalem." To this G. Friedrich remarked: "Also here, as in Mark 6:4, we are dealing not with a self-designation of Jesus, but with the citation of a general view. However, because Jesus not only agrees with this view, but also sets about to realize it, he places himself among the number of the prophets."[33] As Jesus, according to Matt 21:10f., "entered Jerusalem, all the city was stirred, saying, 'Who is this?' And the crowds said, 'This is the prophet Jesus from Nazareth of Galilee.' " And in 21:46 the evangelist Matthew comments: "But when they tried to arrest him, they feared the multitudes, because they held him to be a prophet."

One can in summary say first of all[34] Jesus of Nazareth indeed did not expressly designate himself as "prophet," but the people, the witnesses of his works, held him to be a prophet. In several places of the New Testament Jesus really is seen as the promised prophet of the end of times in reference to Deut. 18:15.[35] At the end Friedrich comes to the conclusion: "That Jesus nowhere expressly designated himself as an eschatological prophet cannot be viewed as evidence that he did not see himself as a prophet, but rather it corresponds to the rest of his proclamation which preserved the messianic secret. However, he did speak and act as a prophet."[36] Many actions of Jesus can be subsumed under the aspect of the prophet. In the prophetic tradition there belong, to name the most important, the following: the call of Jesus, his consciousness of being sent, his critique of the Torah and cult, his instructions to be followed (in any case in part), his condemnatory statements (threats and woes), his symbolic acts and deeds of wonder, his gift of the Spirit, and finally his violent death. [37]

Thus it is understandable that in the beginning, especially in the Palestine Jewish-Christian area of the primitive Church, the prophet Christology widely dominated the field. Was it later driven out by the Son Christology? Perhaps under the influence of Hellenism as the Christian mission crossed the borders of the Holy Land and in defense against tendencies in Jewish Christianity which perhaps showed themselves early as perceiving in Jesus nothing other than a prophet (see the Pseudo Clementines)?[38] Or was there the possibility of an organic transposition of the prophet Christology into the Son Christology? Oscar Cullmann thinks that the presentation of Jesus as "of the prophets" is stated in the New Testament only as an opinion of the people which perhaps "was especially widespread in Galilee."[39] F. Hahn, indeed, sees "that the person and work of Jesus was described in an early stage of the tradition particularly with the help of this image (namely, of the eschatological prophet), but this was wiped out and covered over by later christological statements. But of course the peculiarities of this ancient Christology can still be perceived."[40] I too was for a long time of the same opinion until the book of U. Mauser, *The Image of God and the Incarnation*,[41] came into my hands. This work helped me not only to see the "prophet Christology" in a new light, but also to perceive it as the decisive preliminary step of the "Son Christology" and to grasp this latter finally not merely in its origin, but also in the meaning of its statement. Indeed, it must occur to everyone in the study of the Gospels that the ancient prophet Christology of the initial period of the primitive Church has in no way been suppressed in the redaction of the Gospels. The Gospels indeed are the major source for the knowledge of it. From this, however, there arises the question: Why did the evangelists not suppress it, but rather bind it together with the Son Christology, indeed in such a way that the latter encompasses the former and interprets it in this encompassing and moves beyond it to a higher level? How does Mauser see the question?

Mauser proceeds from an essay of the Old Testament scholar W. Zimmerli, "Verheissung und Erfüllung,"[42] in which Zimmerli establishes a twofold state of affairs (I formulate them according to Mauser): "(1) It can be shown that the apparent fulfillment of a concrete promise in the Old Testament itself is robbed of finality and in turn anew becomes the basis for a new promise which goes far beyond the apparently already-attained fulfillment"; (2) "the expectation of Israel at basis did not turn in general toward this or that item, but rather to the coming of God himself."[43]

Zimmerli cites the word of the prophet Amos (4:12): "Prepare yourselves to meet your God, Israel!" He says "that in the midst of all of the promised things there is the coming Lord himself."[44] Mauser then brings this already proleptic promise into connection with its fulfillment in Jesus Christ: "The coming of God in the New Testament indeed concretely is the coming in the history of a human being, and that is the uniqueness of the New Testament's message, namely, that God does his entire work in the history of a human being."[45] From this perspective Mauser poses the question: "Is it possible—indeed, from the essence of the Old Testament promise, is it demanded—that the expectation that the coming of God as a human being is to be found witnessed to in the Old Testament?"[46] While for Rudolph Bultmann that human life which is bound up with the name of Jesus of Nazareth possesses significance only insofar "as it is the presupposition of the coming of the kerygma,"[47] according to Mauser the eschatological coming of YHWH, predicted by the prophets precisely in the human story of Jesus, is to be seen in his pre-Easter life through his violent death and through his resurrection. "The human story of Jesus Christ is, as the basis of the Christian kerygma, the word of God. This human story, therefore, shows itself as the point of convergence of the directions of the questions which are posed by the Old as well as by the New Testament." With this the question is raised "whether it might not be possible to think through anew the problem of the relationship between the Old and the New Testament from this new convergence point. In reference to the Old Testament the question is raised in this form: If the Old Testament is to be understood as promise which expects the coming of God concretely as his coming in the form of a human history, it must therewith be asked whether the image of God of the Old Testament provides characteristics which point to the inclination of God toward becoming human. At the same time an image of the human would have to correspond to it which showed human life so ordered to the fulfillment of the word of God to become the history of a human being. From the perspective of the New Testament, however, it is to be asked whether the history which Christian theology for centuries described as the becoming human of God can be so understood as an authentically human history, so that it corresponds to the fundamental structures of the Old Testament image of God and humanity."[48]

In order to clarify his program for the reader Mauser points to the so-called anthropomorphisms of the Old Testament, which for him are "signs of a God who is not alien to the human, but rather in the participation in the history of the human associates himself with the human. To this there simultaneously corresponds the human image of the Old Testament which

... in a certain sense is theomorphic," precisely because according to the Creation story the human being is the "image and likeness" of God. With an allusion to the formulation of the Christ hymn in the Epistle to the Philippians, Mauser says: "The Old Testament God *en morphē anthrōpou* is the announcement of the *Deus incarnatus*. And the human being of the Old Testament who in a certain sense experiences his life *en morphē theou* is the messenger of the human being Jesus which corresponds to the Christian confession *vere Deus*."[49] With this Mauser established his theme. In the portion of his book which is devoted to the Old Testament, he carries it out in a threefold move in such a way that he first of all works out further the theological meaning of the "anthropomorphisms," and then interprets the fate of the prophets Hosea and Jeremiah on the basis of their texts so that in their fate the fate of YHWH himself becomes visible in the painful and suffering conversation with his people Israel, and the prophets of the Old Covenant become known not merely as critics of the establishment in Israel and as predictors of salvation and condemnation, but rather as the *representatio* of YHWH. "The God of Israel is a God full of pathos, and prophecy is the inspired communication of the divine pathos through the consciousness of the prophet,"[50] formulates Mauser in agreement with the book of the Jewish scholar Abraham Heschel, *The Prophets*.[51]

Concerning the anthropomorphisms Mauser remarks: "The anthropomorphisms of YHWH stand in a corresponding relationship to the creation of the human being in the image of God and they illuminate each other mutually."[52] Mauser cites J. Hempel: "To be the image of God means for the human being . . . to be God's vizier."[53] The Old Testament anthropomorphisms were "not only not a time-bound naiveté . . ." but rather contained "on the contrary a conscious theology."[54] Mauser refers to the book of the Old Testament scholar H. Wheeler Robinson, *The Cross of Hosea* (1949), in which Robinson, especially in reference to the first three chapters concerning the marriage of the prophet, analyzes them "in a way which opens up an entirely new dimension in the problem of the anthropomorphisms."[55] The history of the marriage of the prophet serves "as a human illustration of a divine truth." "This has first of all a significance for the concept of relevation. As long as revelation is viewed as the communication of truth, the process of revelation continues to be thought of mechanically: The human being who receives the revelation is merely a writer who records a dictation. However, the Book of Hosea allows the judgment that such a mechanical understanding does not correspond to the real process of revelation. For in Hosea"—Mauser here quotes Robinson verbatim—"'We see that the revelation is made in and through a human experience, in which experience the truth to be revealed is first created,' and from this it follows, 'that human experience is capable of representing the divine . . . revelation [which] is made through the unity of fellowship between God and man and is born of their intercourse.' That means nothing less than that already in the Old Testament revelation was essentially related to the incarnation insofar as the transmitter of revelation (the prophet) took a part in the revelation with his own existence, indeed, that his life was the place in which the revelation arose and was the means by which it communicated itself."[56]

For the question concerning anthropomorphisms, it follows from this that the Old Testament anthropomorphisms in no way "are mere accommodations to human weakness which lacks expressive images for the truth of a living God"; rather, the care and love of God express themselves not merely in human speech, but are also representatively reflected in the life experience and in the fate of the prophet. The love and care of Hosea are "not only symbols of a divine attitude toward the world, but real correspondences to an equally completely real love and care of God. If, however, the real love and care of God are to be spoken of in all seriousness, then clearly the dogma of the impassibility of God cannot be maintained."[57] "Anthropomorphism" in this sense is therefore "the announcement of God's becoming human."[58] And the prophet "is the person who not only knows the pathos of God so that he can communicate it, but experiences it in and of itself so that he is impressed by it in his existence."[59] The true mystery of prophecy then may be thus formulated: It is "sympathy with the divine pathos."[60] "If there is however a pathos of God, there is also flowing from it and called forth by it a pathos of the prophet which is related to the pathos of God as a mirror. The prophet therefore is by no means only the proclaimer of the decision and instruction of God; he is at the same time and first of all a presentation of God's true position in the history of his world."[61] From this it follows that the prophet is distinguished from his contemporaries in "that he knows what time it is and proclaims the time as the time of God."[62] The kernel of the prophetic existence "is the participation in the relationship to his human beings in history which is determined by the concrete hour of God."[63] In the prophet God becomes "human in form," he appears in him *en morphē anthrōpou,* which naturally does not mean that the divine nature "confuses" itself with the human, or that God is "taken up into" the prophet.

With this Mauser has pointed out an important path. He himself continues his theses still further with the prophetic figures of Hosea and Jeremiah. Hosea "can act with signs because he himself already has become a sign of God."[64] "The commission of YHWH makes the prophet not only a messenger who repeats what he has heard. Rather, the word of God creates a human life which in a human manner participates in the history of God."[65] The anthropomorphic speech of the Old Testament "intends to present a God who so takes the human to himself that he himself can be represented by a concrete human being."[66] The prophet "takes the position which God in his history takes with his people, and he shares the fate of God which YHWH experiences at the concrete time of his turning toward them. He is therefore not only a speaker for God, but also the representative and parable of YHWH."[67] In this way, "the becoming human of God is prepared in the documents of the faith of Israel."[68]

The New Testament lies completely along this line. For it describes "in the work of Jesus of Nazareth, in his word as well as in his action, the work of God."[69] The New Testament identifies precisely "the event of a human life (namely, that of Jesus of Nazareth) with the word and deed of God. . . . It has thereby spoken of God with much broader and more expressive forms of human language and action, human will and decision, than ever happened in the Old Testament. The anthropomorphism of God in the Old Testament is thus carried to such an extreme in the New Testament that one can grasp the New Testament only as its insurpassable culmination point."[70]

Whoever can agree with what has been laid out up to this point will now also agree to my own thesis: The so-called prophet Christology of the Gospels is in the New Testament no christological "minor crater" which would be quickly covered over; rather, from its essence it quickly leads further christological reflection of the primitive Church logically to the Son Christology. What did the circle of disciples in their vision ultimately experience in Jesus of Nazareth? I would answer: A unity of action extending to the point of congruence of Jesus with God, an unheard-of existential imitation of God by Jesus. But precisely the idea of imitation of God is at home in Jewish thinking.[71] In order to articulate this expression in words in the post-Easter reflection, the title of the Son gradually came forth as if by itself. For ancient oriental sensibilities, the sonship of the first born manifests itself in the precise imitation of the father! If one compares the material in the synoptic tradition for a Messiah Christology with that for a prophet Christology, the latter is by far predominant, as the work of F. Schnider shows. As I emphasized above, almost all of the actions of Jesus can be subsumed under "prophet Christology." "A great prophet has risen among us and God has visited his people" (Luke 7:16); "A prophet mighty in deed and word" (Lk. 24:19): those are the impressions one has of Jesus.

Even in the Gospel of John[72] with its highly reflected Son Christology, the christological prophet model still plays a great role.[73]

In no way do I wish to say that the New Testament Son Christology had as its starting point only the initial prophet Christology. For "Son" is no mere substitution for "prophet." Beyond the experience of Jesus as prophet there was added the experience of Jesus as *meizon* ("greater than") and *pleion* ("more than"), likewise witnessed by the Gospels, which broke through the prophet model. Nevertheless, it should be shown that the christological Son model can *to a large extent* (even if by no means completely) be made understandable by the prophet model, and thereby the New Testament–Christian Son Christology could lose much of its scandalous character for the Jews. The linguistic model for the Son Christology has been provided by the Old Testament and Judaism, especially in the Wisdom teaching.[74] The prophet in his faith is the manifestation of the pathos of God; he moves in a unity of action in his speech and deeds with the one God. Thus seen, the New Testament–Christian Son Christology is not the paganization and the acute Hellenization of strict monotheism as Judaism and Islam represent it. Rather, it lies much more along the line of the teaching of the self-expression and self-emptying of a God into the world. As is well known, the Church as well as Judaism and Islam has through all time held fast to a strict monotheism, although since its beginnings it has proclaimed Jesus of Nazareth as the Son of God and still so proclaims today. The objection of Judaism and of Islam to the Son Christology will also endure. However, the "prophet model" together with the "Wisdom model" can provide a common basis for discussion, and perhaps also create for Jews a certain mental access to the Son Christology, without their having to profess it.[75]

Dialogue with Rosemary Ruether

In her book *Faith and Fratricide*[76] Rosemary Ruether attacks the theological roots of anti-Semitism. The book is doubtless penetrating, disturbing, and upsetting. Whoever engages in a critical dialogue with it must proceed carefully. A refutation is not easy. I shall limit myself essentially to the theses of the author concerning Christology, which in the subtitle to chapter 5, section 4 she designates as "the key issue"—and it is that in fact.

The Theses of Rosemary Ruether

According to Ruether, Christology was "always the other side of anti-Judaism."[77] With this, Christology is above all understood as a "historicizing of the eschatological," that is, as the teaching that with Jesus of

Nazareth the "ultimate," the "redemption" had come into the world, whereas the world in reality showed itself, after as before, in a highly unredeemed condition, to which fact Judaism steadfastly pointed. "Realized eschatology," as Christology largely understood itself, "converts each of the dialectics we have examined—judgment and promise, particularism and universalism, letter and spirit, history and eschatology[78]—into dualisms, applying one side to the 'new messianic people,' the Christians, and the negative side to the 'old people,' the Jews. The message of messianic expectations is imported into history and reified as a historical event in a way that makes it a reality-denying, rather than a reality-discerning principle. Evil is declared to have been conquered once-for-all by the Messiah. His victory has been established as the Catholic Church."[79]

"For Israel, the coming of the Messiah and the coming of the Messianic Age are inseparable. They are, in fact, the same thing. Israel's messianic hope was not for the coming of a redemptive person whose coming would not change the outward ambiguity of human and social existence, but for the coming of that Messianic Age which, as Engels was to put it, is 'the solution to the riddle of history.' "[80] "The attribution of an absolute finality to the heightened expectations surrounding the life and death of Jesus must be regarded as a flawed way of appropriating the real meaning of eschatological encounter. This historicizing of the eschatological has most serious consequences. Both Christian anti-Semitism and patterns of totalitarianism and imperialism that have appeared in Christendom (and its secular revolutionary stepchildren) find their root in this error."[81]

What can be said about this?

A Critical Dialogue with Rosemary Ruether

1. First of all it cannot be denied that the New Testament and Christian proclamation of the "already present" of salvation in Christ has often led to churchly triumphalism and can be a root of theological anti-Judaism: The Messiah has already come, the Jews do not recognize that and are therein themselves guilty, and for this guilt God himself continually punishes them. Jewish existence is really an anachronistic existence! Through their "hardening" the Jews have "outlived" themselves. Their continued existence *post Christum* is therefore a disturbing factor of the first rank, as history shows. "The assertion that the Jews are reprobate because they did not accept Christ as having already come is really a projection upon Judaism of that unredeemed side of itself that Christianity must constantly deny in order to assert that Christ has already come and founded 'the Church.' The Jews represent that which Christianity must repress in itself,

that is to say, the recognition of history and Christian existence as unredeemed."[82]

2. The issue is clearly the disturbing proclamation of the Church that the eschatological salvation in Christ since the death and resurrection of Jesus is already present in the world, that is, it concerns the *Presentia Salutis*. Now that in fact is the faith conviction of the Church. Likewise, since the days of the apostles it is its conviction that eschatological salvation can be proclaimed only in the name of Jesus; cf. Acts 4:12: "And there is salvation in no one else, for there is no other name under heaven given among men by which we must be saved." Even God had ordained it; thus, it "must" be— expressed in the Greek New Testament often with the verb *dei* ("it must"). The Church cannot turn away from this divine ordaining; otherwise it would be directly disobedient to God. It must proclaim in the world: God has already sent the one through whom the world will be saved (cf. John 3:17). "But when the time had fully come, God sent forth his Son, born of woman, born under the law, to redeem those who were under the law, so that we might receive adoption as sons" (Gal. 4:4f.). The latter is indeed a Pauline formation, but with the reception of pre-Pauline, common primitive Church statements of faith.[83] The Son is there. Does this lead to a "false reifying of the experience of the eschatological in history," and does a "false consciousness" thereby arise, as Ruether thinks?[84] It can lead to that, and in the history of the Church and theology it often has led to that, always where the presence of salvation was absolutized or indeed politicized (as in the Byzantine or medieval "kingdom ideology") and the future was forgotten; also, always when the Church identified itself simply with the kingdom of God. The New Testament knows the tension between the "already now" and the "not yet," between the present and the future of salvation. This tension is found in the preaching of Jesus himself.[85]

What does the coming of the Messiah signify? In the understanding of Jesus himself a powerful already-breaking in of the eschatological reign of God in his person;[86] according to the proclamation of the primitive Church it means this, in the formulation of Paul: "The appointed time [left to the world] has [already] grown very short" (1 Cor. 7:29), "for the form of this world [already] is passing away" (1 Cor. 7:31) and we are those "upon whom the end of the ages has [already] come" (1 Cor. 10:11). And the apostle writes this at a time when the "Easter piety," indeed the "*parousia* piety," predominates in him.[87] This means a fundamental formulation that the time between Easter and the *parousia* itself is already eschatologically qualified, and one cannot therefore view this historical consciousness as a "false reifying of the experience of the eschatological in history," even if world history continued to today. It will, however, not continue eternally. The *kairos* is much nearer (Acts 1:3). The end of time is already proclaimed.[88] "The Judge is standing at the doors" [James 5:9]. The time of the Church is not the usual time of history, but the eschatologically qualified time between Easter and the *parousia*.

However, when one speaks of Easter one cannot forget Good Friday, that is, one cannot forget the Crucified One. For the Risen One and the Messiah coming again at the end of these days is at once and forever also the Crucified One. And therefore the theology of the Church can and may never be a pure *theologia gloriae*, but must also be a *theologia crucis*. From an ecclesiological perspective this means that the Church on its pilgrim way through the time which is still at its disposal is accompanied not only by the Risen One, to whom all power in heaven and on earth is given (cf. Matt. 28:18–20), but also by the Crucified One. The Church is becoming more conscious of this than ever before, as Vatican II shows. The Church increasingly understands itself as a pilgrim and no longer as lord. It looks to and calls upon the one who will come to judge the living and the dead, although it knows this one to be always with it, and Christ calls into awareness in its daily Holy Eucharist of the sacrificial meal both his cross and his resurrection. Wherein, therefore, lies the "finality" of the Christ event in which the Church believes and of which Ruether speaks? Not in the world's already being completely redeemed but in the fact that, according to the Christian conviction of faith, Jesus Christ the definitive bringer of salvation (Messiah) has already come and the coming world, the *eschaton*, has already broken into this world of finitude and death; this world, then, stands *sub signo resurrectionis et crucis*, under the sign of the Risen and Crucified One.

That the history of the world continued after the death and resurrection of Jesus is, for the rest, a problem not merely for the Church, but likewise for Judaism insofar as Judaism was filled with an enormous "consciousness of the end" about the "turning of the times," as the Jewish apocalyptic and Qumran writings evidence. Just as the cross of Jesus was a catastrophe for the Church in the year 30, the destruction of the second Temple in the year 70 was a catastrophe for Judaism. This should be much more strongly emphasized. Since then in ways that are particular but connected, both the Church and Judaism stand *sub signo crucis*. The Church was intensely persecuted and is persecuted today more than ever, as everyone who wishes to know knows. I ask, therefore, whether the Christian anti-Judaism really is "the suppression of the unredeemed elements on one's own side and their projection unto that of Judaism," as Ruether believes. Jews and

Christians know about the unredeemed quality of the world. The world does not exist in a saved state. Jews and Christians suffer from this. Therefore both look forward to the coming, or coming again, of the Messiah—and the messianic hope is indeed indissolubly bound up with the knowledge of the lack of salvation in this world—and call for it in their prayers.

Does the Church place the blame for the unredeemed nature of the world on the Jews? For example, because Israel has rejected Jesus as the Messiah and continues to reject him, and because the Jews participated in the violent death of Jesus? The Church sees the cause of the lack of redemption in the sins of the entire world, for which Christ died: "Behold, the Lamb of God, who takes away the sin of the world" (John 1:29); "You know that he appeared to take away sins" (1 John 3:5); "God . . . sent his Son to be the expiation for our sins" (1 John 4:10); "He is the expiation for our sins, and not for ours only but also for the sins of the whole world" (1 John 2:2).

3. Nevertheless, there remains a question, even if it is not answerable: What would have happened to the world if Israel at that time had accepted Jesus as the Messiah? Would the world and its history have taken another course? From the perspective of faith one would like to say: Presumably so. But there is no clear, absolutely certain answer to this question. Only one thing can be said with certainty: Then there would not be a Church! For the Church is the product of the "hardening" of Israel (cf. Acts 28:25–28).[89] Ruether believes that "Judaism, in rejecting Jesus' messianic status, is simply reaffirming the integrity of its own tradition about what the word *Messiah* means."[90] But there was no period of Judaism in which there was an "integrity of its own tradition about what the word *Messiah* means," as even Jewish scholars tell us.[91] The idea of the Messiah in the person of the Messiah Jesus was, at least for Christian faith consciousness, clearly other. However, the major objection of Judaism against the "Messiah dogma" of the Church consists, now as before, in the fact that since the coming of Jesus into the world nothing has changed. It remains unredeemed. Is that really so completely true? In any case two things now exist which were not there previously: The gospel and the Church. Their effective history in the world was much, much greater than one commonly assumes. Without the gospel would one have known, for example, that history really should be the history of freedom? I shall not enter further into these difficult problems.[92]

4. Ruether states: "For Judaism, which had the Torah without the Mes-

siah, Christianity substitutes the Messiah without Torah."[93] This statement
is inaccurate; I shall return to it below (pp. 240f.).

5. Ruether also speaks of the resurrection of Jesus from the dead. "As the
recent Theology of Hope has put it, the Resurrection is not the final
happening of the eschatological event, but the proleptic experiencing of the
final future . . . . The Resurrection reaffirms his hope, in the teeth of
historical disappointment, that evil be overcome and God's will be done on
earth. The messianic meaning of Jesus' life, then, is paradigmatic and
proleptic in nature, not final and fulfilled. It does not invalidate the right of
those Jews not caught up in this paradigm to go forward on earlier foundations."[94] To these "earlier foundations" of Israel there belongs indisputably
the hope of a resurrection of the dead at the end of times by God. This is
simply hope in the future. In contrast, the Church proclaims that this hope
has been already fulfilled in *one*, namely, in Jesus of Nazareth, as God
raised him from the dead, so that the apostle, according to Acts 23:6, could
say to the High Council: "With respect to the hope and the resurrection of
the dead I am on trial." He meant, with respect to the hope in the
resurrection of the dead which he proclaimed had already happened in
Jesus the Crucified One. However, it is first in Jesus that it is fulfilled, and
therefore Ruether correctly says: "But the fulfillment of that hope, the
closing of the gap between what is and what ought to be, remains as much
in the future for the Church as it does for the Jewish people."[95] This hope
binds Israel and the Church together in a completely special way.

I would like to end my critical dialogue with Ruether with the following
statements: The "realized eschatology" in the coming of the Messiah Jesus
and in his resurrection from the dead may have misled the Church at
specific times in its past into a false reifying of the experience of the
eschatological in history, from which at times a self-righteous triumphalism
arose. In reality, however, according to the witness of the New Testament,
the time of the Church is the final and radically eschatologically qualified
time of history. This eschatological qualification of the final time of history
is, however, already effectively prefigured in Abraham's leaving of the land
of his fathers and breaking into the land of promise: With this there begins
the eschatological gathering of Israel and the nations by the God who raises
the dead and calls the things that exist and the things that do not exist
(Rom. 4:17), who is the God of Abraham, the God of Isaac and the God of
Jacob, the God of Israel and Jesus, and the God of all who believe in God
according to the manner of Abraham. And to this a final question: Does
Israel really move always only in so-called history? I would answer this

question strictly negatively. The people of God is no mere "profane" people!

THE RESTRICTION TO A SINGLE TEACHER

"The isolation of the Jesus tradition is the constitutive element of the gospel." Is this sentence which Gerhardt Kittel wrote many years ago[96] correct and verifiable? He means by it that the evangelical Jesus tradition is isolated from the early Jewish tradition, and that the latter was not received by the primitive Church. Rather, a restriction to one single teacher, namely, to Jesus of Nazareth, took place. If Kittel's observation is correct, then it signifies a particular *differentia specifica* between Judaism and Christianity.[97]

The Status "of a Single Teacher" in Judaism

Are there analogies in Judaism for Kittel's assertion? There would at first appear to be. One could for example point to the *Mishnah* tractate "Abot."[98] The tractate begins thus: "Moses received the Torah from Sinai and handed it over to Joshua and Joshua to the elders and the elders to the prophets and the prophets handed it over to the men of the great synagogue." Joshua was the immediate successor of Moses (cf. Num. 28:18ff.; Josh. 1:7ff.); the leadership of the people after the death of Joshua fell to the "elders" (cf. Josh. 24:31; Judg. 2:7). After them "the prophets" are named, "whereby naturally according to the ordering of the Old Testament canon the *rishonim* and the *acharonim* are thought of."[99] Among the "men of the great synagogue" are Ezra and Nehemiah and the first scribes, among whom also there was Shimon the Just One who, according to Abot I, 2, belonged "to the remnant of the great synagogue." There then followed six generations: Antigonos of Sokho and five pairs of scholars (Jose ben Joe'zer and Jose ben Jochanan; Jehoshua ben Perachia and Mattai of Arbela; Jehuda ben Tabai and Shimon ben Shatach; Shemaia and Abtolion; Hillel and Shammai). From Moses this is a tradition chain of twelve links. There then follows a family list of the Hillelites up to Rabbi Judah Ha-nasi and his son.[100] There can be no talk about Moses being declared the only normative teacher of Israel in this series which begins with Moses. Rather the purpose is to lead the Torah back to God as its initiator ("Moses received the Torah on Sinai," that is, from God), and on the other hand, to build up a chain of tradition which begins with Moses and leads to "Rabbi" the "redactor" of the *Mishnah*. Moreover, the tractate "Abot" is a selection of sayings, "only these are not like those of Jesus Sirach, the work of a single man, but rather the collection of statements of around seventy persons, with names named, and also otherwise known outstanding teachers of Torah."[101] Moreover, it relates essentially to the origin and the significance of the Torah and its explanation, so that the chain of tradition that is presented has the purpose of legitimating the explanatory work of the great *Tannaim* through the leading back to Moses and hence to God.

Naturally there is connected with this leading back to Moses the fact that in early Judaism the first teacher and lawgiver of Israel is seen in Moses, as can already be read in Ben Sira 45:5: "[God] gave him [Moses] the commandment face to face, the law of life and knowledge, to teach Jacob the covenant, and Israel his judgments." Moses is "the teacher of Israel par excellence."[102] The phrase "Moses our teacher"[103] is met often. Nevertheless Judaism neither limited itself to Moses as its sole teacher (rather it produced many teachers in the following of Moses,) nor did it declare any man coming after Moses as its exclusive and normative teacher as did the primitive Church in reference to Jesus of Nazareth (more about this below).

This is also not true of the "Teacher of Righteous" of the Qumran-Essene communities.[104] Jeremias remarked: "The community had taken the place of Israel and its scholars, and the Teacher of Righteousness had taken the place of Moses the lawgiver of the community."[105] The classical textual proof for this is found in the Damascus Document VI:2–11:

> God still remembered the Covenant which he had made with their forebears and raised from the priesthood men of discernment and from the laity men of wisdom, and he made them harken to him. And these men "dug the well"— that well whereof it is written, "princes dug it, nobles of the people delved it, with the aid of a staff" (Num. 21:18). The "well" in question is the Law. They that "dug" are those of Israel who repented and departed from the land of Judah to sojourn in "the land of Damascus." God called them all "princes" because they went in search of him, and their glory was never gainsaid by any man's mouth. The term staff refers to the man who expounds the Law. Isaiah has employed an analogous piece of imagery when in allusion to the Law he has spoken of God's "producing a tool for his work" (cf. Isa. 54:16). As for the "nobles of the people," these are the men that come, throughout the Era of Wickedness, to delve the well, using as their staves the statutes which the Lawgiver prescribed for them to walk in. Without such "implements" they would, indeed, never achieve their goal until such time as the true Expositor arises at the end of days.[106]

In this text there are three identifications: (1) "the well"—that is the Torah; (2) "they that 'dig' "—those of Israel who repented (the Essene community); (3) "the staff"—that is the man who expounds the Law (identical with the "Teacher of Righteousness").

The "man who expounds the Law" as the "staff" of God prescribes all the statutes for the community (as once Moses did for the Israelites) for the entire Era of Wickedness. Without the "implement" of his prescriptions, the members of the community would never achieve their goal "until such time as the true Expositor arises at the end of days." Concretely, however, as the rest of the Qumran documents show, the expository activity of the Expositor consists in nothing other than in a laying out of the Scripture with contemporary implications, especially of the prophets (cf. the Habakkuk commentary = 1 Qp Hab) and in an intensified Torah exegesis.[107] It is impressed upon the novices "to convert oneself to the Torah of Moses in all things which he has commanded with your whole heart and your whole soul, following all things which were revealed by it [the Torah] to the sons of Zadik . . . the priests" (1QS V, 8f.). Everything depends on the "doing," the fulfilling of the prescriptions of the Torah, and indeed of all commandments themselves. "The human being is as good as lost then if he does not do *everything*; the fulfillment of merely the preponderance of the commandments is not sufficient."[108]

Did the Essene community fall outside the framework of contemporary Judaism by this? One could answer the question with a yes if one thinks of the exclusive normativeness of the Torah explanation by the "Torah Expositor," the "Teacher of Righteousness," or also of the until now not mentioned separation of the Qumran-Essenes from the Temple and its cult for reasons of the festival calendar and the ancestry of the high priests of a non-Zadok line. However, through its unconditioned loyalty to the Torah of Moses, the Essene community did not fall fundamentally outside the framework of contemporary Judaism. They were a particular group within it. There are also groupings even today in Judaism.

However, today when one speaks of "Judaism," whether Jew or Christian, one thinks primarily of a Judaism that stands in the Pharisaic-Rabbinic tradition as it gradually constituted itself after the destruction of the Temple and as we find it in its early beginnings which go back beyond the year 70 C.E., especially in the *Mishnah*.[109] This Judaism, however, is more or less characterized *by a multiplicity of teachers*. If the *Mishnah* mentions around seventy teachers, the *Talmud* numbers approximately two thousand. However, the individual Rabbi does not stand as the center of interest, but rather the Torah and its explanation.[110] Since the time of the destruction of the Temple Judaism is characterized by its having many teachers who explain the Torah, this fundamental document of Judaism for the Jewish community. Indeed, it is precisely herein that the pluralism of Judaism throughout the centuries is grounded. I ask: Is this principle valid also for the Gospels?

The Fact of "a Single Teacher" in the Gospels

In Matt. 23:8 we find the statement of Jesus: "But you are not to be called rabbi, *for you have one teacher*, and you are all brethren." Therefore, the Christian community has "no rabbinate, but in Jesus its only teacher who speaks to them God's will."[111] The teaching of Jesus then continues: "And call no man your father on earth, for you have one Father, who is in heaven. Neither be called masters, for you have one master, the Christ" (Matt. 23:9f.). Eduard Schweizer attributes vv. 8 and 9 to Jesus, while v. 10 appears to be the making of the community, above all because of the absolute use of the honorific title "the Christ." However that may be, the Matthean redactor directs his addressee community decisively to the fact that they have a single teacher: Jesus, as he has the Risen One say in the "mission command" (Matt. 28:18–20): "Teach them to observe all that I have commanded you," that is, what Jesus and only Jesus has put forth in his pre-Easter teaching. Therefore: restriction to a single teacher—who is called Jesus![112]

The evidence in all four Gospels confirms this affirmation: the consequent restriction to a single teacher, Jesus of Nazareth, is found everywhere. B. Gerhardsson has also pointed this out:

> Characteristic of the books of the New Testament is the central role which they attribute to the figure of Jesus Christ. This is especially striking in the four Gospels; they are written in order to present Jesus alone. To be sure, other persons as well turn up in the Gospels: Jesus had his followers, he early had bitter opponents, and likewise the masses of the people reacted to his works, at first positively and then negatively. As consciously as the roles of the followers as well as the opponents and the masses of the people are outlined in the Gospels, the focus of the spotlight nevertheless is directed the entire time on *Jesus*. The evangelists wish to describe him and nothing other: his rise in Israel, what he said, what he did, what happened to him. Some tradents deal with John the Baptist—that is true—but that rests only on the fact that his fate is positively bound up with Jesus.[113]

Nevertheless, one must look still more closely. One could say that Jesus understands himself, in view of the imminent inbreaking of the eschatological reign of God, as the normative teacher of Torah, indeed as the intensifier of Torah,[114] similar to the "Torah Expositor" of the Essenes, if indeed in the sense of the "Torah sharpening" as it is concretely presented above all in the Sermon on the Mount. However, there is a significant difference: Jesus does not call people back to Moses and he does not call people back to the Torah of Moses in the Jewish sense. He calls them to the will of God as he understands and explains it. Whether he believed that he would thereby fall outside the framework of Judaism is difficult to say. Presumably he wished not to do that—and the present-day Jewish life of Jesus scholarship says: Jesus of Nazareth with his ethical demands is not outside the framework of Judaism!

Still, we have the extraordinary phenomenon in the four Gospels: restriction to a single teacher, Jesus of Nazareth. This restriction naturally had the consequence that in the Gospels only Jesus—no other Jewish rabbi—comes to speak as the normative teacher. In the Gospels the Jesus tradition is handed on in isolated fashion, and this isolation in comparison with Judaism, as Kittel has remarked, is "the constitutive element of the Gospel." This conscious isolation of the Jesus tradition must have taken place very early in the primitive Church, as the early collection of the words of the Lord in the Logia source shows; in it only the words of Jesus are collected! Although it had its origins in Judaism, the primitive Church did not take up the Jewish teaching authorities into its tradition. Conversely Judaism provided Jesus of Nazareth no space in its tradition; it almost appears as if Judaism had suppressed him for a long time, until it today again remembers him. In any case, astounding developments!

I have already discussed in detail the reasons for these developments. They are above all of a "christological" nature. Judaism excluded Jesus—the primitive Church conversely the Jewish teachers.[115] Of course, in the primitive Church there were soon many teachers and "sages"— according to James 3:1, all too many. Moreover, in the New Testament canon alongside the four evangelists, there are the letters of the Apostle Paul and other letters and further literature—in all, twenty-seven "books." However, all apostles and teachers of the Church hold fast to this fundamental decision: restriction to Jesus of Nazareth, which the reference back to the Scripture (the Old Covenant) does not exclude.[116] One could describe the writings of the New Testament canon as explications of the "Jesus phenomenon."

CHRISTIAN FREEDOM AND LAW

For the following reflections I shall proceed from the sentence of Paul: "For freedom Christ has set us free" (Gal. 5:1). According to Pauline theology, the "freedom program" of Christ is one that is comprehensive and multiple, related to past, present and future.[117] The freedom to which Christ has freed us implies, according to Paul, the liberation from Law as a way of salvation. In this tractate on the Jews the fact that the "Law" is a fundamental given of Jewish existence to this very day cannot be overlooked. The Jew takes joy in the Torah; it is for him the instruction for life.[118] According to Pauline teaching, the Law, however, became a factor of death: "The very commandment which promised life proved to be death to me" (Rom. 7:10; cf. Gal. 3:12). The Law became the "Law of sin and of death," from which the "Law of the spirit of life in Jesus Christ . . . has freed us." By the "Law of sin and death" doubtless the Torah is meant, which indeed, according to Rom. 7:12, is "holy and just and good," but which in reality became a factor of death because without the Law the human being would not have known the power of sin; this takes the Law as the starting point *(aphormē)* of its death-bringing attack upon humanity and calls forth from it every kind of covetousness. Thus according to Paul, it was only through the arrival of the Law that the power of sin rose up and brought humanity into death (Rom. 7:7–10); sin "deceived and killed" humanity "through the Law" (7:11). The Law thus became a kind of "power of sin" (1 Cor. 15:56).

Two things in the statement of the apostle about the Law are "un-Jewish": One is the strange judgment of the Law as being a death-bringing agent; the other is the view of human beings who have to do with the Law. For the Jews the Torah is the instruction for life, and the human being, according to Jewish conviction, is capable of carrying out the instructions of the Torah. For Paul it is other: For him the human being who finds himself confronted with the Law is "flesh," and because of the weakness of the flesh he so very often is unable to fulfill the demands of the Law (cf. Rom. 7:18–20). The human being is a sinner: For the apostle this is confirmed from experience and from Scripture (cf. Rom. 1—3:21). The human being cannot free himself from this situation, and it is not necessary for him to do so; for another has freed him: God, specifically in that the crucified Christ "has openly offered himself up as a reconciling sacrifice" (Rom. 3:25) and allowed himself to become "a curse for us" (Gal. 3:13). The moment Paul recognized and witnessed in faith along with the primitive Church that Christ "has died for our sins" (cf. 1 Cor. 15:3), in that moment he saw a totally un-Jewish alternative placed before him, concerning which I have already spoken:[119] eschatological salvation either through the Torah or through the crucified and risen Christ. On the basis of the Damascus experience, Paul decided in favor of the second, and it is *with this decision* that his so un-Jewish-sounding sentences concerning the Torah and (bound up with that) the "justification" of human beings are connected. On the basis of this decision Paul comes to an opposition which is difficult for a Jew to understand: salvation "from faith" (in Christ) and not "from works of the Law." "Even we have believed in Christ Jesus, in order to be justified by faith in Christ, and not by works of the law, because by works of the law shall no one be justified" (Gal. 2:16b). "For if justification were through the law, then Christ died to no purpose" (Gal. 2:21b).

Paul could not avoid these alternatives or seek a harmonization synthesis, as apparently his opponents with whom he battled in the "apostles' council" and later in the Epistle to the Galatians, tried to do. Being placed before these alternatives, Paul decided for the way of faith in Jesus Christ. However, with this he was forced to develop a new and different "Law theology" than Judaism had and has. It was not because he misunderstood the essence of the Law, as for example H.-J. Schoeps among others believes, that Paul came to the new judgment concerning the Law as it is presented in the Epistles to the Romans and Galatians, but rather simply and only on the basis of his christological and soteriological faith convictions.[120]

The primitive Church took over the decision of Paul—even if it was against a strenuous resistance especially from the Jewish Christians—and the Church professes it to the present day. The basis for this decision lies in Christology and in its soteriological implications and nowhere else. With this decision, however, there has come into existence something which forever divides the Church and Judaism.

I return now to the sentence of Rosemary Ruether: "For Judaism which had the Torah without the Messiah, Christianity substituted the Messiah without the Torah."[121] I have already indicated that this sentence is inaccurate. Why is that so? Because Christianity clearly recognizes a "Torah of the Messiah"! The term "Torah of the Messiah" comes from Judaism (*Midrash Qoh.* 11, 8, 52a: "The Torah which a human being learns in this world is nothing compared to the Torah of the Messiah [*torato shel meshiach*]"). As Peter Schäfer has convincingly shown, the "Torah of the Messiah" does not mean a new Torah which would replace the old one, but rather the final fulfillment of the Torah.[122] Paul employs the rabbinic phrase "Torah of the Messiah" in a Greek translation in Gal. 6:2 (*ton nomon tou Christou*), whereby of course he means by the genitive "of Christ" not the Messiah in general, but precisely the Messiah Jesus. The Law of Christ formulated in another way is "the law of the Spirit" (Rom. 8:2) which is identical with the imperative which flows from the new existence in Christ, which, according to Rom. 13:9, is "summed up" in the commandment of love in which the entire Law finds its fulfillment (Gal. 5:14). For Paul, Christ is the "lawgiver" of his community. I have already spelled this out (cf. above, pp. 150ff.). Likewise the Gospel of Matthew understands the Sermon on the Mount as the new Torah of the Messiah, even if this expression is not utilized. Jesus has not come "to abolish the law and the prophets . . . but to fulfill them" (Matt. 5:17). What Matthew understands by this "fulfillment" is to be read in the Sermon on the Mount. I also spoke at length about this (cf. above, pp. 115ff.). With this, however, the aforementioned sentence of Ruether is shown to be inaccurate. Christianity affirms the Messiah, but not without Torah. The instructions of the Messiah Jesus are still more difficult than the instructions of the Torah of Moses. Christian freedom is a freedom that has "the Law *of Christ*" for its norm, which again is connected with the restriction of the primitive Church to a single teacher. Christian freedom is not an anarchic freedom; it has nothing to do with a "utopian Messianism."

VARIOUS UNDERSTANDINGS OF REDEMPTION?— THE "PROMISE EXCESS"

There is a question mark at the end of the title "Various Understandings of Redemption." This is to indicate that we are dealing here with a problem which is not easy to resolve. Even a comprehensive monograph on it presumably would not arrive at an answer which would satisfy all, which would take into consideration all aspects. For to the question of what Judaism understands by "redemption," there is no single answer, but many. If in abstracting fashion one attempted to provide a brief response to this question, then one could perhaps state it thus: Redemption for Judaism is the *establishment of a saved world in justice and peace from which evil has been banned, because then all human beings will live according to the instruction of the Torah.* Immediately the question comes up: Is it the Messiah who establishes this saved world, or is "Messiah" in this only a verbal symbol for the hope that humanity itself will one day succeed in establishing a saved world? Moreover, one must distinguish between what the prophets of the Old Covenant of Israel proclaimed as redemption and what is taught concerning it by postbiblical Judaism, as for example even in the Kabbala.[123]

Redemption in history, at the end of history, through history, beyond history? Judaism knows no "dogma" in the Christian sense, and therefore it is absolutely impossible to present an authentic Jewish definition of "redemption." As in the matter of "Messianology," Christianity is clearer, although even here there are many formulas and definitions (for example, "the childhood of God"; liberation from sin); none of them however can abstract from one thing, namely, from the redeemer Jesus Christ. God "has delivered us from the dominion of darkness and transferred us to the kingdom of his beloved Son, in whom we have redemption, the forgiveness of sins" (Col. 1:13f.). Here it is stated, as in the entire New Testament, that God has already performed his act of redemption, namely, in his Son Jesus Christ. Here indeed Old Testament–Jewish thoughts are taken up which are connected with atonement and representation, [124] but nevertheless distinguishing and dividing elements between the Church and Judaism show up, elements which can be thus briefly formulated: The redeemer has already come into the world in Jesus Christ, even if complete redemption is still awaited—the liberation of all creation from the lot of contingency unto the glory of the children of God, and the redemption of the body in the raising from the dead (cf. Rom. 8:12–23) so that "in this hope we were saved" (Rom. 8:24). [125]

Nevertheless, alongside the dividing and differentiating elements there are large common elements: the hope for an ultimate redemption and definitive establishment of a saved world. There remains the redeeming of the "promise excess," by which the following is meant: The promises of the prophets of Israel have been only partially fulfilled in Jesus of Nazareth. There remains yet an "excess," a large remnant which must yet be brought to fulfillment and to which the Jew constantly points, perhaps even with irony and sarcasm: Jesus indeed has not really fulfilled the promises of the messianic time, and therefore he is not the Promised One, as the Christians maintain.

Even *post Christum* the world continues on its errant course a fact which really no one can dispute. Think only of the world peace which the prophets expressly predicted for the coming time of salvation! [126] Until now there is no indication of its realization! Or, think about death, this most real "non-utopia of human existence" (Ernst Bloch), which after as before still rules, despite the resurrection of Jesus from the dead. The Church cannot deny that there are these "promise excesses" which have not yet been fulfilled. "Judaism intensifies for Christianity the experience of the unredeemed quality of the world. . . . And thus Israel stimulates the Church to hope." [127]

Thus despite all of the dividing and distinguishing elements there remain many hopes which Judaism and the Church have in common and which stem largely from the tradition of Israel. Since the Second Vatican Council the Church has been in the process of giving up all unjustified "already-now triumphalism." It understands itself today more than ever as the pilgrim Church which together with Israel holds in its hand the staff of the wanderer as Abraham going into the Promised Land and Israel wandering through the desert, until the common homeland is reached.

In a tractate on the Jews the dividing and distinguishing elements between the Church and Judaism cannot be glossed over in silence; and there are other things, naturally, which could be introduced here (as, for

example, the Christian doctrine of the Trinity). These dividing and distinguishing elements, however, need not remain "taboo" in the Jewish-
Christian dialogue. Rather, they must be discussed so that mutual knowledge and understanding become possible. I cannot love someone whom I
do not know. In this, however, what is common should never be
forgotten.[128]

UNITY OF HUMANITY IN CHRIST

I have already (pp. 23ff.) dealt with the salvation historical privileges of
Israel according to Rom. 9:4f. and Eph. 2:12. The author of the Epistle to
the Ephesians arrives at the profile of the un-salvation of the Gentiles over
against the horizon of Israel. However, with that he specifies only the
"once" of the Gentile situation; from 2:13 onward he turns toward the
"now" of the Gentiles who "in Christ Jesus" have been from afar brought
close, since Christ "created in himself as a single new human being" (2:15)
the two halves of humanity, the Jews and the Gentiles (and since Abraham
there was, before Christ, only this twofold division), and in this fashion not
only established peace, but "reconciled both to God in one body through
the cross" (2:16). Here the Church is seen as the place in which Christ
gathers the nations *together with the Jews* into a single community and thus
reestablishes the unity of humanity striven for by God but lost by sin. "For
he is our peace" (2:14). He himself, Christ, is therefore the personal "factor
of unity," that is, not an abstract principle (as for example "reason"). This
process has been going on since Christ: In the Church the coming humanity is gathering, united with the heavenly being (2:19).[129]

Therefore what Jewish thinkers have striven for and in part still strive for,
the unity of humanity, is fulfilled since Christ is already in the Church—
even if not in complete fashion, nevertheless in a very tangible manner.
This is so because the Church is not an invisible "spiritual being," but
rather the "body of Christ" which is really and visibly present in the world.
Since the Jews in their great majority reject the "unity factor" Christ, they
stand in a certain measure outside this unification process of humanity—or
they attempt to bring it about, insofar as they do not believe in God, under
atheistic presuppositions, as for example Karl Marx, who has remarked that
"only the *human background* of the Christian religion can express itself in
truly human creations."[130] However, the Church must be on guard not to
automatically connect the Jews, who are unable to believe in Jesus Christ,
with these atheistic strivings for unity.

However, this is true, namely, that the Jewish people as a small "special
people" whom God has not allowed to assimilate themselves to the nations

of the world cannot, like the Church, step forward as the community binding together the nations, despite its scattering throughout the whole world. What has held Judaism together until today, as I have already argued, is the Torah. However, the Torah with its commandments and dispositions, according to Eph. 2:15, has been abolished by Christ and thereby a prerequisite for the unification of the nations has been formed in him.[131] Nevertheless, the Jews together with the Church should be propagandists for the community of nations. For the God of Israel is also the God of the nations, as the prophets of Israel have proclaimed; he also wishes to draw the nations into his salvation.[132] Without this Old Testament knowledge of revelation, Paul and his school would not have been able to develop their ideas concerning the salvation of the nations. With these ideas they do not fall outside the framework of Judaism.[133]

7
Common Tasks and Goals

Martin Buber has remarked: "An Israel striving for the renewal of its faith through the rebirth of the person and a Christianity striving for the renewal of its faith through the rebirth of the nations would have something unsaid to say to one another and would have an assistance to provide one another that is hardly imaginable today."[1] In the previous chapters I have attempted to say, even if in an incomplete manner, that which has long been unsaid, and thereby to provide a measure of assistance. Beyond that, I am convinced that what has now been said could assist the world, presuming that Judaism and Christianity recognize their common tasks toward the modern world. I would like to list several things concerning this task—by no means in an exhaustive manner, but more in the form of theses.[2]

THE "REALIZATION"

"Realization" was a favorite word of Martin Buber. However he was not the first to see in it a word proceeding from the essence of Judaism. In the Holy Scriptures of Israel "realization," "doing" played a central role. For the instructions of the Torah must be realized. Also in the preaching of Jesus, in the synoptic as well as in Johannine, the word "to do," "to realize," played the greatest of roles.[3] For the will of God the Father must be done, must be realized. Believing Judaism is concerned with "learning" the Torah and "doing" the Torah. It is similar with Jesus concerning "learning" and "doing," of course with the distinction that one should learn from *him:* "Learn of me" (Matt. 11:29) and follow my instruction. "Jesus as well as the subsequent tradition clearly give doing a priority over healing and over speaking, and also remain thereby within the area of official Judaism."[4] Jesus belongs to the great ethicists of Judaism, as the Jewish scholars of the life of Jesus have brought to our awareness.[5]

The instructions of the Torah and the instructions of Jesus concern the will of God. The psalmist says: "I delight to do thy will, O my God; thy law is within my heart" (Ps. 40:8); Jesus said: "Not everyone who says to me 'Lord, Lord,' shall enter the kingdom of heaven, but he who does the will of my Father who is in heaven" (Matt. 7:21), and of himself: "My food is to do the will of him who sent me" (John 4:34). The instructions are not the

244

expression of some sort of state or economic rationale. They order the relationships of the individual and of the community to God and to one's fellow human beings. They flow from an obedience toward God; they press toward an ethical behavior in the world. They prevent one from being satisfied with only the discussion of the (to be sure, necessary) "theory." They transform "orthodoxy" ever anew into "orthopraxy." They prevent an esthetic "ritualism" and a dead "only faith," which forgets the works of love. "Be doers of the word, and not hearers only deceiving yourselves" (James 1:22). Thus Judaism and Christianity should not let themselves be outdone by anyone in the world in the practical realization of their theory. Ethical behavior in the world should be their common maxim.

THE PROPHETIC PROTEST

Against what is it directed?[6] It might be that originally YHWH was also honored as a "local God," but YHWH did not remain a "domesticated God." Rather, YHWH was recognized as the God alongside of whom there were no other gods. YHWH alone is the lord of the heavens and the earth, to whom adoration is due. And it is YHWH who will judge not merely Israel but the whole world. YHWH is the creator of the universe. The Baals and the popular divinities will be unmasked as "nothings" and the world will be cleansed of them. With that the world will be disenchanted.

The same YHWH will be experienced by Israel as the God of the "going out," which implies "that religions appear in history not only as world-sustaining but also as world-shaking power. That is, for example, to be seen in the most intimate way with the Exodus event in which God was revealed as the unmanipulable, indecipherable God of history. 'I am who I will be,' says YHWH—the living God who in the breaking out and in the transition time and again is shown as the unmanipulable one."[7] The prophet Amos praises the almighty God thus: "The Lord, YHWH of hosts, he who touches the earth and it melts, and all who dwell in it mourn, and all of it rises like the Nile, and sinks again, like the Nile of Egypt; who builds his upper chambers in the heavens, and founds his vault upon the earth; who calls for the waters of the sea, and pours them out upon the surface of the earth—YHWH is his name" (Amos 9:5f.).

Therefore in the Old Testament the earthquake becomes a symbol of the power of God: by the theophanies (Isa. 6:4; Mic. 1:3f.; Nah. 1:5; Hab. 3:6f.; Pss. 18:8; 97:5), at the final judgment (Isa. 13:13, 24:18f.; Ezek. 38:19f.; Jonah 4:16); it becomes the symbol of terror and misfortune (Isa. 5:25; Amos 8:8; Pss. 46:3f.; 60:3f.); it becomes the image for a political event (Jer. 51:29; Hag. 2:6f., 21f.). YHWH, the God of Israel, lets the earth "quake";

he does not let it come to rest until the time of the earth is at its end when the "day of YHWH" draws the great caesura.[8]

The God who is the God of Israel and also the God of Jesus and of the Church is in no way a God living "in heavenly rest," despite his transcendence beyond the world; rather he is the God who "holds the world in his breath." This is the essential content of the "concept of God" of the prophets of Israel, a theological element of their protest which the Church and Judaism must take up.

This God, according to the prophetic protest, also holds the world in his breath in that he has the prophets of Israel proclaim that there is no true knowledge of God without a practiced justice: "Woe to him who builds his house by unrighteousness, and his upper rooms by injustice; who makes his neighbor serve him for nothing, and does not give him his wages. . . . Do you think you are a king because you compete in cedar? Did not your father eat and drink and do justice and righteousness? . . . *Is not this to know me?* says YHWH" (Jer. 22:13, 15f.).

And Jesus taught: "You have heard that it was said, 'You shall love your neighbor and hate your enemy.' But I say to you, Love your enemies and pray for those who persecute you, so that you may be sons of your Father who is in heaven; for he makes his sun rise on the evil and the good, and sends rain on the just and on the unjust. For if you love those who love you, what reward have you? Do not even the tax collectors do the same? And if you salute only your brethren, what more are you doing than others? Do not even the Gentiles do the same? You, therefore, must be perfect, as your heavenly Father is perfect" (Matt. 5:43–48).

In his great speech in Matt. 25:31–46 Jesus identifies himself as the Son of man with all those who hunger, thirst, are strangers, "naked," sick, and imprisoned in the whole world. This is the Jesus development of the prophetic protest into the whole world. Such a protest allows no religious or churchly "inbreeding." The prophetic protest here is actively critical of rulership. "Religion is not unconditionally an opium for the people. On the contrary, the charismatic leader [the prophet] can overthrow the world order that has been handed on and the legitimation procedures which support it. He can come out in favor of a general religious freedom wherever religions are imprisoned by the states,"[9] as that happens today across the world.

To the implementation of the prophetic protest in the world there also belongs the worldwide making known of the ancient teaching of Israel and the Church that the human being, and indeed every human being, is the image of God,[10] whereby the personal worth of every human being, whoever he or she may be, is set forth. Therefore, Israel and the Church take over a "world responsibility" when they everywhere bring to fruition this dignity of the human being and protest loudly when this dignity is trampled in the dirt, where and whenever that may happen. With this, love "becomes a political entity since it does not allow its limits to be dictated by sociological reality, on which trusting openness and readiness to receive would necessarily shatter."[11]

Said in short: The prophetic protest which the Church and Judaism in following the ancient prophets of Israel must raise directs itself against every suppression of an ideological or social kind. It is a protest for freedom; a protest in favor of true humanity, love, and community; a protest for the truth against the ever-increasing lies of the world and history; a protest against fascism, communism, and capitalism. The Jewish-Christian religion is the antiopium for the people. The gospel is "not according to human taste" (Gal. 1:11).

"SHALOMIZATION OF THE WORLD"

Much has already been written about the Hebrew concept *Shalom*.[12] *Shalom* is a comprehensive, polysemantic concept. At the conclusion of his semantic research into the term *shalom*, R. Friedli comes to the following description: "Peace, joy, freedom, integrity, reconciliation, community, harmony, justice, truth, communication. With this multidimensional description of *shalom* the soteriological dynamic is highlighted on the one hand and the social relationship of *shalom* on the other."[13] *Shalom* is a comprehensive concept of salvation, "salvation" however not as the "salvation of souls," "peace of souls," but as the sign of a world which is in salvation. It concerns the "shalomization of the whole of life" (J. C. Hoekendijk). *Shalom* is realized in the world when all relations to one another are finally in order, the relationship between God and humanity, the relationship between human being and human being. Therefore *shalom* implies "a social action"; it is "an opportunity for fellow humanness."[14] "One cannot have the salvation of God without sharing it with those without salvation"; therefore there is found in the key word *shalom* "a coincidence of salvation history and world event. . . . *Shalom* so encompasses the reign of God and the world that the two are not to be divided."[15] And therefore Israel and the Church cannot reduce "freedom" to *their* peace, because the reign of God does, and intends to, embrace the whole world. It is precisely under the pressure of bitter experiences of persecution that Israel and the Church could succumb to the temptation to direct their peace work only "toward within." The popes have long since recognized that it belongs to the obligatory office of the Church to involve itself for peace everywhere in the world.[16] Israel also must make itself an advocate of peace, and likewise Islam and all the world religions.

There may no longer be any simply ethnocentric notion of peace. The Old Testament, the Holy Scriptures of Israel, lets one see that the world order has for a long time been congruent with the order of the various states or of the various nationality groups. "The 'world' order in Egypt, in Mesopotamia, or in Sumer is the order of the Egyptian, Mesopotamian, or Sumerian world. Therefore the submission of the enemy, the 'pacification' of the other nations, belong to world order precisely there where they speak of peace. The enemy, the strange, the 'unbeliever' belongs on the side of chaos, on the side of the cosmos-threatening powers."[17] The God of Israel, however, who is also the God of Jesus and of the Church, protests against such a concept of peace. He has indeed created the nations, but he does not wish that the nations cut themselves off from each other in hostility. God does not wish an "iron curtain"! What was put forth in the teaching of Israel concerning the image of God in every human being intends to become reality in the whole world through the gospel: *that all human beings recognize each other as brothers and sisters.*

Since God has broken into the Gentile world in Jesus, the national and regional identifications have their borders. Even Israel must see these borders. Zionism would lose its legitimacy if Israel were no longer able to look over its own fence. The Jews especially have passionately confessed to universal humanity, without however assimilating themselves. The human being who is touched by the God of Israel represents, "as a loving human being, a global identification."[18]

Thus it is a special common task of the Church and Israel to employ, together with all men and women of good will in the world, all of their powers for the "shalomization of the world," in service of a political and social ecumenism. What is at stake is that the religions no longer identify with political systems and allow themselves to be coopted by an egoistic politics, "but in prophetic freedom be in solidarity with humanity which does not wish to overpower in proselytizing fashion the world of the other, but rather hopes to point to in symbolic fashion the coming of the reign of God."[19] The Church and Judaism should jointly develop a "world-responsible cooperation theology" without therefore having to give up their own proper characteristics in a false ecumenism. The dividing and differentiating elements which have not been ignored in this book are not a hindrance to such a cooperation theology. Its development is urgent.[20]

THE "ESCHATOLOGICAL RESERVATION"

With this theological technical expression I understand that "reservation" which is pronounced concerning all world and life plans which claim to be able to bring the world into its final salvation through human wisdom and efforts alone.[21] The "YHWH religion" of Jewish and Christian provenance is convinced that humanity is not in a position to do this. The experience of history supports this. The egoism and the power of sin are too great to attain that ultimate "shalomization of the world" as only God with his power can attain it and wishes to attain it according to the prophetic predictions. He brings the world into ultimate salvation just because he alone possesses the power to overcome death, which indeed is the real frustrator of all human history.

Neither through evolution nor revolution can the world arrive at ultimate salvation. Evolution produces "nature," not however "salvation." As is known, revolution eats its own children; it indeed changes the present condition, but in the place of the old class there comes forth a new; love is not its slogan, but rather "liquidation."[22] Revolution is understandable as the pushing back by the suppressed against the pressure of the suppressor; but it produces nothing final. Revolution makes the world into a "slaughter house" (Hegel), not into a home. Humanity, however, yearns toward home and happiness. The presupposition for home and happiness is, briefly stated, the presence of loving persons. For the loving person is "the presence of everything" (A. Stifter). According to the prophetic prediction of the Scriptures of Israel and the Church, this presence will first be realized in the "new heaven and new earth." Only then will the "shalomization of the world" be ultimately completed.[23]

The Church and Israel are called by their Holy Scriptures to announce always and everywhere in the world the "eschatological reservation." This belongs to their common tasks in this time which continually gives itself over to the illusion that "it can go it alone."

"GOD IS ALL IN ALL"

The Apostle Paul has expressed the final goal of all history and salvation history in classical brevity in the formula of 1 Cor. 15:28: "God is all in all." Jews and Christians can unhesitatingly affirm this formula. It affirms God, it affirms his unlimited power, it affirms the universality of salvation. It lets it be seen that even for Christian theology, it is not Christology but rather Theo-logy, talk about God, that is the final concern of its efforts of thought.[24] It affirms God as Israel has experienced him in its history and has proclaimed him in its Holy Scriptures. In the context of this formula there is also the sentence: "As a final enemy death will be annihilated" (15:25). It is precisely in this that the divinity of God is revealed: He will raise up the dead as he, according to the Christian proclamation of faith, has raised Jesus from the dead.

"I believe in the resurrection of the flesh and eternal life": Israel as well as the Church professes these statements of the Credo. This common confession gives the world hope and promises it a future.[25] "I wish to give you a future and a hope" (Jer. 29:11).

8

The Church and Israel:
A Brief Commentary on Nostra Aetate, 4

Instead of a summary of the analyses in this tractate on the Jews, I shall present a brief commentary on the most important statements of the Second Vatican Council concerning Judaism as it is found in the conciliar decree *Nostra Aetate*, No. 4.[1]

The Church Is "Spiritually Linked with the Stock of Abraham." The "stock" is the Jewish people, which can trace its origin back to Abraham. Through faith in the manner of Abraham the members of the Church, according to the teaching of the Apostle Paul, have become the spiritual sons of Abraham (Gal. 3:7). Through its spiritual connection with the stock of Abraham the Church participates in the election of Israel; it together with Israel belongs to one people of God.[2]

The Church Has Received from Israel the Revelation of the Old Covenant Which Has Found Its Written Form in the Old Testament. The Holy Scripture of Israel is an essential portion of the Holy Scriptures of the Church. The Old Testament is, however, not the sole property of the Church; it is rather a loan of Israel to the Church, which is important for the Church because without the Old Testament the Church loses its identity and its self-understanding, as the experience of history shows.[3] "The Old Testament is the common foundation, the theological and historical root of Judaism and Christianity."[4]

The Church Is Nourished by the "Root of the Good Olive Tree." The good olive tree is Israel.[5] The nourishment which the Church received from it is not the merely the Holy Scripture of the ancient covenant, but also "the Jewish categories," of which humanity has need in order to be able to think in a saving way. It is precisely in view of that great heritage of faith of Israel which has gone over into the Church that Israel shows itself as the good olive tree.

The Church acknowledges the continuing "privileges of Israel," as they are enumerated by the apostle in Rom. 9:4f.[6] They have not been transferred to the Church, as some Christian theologians believe.

Christ, His Mother Mary, His Apostles, and "Most of Those First Disciples Who Proclaimed the Gospel of Christ to the World" Stem from Judaism. They have brought the great spiritual heritage of Israel to the world of the Gentiles. Through them the faith heritage of Israel has remained fermentive in the Gentile world. It penetrates the whole world like yeast and makes the world "Jewish" in a Jesus sense.

The Jews Are "Still Always Beloved of God for the Sake of the Fathers." God has not rejected or forgotten his people Israel. God holds his hand protectingly over his people and will save all Israel in the end (Rom. 11:26). In the continuation of Israel through all ages the loyalty of God to his promises is shown. Israel is the continuing witness to the loyalty and truthfulness of God in the world.

The Church Waits Together with Judaism for the "Day of the Lord." Both know of no self-fulfillment of history; both know of the "eschatological reservation" of God toward all attempts to fulfill human history on an innerworldly basis. Rather, both view the "day of the Lord" as the day of the great caesura, in which God intervenes in the history of this world and prepares for it an abrupt end. The knowledge of the "day of the Lord" makes the Church and Israel sober and watchful.

In View of the Rich Spiritual Heritage of Israel, the Church Is Obliged "to Foster Mutual Knowledge and Respect," which above all through an intense dialogue and through a likewise intense study of the Jewish tradition takes place.[7]

Despite the Death of Jesus on the Cross the Jews May Not be Seen as "Rejected or Accursed by God." The remembrance of the crucifixion of Jesus, which was the work of the pagan Roman state power, misleads Christianity time and again to legitimate in a pseudo-theological way its anti-Semitism and to hold up the thesis of "deicide" and of "self-cursing" by the Jews. The Council "deplores all hatreds, persecutions, displays of anti-Semitism leveled at any time or from any source against the Jews." The anti-Semitism which has fed the Church for centuries belongs to its great sins in history. The Church must constantly ask God for forgiveness for this guilt.

Christ Has Died for the Sins of All Human Beings. "Therefore it is the task of the preaching of the Church to proclaim the cross of Christ as the sign of the universal love of God and as the source of all grace." Christ died not only for the sins of the pagans, but also for the sins of the Jews. His blood comes as a redeemer's blood likewise over the Jews. In addition the Council expressly teaches that "neither all Jews indiscriminately at that time, nor Jews today, can be charged with the crimes committed during his passion." Israel also is not weighed down with a "collective guilt."

From this teaching of the Council there results finally the possibility of not merely a new next-to-one-another, but also a new with-one-another of the Church and Israel. The Church and Israel belong together; they form a community of fate. The Church can no longer overlook Israel, its "root." Is that not also true for Israel concerning the Church? Jews should reflect on this.

9
Psalm 129

" 'Sorely have they afflicted me from my youth,' let Israel now say—
'Sorely have they afflicted me from my youth, yet they have not prevailed
against me. The plowers plowed upon my back; they made long their
furrows.' The Lord is righteous; he has cut the cords of the wicked. May all
who hate Zion be put to shame and turned backward! Let them be like the
grass on the housetops, which withers before it grows up, with which the
reaper does not fill his hand or the binder of sheaves his bosom, while those
who pass by do not say,

'The blessing of the Lord be upon you!

We bless you in the name of the Lord!' "

Notes

NOTES FOR CHAPTER 1

1. Reference is made here first of all to the major investigations by H. G. Adler which contain a large amount of material and comprehensive bibliographies: *Theresienstadt 1941–1945. Das Antlitz einer Zwangsgemeinschaft* (Tübingen, 1955); *Der verwaltete Mensch. Studien zur Deportation der Juden aus Deutschland* (Tübingen, 1974). Also see G. Reitlinger, *Die Endlösung. Hitlers Versuch der Ausrottung der Juden Europas 1939–1945* (Berlin, 1953); A. Rückerl, *NS-Vernichtungslager im Spiegel deutscher Strafprozesse*, 2d ed. (Munich, 1978).

2. In *Lexikon für Theologie und Kirche*, supplementary vol.; *Das Zweite Vatikanische Konzil* (Freiburg, 1967), 2:406–478. See also Augustin Bea, *The Church and the Jewish People* (New York, 1966).

3. Reprinted in ibid., pp. 440f.

4. English translation available in Austin Flannery, ed., *Vatican Council II: The Conciliar and Post Conciliar Documents* (Collegeville, Minn., 1975), pp. 743–749.

5. Even before the appearance of the "Vatican Guidelines," the French Bishops' Commission issued on 16 April 1973 an important declaration on the attitude of Christians toward Judaism. Reference is also expressly made to the Working Paper of the Dialogue Circle "Jews and Christians" of the Central Committee of German Catholics entitled "Theologische Schwerpunkte des jüdisch-christlichen Gesprächs" from 8 May 1979.

6. See above all the following statements: "Israel: People, Land, and State," by the Synod of the Reformed Church, Holland, 1970; "Christians and Jews," a study by the Council of the Evangelical Church in Germany, 1975 (and the related "*Arbeitsbuch*" *Christen und Juden. Zur Studie des Rates der EKD*, ed., Rolf Rendtorff [Gütersloh, 1979]). These and other pertinent documents are printed in Helga Croner, *Stepping Stones to Further Jewish-Christian Relations: An Unabridged Collection of Christian Documents* (London and New York, 1977). Also see: "Überlegungen zum Problem Kirche-Israel," ed. by the Vorstand des Schweizerischen Evangelischen Kirchenbundes in May 1977, printed in the *Freiburger Rundbrief* 29 (1977): 108–111. Concerning the situation in the German-language area, see also Eva Fleischner, *Judaism in German Christian Theology since 1945: Christianity and Israel Considered in Terms of Mission* (Metuchen, N.J., 1975). On the image of Judaism of specific Christian theologians in the Nazi period, see F. Werner, "Das Judentumsbild der Spätjudentumsforschung im Dritten Reich. Dargestellt anhand der 'Forschungen zur Judenfrage,'" *Kairos* 13 (1971): 161–194.

7. Croner, *Stepping Stones*, p. 66.

8. According to G. Klein, Auschwitz does not prejudice "the intentions of our

texts," namely, in the New Testament: "Präliminarien zum Thema 'Paulus und die
Juden,'" in *Rechtfertigung. Festschrift für Ernst Käsemann* (Tübingen, 1976), pp.
229–243. Klein argues against an "argumentative one-upmanship after genocide."
"Methodical clarity and verifiability of exegesis were gambled away and arbitrariness dominated the field" (ibid.). These sentences were directed above all
against the writing of H. Gollwitzer, M. Palmer, V. Schliski, "Der Jude Paulus und
die deutsche ntl. Wissenschaft," *Evangelische Theologie* 34 (1974): 276–304.
Against Klein I would like to say: It does concern precisely the "verifiability of
exegesis" in the text of the New Testament, which often and for centuries was read
under a false hermeneutical a priori, namely, the a priori of a conscious or unconscious anti-Judaism, for which the text itself often offered no basis. The *text* was read
with anti-Judaistic glasses and then provided what one wished to hear. The classical
example of this is the interpretation of the sentence in Romans 11:26: "All Israel will
be saved," which up to the most recent commentaries, such as that of Otto Kuss,
Regensburger Neues Testament (Regensburg, 1965; 3rd printing, 1978), was interpreted as the conversion of Israel through the gospel. Every interpretation of a
text—modern hermeneutics since Schleiermacher has shown us this (see Franz
Mussner, *Geschichte der Hermeneutik von Schleiermacher bis zur Gegenwart*, 2d
ed. [Freiburg, 1976]—also stands under the prejudgment of the interpreter. This
prejudgment can, however, be submitted to a conversion—and the giving up of
theological anti-Judaism is a genuine conversion event, as I know from my own
experience. That prejudgment can be dismantled and the anti-Judaistic glasses laid
aside. All at once the text shows its true face. That prejudgment in the matter of
interpretation can also be nourished by tradition, as Gadamer has taught us beyond
Heidegger—and in our case by an almost two-thousand-year-long anti-Judaistic
tradition. Thus, ongoing experience—and to it belongs above all in our time
Auschwitz—can finally free the vision to see "the intention of our texts." See F.-W.
Marquardt, *Die Juden im Römerbrief* (Zurich, 1971). From the prompted re-
sponses, in part very strenuously argued, the following should be noted: G. Klein,
"Erbarmen mit den Juden!" *Evangelische Theologie* 34 (1974): 201–218; D. Flusser,
"Ulrich Wilkens und die Juden," *Evangelische Theologie* 34 (1974): 236–243;
U. Wilkens, "Das Neue Testament und die Juden," *Evangelische Theologie* 34
(1974): 602–611; R. Rendtorff, "Die neutestamentliche Wissenschaft und die Ju-
den. Zur Diskussion zwischen David Flusser und Ulrich Wilkens," *Evangelische
Theologie* 34 (1974): 191–200.

9. Concerning this, see also I. Maybaum, *The Face of God after Auschwitz*
(Amsterdam, 1965): Alan Davies, *Anti-Semitism and the Christian Mind* (New York,
1969), with an annotated bibliography; Johannes B. Metz et al., *Gott nach Auschwitz* (Freiburg, 1979). With regard to Auschwitz, one even speaks of the "Beginning
of a new era"; see Eva Fleischner, ed., *Auschwitz: Beginning of a New Era:
Reflections on the Holocaust* (New York, 1977)—papers from a symposium on the
Holocaust in New York, 3–6 June 1974.

10. Everyone must agree with Clemens Thoma when he remarks: "A Christian
who *after* Auschwitz speaks anti-Jewishly behaves essentially less responsibly than
any Church Father who thought that the degradation of the Jews belonged in
Christian preaching and who could still not foresee the evil consequences of his
words" (*Christliche Theologie des Judentums*) [Aschaffenburg, 1978], pp. 142f.; for

an English paraphrase, see *A Christian Theology of Judaism*, tr., Helga Croner (New York, 1980), p. 160.

11. An overview of the anti-Jewish writings is provided by A. L. Williams, *Adversus Judaeos: A Bird's-Eye View of Christian Apologiae until the Renaissance* (Cambridge, 1935). See also K. H. Rengstorf and S. von Kortzfleisch, eds., *Kirche und Synagoge* (Stuttgart, 1968), I: 50–209; Kurt Hruby, *Juden und Judentum bei den Kirchenvätern* (Zurich, 1971); Rosemary Ruether, *Faith and Fratricide* (New York, 1974), pp. 117–182 (with a wealth of material). Specifically concerning John Chrysostom, see C. M. Maxwell, "Chrysostom's Homilies Against the Jews" (Ph.D. diss., University of Chicago, 1966); concerning Augustine, see B. Blumenkranz, *Die Judenpredigt Augustins. Ein Beitrag zur Geschichte der jüdisch-christlichen Beziehungen in den ersten Jahrhunderten* (Paris, 1973). Concerning the totality, see also M. Simon, *Verus Israel. Etude sur les relations entre Chrétiens et Juifs dans l'Empire Romain*, 2d ed., (Paris, 1964). See also O. Knoch, "Die Stellung der apostolischen Väter zu Israel und zum Judentum," in *Begegnung mit dem Wort. Festschrift für H. Zimmermann*, ed. J. Zmijewski and E. Nellessen (Bonn, 1980), pp. 347–378, with bibliography.

12. See Norbert Lohfink, "Methodenprobleme zu einem christlichen 'Traktat über die Juden,'" in *Bibelauslegung im Wandel*, ed. Norbert Lohfink (Frankfurt, 1967), pp. 214–237.

13. Important literature includes Martin Buber, "Die Erwählung Israels," *Werke* (Munich and Heidelberg, 1964), 2: 1037–1051; Kurt Galling, *Die Erwählungstraditionen Israels* (Giessen, 1928); T. C. Vriezen, *Die Erwählung Israels nach dem AT* (Zurich, 1953); K. Koch, "Zur Geschichte der Erwählungsvorstellung in Israel," *Zeitschrift für alttestamentliche Wissenschaft* 67 (1955): 205–226; H. Wildberger, *Jahwehs Eigentumsvolk* (Zurich and Stuttgart, 1960) H. J. Zobel, "Ursprung und Verwurzelung des Erwählungsglaubens Israels," *Theologische Literaturzeitung* 93 (1968): 1–12; H. Wildberger, "Die Neuinterpretation des Erwählungsglaubens Israels in der Krise der Exilszeit, in *Wort-Gebot-Glaube, Festschrift für W. Eichrodt* (Zurich, 1970), pp. 307–324; H. Wildberger, Article בחר ("to choose") in *Theologisches Handwörterbuch zum AT*, ed. G. J. Botterweck and H. Ringgren, (Munich and Zurich, 1971), 1: 275–300; H. Seebas, Article בחר in ibid., pp. 592–608.

14. Wildberger, "Neuinterpretation," p. 309.

15. With this Israel, not Abraham, is addressed (see J. Ziegler, "Isaias" *Echter-Bibel* (Würzburg, 1948).

16. Concerning this, see further pp. 28ff.

17. Important literature includes G. von Rad, "Das Gottesvolk im Deuteronomium," *Beiträge zur Wissenschaft vom Alten und Neuen Testament* 47 (Stuttgart, 1929); H. Wildberger, "Jahwes Eigentumsvolk," *Abhandlungen zur Theologie des Alten und Neuen Testaments* 37 (Zurich and Stuttgart, 1960); O. Bächli, "Israel und die Völker," ibid. 41 (1962); N. Lohfink, "Beobachtung zur Geschichte des Ausdrucks עם יהוה," in *Probleme biblischer Theologie, Festschrift für G. von Rad*, ed. H. W. Wolff (Munich, 1971), pp. 275–305.

18. Cf. R. Smend, *Die Mitte des Alten Testaments* (Zurich, 1970), pp. 48, 52.

19. Bächli, "Israel und die Völker," p. 140.

20. Wildberger, "Jahwes Eigentumsvolk," p. 52.

21. G. Wanke, Article " נַחֲלָה ," in *Theologisches Handwörterbuch zum Alten Testament* 2:58.

22. Clemens Thoma, *Theologische Berichte*, 3 (special volume, *Judentum und Kirche: Volk Gottes*) (Einsiedeln, 1974), p. 107. For a view of so-called early Judaism, see above all N. A. Dahl, *Das Volk Gottes. Eine Untersuchung zum Kirchenbewusstsein des Urchristentums*, 2d ed. (Darmstadt, 1963), pp. 51–143.

23. Ibid., pp. 144–263; F. Mussner, *Praesentia Salutis. Gesammelte Studien zu Fragen und Themen des Neuen Testaments* (Düsseldorf, 1967), pp. 244–252 (biblio); T. C. Kruiff, "Das Volk Gottes im Neuen Testament," *Theologische Berichte*, 3 (see note 22), pp. 119–133.

24. Kruiff, "Das Volk Gottes," p. 128.

25. "Paul follows neither the Hebrew text nor the LXX, but another translation" (H. Conzelmann, *Der erste Brief an die Korinther* [Göttingen, 1969]).

26. E. Käsemann, *An die Römer*, 3d ed. (Tübingen, 1974), p. 263.

27. M. Görg, "Anfängeisraelitischen Gottesglaubens," *Kairos* 18 (1976): 264.

28. R. Rendtorff, "Das Land Israel im Wandel der alttestamentlichen Geschichte," in *Jüdisches Volk—gelobtes Land*, ed. W. Eckert, N. P. Levinson, and M. Stöhr (Munich, 1970), pp. 153–168. See also A. Ohler, *Israel, Volk und Land. Zur Geschichte der wechselseitigen Beziehungen zwischen Israel und seinem Land in alttestamentlicher Zeit* (Stuttgart, 1979).

29. Selected bibliography: G. von Rad, "Verheissenes Land und Jahwes Land," in *Gesammelte Studien zum Alten Testament*, ed. G. von Rad (Munich, 1958), pp. 87–100; M. Buber, *Israel und Palästina. Zur Geschichte einer Idee* (Zurich, 1959); H. Wildberger, "Israel und sein Land, *Evangelische Theologie* 16 (1956): 404–422; D. Ben-Gurion, *Rebirth and Destiny of Israel* (New York, 1954); M. Y. Ben-Gavriel, *Israel. Wiedergeburt eines Staates* (Munich, 1957); E. Rothschild, *Die Juden und das Heilige Land. Zur Geschichte des Heimkehrwillens eines Volkes* (Hanover, 1964); W. Zimmerli, "Der Staat Israel—Erfüllung biblischer Verheissungen," in *Israel und die Christen*, ed. W. Zimmerli (Neukirchen, 1964); F.-W. Marquardt, *Die Bedeutung der biblischen Landverheissungen für die Christen* (Munich, 1964), with extensive bibliography; Eckert et al., eds., *Jüdisches Volk—gelobtes Land. Die jüdischen Landverheisungen als Problem des jüdischen Selbstverständnisses und der christlichen theologie* (Munich, 1970); U. Tal, "Jüdisches Selbstverständnis und das Land und der Staat Israel," *Freiburger Rundbrief* 23 (1971): 27–32; P. Diepold, *Israels Land* (Stuttgart, 1972); M. H. Tanenbaum and R. J. Zwi Werblowsky, eds., *The Jerusalem Colloquium on Religion, Peoplehood, Nation and Land* (Jerusalem, 1970); W. D. Davies, *The Gospel and the Land* (London, 1974); R. Rendtorff, *Israel und sein Land (Theol. Existenz heute 188)* (Munich, 1975); P. Navé, "Jerusalem—Zion und das Land Israel im jüdischen Glauben," *Lebendiges Zeugnis* 32 (1977): 87–97; F.-W. Marquardt, *Die Juden und ihr Land* (Hamburg, 1975); R. Mosis, ed., *Exil-Diaspora-Rückkehr. Zum theologischen Gespräch zwischen Juden und Christen* (Düsseldorf, 1977); H. Seebass, "Landverheissung an die Väter," *Evangelische Theologie* 37 (1977): 210ff.; R. J. Zwi Werblowsky, "Prophetie, das Land und das Volk," *Freiburger Rundbrief* 23 (1971): 33–35; F.-W. Marquardt, "Gottes Bundestreue und die biblischen Landverheissungen," in *Jüdische Hoffnungskraft und christlicher Glaube*, ed. W. Strolz (Freiburg, 1971), pp. 80–133; R. Rendtorff, "Die religiösen und geistigen Wurzeln des Zionismus,"

Aus Politik und Zeitgeschichte B 49/76, pp. 3–17; R. Pfisterer, "Der Zionismus— die nationale Befreiungsbewegung des jüdischen Volkes," ibid., pp. 1–39; H. J. Schoeps, ed., *Zionismus, 34 Aufsätze* (Munich, 1973); *Zionismus. Befreiungsbewegung des jüdischen Volkes* (Veröffentlichungen aus dem Institute Kirche und Judentum bei der kirchlichen Hochschule Berlin, 5, Berlin, 1977); B. Klappert, *Israel und die Kirche. Erwägungen zur Israellehre Karl Barths* (Munich, 1980); A. Ohler, *Israel, Volk und Land. Zur Geschichte der wechselseitigen Beziehungen zwischen Israel und seinem Land in alttestamentlicher Zeit* (Stuttgart, 1979).

30. See above all Diepold, *Israels Land.*

31. W. Zimmerli, *Grundriss der alttestamentlichen Theologie* (Stuttgart, 1972), p. 55.

32. Rendtorff in Eckert et al., *Jüdisches Volk—gelobtes Land*, p. 164.

33. Ibid.

34. This material is gathered in E. L. Dietrich, שׁוּב שְׁבוּת. *Die endzeitliche Wiederherstellung bei den Propheten* (Giessen, 1928), pp. 38–51; W. D. Davies, *Paul and Rabbinic Judaism*, 2d ed. (London, 1955), pp. 79–82.

35. Rendtorff in Eckert et al., *Jüdisches Volk—gelobtes Land*, p. 168.

36. Ibid.

37. H. Schmid, "Messiaserwartung und Rückkehr in das Land Israel nach dem Alten Testament," in ibid., pp. 188–196.

38. Cf. F. J. Schierse, *Verheissung und Heilsvollendung. Zur theologischen Grundfrage des Hebräerbriefes* (Munich, 1955).

39. Cf. the material in P. Billerbeck, *Kommentar zum Neuen Testament aus Talmud und Midrasch* (Munich, 1922), 1: 199f.

40. Cf. B. H. Ausserhofer, "Joseph Roth im Widerspruch zum Zionismus," *Emuna. Horizonte* 5 (1970): 325–330.

41. Cf. J. Jeremias, *Jesu Verheissung für die Völker* (Stuttgart, 1956).

42. H. U. von Balthasar, *Einsame Zwiesprache. Martin Buber und das Christentum* (Cologne and Olten, 1958), p. 54.

43. Ibid., pp. 52f.

44. Buber, *Israel und Palästina* (Zurich, 1950).

45. See the illuminating dual biography by the Jewish scholar R. Kallner, *Herzl und Rathenau. Wege jüdischer Existenz an der Wende des 20. Jahrhunderts* (Stuttgart, 1976).

46. See also the enlightening book by M. Sallis-Freudenthal, *Ich habe mein Land gefunden. Autobiographischer Rückblick* (Frankfurt, 1977).

47. Klappert, *Israel und die Kirche*, pp. 70–76.

48. Ibid.

49. Certainly Peter encouraged the Jews in 3:19 to conversion (namely, to the gospel) and spoke to them in 3:23 with a citation from Lev. 23:19: "And it shall be that every soul that does not listen to that prophet [Jesus] shall be discharged from the people," whereto E. Haenchen in his Acts commentary remarks: "The Jew who does not confess to Christ ceases to be a member of the people of God! With this it is made clear to the listeners just what is at stake." However, there is neither here nor anywhere else in Acts a single syllable about God excluding his people Israel in fact from eschatological salvation, even though it rejected Jesus as Messiah. Cf. F.

Mussner, "Wohnung Gottes und Menschensohn nach der Stephanusperikope (Acts 6:8—8:2)," in *Jesus und der Menschensohn. Festschrift für A. Vögtle*, ed. R. Pesch and R. Schnackenburg (Freiburg, 1975), pp. 283–299. Such juridical threats in the Old Testament also belong to the prophetic style of teaching.

50. E. Käsemann and H. Schlier in their translation of the original text understand the statement about the covenant to be future ("and this will be my covenant for you").

51. H. Schlier, *Der Römerbrief* (Freiburg, 1977), p. 340.

52. Cf. especially the article on *"tōrā"* by G. Liedke and C. Petersen in the *Theologisches Handwörterbuch zum Alten Testament.* (Munich and Zurich, 1976), 2: 1032–1043 (with comprehensive bibliography on the history of research).

53. Cf. ibid., p. 1035.

54. Ibid., p. 1036.

55. Cf. ibid.

56. Ibid., p. 1037.

57. Ibid.

58. Ibid.

59. Ibid., p. 1039.

60. Ibid., p. 1040.

61. Cf. also H. J. Kraus, "Freude an Gottes Gesetz," *Evangelische Theologie* 10 (1951/52): 337–351.

62. Liedke and Petersen, *"tōrā."*

63. Ibid., p. 1042.

64. W. Gutbrod, *"Nomos,"* in *Theological Dictionary of the New Testament*, ed. G. Kittel (Grand Rapids, 1967), 4: 1047.

65. See specifics with references in ibid.

66. Ibid., p. 1048.

67. Ibid. Cf. also R. Meyer, "Tradition und Neuschöpfung im antiken Judentum," *Berichte über die Verhandlungen der Sächssichen Akademie* 110, no. 2 (1965): 7–88.

68. Cf. M. Hengel, *Judentum und Hellenismus. Studien zu ihrer Begegnung unter besonderer Berücksichtigung Palästinas bis zur Mitte des 2. Jahrhunderts v. Chr.*, 2d ed. (Tübingen, 1973), pp. 105ff., 453–463. English translation: *Judaism and Hellenism* (Philadelphia, 1974), 1: 55f., 247–254.

69. Cf. ibid., pp. 169–175; H.-Fr. Weiss, *Untersuchungen zur Kosmologie des hellenistischen und palästinischen Judentums. Texte und Untersuchungen zur Geschichte der altchristlichen Literatur* (Berlin, 1966), 97: 283–304; M. Limbeck, *Die Ordnung des Heils. Untersuchungen zum Gesetzesverständnis des Frühjudentums* (Düsseldorf, 1971); M. Limbeck, *Von der Ohnmacht des Rechts. Zur Gesetzeskritik des Neuen Testaments* (Düsseldorf, 1972); L. Mack, *Logos und Sophia. Untersuchungen zur Weisheitstheologie im hellenistischen Judentum* (Göttingen, 1973); E. Zenger, "Die späte Weisheit und das Gesetz," in *Literatur und Religion des Frühjudentums*, ed. J. Maier and J. Schreiner (Würzburg and Gütersloh, 1973), pp. 43–56—with extensive bibliography.

70. M. Limbeck developed this often-overlooked aspect in Law piety.

71. Limbeck, *Von der Ohnmacht des Rechts*, p. 34.

72. Ibid.

73. See W. Zimmerli, *Das Gesetz und die Propheten* (Göttingen, 1963), pp. 81–93.

74. Ibid.

75. Cf. H. Gross, "Tora und Gnade im Alten Testament," *Kairos* 14 (1972): 220–231; R. J. Zwi Werblowsky, "Tora als Gnade," *Kairos* 15 (1973): 156–163; H. Schmid, "Gesetz und Gnade im Alten Testament," *Judaica* 25 (1969): 3–29; K. Hruby, "Gesetz und Gnade in der rabbinschen Überlieferung," *Judaica* 25 (1969): 30–63; J. Maier, "'Gesetz' und 'Gnade' im Wandel des Gesetzesverständnisses der nachtalmudischen Zeit," *Judaica* 25 (1969): 64–176; E. L. Ehrlich, "Tora im Judentum," *Evangelische Theologie* 37 (1977): 536–549; P. von der Osten-Sacken, "Das paulinische Verständnis des Gesetzes im Spannungsfeld von Eschatologie und Geschichte. Erläuterungen zum Evangelium als Faktor von theologischen Antijudaismus," *Evangelische Theologie* 37 (1977): 549–587.

76. See M. Buber, *Two Types of Faith* (New York, 1951); L. Baeck, *Aus drei Jahrtausenden* (Tübingen, 1957); H. Kosmala, *Hebräer—Essener—Christen* (Leiden, 1957), pp. 97–116; N. Oswald, "Grundgedanken zu einer pharisäisch-rabbinischen Theologie," *Kairos* 6 (1963): 40–58.

77. See the further discussion on pp. 68ff.

78. Ibid., p. 57.

79. See A. H. Friedlander, "Zeitlosigkeit und geschichtliche Wirksamkeit der Torah," in *Drei Wege zu dem einen Gott*, ed. A. Falaturi, J. J. Petuchowski, W. Strolz (Freiburg, 1976), pp. 33–44.

80. E. Simon, *Brücken. Gesammelte Aufsätze* (Heidelberg, 1965), p. 468.

81. Oswald, "Grundgedanken."

82. I am grateful here for the early Judaism materials from Reinhold Mayer of Tübingen.

83. Friedlander, "Zeitlosigkeit," p. 36.

84. See below, pp. 134ff.

85. Besides the commentaries, see especially M. Rese, "Die Vorzüge Israels in Röm 9,4f. und Eph 2,12. Exegetische Anmerkungen zum Thema Kirche und Israel," *Theologische Zeitschrift* 31 (1975): 211–222; Karl Barth, *Church Dogmatics* II/2 (Edinburgh, 1957): 202–205.

86. H. Schlier, *Der Römerbrief* (Freiburg, 1977), p. 92.

87. Rese, "Vorzüge."

88. See also C. Roetzel, "Diathekai in Romans 9,4," *Biblica* 51 (1979): 377–390.

89. See also F. W. Maier, *Israel in der Heisgeschichte nach Röm 9—11* (Münster, 1929).

90. Schlier, *Römerbrief*, pp. 286f.

91. Rese, "Vorzüge," p. 218.

92. See also Joseph Blank, "Das Mysterium Israel," in *Jüdische Hoffnungskraft*, ed. Strolz, pp. 134–190.

93. "The pagan relationship toward the future was completely different from that of Israel, so that in the end it can be described only as 'hopelessness,'" ibid., p. 136.

94. Concerning this extraordinary affirmation, cf. J. Gnilka, *Der Epheserbrief*, 2d ed. (Freiburg, 1977), pp. 136f. Joseph Blank interprets this extremely well as follows: "Not that pagans had no religion or no gods. On the contrary, their world was overfilled with them. However, precisely this pagan overabundance of gods and

religions was and is the sign of a profound godlessness, of a missing community with God, so that the human being in paganism created for himself with his gods a substitute for the missing community with God; he had to cover up the existing distance from God with the pressing nearness of the gods" ("Mysterium Israel").

95. See further details on pp. 243ff.

96. Blank, "Mysterium Israel," p. 137.

97. See further details on pp. 134ff.

98. See also F. Hahn, "'Das Heil kommt von den Juden.' Erwägungen zu Joh 4,22b," *Wort und Wirklichkeit. Festschrift für Eugen Ludwig Rapp* (Meisenheim, 1976), 1: 67–84.

99. See, for example, Burger, *Jesus als Davidsohn. Eine traditionsgeschichtliche Untersuchung* (Göttingen, 1970).

100. C. H. Dodd, *The Interpretation of the Fourth Gospel* (Cambridge, 1954), p. 296.

101. For example, R. Bultmann, among others.

102. For example, G. Friedrich, *Wer ist Jesus? Die Verkündigung des vierten Evangelisten, dargestellt an Joh 4,4–42* (Stuttgart, 1967), p. 43.

103. See also R. Schnackenburg, *Das Johannesevangelium*, 3d ed. (Freiburg, 1972), 1: 471; C. K. Barrett, *The Gospel According to St. John* (London, 1955), p. 198.

104. See further details on pp. 38ff.

105. Cf. concerning this F. Mussner, "Ganz Israel wird gerettet werden' (Röm 11,26)," *Kairos* 18 (1976): 241–255. What is presented there in a more scholarly fashion will here be repeated in abbreviated form and in a more generally understandable manner, along with a few expansions. I shall take a position regarding only some of the comprehensive literature on Rom. 9—11 (on this see note 132).

106. G. von Rad, "*Israēl*," in Kittel, ed., *Theological Dictionary*, 3: 357f.

107. "All Israel" 148 times, "the entire people" (Israel) 119 times, "the entire house of Israel" 20 times, "the entire community" (Israel) 84 times, "all the sons of Israel," "all the offspring of the sons of Israel," etc.

108. On the various interpretations of the formula "all Israel" in exegesis, see the analysis in B. Mayer, *Unter Gottes Heilsratschluss. Prädestinationsgedanken bei Paulus* (Würzburg, 1974), pp. 285ff.

109. See further details on pp. 23ff.

110. See the references in my article, "Ganz Israel wird gerettet werden," pp. 247–249.

111. D. Zeller, *Juden und Heiden in der Mission des Paulus. Studien zum Römerbrief* (Stuttgart, 1973), p. 245. Zeller himself does not believe in a "special way"; rather he believes that Israel will "come to salvation through faith in the gospel" (p. 257).

112. Mayer, *Unter Gottes Heilsratschluss*, p. 284.

113. Reference is also made to 4Qflor I, 11b–13: "That is the descendant of David [the David Messiah] who along with the researchers of the Law will appear . . . in Zion at the end of days, as it is written: and I will set up again the fallen hut of David (Amos 9:11). That is the fallen hut of David which will stand in order to save Israel." Here very obviously a connection is established between the rise of the Messiah in Zion at the end of days and the saving of Israel.

114. Maier, *Israel in der Heilsgeschichte*.

115. See also the formation in Acts 3:20, according to which God sends at the *parousia* "the Christ appointed *for you*, Jesus," that is, the *parousia* Christ also comes primarily for Israel!

116. Reference can also be made to Luke 21:24: "And they [the Jews] will fall by the edge of the sword, and be led captive among all nations; and Jerusalem will be trodden down by the Gentiles, *until the times of the Gentiles are fulfilled.*" Here Jesus appears to be predicting that the times of un-salvation will be followed by a time of salvation for Israel, especially if one compares this prediction with that of Luke 13:35, where the same promise as in Matt. 23:39 is encountered.

117. See further details on pp. 209ff.

118. See also the study document by Tommaso Federici, "Study Outline on the Mission and Witness of the Church, *Sidic* II, no. 3 (1978): 25–34. This is a highly thought of lecture which Federici delivered on the sixth day of the Catholic-Jewish Liaison Committee Meeting in March 1977 at Venice. See further U. Luz, "Judenmission im Lichte des Neuen Testaments," *Zeitschrift für Mission* 4 (1978): 127–133; Heinz Kreimers, *Judenmission heute: Von der Judenmission zur brüderlichen Solidarität und zum ökumenischen Dialog* (Neukirchen, 1979).

119. Cf. also O. Hofius, "Die Unabänderlichkeit des göttlichen Heilsratschlusses. Erwägungen zur Herkunft eines neutestamentlichen Theologumenon," *Zeitschrift für die neutestamentliche Wissenschaft* 64 (1973): 135–145. "Only because God is loyal to Israel do the Gentile Christians have a basis to trust in him; or, negatively phrased: If God were not loyal to his people chosen in an earlier time, the Gentile Christians who had been engrafted onto that same people would have no basis to believe that the election of God is any different from a changing arbitrariness and that God will also maintain loyalty to them. The basis and the content of faith . . . is dependent on the mercy of God on all Israel" (Markus Barth, "Das Volk Gottes. Juden und Christen in der Botschaft des Paulus," in *Paulus—Apostat oder Apostel?*, ed. Markus Barth et al. [Regensburg, 1977], pp. 75f.).

120. The apostle affirms this in opposition to his immediately preceding formulation: "In regard to the gospel [they are] indeed enemies for your sakes," that is, for the sake of the Christianized Gentiles. This addition of the apostle, "for your sakes," "had been suppressed in the 2,000-year history of Christian anti-Judaism" (Peter von der Osten-Sacken, "Rückzug ins Wesen und aus der Geschichte. Antijudaismus bei Adolf von Harnack und Rudolf Bultmann," *Wissenschaft und Praxis in Kirche und Gesellschaft* 67 [1978]: 106–122). Cf. also the penetrating analysis of F.-W. Marquardt, "'Feinde um unseretwillen.' Das jüdische Nein und die christliche Theologie," in *Treue zur Thora. Festschrift für G. Harder*, ed. Peter von der Osten-Sacken (Berlin, 1977), pp. 174–193. Marquardt points out the positive impact on Christian theology that should arise from the formulation "enemies for our sake." E. P. Grässer convincingly showed that with reference to Bultmann, one may not speak of anti-Judaism: "Antijudaismus bei Bultmann? Eine Erwiderung," *Wissenschaft und Praxis in Kirche und Gesellschaft* 67 (1978): 419–429. The "existential interpretation" of the Bible need by no means carry with it an anti-Judaism, even though the salvation historical phenomenon of Israel necessarily disappears in it; it means a retreat from history into existence.

121. The Church should reflect on this. It also makes little sense to speculate on the question: What would have happened if . . . (if Israel had accepted Jesus and gospel?)

122. See Maier, *Israel in der Heilsgeschichte*, p. 139, n. 141.

123. See further details on pp. 38ff.

124. See J. Gnilka, *Die Verstockung Israels. Isaias 6,9–10 in der Theologie der Synoptiker* (Munich, 1961).

125. Lohfink, *Bibelauslegung*, p. 234.

126. See F. Mussner, "Die Idee der Apokatastasis in der Apostelgeschichte," in *Praesentia Salutis. Gesammelte Studien zu Fragen und Themen des Neuen Testaments*, ed. F. Mussner (Düsseldorf, 1967), pp. 223–234; G. Voss, *Die Christologie der lukanischen Schriften in Grundzügen* (Paris and Brügge, 1965), pp. 28–31; G. Lohfink, "Christologie und Geschichtsbild in Apg 3,19–21," *Biblische Zeitschrift* 13 (1969): 223–241.

127. See F. Mussner, "'In den letzten Tagen' (Apg 2, 17a)," *Biblische Zeitschrift* 5 (1961): 263–265.

128. A. Wikenhauser, *Die Apostelgeschichte*, 3d ed. (Regensburg, 1956).

129. E. Stauffer, "Agnostos Christos," in *The Background of the New Testament and Its Eschatology: Studies in Honour of C. H. Dodd* (Cambridge, 1956), p. 286.

130. Material for this restoration *(apokatastasis)* idea are found in E. L. Dietrich, *Shuv Shevut. Die endzeitliche Wiederherstellung bei den Propheten* (Giessen, 1928), pp. 38–51; W. D. Davies, *Paul and Rabbinic Judaism*, 2d ed. (London, 1955), pp. 79–82. The term *shuv shevut* occurs 27 times in the Old Testament. On the controversy concerning its precise meaning, see the brief report by J. A. Soggin in *Theologisches Handwörterbuch zum Alten Testament*, ed. Ernst Jenni and Claus Westermann (Munich, 1971), 2: 886–888. In any case, the term appears to belong to the image field of a "restorative eschatology" (Fohrer).

131. See also J. R. Garcia, "La restauración de Israel (Act. 1,4–9)," *Estudios bíblicos* 8 (1949): 75–133.

132. Recent literature on Rom. 9—11 (selection without commentary): W. Fischer, "Das Geheimnis Israels. Eine Erklärung der Kapitel 9—11 des Römerbrief," *Judaica* 6 (1950): pp. 81–132. L. Goppelt, "Israel und die Kirche, heute und bei Paulus," in *Christologie und Ethik. Aufsätze zum Neuen Testament*, ed. L. Goppelt (Göttingen, 1968), pp. 165–189. E. Käsemann, "Rechtfertigung und Heilsgeschichte im Römerbrief," in *Paulinische Perspektiven*, ed. E. Käsemann, 2d ed. (Tübingen, 1972), pp. 108–139. U. Luz, "Das Geschichtsverständnis des Paulus," *Beiträge zur evangelischen Theologie* 49 (Munich, 1968). Maier, *Israel in der Heilsgeschichte*. Mayer, *Unter Gottes Heilsratschluss*, pp. 167–313, with comprehensive bibliography. Müller, *Gottes Gerechtigkeit und Gottes Volk. Eine Untersuchung zu Römer 9—11. Forschungen zur Religion und Literatur des Alten und Neuen Testaments* 86 (1964). J. Munck, *Christus und Israel. Eine Auslegung von Röm 9—11. Acta Jutlantica, Teol. Ser. 7* (Copenhagen, 1956). E. Peterson, "Die Kirche aus Juden und Heiden," *Theologische Traktate*, ed. E. Peterson (Munich, 1951), pp. 239–292. Plag, *Israels Wege zum Heil. Eine Untersuchung zu Römer 9—11. Arbeiten zur Theologie* 1, no. 40 (Stuttgart, 1969). P. Richardson, *Israel in the Apostolic Church* (Cambridge, 1969), pp. 126–147. K. L. Schmidt, *Die Judenfrage im Lichte der Kapitel 9—11 des Römerbriefes. Theologische Studien* 13 (Zollikon

and Zurich, 1943). H. J. Schoeps, *Paulus. Die Theologie des Apostels im Lichte der jüdischen Religionsgeschichte* (Tübingen, 1959), pp. 248–259. G. Schrenk, *Die Weissagung über Israel im Neuen Testament* (Zurich, 1951). P. Stuhlmacher, "Zur Interpretation von Römer 11, 25–32," in *Probleme biblischer Theologie. Festschrift für G. von Rad*, ed. H. W. Wolff (Munich, 1971), pp. 555–570. D. Zeller. *Juden und Heiden in der Mission des Paulus. Studien zum Römerbrief. Forschung zur Bibel 1* (Stuttgart, 1973). D. Zeller, "Israel unter dem Ruf Gottes (Röm 9—11)," *Internationale Katholische Zeitschrift* 4 (1973): 289–301. K. Barth, *Church Dogmatics*, II/2: 294–336. M. Barth, "Das Volk Gottes. Juden und Christen in der Botschaft des Paulus," in *Paulus—Apostat oder Apostel? Jüdische und christliche antworten*, ed. M. Barth et al. (Regensburg, 1977) pp. 45–134 (81–79). W. D. Davies, "Paul and the People of Israel," *New Testament Studies* 24 (1977/78): 4–39. L. De Lorenzi, ed., *Die Israelfrage nach Röm 9–11* (Rome, 1977) with the following contributions: L. De Lorenzi, "Il problema d'Israele," pp. 1–12e; W. G. Kümmel, "Die Probleme von Römer 9–11 in der gegenwärtigen Forschungslage," pp. 13–33; F. Montagnini, "Elezione e libertà, grazia e predestinazione a propositio di Rom 9,6–29," pp. 56–86; C. K. Barrett, "Romans 9,30—10,21: Fall and Responsibility of Israel," pp. 99–121; F. Dreyfus, "Le passé et le présent d'Israel (Rom. 9,1–5; 11,1–24)," pp. 131–151; J. Jeremias, "Einige vorwiegend sprachliche Beobachtungen zu Röm 11,25–36," pp. 193–205; P. Benoit, "Conclusion par mode de synthèse," pp. 217–236; M. Barth, "Die Stellung des Paulus zu Gesetz und Ordnung," pp. 145–187 (the comprehensive and lively discussion of the conference participants is added to each contribution). B. Klappert, *Israel und die Kirche. Erwägungen zur Israellehre Karl Barths* (Munich, 1980). B. Klappert, "Traktat für Israel (Römer 9—11)," in *Jüdische Existenz und die Erneuerung der christlichen Theologie*, ed. M. Stöhr (Munich, 1982), pp. 58–137. F. Mussner, "Heil für alle. Der Grundgedanke des Römerbriefs," *Kairos* 23 (1981): 207–214.

133. For its exegesis, see the commentaries on the Epistle to the Romans, especially the careful analyses which pursue the finest nuances of the text by Maier, *Israel in der Heilsgeschichte*, pp. 125ff; also see the works on Romans 9—11 in ibid.; further, see K. H. Rengstorf, "Das Ölbaum-Gleichnis in Röm 11,16ff. Versuch einer weiterführenden Deutung," in *Donum Gentilicium. Festschrift für D. Daube*, ed. C. K. Barrett (Oxford, 1978), pp. 127–264.

134. For it, see Maurer, "Hriza," in Kittel, ed., *Theological Dictionary* 6: 985–991; J. Becker, "Wurzel und Wurzelspross. Ein Beitrag zur hebräischen Lexikographie," *Biblische Zeitschrift* 20 (1976): 22–44.

135. Ibid., p. 43.

136. Ibid., p. 44.

137. In the essay referred to in note 133 K. H. Rengstorf attempts to show that in Rom. 11:16f. Paul "not only uses several traditional metaphors, but that within it he moves from beginning to end within the area of Rabbinic *haggadah* and places it at the service of his proclamation" (p. 163).

138. E. Käsemann, *An die Römer*, 2d ed. (Tübingen, 1974), pp. 299f. Likewise, Maier should be cited here: "The thought of the present dependence of Gentile and Jewish salvation history on the one side and the eschatological 'fulfilling' of the hope of Israel connected with it on the other, do not stand as two separated, unconnected circles of images alongside of each other; rather this is a connecting, interpenetrat-

ing development whose beginning and end point is *Israel*," and "*Israel at the same time is the alpha and omega of all salvation history*" (*Israel in der Heilsgeschichte*, p. 123). Of course, I cannot share Maier's opinion of a final "total" conversion of Israel to the gospel because in reality the apostle did not predict this, if one listens carefully to the texts (concerning this, see my analyses on pp. 28ff.).

139. Käsemann, *An die Römer*, p. 297.

140. Cf. Rengstorf, "Das Ölbaum-Gleichnis," p. 155: "The coming universal community of God, united in faith in Jesus as the Christ, and in whom the renewed single humanity will not be without the descendants of Abraham according to the flesh. That was thus willed by God, and if it remains so, that means that Israel will form the core of the new humanity which, when it is there, will gather itself around God." This means, however, also, "that there can be no Christian Church without a relationship back to the pre-Christian revelation, and that a Christianity which believes that it can be without the Old Testament for the sake of the world which stands in rejection over against Judaism loses the ground under its feet and runs the danger sooner or later of also losing the God who is the Father of Jesus Christ."

141. B. Klappert, "Der Verlust und die Wiedergewinnung der israelitischen Kontur der Leidensgeschichte Jesu (das Kreuz, das Leiden, das Paschamahl, der Prozess Jesu)," in *Exodus und Kreuz im ökumenischen Dialog zwischen Juden und Christen*, ed. H. H. Henrix and M. Stöhr (Aachen, 1978), pp. 107–153. Cf. also Klappert, *Israel und die Kirche*.

142. See, for example, H. Haag, "Ebed Jahwe-Forschung 1948–1958," *Biblische Zeitschrift* 3 (1959): 174–204; O. Kaiser, *Der Königliche Knecht. Eine traditionsgeschichtlich-exegetische Studie über die Ebed-Jahwe-Lieder bei Deuterojesaja* (Göttingen, 1959).

143. See, for example, P. Seidelin, "Der Ebed Jahwe und die Messiasgestalt im Jesajatargum," *Zeitschrift für die neutestamentliche Wissenschaft* 35 (1936): 194–231; J. Jeremias, "pais theou," in Kittel, ed., *Theological Dictionary*, 5: 677–717; H. Hegemann, *Jesaja 53 in Hexapla, Targum und Peschitta* (Gütersloh, 1954); M. Rese, "Überprüfung einiger Theses von Joachim Jeremias zum Thema des Gottesknechts im Judentum," *Zeitschrift für Theologie und Kirche* 60 (1963): 21–41; K. Baltzer, "Zur formgeschichtlichen Bestimmung der Texte vom Gottes-Knecht im Deuterojesaja-Buch," in *Probleme biblischer Theologie. Festschrift für G. von Rad* (Munich, 1971), pp. 27–43.

144. See J. Jeremias, "Pais (theou) im Neuen Testament," in *Abba. Studien zur neutestamentlichen Theologie- und Zeitgeschichte*, ed. J. Jeremias (Göttingen, 1966), pp. 191–216 (revision of the "pais theou D," in Kittel, ed., *Theological Dictionary*, 5: 698–713).

145. See Thoma, *Christian Theology of Judaism*, p. 132.

146. Leo Baeck, *Das Wesen des Judentums*, 4th ed. (Frankfurt, 1926), pp. 202–205. See also H. Wittenberg, *Jüdische Existenz nach Leo Baeck* (Neuendettelsau, 1955).

147. Joseph Klausner, *The Messianic Idea in Israel* (New York, 1955), p. 163.

148. See H.-M. Rotermund, *Marc Chagall und die Bibel* (Lahr, 1970), pp. 111–138.

149. Ibid., p. 138.

150. "The appearance of the crematorium ovens of Auschwitz is for me the light

tower which directs all my thoughts. O my Jewish brothers, and also you, my Christian brothers, do you not believe that it is with another appearance with which the cross is confused?" wrote the Jew Jules Isaac, *Jesus and Israel* (New York, 1971), p. 400.

151. Apparently Jesus had understood himself as the "servant of God" predicted by Deutero-Isaiah. The Jewish scholar M. Friedländer has remarked: "There can . . . be no doubt that Jesus was very clearly aware of it. The 'servant of God' in Isaiah was the great prototype according to which he lived and worked. The impression which this prophetic vision exercised on him appears to have been a powerful one from the beginning" *(Synagoge und Kirche in ihren Anfängen* [Berlin, 1908], p. 178).

152. Schalom Ben-Chorin, "Der leidende Mensch. Von Hiob bis zum Knecht Gottes," in *"Dass dein Ohr auf Weisheit achtet"* (Wuppertal-Barmen, 1966), p. 24.

153. Concerning Holocaust theology see, for example, E. Berkovits, *Faith after the Holocaust* (New York, 1973); E. Fleischner, ed., *Auschwitz: Beginning of a New Era?* *Reflections on the Holocaust* (New York, 1977); *Freiburger Rundbrief* 27 (1975): 20–27; Thoma, *Christian Theology of Judaism*, pp. 152–155, 159f.; E. L. Ehrlich and C. Thoma, *Gibt es eine Holocaust-Theologie?* (Vienna, n.d.).

154. Thoma, *Christian Theology of Judaism*, p. 159.

155. See also J. Oesterreicher, *Auschwitz, der Christ und das Konzil* (Meitingen, 1964) and, in addition, my own specifics on pp. 131ff., "Jesus as Israel."

156. B. Engelmann, *Deutschland ohne Juden. Eine Bilanz*, Deutscher Taschenbuchverlag 979 (Munich, 1973).

157. With a view to Ps. 59:10f.: "My God in his steadfast love will meet me; my God will let me look in triumph on my enemies. Slay them not, lest my people forget; make them totter by thy power, and bring them down," Augustine remarked: "God had, therefore, shown the grace of his mercy to the Church in its enemies, the Jews, since, as the apostle says (in Rom. 11:11), 'Their sins are unto salvation for the Gentiles'; and therefore he did not kill them, that is, he did not destroy their character as Jews, although they were conquered by the Romans and were suppressed, so that they might not, by forgetting the Law of God, become unfit to bear the witness which we here mean" *(The City of God*, 18: 46). In this Augustine is thinking of the witness of the Jews scattered among the Gentiles to the authenticity of the prophecies "which were issued previously about Christ" (ibid.): "They are not the inventions of the Church." Therefore, for Augustine the Jew is the witness to the remaining validity of the Scriptures.

158. For Hegel's image of Judaism see H. Liebeschütz, *Das Judentum im deutschen Geschichtsbild von Hegel bis Max Weber* (Tübingen, 1967), pp. 1–42.

159. E. Jünger, *Eumeswil* (Stuttgart, 1977).

160. Marquardt, "'Feinde um unsretwillen,'" pp. 174–193. J. Blank formulates the matter thus: "A state or a society which understands itself as something absolutely perfect cannot bear a group which through its mere existence contradicts this ideal" *(Das Mysterium Israel*, p. 189).

161. See also L. Perlitt, "Die Verborgenheit Gottes," in Wolff, ed., *Probleme biblischer Theologie*, pp. 367–382.

162. Schoeps, *Paulus*, p. 274.

163. D. Flusser, "Inwiefern kann Jesus für Juden eine Frage sein?" *Concilium* 10 (1974): 596–599.

164. P. Lapide and H. Küng, "Is Jesus a Bond or a Barrier? A Jewish-Christian Dialogue," *Journal of Ecumenical Studies* 14 (1977): 482.

165. Marquardt, " 'Feinde um unsretwillen,' " p. 192.

166. Ibid.

167. Concerning this see pp. 28ff.

168. Thoma, *Christian Theology of Judaism*, p. 176.

169. M. Hess, *Rom und Jerusalem. Die letzte Nationalitätsfrage*, 2d ed. (Leipzig, 1899), p. 57.

170. Concerning this see pp. 243ff.

171. See further details on pp. 42ff.

172. Additional profound reflections on this theme can be found in J. Moltmann, *Kirche in der Kraft des Geistes. Ein Beitrag zur messianischen Ekklesiologie* (Munich, 1975), pp. 156–171.

173. Cf. F. Rosenzweig, *Der Stern der Erlösung*, 4th ed. (Haag, 1976), p. 460.

174. Ibid., p. 461. I agree completely with the statements of Markus Barth: "The existence of the people of God is not only inseparable from the completion of, but also identical with, the history of the election, condemnation, maintenance, and mission of Israel in the midst of the Gentile world. Therefore this people is neither a timeless idea nor a utopia. Its history in fact shows it to be so unique, inexplicable, and goal-oriented that it is not to be compared with another history and in no way can be manipulated" ("Das Volk Gottes," p. 96). Barth speaks also of a "*character indelibilis* of the Jewish people . . . which distinguishes this people from all other peoples: The consolation and the claim of being the chosen people of God is affirmed of it—regardless of whether the Jews themselves, the Gentiles, or the Christians greet this and acknowledge it in word and deed" (ibid., p. 106).

NOTES FOR CHAPTER 2

1. See P. van Imschoot, "Monotheism," in *Bibel-Lexikon*, ed. H. Haag, 2d ed. (Einsiedeln, 1968), pp. 1167–1170; F. Baumgärtel, "Monotheismus im AT," in *Religion in Geschichte und Gegenwart*, 3d ed. (Tübingen, 1960), 4: 1113–1115; M. Gusinde, V. Hamp, J. Schmid, K. Rahner, "Monotheismus," in *Lexikon für Theologie und Kirche*, 2d ed. (Freiburg, 1962), 7: 565–570—each with bibliography. See further M. Vorländer, *Mein Gott. Die Vorstellungen vom persönlichen Gott im Alten Orient und im Alten Testament* (Neukirchen, 1975); M. Görg, "Anfänge israelitischen Gottesglaubens," *Kairos* 18 (1976): 256–264; C. J. Labuschagne, *The Incomparability of Yahweh in the Old Testament* (Leiden, 1966); H. Gross, "Gotteserfahrung im Alten Testament," in *Suche nach Sinn. Suche nach Gott*, ed. A. Paus (Graz, 1978), pp. 139–175; M. Buber, "Die Götter der Völker und Gott," in *Werke* (Munich, 1964), 2: 1066–1083.

2. Philo, *De opificio mundi*, 171.

3. V. Hamp, "Monotheismus," *Lexikon für Theologie und Kirche*, 2d ed. (Freiburg, 1962), 7: 567.

4. Ibid.

5. For the following see especially van Imschoot, "Monotheismus"; see further L. Ruppert, "Jahwe und die Götter. Zur religionskritischen Funktion des Jahweglaubens," *Trierer theologische Zeitschrift* 84 (1975): 1–13.

6. See further details in G. Sauer in *Theologisches Handwörterbuch zum Alten Testament*, ed. E. Jenni and C. Westermann, 1: 106f., with bibliography.

7. See E. Zenger, "Die Mitte der alttestamentlichen Glaubensgeschichte," *Katechetische Blätter* 101 (1976): 3–16; Görg, "Anfänge israelitischen Gottesglaubens," p. 264.

8. See, for example, C. Westermann, *Genesis I* (Neukirchen, 1974), p. 131; O. H. Steck, *Der Schöpfungsbericht der Priesterschrift* (Göttingen, 1975), p. 226.

9. Ibid., p. 227.

10. *Midrash Bereshit Rabba* on Genesis 1:1.

11. See, for example, G. J. Botterweck, "Die Entstehung der Welt in den altorientalischen Kosmogonien," *Bibel und Leben* 6 (1965): 184–191.

12. H. Gunkel.

13. See, for example, Westermann, *Genesis I*, pp. 136–139; A. Angerstorfer, *Der Schöpfergott des Alten Testaments. Herkunft und Bedeutungsentwicklung des hebräischen Terminus (Bara) "Schaffen"* (Frankfurt, 1979); W. H. Schmidt, *"Bara"* in Jenni and Westermann, eds., *Theologisches Handwörterbuch zum Alten Testament*, 1: 336–339, with bibliography.

14. Westermann, *Genesis I*, p. 136.

15. Cf. ibid., p. 150: "The sentence that God had created the world from nothing says not more, but rather says less than the sentence that God had created the world. The question whether *creatio* is *ex nihilo* or not is not appropriate to the text." It is in 2 Macc. 7:28 that the idea of *creatio ex nihilo* is first thus formulated: "I beseech you, my child, to look at heaven and the earth and see everything that is in them, and recognize that God did not make them out of things that existed *(hoti ouk ex ontōn epoiēsen auta ho theos)."* Nevertheless, when one looks carefully, this idea is not present; cf. G. Schmuttermayr, " 'Schöpfund aus dem Nichts' im 2 Makk 7,28? Zum Verhältnis von Position und Bedeutung," *Biblische Zeitschrift* 17 (1973): 203–228, with the result: "For the presentation and teaching of creation from nothing 2 Macc. 7:28 cannot qualify as the 'locus classicus.' "

16. W. Zimmerli, *Grundriss der alttestamentlichen Theologie* (Berlin, 1972), p. 27. For the concept and principle of "separation" here and elsewhere in the Old Testament, see P. Beauchamp, *Création et séparation. Étude exégétique du chapitre premier de la Genèse* (Paris, 1969).

17. Zimmerli, *Grundriss*, p. 28.

18. Ibid.

19. Ibid., p. 30. See also H. Haag, "Gott als Schöpfer und Erlöser in der Prophetie des Deuterojesaja," *Trierer theologische Zeitschrift* 85 (1976): 193–213.

20. See Zimmerli, *Grundriss*, pp. 31f., 136–146 (further bibliography); G. von Rad, *Weisheit in Israel* (Neukirchen, 1970), pp. 189–228.

21. Ibid., p. 200.

22. Ibid., p. 204.

23. Ibid., p. 228.

24. Ibid.

25. Outside of the commentaries on Genesis see, for example, J. J. Stamm, "Die Imago-Lehre von Karl Barth und die alttestamentliche Wissenschaft," in *Antwort. Festschrift für Karl Barth* (Zollikon, 1956), pp. 84–98; J. J. Stamm, *Die Gottebenbildlichkeit des Menschen im Alten Testament. Theologische Studien* 54 (Zollikon,

1959); H. Gross, "Die Gottebenbildlichkeit des Menschen," in *Lex tua veritas. Festschrift für H. Junker*, ed. H. Gross and F. Mussner (Trier, 1961), pp. 89–100; H. Wildberger, "Das Abbild Gottes," *Theologische Zeitschrift* 21 (1965): 245–259, 481–501; H. Wildberger, *"Tzelem"* in *Theologisches Handwörterbuch zum Alten Testament*, 2: 556–563; O. Loretz, *Die Gottebenbildlichkeit des Menschen* (Stuttgart, 1967); H. W. Wolff, *Anthropologie des Alten Testaments* (Munich, 1973), pp. 233–242; J. Jervell, *Imago Dei. Gen 1,26f. im Spätjudentum, in der Gnosis und in den paulinischen Briefen* (Göttingen, 1960).

26. See Wildberger, *"Abbild Gottes,"* pp. 559f.

27. See further details in Gross, "Gottebenbildlichkeit," pp. 96–98.

28. Ibid., p. 98.

29. Wolff, *Anthropologie*, p. 235.

30. See ibid., p. 237.

31. Ibid., p. 238.

32. See Jervell, *Imago Dei*, pp. 71–84.

33. Ibid., p. 79.

34. See ibid., pp. 86–96.

35. Ibid., p. 96, with Rabbinic references.

36. See ibid., p. 95.

37. See pp. 7ff.

38. Zimmerli, *Grundriss*, p. 36. See further O. Procksch and K. G. Kuhn, "Hagios," in *Theological Dictionary of the New Testament*, ed. G. Kittel (Grand Rapids, 1967), 1: 88–115; O. Schilling, *Das Heilige und Gute im Alten Testament* (Leipzig, 1956); F. Nötscher, "Heiligkeit in den Qumranschriften," in *Vom Alten zum Neuen Testament*, ed. F. Nötscher (Bonn, 1962), pp. 126–174.

39. See pp. 18ff.

40. See J. Schreiner, "Hören auf Gott und sein Wort in der Sicht des Deuteronomiums," in *Miscellanea Erfordiana* (1962), pp. 27–47; M. Lohfink, *Das Hauptgebot* (Rom, 1963), pp. 66ff., 299ff.; A. K. Fenz, *Auf Jahwes Stimme hören* (Vienna, 1964).

41. J. Vollmer, *"asah,"* in *Theologisches Handwörterbuch zum Alten Testament:* 2: 359–370. See also H. Braun, *"Poieō,"* in Kittel, ed., *Theological Dictionary*, 6: 458–484.

42. Braun, ibid., p. 478.

43. H. Braun, *Spätjüdisch-häretischer und frühchristlicher Radikalismus* (Tübingen, 1957), 2: 30.32.

44. See further details on pp. 134ff.

45. Zimmerli, *Grundriss*, p. 128.

46. Ibid.

47. For further details, see J. Becker, *Gottesfurcht im Alten Testament* (Rome, 1965).

48. See G. J. Botterweck, *"Gott erkennen" im Sprachgebrauch des Alten Testaments* (Bonn, 1951); W. Zimmerli, *Erkenntnis Gottes nach dem Buche Ezechiel* (Zurich, 1954); H. W. Wolff, "Erkenntnis Gottes im Alten Testament," *Evangelische Theologie* 15 (1955): 426–431; S. Wagner, *"Yada"* in dem Loblieden von Qumran," in *Bibel und Qumran*, ed. H. Bardtke (Berlin, 1968), pp. 232–252; W. Schottroff, *"Yada,"* in *Theologisches Handwörterbuch zum Alten Testament* 1: 682–701;

B. Reike, "Da'at and Gnosis in Intertestamental Literature," in *Neotestamentica et Semitica. Festschrift for M. Black*, ed. E. Earle Ellis and M. Wilcox (Edinburgh, 1969), pp. 245–255.

49. See F. Mussner, ZOE. *Die Anschauung vom "Leben" im vierten Evangelium unter Berücksichtigung der Johannesbriefe* (Munich, 1952), pp. 172–176.

50. Schottroff, "Yada," p. 695.

51. See E. Jenni, "Ahav," in *Theologisches Handwörterbuch zum Alten Testament*, 1: 60–73, with further bibliography.

52. Ibid.

53. Ibid.

54. See J. Fichtner, "Der Begriff des 'Nächsten' im Alten Testament," *Wort und Dienst, Jahrbuch der Theologischen Schule Bethel* 4 (1955): 23–52.

55. See pp. 121ff.

56. Jenni, "Ahav."

57. F. Rosenzweig, *Der Stern der Erlösung*, 4th ed. (Haag, 1976), p. 239.

58. Concerning this see, for example, H. Wildberger, "'Glauben' im Alten Testament," *Zeitschrift für Theologie und Kirche* 65 (1968): 129–159; R. Smend, "Zur Geschichte von He-emin," in *Hebräische Wortforschung. Festschrift für W. Baumgartner* (Leiden, 1967), pp. 284–290; J. Barr, *Bibelexegese und moderne Semantik* (Munich, 1965), pp. 164–206; H. Wildberger, "Aman," in *Theologisches Handwörterbuch zum Alten Testament*, 1: 177–209.

59. G. von Rad, *Das erste Buch Mose (Genesis)*, 9th ed. (Göttingen, 1972), p. 142.

60. R. Kilian, *Die vorpriesterlichen Abrahamsüberlieferungen. Literarkritisch und traditionsgeschichtlich untersucht* (Bonn, 1966), p. 65.

61. W. Eichrodt, *Theologie des Alten Testaments* (Berlin, 1948), 3: 26.

62. For the whole matter, see ibid., pp. 23–30.

63. M. Buber, *Two Types of Faith* (New York, 1951).

64. See, for example, L. Wachinger, *Der Glaubensbegriff Martin Bubers* (Munich, 1970); E. Lohse, "Emuna und Pistis—Jüdisches und christliches Verständnis des Glaubens," *Zeitschrift für neutestamentliche Wissenschaft* 68 (1977): 147–163; C. Thoma, *A Christian Theology of Judaism*, tr. Helga Croner (New York, 1980), pp. 108–110 (the Jewish scholars S. H. Bergmann and D. Flusser have subjected the views of Buber to significant criticism).

65. See C. Schütz, *Verborgenheit Gottes. Martin Bubers Werk. Eine Gesamtdarstellung* (Zurich, 1975).

66. See especially D. Lührmann, *Glaube im frühen Christentum* (Gütersloh, 1976).

67. U. Wilkens, "Glaube nach urchristlichem und frühjüdischem Verständnis," in *Was Juden und Christen voneinander denken*, ed. P. Lapide, F. Mussner, and U. Wilkens (Freiburg, 1978), p. 95.

68. Ibid., p. 96.

69. See F. Mussner, "Der Glaube Mariens im Lichte des Römerbriefs," in *Praesentia Salutis. Gesammelte Studien und Themen des Neuen Testaments* (Düsseldorf, 1967), pp. 284–292.

70. A select bibliography: E. K. Dietrich, *Die Umkehr (Bekehrung und Busse) im Alten Testament und im Judentum* (Stuttgart, 1936); G. Fohrer, "Umkehr und

Erlösung beim Propheten Hosea," *Theologische Zeitschrift* 11 (1955): 161–185; H. W. Wolff, "Das Thema 'Umkehr' in der alttestamentlichen Prophetie," in *Gesammelte Studien zum Alten Testament* (Munich, 1964), pp. 130–150; H. W. Wolff, "Das Kerygma des deuteronomistischen Geschichtswerks," ibid., pp. 308–324; E. Würthwein, "metanoia," in Kittel, ed., *Theological Dictionary*, 4: 980–989; H. Gross, "Umkehr im Alten Testament in der Sicht der Propheten Jeremia und Ezechiel," in *Zeichen des Glaubens. Festschrift für B. Fischer*, ed. H. auf der Maur and B. Keinheyer (Einsiedeln, 1972), pp. 19–28, with further bibliography.

71. See Dietrich, *Umkehr*, pp. 319ff.

72. Wolff, "Thema 'Umkehr,' " p. 135.

73. Ibid., p. 143.

74. See ibid., pp. 144f.

75. Ibid., p. 145.

76. Wolff, "Das Kerygma," p. 315.

77. See ibid., pp. 321f.

78. J. Behm, "Metanoia," in Kittel, ed., *Theological Dictionary.* 4: 997.

79. See G. von Rad, *Theologie des Alten Testaments*, 5th ed. (Munich, 1966), 1: 353–367; C. Westermann, *Lob und Klage in den Psalmen*, 5th ed. (Göttingen, 1977); C. Westermann, "*Halal*," in *Theologisches Handwörterbuch zum Alten Testament*, 1: 493–502; C. Westermann, "*Yadah*," in ibid., pp. 674–682; F. Crüsemann, *Studien zur Formgeschichte von Hymnus und Danklied in Israel* (Neukirchen, 1969).

80. Von Rad, *Theologie des Alten Testaments*, p. 367.

81. Westermann, *Lob und Klage*, p. 495.

82. The verbs parallel to "praise" are "sing," "play," "praise," and are accompanied by musical instruments.

83. Westermann, *Lob und Klage*.

84. Ibid., p. 499.

85. See ibid., pp. 499f.

86. Concerning this see, for example, D. Michel, "Studien zu den sogenannten Thronbesteigungspsalmen," *Vetus Testamentum* 6 (1956): 40–58.

87. Westermann, *Lob und Klage*, pp. 110–115.

88. For further details see pp. 110ff.

89. From the comprehensive literature on the theme "covenant" according to the Old Testament the following are to be mentioned: N. Lohfink, "Bund," in *Bibel-Lexikon*, ed. H. Haag, 2d ed. (Einsiedeln, 1968), pp. 267–273, with comprehensive bibliography; D. J. McCarthy, *Der Gottesbund im Alten Testament. Ein Bericht über die Forschung der letzten Jahre. Stuttgarter Bibelstudien* 13 (Stuttgart, 1967); E. Kutsch, "*Berit*," in *Theologisches Handwörterbuch zum Alten Testament*, 1: 339–352; M. Weinfeld, "*Berit*," in ibid., pp. 781–808; H. Gross, "Glaube und Bund—Theologische Bemerkungen zu Genesis 15," in *Studien zum Pentateuch. Festschrift für W. Kornfeld* (Vienna, 1977), pp. 25–35, with extended bibliography; R. Buis, *La notion d'alliance dans l'Ancien Testament* (Paris, 1976); J. Halbe, *Das Privilegrecht Jahwes Ex 34, 10–26. Gestalt und Wesen, Herkunft und Wirken in vordeuteronomischer Zeit* (Göttingen, 1975); W. Gross, "Bundeszeichen und Bundesschluss in der Priesterschrift," *Trierer Theologische Zeitschrift* 87 (1978): 98–115.

90. See above all C. Westermann, *Genesis I* (Neukirchen, 1974), pp. 615–643, with abundant bibliography; S. Grill, "Die religionsgeschichtliche Bedeutung der vormosaischen Bündnisse (Gen 9,9–17)," *Kairos* 2 (1960): 17–22.

91. It is not a question of what historical experience lies behind the story of the flood of the "priestly writer," but rather of the interpretation which is given it by the "priestly writer." Doubtless this latter is connected with the entire earth.

92. Westermann, *Genesis I*, pp. 633f.

93. For further details see pp. 96ff.

94. See, for example, J. Ziegler, *Isaias, Echter-Bibel* (Würzburg, 1948).

95. See W. Thiel, "Hēfēr Berît. Zum Bundesbrechen im Alten Testament," *Vetus Testamentum* 20 (1970): 214–229.

96. Westermann, *Genesis I*, p. 624.

97. "The encompassing circle of all humanity and the inner circle of Israel are each referred to in an eternal *berit* with YHWH" (Gross, "Bundeszeichen," p. 102).

98. From it the following are referred to: H. Gressmann, *Der Messias* (Göttingen, 1929); L. Dürr, *Ursprung und Ausbau der israelitisch-jüdischen Heilandserwartung* (Berlin, 1925); S. Mowinckel, *He That Cometh: The Messianic Concept in the Old Testament and Later Judaism* (Oxford, 1956); M. Rehm, *Der königliche Messias im Licht der Immanuel-Weissagungen des Buches Jesaja* (Kevelaer, 1968), with comprehensive bibliography; E. König, *Die messianischen Weissagungen des Alten Testaments* (Stuttgart, 1925); A. S. van der Woude, *Die messianischen Vorstellungen der Gemeinde von Qumran* (Assen, 1957); A. Caquot, "Le messianisme qumrânien," in *Qumrân. Sa piété, sa théologie et son milieu* (Gembloux, 1978), pp. 231–247; W. H. Schmidt, "Die Ohnmacht des Messias. Zur Überlieferungsgeschichte der messianischen Weissagungen im Alten Testament," *Kerygma und Dogma* 15 (1969): 18–34; H. Gross, "Der Messias im Alten Testament," in *Kernfragen des Alten Testaments,* ed. H. Gross (Regensburg, 1977), pp. 66–84; J. Klausner, *The Messianic Idea in Israel: From Its Beginning to the Completion of the Mishnah* (New York, 1955); G. Friedrich, *Utopie und Reich Gottes. Zur Motivation politischen Verhaltens* (Göttingen, n.d.); J. H. Greenstone, *The Messiah Idea in Jewish History* (Philadelphia, 1943); F. Dexinger, "Die Entwicklung des jüdisch-christlichen Messianismus," *Bibel und Liturgie* 47 (1974): 5–31, 239–366; K. Hruby, "Die Messiaserwartung in der talmudischen Zeit," *Judaica* 20 (1964): 6–22; U. B. Müller, *Messias und Menschensohn in jüdischen Apokalypsen und in der Offenbarung des Johannes* (Gütersloh, 1972); Thoma, *Christian Theology of Judaism,* pp. 59–64, 168f.; A. H. Silver, *A History of Messianic Speculation in Israel* (Boston, 1959); P. Schäfer, "Die messianischen Hoffnungen des rabbinischen Judentums zwischen Naherwartung und religiösem Pragmatismus," in *Zukunft in der Gegenwart. Wegweisungen in Judentum und Christentum,* ed. C. Thoma (Bern, 1976), pp. 95–126; R. Mosis, "Die messianische Erwartung als haltende Macht. Am Beispiel des Volkes Israel und seines Geschichtsverständnisses," in *Ich will euch Hoffnung und Zukunft geben. 85. Deutscher Katholikentag vom 13. September bis 17. September 1978 in Freiburg,* 2d ed. (Paderborn, 1978), pp. 171–184; H. Gese, "Der Messias," in *Zur biblischen Theologie. Alttestamentliche Vorträge. Beiträge zur evangelischen Theologie* 78 (Munich, 1977): 128–151; G. Stemberger, "Heilsvorstellungen im nachbiblischen Judentum," *Bibel und Kirche* (1978), pp. 115–121; H. Frankemölle, "Jüdische

Messiaserwartung und christlicher Messiasglaube. Hermeneutische Anmerkungen im Kontext des Petrus bekenntnisses Mk 8,29," *Kairos* 20 (1978): 97–109; L. Landman, *Messianism in the Talmudic Era: Selected with an Introduction* (New Jersey, 1979).

99. In addition to Klausner, *Messianic Idea in Israel*, see especially G. Scholem, "Toward an Understanding of the Messianic Idea in Judaism," in *The Messianic Idea in Judaism*, ed. G. Scholem (New York, 1971), pp. 1–36; further, J. Sarachek, *The Messianic Idea in Medieval Jewish Literature* (New York, 1932); A. S. van der Woude, *Die messianischen Vorstellungen der Gemeinde von Qumran* (Assen, 1957); S. Talmon, "Typen der Messiaserwartung um die Zeitenwende," in *Probleme biblischer Theologie. Festschrift für G. von Rad*, ed. H. W. Wolff (Munich, 1971), pp. 571–588; E. F. von Hammerstein, *Das Messiasproblem bei Martin Buber* (Stuttgart, 1958); L. Wächter, "Jüdischer und christlicher Messianismus," *Kairos* 18 (1976): 119–134.

100. Scholem, "Toward an Understanding," p. 3.

101. See pp. 35f.

102. Scholem, "Toward an Understanding," p. 4.

103. Ibid., p. 10.

104. Ibid., p. 26.

105. Ibid., p. 7.

106. Ibid., p. 14

107. Ibid., p. 15. "The messianic expectations, already before Christ, but also later at the time of the Church and of post-biblical Judaism, released in the people of God incredible powers of hope and of ferment. However, tragedy, impatience, division and ideologies likewise resulted from the messianic expectations, (Thoma, *Christian Theology of Judaism*, p. 63).

108. Scholem, "Toward an Understanding," pp. 35f.

109. Messianism wants to contradict the statement that there is nothing new under the sun and that the structures of the world and its history never change fundamentally, or at most do so only in name. Cf. concerning this the interesting dispute of the structuralist Claude Lévi-Strauss with Sartre in his book *The Savage Mind* (Chicago, 1966), especially the concluding chapter, "History and Dialectic." Naturally it is true that every attempt is doomed to failure which undertakes to argue that "historicity can be made into the final refuge of a transcendental humanism . . . as if human beings, if they would only renounce the ego, which already has lost all too much by consistency, could again find the illusion of freedom on the level of the we" (ibid., p. 302) as Hegel and Marxism believe. Biblical Messianism indeed does not know of any evolutionary continuum of history, but rather an absolute break in it which is designated by the Old Testament prophets as the "day of YHWH" and by the Jewish and Christian apocalyptics as "the end" (for further details see pp. 81ff.).

110. See for example O. Betz, "Die Frage nach dem messianischen Bewusstsein Jesu," *Novum Testamentum* 6 (1963): 20–48; N. Brox, "Das messianische Selbst-verständnis des historischen Jesus," in *Vom Messias zu Christus*, ed. K. Schubert (Vienna, 1964); E. Dinkler, "Petrusbekenntnis und Satanswort. Das Problem der Messianität Jesu," in *Zeit und Geschichte. Dankesgabe an R. Bultmann* (Tübingen, 1964), pp. 127–153. There are, however, reputable scholars, Jewish and Christian,

who are convinced that Jesus did not think of himself or claim to be the Messiah, e.g., Pinchas Lapide, *Der Jude Jesus* (Zurich, 1979), p. 29, and Ulrich Luz in ibid., p. 130: "Not only did Jesus not proclaim himself to be the Messiah of his people, but he most probably did not even consider himself the Messiah at all."

111. For further details see pp. 81ff.

112. A select bibliography: N. Lohfink, "Eschatologie im Alten Testament," in *Bibelauslegung im Wandel*, ed. N. Lohfink (Frankfurt, 1967), pp. 158–184; H. D. Preuss, *Jahweglauben und Zukunftserwartung* (Stuttgart, 1968); H. Gross, "Grundzüge alttestamentlicher und frühjüdischer Eschatologie," in *Mysterium Salutis. Grundriss heilsgeschichtlicher Dogmatik*, ed. J. Feiner and M. Löher (Zurich, 1976), 5: 701–722; Schütz, "Allgemeine Grundlegung der Eschatologie," in ibid., pp. 553–700, with comprehensive bibliography; J. Ratzinger, "Heilsgeschichte und Eschatologie," in *Theologie im Wandel*, ed. J. Ratzinger and J. Neumann (Munich, 1967), pp. 68–89; J. Ratzinger, *Eschatologie—Tod und ewiges Leben. Kleine Katholische Dogmatik* (Regensburg, 1977), vol. 9; J. Ratzinger, "Eschatologie und Utopie," *Internationale Katholische Zeitschrift* 6 (1977): 97–110; J. Moltmann, *Theologie der Hoffnung*, 7th ed. (Munich, 1968); J. Pieper, *Hoffnung und Geschichte* (Munich, 1967); W. Kamlah, *Utopie, Eschatologie und Geschichtstheologie* (Mannheim, 1969); K. Löwith, *Weltgeschichte und Heilsgeschehen. Die theologischen Voraussetzungen der Geschichtsphilosophie*, 5th ed. (Stuttgart, 1967); S. Herrmann, *Die prophetische Heilserwartung im Alten Testament* (Stuttgart, 1965); A. Jepsen, "Eschatologie im Alten Testament," in *Religion in Geschichte und Gegenwart* (Tübingen, 1958), 2:655–662; R. Meyer, "Eschatologie im Judentum," in ibid., pp. 662–665.

113. See J. Schreiner, "Führung—Thema der Heilsgeschichte im Alten Testament," *Biblische Zeitschrift* 5 (1961): 2–18.

114. A select bibliography on the "day of Yahweh": L. Cerny, *The Day of Jahwe and Some Relevant Problems* (Prague, 1948); G. von Rad, "The Origin of the Concept of the Day of Jahwe," *Journal of Semitic Studies* 4 (1959): 91–101; G. von Rad, *Theologie des Alten Testaments*, 5th ed. (Munich, 1968), 2: 129–133; K.-D. Schunck, "Strukturlinien in der Entwicklung der Vorstellung vom 'Tag Jahwes,'" *Vetus Testamentum* 14 (1964): 319–330; M. Weiss, "The Origin of the 'Day of the Lord' Reconsidered," *Hebrew Union College Annual* 37 (1966): 29–72; J. Bourke, "Le Jour de Yahvé dans Joël," *Revue Biblique* 66 (1959): 5–31, 191–212.

115. See K. Koch, "Biblischer Ursprung des geschichtlichen Bewusstseins," in *Christentum und Gesellschaft*, ed. W. Lohff and B. Lohse (Göttingen, 1969), pp. 27–45.

116. On the topic of hope in Old Testament theology, see C. Westermann, "Das Hoffen im Alten Testament. Eine Begriffsuntersuchung," in *Forschung am Alten Testament. Gesammelte Studien*, ed. C. Westermann (Munich, 1964), pp. 219–265; A. Deissler, "Das Israel der Psalmen als Gottesvolk der Hoffenden," in *Die Zeit Jesu. Festschrift für Heinrich Schlier*, ed. G. Bornkamm and K. Rahner (Freiburg, 1970); W. Zimmerli, *Der Mensch und seine Hoffnung im Alten Testament* (Göttingen, 1968).

117. See N. Lohfink, "Zukunft. Zur biblischen Bezeugung des Ideals einer stabilen Welt," in *Unsere grossen Wörter. Das Alte Testament zu Themen dieser Jahre*, ed. N. Lohfink (Freiburg, 1977), pp. 172–189.

118. With this of course the question of how far the Jewish background in his heritage was influential in the thinking of Karl Marx is by no means clarified. Did "Messianism" run in his blood? In any case Marx received decisive philosophical stimulation from Hegel, especially from his idea of a "final goal" of history and from his process thinking with its dialectic. Hegel himself, however, cannot be understood without the influence of the Christian tradition. "The kingdom of God" was the common word of solution of the three Tübingen friends—Hegel, Schelling, and Hölderlin! Likewise for Ernst Bloch "the kingdom" is the religious core concept; however, "*the religious intention of the kingdom as such*," Bloch thinks, "*involves atheism, finally grasped*," (Ernst Bloch, *Das Prinzip Hoffnung* [Frankfurt, 1967], pp. 1411f.).

119. Ibid., p. 711.

120. On this and the following see G. Delling, "Hēmera," in Kittel, ed., *Theological Dictionary*, 2: 950–953; H. Riedlinger, "Jesus und die Zukunft," in *Wer ist Jesus Christus?*, ed. J. Sauer (Freiburg, 1977), pp. 93–120.

121. See also G. Sauer, *Zukunft und Verheissung* (Zurich, 1965); H. Kimmerle, *Die Zukunftsbedeutung der Hoffnung* (Bonn, 1966); J. Moltmann, "Die Zukunft als neues Paradigma der Transzendenz," *Internationale Dialog-Zeitschrift* 22 (1969): 2–13; W. D. Marsch, *Zukunft* (Stuttgart, 1969).

122. A select bibliography: H. J. Kraus, "Die prophetische Botschaft gegen das soziale Unrecht Israels," *Evangelische Theologie* 15 (1965): 295–307; O. H. Steck, "Prophetische Kritik der Gesellschaft," in *Christentum und Gesellschaft*, ed. W. Lohff and B. Lohse (Göttingen, 1969), pp. 46–62; K. Koch, "Die Entstehung der sozialen Kritik bei den Propheten," in Wolff, ed., *Probleme biblischer Theologie*, pp. 236–257; F. L. Hossfeld and I. Meyer, *Prophet gegen Prophet. Eine Analyse der alttestamentlichen Texte zum Thema: Wahre und falsche Propheten* (Freiburg, 1973); G. J. Botterweck, " 'Sie verkaufen den Unschuldigen um Geld.' Zur sozialen Kritik des Propheten Amos," *Bibel und Leben* 12 (1971): 215–231; H. Donner, "Die soziale Botschaft der Propheten im Lichte der Gesellschaftsordnung in Israel," *Oriens Antiquus* 2 (1963): 229–245; H. W. Wolff, *Die Stunde des Amos. Prophetie und Protest* (Munich, 1969), pp. 54–67 ("Kritik der Gesellschaft"); S. Holm-Nielsen, "Sozialkritik der Propheten," in *Denkender Glaube. Festschrift für C. H. Ratschow*, ed. O. Kaiser (Berlin, 1976), pp. 7–23.

123. Wolff, *Anthropologie*, pp. 296f.

124. Cf. ibid.

125. Wolff, *Die Stunde des Amos*, p. 63.

126. See K. Koch, "*Tzadak*," in *Theologisches Handwörterbuch zum Alten Testament*, 2: 507–530; G. Liedke, "*Shafat*," in ibid., pp. 999–1009; H. H. Schmid, *Gerechtigkeit als Weltordnung, Hintergrund und Geschichte des alttestamentlichen Gerechtigkeitsbegriffes* (Tübingen, 1968).

127. Koch, "*Tzadak*," p. 526.

128. Ibid., p. 527.

129. For further details, see J. Swetnam, "Some Observations on the Background of *tzadik* in Jeremiah 23,5a," *Biblica* 46 (1965): 29–40.

130. For further details, see H. Gross *Die Idee des ewigen und allgemeinen Weltfriedens im Alten Orient und im Alten Testament*, 2d ed. (Trier, 1967).

131. See G. Schrenk, "*Dikaioō*," in Kittel, ed., *Theological Dictionary*, 2: 212ff.

132. Thus the majority of the founders of "Critical Theory" ("Frankfurt School") were Jews—M. Horkheimer, T. W. Adorno, W. Benjamin, H. Marcuse.

133. See also G. Dietrich, "Das jüdisch-prophetische Erbe in den neueren revolutionären Bewegungen," in *Jüdische Hoffnungskraft und christlicher Glaube*, ed. W. Strolz (Freiburg, 1971), pp. 191–243; W. Strolz, "Sinnfragen nichtglaubender Juden," *Frankfurter Hefte* 31 (1976): 25–34.

134. According to G. Dietrich there are in Jewish prophecy "those three elements which were contained in the presuppositions of the Marxist critique of religion: first of all the struggle against the idols, the self-made religion, the opium of the people; second, the struggle against the inauthentic in religion, which makes sacrality into an end in itself and thereby sanctions asocially existing injustice; third, the struggle against a false dependence, for a responsible autonomy of humanity" ("Jüdisch-prophetische Erbe," p. 216). In this, however, Dietrich also does not forget the "weighty distinction"; according to him it lies "in the fact that for Marx the ultimate agency is the Communist society, whereas for the prophets it is YHWH, the living God, who calls the human being to the carrying out of his critical function."

135. See also U. Hommes and J. Ratzinger, *Das Heil des Menschen. Innerweltlich—Christlich* (Munich, 1975); J. Ratzinger, *Glaube und Zukunft* (Munich, 1970).

136. A select bibliography: E. Lohse, *Märtyrer und Gottesknecht. Untersuchungen zur urchristlichen Verkündigung vom Sühnetod Jesu Christi* (Göttingen, 1955); J. Sharbert, *Heilsmittler im Alten Testament und im Alten Orient. Questiones Disputatae* 23/24 (Freiburg, 1964); N. Brox, *Zeuge und Märtyrer. Untersuchungen zur frühchristlichen Zeugnis-terminologie* (Munich, 1961); E. Sjöberg, *Gott und die Sünder im palästinenischen Judentum* (Stuttgart, 1938); H. Thyen, *Studien zur Sündenvergebung im Neuen Testament und seinen alttestamentlichen und jüdischen Voraussetzungen* (Göttingen, 1970); J. Gnilka, "Martyriumsparänese und Sühnetod in synoptischen und jüdischen Traditionen," in *Die Kirche des Anfangs. Festschrift für H. Schürmann*, ed. R. Schnackenburg, J. Ernst, and J. Wanke (Leipzig, 1977), pp. 223–246; H. Gese, "Die Sühne," in *Zur biblischen Theologie. Alttestamentliche Vorträge* (Munich, 1977), pp. 85–106.

137. See F. Büchsel and J. Herrmann, "*Hileōs*," in Kittel, ed., *Theological Dictionary*, 3: 300–322; F. Maass, "*Kafar*," in *Theologisches Handwörterbuch zum Alten Testament*, 1: 842–857.

138. See above all, Lohse, *Märtyrer und Gottesknecht*, pp. 13–110.

139. Ibid., p. 20.

140. On this see ibid., pp. 23–37.

141. For further details on this see ibid., pp. 33-37.

142. Cited in ibid., pp. 26f.

143. The entire New Testament material is gathered together and discussed in ibid., pp. 113–187.

144. See ibid., pp. 75–87.

145. Ibid., p. 75.

146. Ibid.

147. See the important book by R. Schwager, *Brauchen wir einen Sündenbock? Gewalt und Erlösung in den biblischen Schriften* (Munich, 1978).

278   NOTES FOR CHAPTER 2

148. See C. Maurer, "*Synoida, Syneidēsis,*" in Kittel, ed., *Theological Diction-ary,* 7: 899–919, with extensive bibliography; J. Schreiner, "Persönliche Ent-scheidung vor Gott nach biblischen Zeugnis," *Bibel und Leben* 6 (1965): 107–121.
149. See, for example, F. Baumgärtel and J. Behm, "*Kardia,*" in Kittel, ed., *Theological Dictionary,* 3: 605–614, with bibliography.
150. A. Schlatter, *Theologie des Judentums nach dem "Bericht des Josephus"* (Gütersloh, 1932), p. 21.
151. See J. Schreiner, "Hören auf Gott und sein Wort in der Sicht des Deu-teronomiums," in *Miscellanea Erfordiana* (Leipzig, 1962), pp. 27–47; A. K. Fenz, *Auf Jahwes Stimme hören. Eine biblische Begriffsuntersuchung* (Vienna, 1964).
152. Schreiner, "Hören auf Gott," p. 114.
153. Ibid., p. 111.
154. Concerning this see, for example, J. J. Stamm, *Der Dekalog im Lichte der neueren Forschung* (Bern, 1958); E. Nielsen, *Die Zehn Gebote* (Copenhagen, 1965); J. Schreiner, *Die Zehn Gebote im Leben des Gottesvolkes* (Munich, 1966); N. Lohfink, "Die Zehn Gebote ohne den Berg Sinai," in *Bibelauslegung im Wandel,* ed. N. Lohfink (Frankfurt, 1967), pp. 129–157; B. Reike, *Die zehn Wörte in Geschichte und Gegenwart* (Tübingen, 1873); A. Deissler, *Ich bin dein Gott, der dich befreit hat. Wege zur Meditation über das Zehngebot* (Freiburg, 1975); H. Gross, "Die Zehn Gebote damals und heute. Bleibendes und Wandelbares im Dekalog," in H. Gross, *Die Zehn Gebote. Topos* 48 (Mainz, 1976); S. Ben-Chorin, *Die Tafeln des Bundes. Das Zehnwort vom Sinai* (Tübingen, 1979); E. L. Ehrlich, "Die 10 Gebote," in G. Müller, ed., *Israel hat dennoch Gott zum Trost. Festschrift für Schalom Ben-Chorin,* ed. G. Müller (Trier, 1978), pp. 11–19.
155. Taken from the German translation by J. Winter and A. Wünsche (Leipzig, 1909).
156. See Lohfink, "Die Zehn Gebote," pp. 135ff.
157. Ibid., p. 143.
158. Ibid., pp. 145–149.
159. See H. Gross, "Zur Wurzel zurück," *Biblische Zeitschrift* 4 (1960): 227–237, reprinted in Gross, *Kernfragen des Alten Testaments,* pp. 30–41; P. A. H. de Boer, *Gedenken und Gedächtnis in der Welt des Alten Testaments* (Stuttgart, 1962); B. S. Childs, *Memory and Tradition in Israel* (London, 1962); W. Schottroff, *"Gedenken" im Alten Orient und im Alten Testament* (Neukirchen, 1963); W. Schottroff, "*Zachar,*" in *Theologisches Handwörterbuch zum Alten Testament,* 1: 507–518; R. Le Déaut, *La Nuit Pascale. Essai sur la signification de la Pâque juive à partir du Targum d'Exode 12,42* (Rome, 1963), pp. 66–71; H. Zirker, *Die kultische Vergegenwärtigung der Vergangenheit in den Psalmen* (Bonn, 1964); C. Wester-mann, "Vergegenwärtigung der Geschichte in den Psalmen," in *Forschung am Alten Testament,* ed. C. Westermann (Munich, 1964), pp. 306–335.
160. Westermann, "Vergegenwärtigung," p. 309.
161. See pp. 28ff.
162. Westermann, "Vergegenwärtigung," p. 313.
163. Zirker, *Die kultische Vergegenwärtigung,* p. 70.
164. See *Exodus Rabbah* 15,11: "The Holy One . . . stipulated for Israel a month of redemption, in which it was liberated from Egypt and in which it was [once] redeemed." See also N. Füglister, *Die Heilsbedeutung des Pascha* (Munich, 1963),

esp. pp. 218–226 ("Pascha und Heilszukunft"); R. Le Déaut, *La Nuit Pascale;*
R. Schmitt, *Exodus und Passah. Ihr Zusammenhang im Alten Testament* (Freiburg,
1975).

165. Füglister, *Heilsbedeutung,* pp. 199–294.

166. See also E. Werner, *The Sacred Bridge: The Interdependence of Liturgy
and Music in Synagogue and Church during the First Millennium* (New York,
1959); and the research report of J. Hennig, "Liturgie und Judentum," *Archiv für
Liturgiewissenschaft,* 20 (1979).

167. A select bibliography: E. Jenni, *Die theologische Begründung des Sab-
batgebotes im Alten Testament. Theologische Studien* 46 (Zurich, 1956); A. J.
Heschel, *The Sabbath: Its Meaning for Modern Man* (New York, 1951/52); G. von
Rad, "Es ist noch eine Ruhe vorhanden im Volke Gottes," in *Gesammelte Studien
zum Alten Testament,* ed. G. von Rad, 4th ed. (Munich, 1971), pp. 101–108;
E. Lohse, "Sabbaton," in Kittel, ed., *Theological Dictionary,* 7: 1–34, with com-
prehensive bibliography; Wolff, *Anthropologie,* pp. 200–210; J. Halperin, ed., *Le
Shabbat dans la Conscience Juive. Données et Textes* (Paris, 1975).

168. R. H. Charles, *The Apocrypha and Pseudepigrapha of the Old Testament*
(Oxford, 1913), 2: 14f. The Book of Jubilees is a haggadic-halachic midrash on
Genesis 1 to Exodus 12; it was probably written in the first half of the first century
before Christ within Essene circles.

169. "With us": with God and the higher classes of angels.

170. "This one": the Sabbath; "That one": Jacob.

171. See also Exod. 20: 12, 20: "I gave them my sabbaths, as a sign between me
and them, that they might know that I YHWH sanctify them" (Exod. 31:13).

172. Wolff, *Anthropologie,* p. 202.

173. Ibid., p. 203.

174. Philo, *De spec. leg.,* 2: 59.

175. Ibid., p. 70.

176. See von Rad, "Es ist noch eine Ruhe"; O. Hofius, *Katapausis. Die
Vorstellung vom endzeitlichen Ruheort im Hebräerbrief* (Tübingen, 1970).

177. See F. Mussner, *Die Auferstehung Jesu* (Munich, 1969), pp. 30–48; further,
R. Martin-Achard, *De la mort à la résurrection d'après l'Ancien Testament* (Neu-
chatel, 1956); K. Schubert, "Die Entwicklung der Auferstehungslehre von der
nachexilischen bis zur frührabbinischen Zeit," *Biblische Zeitschrift* 6 (1962): 177–
214; W. Zimmerli, *Der Mensch und seine Hoffnung im Alten Testament* (Göttingen,
1968), pp. 149–162; G. Fohrer, "Das Geschick des Menschen nach dem Tod im
Alten Testament," *Kerygma und Dogma* 14 (1968): 249–262; G. Stemberger, "Das
Problem der Auferstehung im Alten Testament," *Kairos* 14 (1972): 273–290; G.
Stemberger, *Der Leib der Auferstehung. Studien zur Anthropologie und Eschatologie des palästinischen Judentums im neutestamentlichen Zeitalter* (Rome,
1972); U. Kellermann, "Überwindung des Todesgeschicks in der alttestamentlichen
Frömmigkeit vor und neben dem Auferstehungsglauben," *Zeitschrift für Theologie
und Kirche* 73 (1976): 259–282; H. Wahle, "Die Lehren des rabbinischen Judentums über das Leben nach dem Tod," *Kairos* 14 (1972): 291–309.

178. See F. Mussner, "Jesu Lehre über das kommende Leben nach den Synop-
tikern," *Concilium* 6 (1970): 692-695.

179. See P. Lapide, *Auferstehung. Ein jüdisches Glaubensbekenntnis* (Stuttgart,
1977).

180. The following quotation is cited in ibid., pp. 27f.
181. For further details see S. Ben-Chorin, *Jüdischer Glaube. Struktur einer Theologie des Judentums anhand des Maimonidschen Credo* (Tübingen, 1975), pp. 299–320.
182. Ibid., p. 319.
183. E. Käsemann, *An die Römer* (Tübingen, 1974).
184. See the documentation for this in E. Schweizer, "Sōma," in Kittel, ed., *Theological Dictionary*, 7: 1036.
185. See R. Meyer, "Sarx," in ibid., pp. 116–118.
186. Ibid., p. 118.
187. On how this resurrection body is made according to the view of early Judaism, see details in Stemberger, *Der Leib der Auferstehung*.
188. On this see pp. 81ff.
189. To the great annoyance of the Enlightenment and reason theologians. Thus their great master H. S. Reimarus wrote: "The pure teaching of Christ, which has flowed from his own mouth, *insofar as it is not especially enclosed in Judaism,* but rather can be general, contains nothing other than a reasonable practical religion," *Apologie oder Schutzschrift für die vernünftigen Verehrer Gottes,* ed. G. Alexander (Frankfurt, 1972), 1: 126.
190. K. Marx, "On the Jewish Question," in *Karl Marx, Selected Writings,* ed. D. McLellan (London, 1977), p. 58.
191. The correspondence of G. Scholem with W. Benjamin on historical and dialectical materialism is printed in G. Scholem, *Walter Benjamin—Die Geschichte einer Freundschaft.* Bibliothek Suhrkamp 467 (Frankfurt, 1975), pp. 283–292. On W. Benjamin see also P. Bulthaup, ed., *Materialien zu Benjamins Theses "Über den Begriff der Geschichte." Beiträge und Interpretationen* (Frankfurt, 1975). R. Tiedemann remarked in his contribution "Historischer Materialismus oder politischer Messianismus? Politische Gehalte in der Geschichtsphilosophie Walter Benjamins," pp. 77–121: "The danger cannot be shrugged off that with the retranslation of materialism into theology both will be lost: the secularized content dissolves and the theological idea vanishes" (p. 100).
192. See, for example, F. Belo, *Lecture matérialiste de l'Evangile de Marc* (Paris, 1974); M. Clévenot, *So kennen wir die Bibel nicht. Anleitung zu einer materialistischen Lektüre biblischer Texte* (Munich, 1978); K. Füssel, "Was heisst materialistische Bibelauslegung?" *Una Sancta* 32 (1977): 46–54.
193. See also Thoma, *Christian Theology of Judaism,* p. 174.

NOTES FOR CHAPTER 3

1. I shall present first of all a selection of books written for the most part in German and essays by Jewish authors on Jesus of Nazareth which have appeared since around 1920. The standard work is still J. Klausner, *Jesus of Nazareth: His Times, His Life and His Teaching* (Hebrew: Jerusalem, 1907; English: New York, 1925). Further, L. Baeck, "Das Evangelium als Urkunde der jüdischen Glaubensgeschichte," in *Paulus, die Pharisäer und das Neue Testament,* ed. L. Baeck (Frankfurt, 1961), pp. 99–196; D. Flusser, *Jesus* (New York, 1969); S. Sandmel, *We Jews and Jesus* (London, 1972); P. Lapide, *Der Rabbi Jesus von*

Nazareth (Trier, 1974); P. Lapide and U. Luz, *Der Jude Jesus* (Einsiedeln, 1979); S. Ben-Chorin, *Bruder Jesus. Der Nazarener in jüdischer Sicht* (Munich, 1967); S. Ben-Chorin, *Jesus im Judentum* (Wuppertal, 1970); J. Isaac, *Jesus and Israel* (New York, 1971); E. L. Ehrlich, "Eine jüdische Auffassung von Jesus," in *Jesu Jude-Sein als Zugang zum Judentum*, ed. W. P. Eckert and H. H. Henrix (Aachen, 1976); pp. 35–49; G. Vermés, *Jesus the Jew* (London, 1973). From among the reviews of Jewish life-of-Jesus research the following should be mentioned: G. Lindeskog, *Die Jesusfrage im neuzeitlichen Judentum. Ein Beitrag zur Geschichte der Leben-Jesu-Forschung* (Uppsala, 1938; 2d ed.: Darmstadt, 1973, with an afterword); M. Brocke, "Das Judentumsbild neuer Jesusbücher. Kritische Beobachtung christlicher Literatur," *Freiburger Rundbrief* 23 (1971): 50–59; G. Jasper-Bethel, *Stimmen aus dem neureligiösen Judentum in seiner Stellung zum Christentum und zu Jesus* (Hamburg, 1958); R. Gradwohl, "Das neue Jesus-Verständnis bei jüdischen Denkern der Gegenwart," *Freiburger Zeitschrift für Philosophie und Theologie* 20 (1973): 306–323; S. Ben-Chorin, "The Image of Jesus in Modern Judaism," *Journal of Ecumenical Studies* 11 (1974): 401–430; P. Lapide, *Jesus, Jews and Israelis* (New York, 1978); J. Maier, "Gewundene Rezeption. Zur neueren jüdischen Jesusforschung," *Herder-Korrespondenz* 30 (1976): 313–319; A. Sand, "Jesus im Urteil jüdischer Autoren der Gegenwart (1930–1976)," *Catholica* 31 (1977): 29–38; G. Baumbach, "Fragen der modernen jüdischen Jesusforschung an die christliche Theologie," *Theologische Literatur Zeitung* 102 (1977): 625–636; J. Jocz, *The Jewish People and Jesus Christ: A Study in the Relationship between the Jewish People and Jesus Christ* (London, 1949); K. Schubert, *Jesus im Lichte der Religionsgeschichte des Judentums* (Vienna, 1973); J. Maier, *Jesus im Talmud* (Darmstadt, 1977); D. R. Catchpole, *A Study in the Gospels and Jewish Historiography from 1770 to the Present Day* (Leiden, 1971); C. Thoma, *A Christian Theology of Judaism* (New York, 1980), pp. 106–136.

2. Klausner, *Jesus of Nazareth*, p. 413.
3. Ibid.
4. Ibid., p. 414.
5. Ibid.
6. See ibid., p. 371.
7. Flusser, *Jesus*, p. 10.
8. Ibid., p. 12.
9. Ibid., p. 46.
10. Ibid., p. 50.
11. Ibid., p. 61.
12. Ibid., p. 65.
13. Ibid., p. 84.
14. Ibid., p. 90.
15. Ibid., p. 98.
16. Ibid.
17. Ibid., pp. 103f.
18. See ibid., pp. 111ff.
19. Ibid., pp. 128f.
20. Ibid., p. 122.
21. Ibid., p. 72.

22. Ben-Chorin, *Bruder Jesus*, p. 11.

23. Ibid., p. 12.

24. Ibid., p. 14.

25. Ibid., p. 16.

26. Ibid., p. 17.

27. Ibid., p. 26.

28. Ibid., p. 27.

29. Ibid., p. 12.

30. M. Buber, *Two Types of Faith* (New York, 1951), pp. 12f.

31. Baeck, "Das Evangelium," pp. 99–196.

32. P. 388. The French appeared under the title *Jésus et Israël* (Paris, 1946); the German translation appeared in 1968 (Zurich and Vienna) and the English in 1971 (New York). See also E. H. Flannery, "Jesus, Israel, and Christian Renewal," *Journal of Ecumenical Studies* 9 (1972): 74–93.

33. See pp. 155ff.

34. See, for example, F. Mussner, "Der Jude Jesus," *Freiburger Rundbrief* 23 (1971): 3–7; F. Lentzen-Deis, "Der Glaube Jesu. Das Gottesverhältnis Jesu als Erfüllung alttestamentlichen Glaubens," *Trierer Theologische Zeitschrift* 80 (1971): 141–155; L. Volken, "Jesus der Jude," *Lebendiges Zeugnis* 32 (1977): 64–77.

35. See F. Mussner, *Der Jacobusbrief*, 3d ed. (Freiburg, 1975), pp. 76–84, with bibliography; M. Schwantes, *Des Recht der Armen* (Bern, 1977).

36. See also A. George, "Jésus et les Psaumes," in *À la recontre de Dieu. Mémorial A. Gelin* (LePuy, 1961), pp. 297–308.

37. F. D. E. Schleiermacher, *Hermeneutik*. Newly edited from the autograph and introduced by H. Kimmerle, 2d ed. (Heidelberg, 1974), p. 38.

38. Certainly the "Jewish categories," as the New Testament shows, have experienced certain christological transformations, as can be observed in the New Testament canon, especially in the example of the Epistle to the Hebrews—all of which needs to be investigated more thoroughly. However, Israel has largely contributed the "lexicon" to the "linguistic material."

39. Baeck, "Das Evangelium als Urkunde," p. 70.

40. H. Schürmann, *Das Lukasevangelium* (Freiburg, 1969), 1: 126.

41. See, for example, A. von Harnack, *Geschichte eines programmatischen Wortes Jesu (Matth 5,17) in der ältesten Kirche*. Sitzungsberichte der Preussischen Akademie der Wissenschaft I (Berlin, 1912); H. Ljungman, *Das Gesetz erfüllen. Matth 5,17ff. und 3.15* (Lund, 1954), pp. 19–36; E. Schweizer, "Mt. 5,17–20," *Theologische Literatur Zeitung* 77 (1952): 475–484; W. Trilling, *Das Wahre Israel*, 3d ed. (Munich, 1964), pp. 167–186; G. Harder, "Jesus und das Gesetz (Matthäus 5,17–20)," in *Antijudaismus im Neuen Testament*, ed. W. P. Eckert et al. (Munich, 1967), pp. 105–118; J. Jocz, "Jesus and the Law," *Judaica* 26 (1970): pp. 105–124; O. Hanssen, "Zum Verständnis der Bergpredigt. Eine missionstheologische Studie zu Mt 5,17–18," in *Der Ruf Jesu und die Antwort der Gemeinde. Festschrift für J. Jeremias*, ed. E. Lohse (Göttingen, 1970), pp. 94–111; H. Hübner, *Das Gesetz in der synoptischen Tradition. Studien zur These einer progressiven Qumranisierung und Judaisierung innerhalb der synoptischen Tradition* (Witten, 1973), pp. 15–39; A. Sand, *Das Gesetz und die Propheten. Untersuchungen zur Theologie des Evangeliums nach Matthäus* (Regensburg, 1974), pp. 33–45, 183–205; S. Légasse, "L'

'antijudaisme' dans l'Evangile selon Matthieu," in *L'Evangile selon Matthieu. Radaction et theologie*, ed. M. Didier (Gembloux, 1972), pp. 417–428; M. Lehmann-Habeck, "Das Gesetz als der gute Gotteswille für meinen Nächsten. Zur bleibenden Bedeutung des Gesetzes nach dem Matthäus-Evangelium," in *Treue zur Thora. Festschrift für G. Harder*, ed. P. von der Osten-Sacken (Berlin, 1977), pp. 47–53; W. D. Davies, *Christian Origins and Judaism* (Philadelphia, 1962), pp. 31–66; M. Hengel, "Jesus und die Tora," *Theologische Beiträge* 9 (1978): 152–172; U. Luz, "Die Erfüllung des Gesetzes by Matthäus (Mt 5,17–20)," *Zeitschrift für Theologie und Kirche* 75 (1978): 398–435.

42. R. Bultmann, *Die Geschichte der synoptischen Tradition*, 8th ed. (Göttingen, 1970), pp. 146f.

43. E. Schweizer, *Das Evangelium nach Matthäus* (Göttingen, 1973), p. 62.

44. Hanssen, "Zum Verständnis der Bergpredigt," p. 109.

45. Klausner, *Jesus of Nazareth*, p. 366.

46. Flusser, *Jesus*, p. 61.

47. On this see, for example, S. J. Schmidt, " 'Text' und 'Geschichte' als Fundierungskategorien," in *Beiträge zur Textlinguistik*, ed. W.-D. Stempel (Munich, 1971), pp. 31–52.

48. On this see pp. 234ff.

49. H. Schürmann had presumed that behind Luke 16:17 and Matt. 5:19 there lay a debate "within the oldest Palestinian community": A strict group stood in opposition to another one which carried out a freer practice. See H. Schürmann, " 'Wer daher eines dieser geringsten Gebote auflöst . . . .?' Wo fand Mt das Logion Mt 5,19?" *Biblische Zeitschrift* 4 (1960): 238–250.

50. A selected bibliography on the "antitheses": V. Hasler, "Das Herzstück der Bergpredigt. Zum Verständnis der Antitheses in Matth 5,21–48," *Theologische Zeitschrift* 15 (1959): 90–106; E. Lohse, " 'Ich aber sage euch,' " in *Der Ruf Jesu und die Antwort der Gemeinde. Festschrift für J. Jeremias*, ed. E. Lohse (Göttingen, 1970), pp. 189–203; G. Schmahl, "Die Antithesen der Bergpredigt. Inhalt und Eigenart ihrer Forderungen," *Trierer Theologische Zeitschrift* 83 (1974): in *Jesus Christus in Historie und Theologie. Festschrift für H. Conzelmann* (Tübingen, 1975), pp. 433–444; J. Eckert, "Wesen und Funktion der Radikalismen in der Botschaft Jesu," *Münchner Theologische Zeitschrift* 24 (1973): 301–325; G. Strecker, "Die Antitheses der Bergpredigt (Mt 5,21–48 parr.)," *Zeitschrift für die neutestamentliche Wissenschaft* 69 (1978): 36–72, with comprehensive bibliography; A. B. du Toit, "The Self-Revelation of Jesus in Matthew 5–7," *Neotestamentica* 1 (1967): 66–72; H. Hübner, *Das Gesetz in der synoptischen Überlieferung* (Witten, 1973), pp. 40–112.

51. See Billerbeck, *Kommentar*, I, p. 253.

52. See the Damascus Document 4, 10: "The *predecessors* who have entered into the Covenant"; 8, 4: "And God recalled the Covenant with the *predecessors*."

53. See, for example, E. Mayser, *Grammatik der griechischen Papyri aus der Ptolemäerzeit* (Berlin, 1934), 2: 125ff.

54. I call attention above all to the careful and expert analyses by Strecker, "Die Antitheses der Bergpredigt."

55. Ibid., p. 70.

56. Ibid.

57. Ibid., p. 71.

58. Ibid.

59. Ben-Chorin, *Bruder Jesus*, p. 76.

60. "With *pistis* the question remains open as to what content to give the word here. In connection with *chesed* and *emet*, *pistis* can also designate the attitude of one human to another. Then to mercy, which is called forth by an emergency, there is added loyalty, which gives our communion with one another stability" (A. Schlatter, *Der Evangelist Matthäus* [Stuttgart, 1948], pp. 679f.).

61. On this see, for example, N. Lohfink, "Altes Testament—Die Entlarvung der Gewalt," *Herder-Korrespondenz* 32 (1978): 187–193.

62. On this see pp. 234ff.

63. On this see pp. 155ff.

64. Thoma, *Christian Theology of Judaism*, p. 115. "In reference to the Torah it is first of all to be said that Jesus—like every Palestinian Jew—naturally presumed its previous validity and application" (M. Hengel, "Jesus und die Tora," *Theologische Beiträge* 9 [1978]: p. 157). Of course in this it must always be remembered that with Jesus "the fundamental theme is precisely not the Torah, but the coming of the lordship of God" (ibid., p. 153).

65. On this see, for example, Billerbeck, *Kommentar*, 1: 900–908; R. Schnackenburg, *Die sittliche Botschaft des Neuen Testaments*, 2d ed. (Munich, 1962), pp. 65–71, 172–178, with bibliography; G. Bornkamm, "Das Doppelgebot der Liebe," in *Gesammelte Aufsätze* (Munich, 1968), 3: 37–45; C. Burchard, "Das doppelte Liebesgebot in der frühen christlichen Überlieferung," in *Der Ruf Jesu und die Antwort der Gemeinde. Festschrift für J. Jeremias* pp. 39–62; J. B. Stern, "Jesus' Citation of Dt 6,5 and Lv 19,18 in the Light of Jewish Tradition," *Catholic Biblical Quarterly* 28 (1966): 312–316; K. Berger, *Die Gesetzesauslegung Jesu. Ihr historischer Hintergrund im Judentum und im Alten Testament* (Neukirchen, 1972), 1: 56–257; G. Friedrich, "Das Doppelgebot der Liebe (Lk 10,25–29)," in *Was heisst das: Liebe?* ed. G. Friedrich (Stuttgart, 1972), pp. 7–15; M. Limbeck, *Von der Ohnmacht des Rechts. Untersuchungen zur Gesetzeskritik des Neuen Testaments* (Düsseldorf, 1972), pp. 77–83; R. H. Fuller, "Das Doppelgebot der Liebe. Ein Testfall für die Echtheitskriterien der Worte Jesu," in *Jesus Christus in Historie und Theologie. Festschrift für H. Conzelmann*, ed. G. Strecker (Tübingen, 1975), pp. 317–320; A. Nissen, *Gott und der Nächste im antiken Judentum. Untersuchungen zum Doppelgebot der Liebe* (Tübingen, 1974); R. Pesch, *Das Markusevangelium* (Freiburg, 1977), vol. 2; G. Schneider, "Die Neuheit der christlichen Nächstenliebe," *Trierer Theologische Zeitschrift* 82 (1973): 257–275; F. Prast, "Ein Appell zur Besinnung auf das Juden wie Christen gemeinsam verpflichtende Erbe im Munde Jesu. Das Anliegen einer alten vormarkinischen Tradition (Mk 12,28–34)," in *Gottesverächter und Menschenfeinde? Juden zwischen Jesus und frühchristlicher Kirche*, ed. Goldstein (Düsseldorf, 1979), pp. 79–98.

66. Burchard, "Das doppelte Liebesgebot," p. 57.

67. Berger, *Die Gesetzesauslegung Jesu*, pp. 26–277.

68. E. Haenchen, *Der Weg Jesu* (Berlin, 1966), p. 414.

69. Pesch, *Das Markusevangelium*, 2: 244.

70. Ibid., pp. 239, 244, 248.

71. According to Pesch, ibid., p. 247: "The traditioned formulation of the double

commandment might go back to Jesus himself." One sees in this that one may not go further than "might."

72. Shab. 31a Bar.

73. SLev 19:18.

74. Berakh 63a.

75. Pesch, *Das Markusevangelium* 2: 248.

76. See, above all, A. Vögtle, "The Lord's Prayer: A Prayer for Jews and Christians?" in *The Lord's Prayer and Jewish Liturgy*, ed. J. Petuchowski and M. Brocke (New York, 1974), pp. 93–117, with extensive bibliography.

77. For various interpretations of the attributive *ton epiousion* see, for example, ibid., pp. 98–100. I shall not go further into the matter.

78. Thus, J. Jeremias, as is known. See J. Jeremias, "Kennzeichen der ipsissima vox Jesu," *Abba. Studien zur neutestamentlichen Theologie und Zeitgeschichte* (Göttingen, 1966), pp. 145–152; J. Jeremias, "Abba," ibid., pp. 15–67.

79. Thus, J. Becker, "Das Gottesbild Jesu und die älteste Auslegung von Ostern," in Strecker, ed., *Jesus Christus*, pp. 105–126.

80. Ibid., pp. 107f.

81. Ibid., p. 109.

82. Ibid., pp. 110f.

83. Ibid., p. 110.

84. Ibid., p. 114.

85. Ibid., p. 110.

86. A. Deissler, "The Spirit of the Lord's Prayer in the Faith and Worship of the Old Testament," in Petuchowski and Brocke, eds., *Lord's Prayer*, pp. 3–17.

87. Ibid., pp. 16f.

88. Concerning this see H. Schürmann, *Das Gebet der Herrn. Aus der Verkündigung Jesu erläutert* (Freiburg, 1957). Tertullian had described the Our Father as "breviarium totius Evangelii."

89. On this see the material in Jeremias, "Abba," pp. 33ff.

90. See the overview in ibid., pp. 16–33.

91. Concerning this see ibid., pp. 20–22; G. Dalman, *Die Worte Jesu* (Darmstadt, 1965), pp. 150–155, 296–304. M. McNamara found in the Palestinian targumim 20 passages with the expression "Father in heaven" as a reference to God: 3 in Targum Ps.-Jon, 10 in the "targum fragments," and 3 in Targum Neofiti— *Targum and Testament. Aramaic Paraphrases of the Hebrew Bible: A Light on the New Testament* (Shannon, 1972), p. 116, complete with precise references. Of course a gradual tendency to avoid the term "Father" for God, especially in the targum of the prophets, is exhibited. Ibid., p. 115.

92. Jeremias, "Abba," p. 29.

93. Why one in Israel for a long time had certain hesitations about addressing God as "Father" doubtless has its foundation in the desire to prevent God from being seen as a physical father (a begetter God), to which the surrounding pagan world gave Israel sufficient stimuli (fertility cults!). In the eyes of Israel God is first of all the "Father" as the creator, who in no way is identical with creation and therefore also may not be confused with it.

94. Ibid., p. 33.

95. Thus according to Jeremias, ibid., p. 56.

96. Ibid., p. 34.
97. Ibid., pp. 35f.
98. Ibid., p. 36.
99. Concerning this see ibid., pp. 59f.
100. "Father in heaven" (*ho patēr ho en [tois] ouranois, ho patēr ho ouranios*) is encountered in the words of Jesus twenty times in Matthew, once in Mark (11:25), and never in Luke.
101. There is no further need for specific proofs for the individual petitions of the Our Father. These proofs have been amply presented, as for example in the work referred to in note 76, *The Lord's Prayer.* Concerning this see also the book by P. Navé, *Du, unser Vater. Jüdische Gebete für Christen,* 3d ed. (Freiburg, 1978).
102. K. Barth, *Church Dogmatics* (Edinburgh, 1957), II/2 in the discussions about God's graceful election.
103. See Fr.-W. Marquardt, *Die Entdeckung des Judentums für die christliche Theologie. Israel im Denken Karl Barths* (Munich, 1967), esp. pp. 175ff., 209ff., 242ff.; B. Klappert, *Israel und die Kirche. Erwägungen zur Israellerhe Karl Barths* (Munich, 1980).
104. Concerning this see the book by the Jew R. Aron, *Jesus of Nazareth: The Hidden Years* (London, 1962).
105. Concerning this see Barth, *Church Dogmatics,* II/2, p. 200.
106. H. Urs von Balthasar, *Einsame Zwiespräche,* p. 83.
107. Barth, *Church Dogmatics,* II/2, pp. 286f.

NOTES FOR CHAPTER 4

1. On the theme "Paul and Israel" there is an immense literature from which in the treatment of Romans 11:26 (see pp. 28ff.) a selection has already been listed. In addition to those the following works must be noted: J. Klausner, *From Jesus to Paul* (Boston, 1943); S. Ben-Chorin, *Paulus. Der Völkerapostel in jüdischer Sicht* (Munich, 1970); H.-J. Schoeps, *Die Theologie des Apostels im Licht der jüdischen Religionsgeschichte* (Tübingen, 1959); D. Zeller, *Juden und Heiden in der Mission des Paulus. Studien zum Römerbrief,* 2d ed. (Stuttgart, 1976); M. Barth et al., *Paulus—Apostat oder Apostel? Jüdische und christliche Antworten* (Regensburg, 1977); F.-W. Marquardt, *Die Juden im Römerbrief* (Zurich, 1971)—and concerning it, G. Klein, "Erbarmen mit den Juden! Zu einer 'historisch-materialistischen' Paulusdeutung," *Evangelische Theologie* 34 (1974): 201–218; H. Gollwitzer, M. Palmer, V. Schliski, "Der Jude und die deutsche neutestamentliche Wissenshaft," ibid., pp. 276–304; G. Klein, "Präliminarien zum Thema 'Paulus und die Juden," in *Rechtfertigung. Festschrift für E. Käsemann,* ed. J. Friedrich, W. Pöhlmann, P. Stuhlmacher (Tübingen and Göttingen, 1976), pp. 229–243; J. Eckert, "Paulus und Israel. Zu den Strukturen paulinischer Rede und Argumentation," *Trierer Theologische Zeitschrift* 87 (1978): 1–13, without depth; K. Stendahl, *Paul among Jews and Gentiles* (Philadelphia, 1976); P. von der Osten-Sacken, "Das paulinische Verständnis des Gesetzes im Spannungsfeld von Eschatologie und Geschichte, Erläuterungen zum Evangelium als Faktor von theologischem Antijudaismus," *Evangelische Theologie* 37 (1977): 549–587; W. D. Davies, "Paul and the People of Israel," *New Testament Studies* 24 (1977/78): 4–39, with further

bibliography (the two essays by P. von der Osten-Sacken and W. D. Davies are important contributions to the theme "Paul and Israel"); O. Betz, "Paulus als Pharisäer nach dem Gesetz. Phil 3,5–6 als Beitrag zur Frage des frühen Pharisäismus," in *Treue zur Thora. Festschrift für G. Harder* (Berlin, 1977), pp. 54–64; M. Barth, "Die Stellung des Paulus zu Gesetz und Ordnung," *Evangelische Theologie* 33 (1973): 496–526; F. Hahn, "Das Gesetzesverständnis im Römer- und Galaterbrief," *Zeitschrift für die neutestamentliche Wissenschaft* 67 (1976): 29–63; E. Lohse, "'Wir richten das Gesetz auf!' Glaube und Thora im Römerbrief," in *Treue zur Thora. Festschrift für G. Harder*, ed. P. von der Osten-Sacken (Berlin, 1977), pp. 65–71; E. P. Sanders, *Paul and Palestinian Judaism. A Comparison of Patterns of Religion* (London, 1977); W. Wiefel, "Paulus in jüdischer Sicht," *Judaica* 31 (1975): 109–115, 151–172; L. Baeck, "Der Glaube des Paulus," in *Paulus, die Pharisäer und das Neue Testament*, ed. L. Baeck (Frankfurt, 1961), pp. 7–37; H. Hübner, *Das Gesetz bei Paulus. Ein Beitrag zum Werden der paulinischen Theologie* (Göttingen, 1978); H. Ronning, "Some Jewish Views of Paul," *Judaica* 24 (1968): 82–97; K. Haacker, "Paulus und das Judentum," *Judaica* 33 (1977): 161–177; W. D. Davies, *Paul and Rabbinic Judaism: Some Rabbinic Elements in Pauline Theology*, 2d ed. (London, 1955); A. Mamorstein, "Paulus und die Rabbinen," *Zeitschrift für die neutestamentliche Wissenschaft* 30 (1931); 271–285; M. Barth, "Paulus und die Juden," in *Jesus, Paulus und die Juden*, ed. M. Barth (Zurich, 1967), pp. 40–82; W. Wuellner, "Toposforschung und Thorainterpretation bei Paulus und Jesus," *New Testament Studies* 24 (1977/78): 463–483; K. Stendahl, *Der Jude Paulus und wir Heiden. Kaiser Traktate* 36 (Munich, 1978); U. Wilkens, "Glaube nach urchristlichem und frühjüdischem Verständnis," in *Was Juden und Christen voneinander denken. Bausteine zum Brükenschlag*, ed. P. Lapide, F. Mussner, U. Wilkens (Freiburg, 1978), pp. 72–96; D. Zeller, "Christus, Skandal und Hoffnung. Die Juden in den Briefen des Paulus," in *Gottesverächter und Menschenfeinde? Juden zwischen Jesus und frühchristlicher Kirche*, ed. H. Goldstein (Düsseldorf, 1979), pp. 256–278.

2. Concerning this see specifics in F. Mussner, *Der Galaterbrief*, 3d ed., (Freiburg, 1977), pp. 184–186.

3. Concerning this see, for example, H. Riesenfeld, "*Hyper*," in *Theological Dictionary of the New Testament*, ed. G. Kittel (Grand Rapids, 1967), 8: 510–513; K. H. Schelkle, *Die Passion Jesu in der Verkündigung des Neuen Testaments* (Heidelberg, 1949), pp. 132ff.

4. H.-J. Schoeps, *Paulus. Die Theologie des Apostels im Licht der jüdischen Religionsgeschichte* (Tübingen, 1959), pp. 224–230.

5. Ibid., pp. 95–110.

6. Ibid., p. 221.

7. Here, however, Paul could join with the Jewish tradition, especially the Yom Kippur theology with its images of atonement, the prophetic proclamation of the suffering servant of God (Isa. 53), and the Jewish martyr theology. Something similar is true for his "concept of faith." See, for example, Wilkens, "Glaube nach urchristlichem und frühjüdischem Verständnis"; D. Lührmann, *Glaube im frühen Christentum* (Gütersloh, 1976); F. Mussner, "Der Glaube Mariens im Lichte des Römerbriefs," in *Praesentia Salutis. Gesammelte Studien zu Fragen und Themen des Neuen Testaments*, ed. F. Mussner (Düsseldorf, 1967), pp. 284–292. Likewise,

the Jewish conviction of the atonement character of the "Aqedath Yishaq" provided the primitive Church hermeneutical assistance in the theological interpretation of the violent death of Jesus (see on this, for example, Schoeps, *Paulus*, pp. 144–152). If all this were taken into consideration, the Jewish contours of the passion of Jesus could again be regained (concerning this see B. Klappert, "Der Verlust und die Wiedergewinnung der israelitischen Kontur der Leidengeschichte Jesu [das Kreuz, das Leiden, das Paschamahl, der Prozess Jesu]," in *Exodus und Kreuz im ökumenischen Dialog zwischen Juden und Christen*, ed. H. H. Henrix and M. Stöhr [Aachen, 1978], pp. 107–153; P. Lapide, "Das Leiden und Sterben Jesu von Nazareth. Versuch einer jüdischen Sinngebung," in ibid., pp. 94–106).

8. G. Klein, "Römer 4 und die Idee der Heilsgeschichte," in *Rekonstruktion und Interpretation. Gesammelte Aufsätze zum Neuen Testament*, ed. G. Klein (Munich, 1969), p. 158.

9. See also N. A. Dahl, "Die Messianität Jesu bei Paulus," in *Studia Paulina. Festschrift für J. de Zwaan* (Haarlem, 1953), pp. 83–95.

10. Baeck, "Der Glaube des Paulus," p. 9.

11. Ibid., p. 10.

12. Ibid., p. 11.

13. Ibid., p. 10.

14. Von der Osten-Sacken, "Paulinische Verständnis des Gesetzes," pp. 549–587.

15. Cf. ibid.

16. Concerning this see pp. 28ff.

17. Dahl, "Messianität Jesu," p. 94.

18. Concerning this see, for example, F. J. Schierse, "Oster- und Parusiefrömmigkeit im Neuen Testament," in *Strukturen christlicher Existenz. Festschrift für Fr. Wulf* (Würzburg, 1968), pp. 37–57, esp. p. 42.

19. Concerning this see, for example, O. Kuss, *Der Römerbrief* (Regensburg, 1957ff.), pp. 268f.

20. For specifics see pp. 175ff. In bBer. Jochanan ben Zakkai is called a "light of Israel, an upright pillar."

21. For specifics see Mussner, *Galaterbrief*, Exkurs 4: "Hat Paulus das Gesetz 'missverstanden'?; G. Jasper, "Das 'grundlegende Missverständnis' des Paulus nach jüdischer Sicht," *Judaica* 15 (1959): 143–161.

22. E. Käsemann, *An die Römer*, 3d ed. (Tübingen, 1974), p. 190.

23. Concerning this see, for example, H. Schlier, "Von den Heiden. Römerbrief 1,18–32," in *Die Zeit der Kirche*, ed. H. Schlier (Freiburg, 1956), pp. 29–37; H. Schlier, "Von den Juden. Römerbrief 2,1–29," in ibid., pp. 38–47; O. Kuss, "Die Heiden und die Werke des Gesetzes (nach Röm 2,14–16)," *Münchner Theologische Zeitschrift* 5 (1954): 77–98; G. Eichholz, *Die Theologie des Paulus im Umriss* (Neukirchen, 1972), pp. 63–81 ("Der Mensch der Völkerwelt als Gottes Angeklagter"); pp. 82–100 ("Der Jude als Gottes Angelklager"); pp. 221–226; von der Osten-Sacken, "Paulinische Verständnis des Gesetzes," pp. 562–569.

24. See Rom. 2:14f.: "When Gentiles who have not the law do by nature what the law requires, they are a law to themselves, even though they do not have the law. They show that what the law requires is written on their hearts, while their conscience also bears witness and their conflicting thoughts accuse or perhaps

excuse them." Concerning this see Kuss, *Der Römerbrief,* pp. 72–82; R. Walker, "Die Heiden und das Gericht. Zur Auslegung von Röm 2,12–16," *Evangelische Theologie* 20 (1960): 302–314; Käsemann, *An die Römer,* pp. 57–63.

25. See Mussner, *Galaterbrief,* p. 29. In this commentary I attempted in the explanation to be seriously consistent with this insight.

26. See F. Mussner, *Petrus und Paulus—Pole der Einheit. Eine Hilfe für die Kirchen* (Freiburg, 1976), pp. 86, 137.

27. J. Blank, in his review of my commentary in *Biblische Zeitschrift* 20 (1976): 291–301.

28. On this also see the formulation of the apostle in Rom. 9:6: "not all who are descended from Israel belong to Israel."

29. A. Schlatter remarks on Rom. 2:28f.: "Paul did not dispute the national existence of Judaism, but acknowledged it as a fact willed by God. Further, he laid on top of this the goal of God with Israel. The meaning of the call of Israel is the community, which receives its interior life from the Spirit of God. The work of God is greater than that which is communicated by nature. . . . However, the sentence that according to the judgment of Paul there is nothing effective in Judaism which is of the flesh, is not seriously reconcilable with what Paul had affirmed about the word being delivered to Israel as the word of God" (*Gottes Gerechtigkeit. Ein Kommentar zum Römerbrief* [Stuttgart, 1952], pp. 111f.).

30. On this see our discussion on pp. 28ff.

31. Thus, for example, Klein, ed., *Rekonstruktion und Interpretation,* p. 203.

32. See specifics in Mussner, *Galaterbrief,* pp. 219–274.

33. Also Rabbi Nechemya (around 150) taught: "Thus you find with Abraham that he had taken possession of this and the world to come as a reward of faith, as it says: He believed in God and he reckoned it as righteousness to him" (*Mekilta Ex.* 14:31).

34. For specifics see F. Mussner, "Wer ist 'der ganze Samen' in Röm 4,16?" in *Begegnung mit dem Wort. Festschrift für H. Zimmermann* (Bonn, 1980), pp. 213–217.

35. Concerning this see, for example, O. Michel, *Paulus und seine Bibel* (Augsburg, 1929; photo reprint, 1972).

36. Concerning this see, for example, W. Windfuhr, "Paul als Haggadist," *Zeitschrift für alttestamentliche Wissenschaft* 3 (1926): 327ff.; Mamorstein, "Paulus und die Rabbinen," pp. 271–285; J. Bonsirven, *Exégèse Rabbinique et Exégèse Paulinienne* (Paris, 1939); Davies, *Paul and Rabbinic Judaism;* C. Maurer, "Der Schluss 'a minore ad majus' als Element paulinischer Theologie," *Theologische Literatur Zeitung* 85 (1960): 149–152; J. Jeremias, "Paulus als Hillelit," in *Neotestamentica et Semitica. Festschrift for M. Black* (Edinburgh, 1969), pp. 88–94; E. P. Sanders, *Paul and Palestinian Judaism* (London, 1977). According to Acts 22:3, Paul was "a Jew, born at Tarsus in Cilicia, but brought up in this city [Jerusalem] at the feet of Gamaliel, educated according to the strict manner of the law of our fathers, being zealous for God."

37. Käsemann, *An die Römer,* p. 348.

38. Ibid., p. 349.

39. See specifics in Mussner, *Galaterbrief,* pp. 351–354.

40. *Ho nomos tou Christou* = *torato shel meshiach,* meeting in MidrQoh

11,8,5a: "The Torah which a man learns in this world is a nothing compared with the Torah of the Messiah." On the problem of a coming "Torah of the Messiah" see especially P. Schäfer, "Die Torah der messianischen Zeit," *Zeitschrift für die neutestamentliche Wissenschaft* 65 (1974): 27–42.

41. H. Lietzmann, *An die Galater*, 4th ed. (Tübingen, 1971), p. 41. H. Schürmann in his essay, " 'Das Gesetz des Christus' (Gal 6,2). Jesu Verhalten und Wort als letzgültige sittliche Norm nach Paulus," in *Jesu ureigener Tod. Exegetische Besinnungen und Ausblick*, ed. H. Lietzmann (Freiburg, 1975), pp. 97–120, undertook the important attempt to spell out more precisely the content of the "law of Christ," of which Paul in Gal. 6:2 speaks. According to him, the word structure "the law of Christ" says "two things: formally the teaching of Jesus as the highest authority attributed to it; in content it is strongly differentiated from the Torah of Moses" (p. 106). What is new is that for Christians moral demands are now no longer the law of Moses, but the law of Christ, of the Messiah and of his God, or "the law of faith" (Rom. 3:27), or "the spiritual law of life" (Rom. 8:2), but nevertheless as a "summing up" and "fulfilling" of the Torah, summed up and fulfilled in the law of love. "With the word structure 'the law of Christ' Paul succeeded in bringing together in a 'brief formula' and with great pregnancy the moral demands which at the same time concentrate and intentionalize the Old Testament instructions in the command of love, having thus adopted the latter" (p. 112). Then, of course, it is true: "But if you are led by the Spirit you are not under the Law" (Gal. 5:18), namely, under the old Law which was not able to bring life. "For the law of the spirit of life in Christ Jesus has set me free from the law of sin and death" (Rom. 8:2). A paradox is again shown here in the Pauline theology of the Law; for on this one side the old Torah in fact is "set aside" (H. Schürmann), and on the other side it is "fulfilled": discontinuity in continuity. Who can really grasp these paradoxes? Paul could speak of this only in a dialectic fashion.

42. Käsemann, *An die Römer*, p. 179.

43. Concerning the Synagogue penalty of flogging, see Billerbeck, *Kommentar zum Neuen Testament*, III, pp. 527–530.

44. O. Michel, "Fragen zu 1 Thessalonicher 2,14–16: Antijüdische Polemik bei Paulus," in *Antijudaismus im Neuen Testament? Exegetische und systematische Beiträge*, ed. W. Eckert, N. P. Levinson, M. Stöhr, (Munich, 1967), pp. 50–59.

45. E. Bammel, "Judenverfolgung und Naherwartung," *Zeitschrift für Theologie und Kirche* 56 (1959); 294–315.

46. Davies, "Paul and the People of Israel," pp. 6–9. I am particularly following W. D. Davies here, though perhaps not in everything.

47. Concerning this see also O. H. Steck, *Israel und das gewaltsame Geschick der Propheten* (Neukirchen, 1967).

48. Ibid., p. 8.

49. Ibid.

50. See also M. Barth, "Was Paul an anti-Semite?" *Journal of Ecumenical Studies* 5 (1968); 78–104.

NOTES FOR CHAPTER 5

1. Concerning this see, for example, F. Mussner, "Die Gemeinde des Lukasprologs," in *Festschrift für Bo Reike* (not yet published).

2. See F. Mussner, "Christologische Homologese und evangelische Vita Jesu," in *Zur Frühgeschichte der Christologie. Ihre biblische Anfänge und die Lehrformel von Nikaia*, ed. B. Welte (Freiburg, 1970), pp. 59–73; G. Lohfink, "Erzählung als Theologie. Zur sprachlichen Grundstruktur der Evangelien," *Stimmen der Zeit* 99 (1974): 521–532. E. Käsemann has remarked: "If primitive Christianity has identified the lowly with the mighty Lord, it announces with this that in the presentation of its history it is not able to abstract from its faith. At the same time, however, it announces with this that it is not willing to allow a myth to stand in the place of history, a heavenly being in the place of the Nazarene" ("Das Problem des historischen Jesus," in E. Käsemann, *Exegetische Versuche und Besinnungen*, ed. E. Käsemann [Göttingen, 1960], 1:196).

3. J. Isaac, *Jesus and Israel* (New York, 1971), pp. 391, 398f.

4. With this Isaac means Jewish Christianity.

5. Isaac is thinking here of "heterodox" Jewish Christianity. On this see, for example, H. J. Schoeps, *Theologie und Geschichte des Judenchristentums* (Tübingen, 1949); G. Strecker, *Das Judenchristentum in den Pseudoklementinen* (Berlin, 1958); J. Daniélou, *Théologie du Judeo-Christianisme* (Tournai, 1958); G. Schille, *Das vorsynopstische Judenchristentum* (Berlin, 1970); B. Bagatti, *The Church from the Circumcision: History and Archaeology of the Judaeo-Christians* (Jerusalem, 1971); A. F. Klijn and G. J. Reinink, *Patristic Evidence for Jewish-Christian Sects* (Leiden, 1973).

6. Among Christian scholars, W. Feneberg in his book *Der Markusprolog. Studien zur Formbestimmung des Evangeliums* (Munich, 1974)—here see particularly pp. 121–144—has drawn attention in a special manner to this "Sitz im Leben" in the process of the origin of the Gospels. He was inspired in part by K. L. Schmidt, "Die Stellung der Evangelien in der allgemeinen Literaturgeschichte," in *Eucharisterion. Festschrift für H. Gunkel,* ed. H. Schmidt (Göttingen, 1923), 2: 50–134.

7. See also C. Thoma, "Auswirkungen des jüdischen Krieges gegen Rom (66–70/73 n. Chr.) auf das rabbinische Judentum," *Biblische Zeitschrift* 12 (1968): pp. 30–54, 186–210.

8. Feneberg, *Der Markusprolog.*, p. 123.

9. See J. Jeremias, *Jesu Verheissung für die Völker* (Stuttgart, 1956); H. Rusche, "Für das 'Haus Israel' vom 'Gott Israels' gesandt. Jesus und die Juden in der Deutung von Mt 15,21–28," in *Gottesverächter und Menschenfeinde? Juden zwischen Jesus und der frühchristlichen Kirche,* ed. H. Goldstein (Düsseldorf, 1979), pp. 99–122.

10. F. Schnider, *Die verlorenen Söhne. Strukturanalytische und historisch-kritische Untersuchungen zu Lk 15* (Freiburg and Göttingen, 1977), has shown this in the traditioned material with Luke 15 as an example.

11. Concerning this see F. Mussner, "Gab es eine 'galiläische Krise'?" in *Orientierung an Jesus. Zur Theologie der Synoptiker. Festschrift für J. Schmid,* ed. P. Hoffman (Freiburg, 1973), pp. 238–252.

12. For specifics, see pp. 216ff.

13. See Mussner, "Gab es eine 'galiläische Krise'?" pp. 247f.

14. See H. Schürmann, "Die vorösterlichen Anfänge der Logientradition," in *Traditionsgeschichtliche Untersuchungen zu den synoptischen Evangelien,* ed. H. Schürmann (Düsseldorf, 1968), pp. 39–65.

NOTES FOR CHAPTER 5

15. See above all J. Maier, *Jesus im Talmud* (Darmstadt, 1977).

16. See specifics on pp. 216ff.

17. D. Michel, "Polemik und Scheidung," in *Basileia. Festschrift für W. Freytag* (Stuttgart, 1959), pp. 185–198.

18. See for further details F. Schnider, *Jesus, der Prophet* (Freiburg and Göttingen, 1973).

19. See F. Mussner, "Die bösen Winzer nach Matthäus 21,33–46," in *Antijudaismus im Neuen Testament?*, ed. W. P. Eckert, N. P. Levinson, M. Stöhr (Munich, 1976), pp. 129–134.

20. Feneberg, *Der Markusprolog*, p. 139.

21. Ibid., p. 140. Feneberg then exemplified this orientation in the "Markan Prologue" (Mark 1:1–11) with his new historical picture of how the primitive Church gradually developed.

22. Concerning this see also E. Janssen, *Das Gottesvolk und seine Geschichte. Geschichtsbild und Selbstverständnis im palästinenischen Schrifttum von Jesus Sirach bis Jehuda na-Nasi* (Neukirchen, 1971); G. Lindeskog, "Anfänge des jüdisch-christlichen Problems. Ein programmatischer Entwurf," in *Donum Gentilicium. New Testament Studies in Honour of David Daube*, ed. E. Bammel et al. (Oxford, 1978), pp. 225–275.

23. From the wealth of material the following are selected: R. Travers Herford, *The Pharisees* (Boston, 1962); A Finkel, *The Pharisees and the Teacher of Nazareth* (Leiden, 1964); J. Neusner, *The Rabbinic Traditions about the Pharisees*, 3 vols. (Leiden, 1971); J. Neusner, "Die Verwendung des späteren rabbinischen Materials für die Erforschung des Pharisäismus im 1. Jhd. n. Chr.," *Zeitschrift für Theologie und Kirche* 76 (1979): 292–309; L. Finkelstein, *The Pharisees*, 2 vols., 3d ed. (Philadelphia, 1962); G. Allon, "The Attitude of the Pharisees to the Roman Government and the House of Herod," in *Scripta Hierosolymitana* 7 (1961): 53–78; L. Baeck, *The Pharisees* (New York, 1947); L. Baeck, "Die Pharisäer," in *Paulus, die Pharisäer und das Neue Testament* (Frankfurt, 1961); I. Abrahams, *Studies in Pharisaism and the Gospels*, 2 vols., 2d ed. (Cambridge, 1967); E. Bickermann, *Die Makkabäer* (Berlin, 1935); J. Jeremias, *Jerusalem in the Time of Jesus* (Philadelphia, 1969); K. Schubert, "Die jüdischen Religionsparteien im Zeitalter Jesu," in *Der historische Jesus und der Christus des Glaubens* (Vienna, 1962), pp. 15–101 (more specifically, pp. 57–80); L. Ehrlich, "Zur Geschichte der Pharisäer," *Freiburger Rundbrief* 29 (1977): 46–52; C. Thoma, "Der Pharisäismus," in *Literatur und Religion des Frühjudentums*, ed. J. Maier and J. Schreiner (Würzburg, 1973), pp. 254–272; R. Meyer, "Die Bedeutung des Pharisäismus für Geschichte und Theologie des Judentums," *Theologische Literatur Zeitung* 77 (1952): 677–684; R. Meyer, *Tradition und Neuschöpfung im antiken Judentum. Dargestellt an der Geschichte der Pharisäer. Mit einem Beitrag von H. F. Weiss, "Der Pharisäismus im Lichte der Überlieferung des NT,* (Sitzungsbericht der Sächsischen Akademie der Wissenschaften zu Leipzig, philo.-histor. Kl. 110.2 (Berlin, 1965); R. Meyer and K. Weiss, "Pharisaios," in *Theological Dictionary of the New Testament*, ed. G. Kittel (Grand Rapids, 1967), 9: 11–51, with comprehensive bibliography; W. Beilner, *Christus und die Pharisäer. Exegetische Untersuchung über Grund und Verlauf der Auseinandersetzungen* (Vienna, 1959), also with comprehensive bibliography; W. Beilner, "Der Ursprung des Pharisäismus," *Biblische Zeitschrift* 3 (1959): 235–251;

H. Merkel, "Jesus und die Pharisäer," *New Testament Studies* 14 (1967/68): 194–208; F. Mussner, "Jesus und die Pharisäer," in *Praesentia Salutis. Gesammelte Studien zu Fragen und Themen des Neuen Testaments*, ed. F. Mussner (Düsseldorf, 1967), pp. 99–112 (I would no longer write this essay in this manner today); J. Bowker, *Jesus and the Pharisees* (Cambridge, 1973); B. Lindars, "Jesus and the Pharisees," in *Donum Gentilicium. New Testament Studies in Honour of David Daube*, ed. E. Bammel, C. K. Barret, W. D. Davies (Oxford, 1978), pp. 51–63; G. Baumbach, "Volk Gottes im Frühjudentum," *Kairos* 21 (1979): 30–47; H. Frankemölle, " 'Pharisäismus' in Judentum und Kirche. Zur Tradition und Redaktion in Matthäus 23," in Goldstein, ed., *Gottesverächter*, pp. 123–189—with abundant bibliography. The history of the research on the Pharisees is briefly outlined by N. N. Glatzer in his introduction to the 1962 edition of R. T. Herford's book *The Pharisees*, and by R. Mayer, "Das frühere und gegenwärtige Bild der Pharisäer," the manuscript of a lecture in Regensburg which the author graciously put at my disposal. See also the persuasive and revolutionary treatment of the Pharisees by the Jewish scholar Ellis Rivkin, *The Hidden Revolution* (Nashville, 1978); also excellent is John T. Pawlikowski, *Christ in the Light of Christian-Jewish Dialogue* (New York, 1982), pp. 76–107; likewise, Leonard Swidler, "The Pharisees in Recent Catholic Writing," *Horizons* 10, 2 (Fall, 1983).

24. Josephus, *De Bello Judaico*, 2: 14, 162. See also *Antiquitates*, 17: 2,41.

25. Thus in any case Rabbi Akiba taught: "Just as the entire Torah is the Law given to Moses on Sinai, so also a lesser teaching statement is a statement given to Moses on Sinai" (bT Niddah 45a). "Whereby Levi ben Chama spoke in the name of Rabbi Shimon ben Laqish: it says: 'I will give you the tables of stone, with the Law and the commandment, which I have written for your instruction' (Exod. 24:12). With the 'tables of stone' the ten commandments are meant, with the 'Law' the Holy Scriptures, with the 'commandment' the Mishnah, with 'which I have written' the prophetic books and writings, and 'for their instruction' the Talmud. This teaches that they all were handed over to Moses on Mt. Sinai" (bBer. 5a). Consequently the "tradition of the elders" as the total oral tradition on "the elders" is also traced back to Moses (cf. Abot 1,1). Concerning this whole issue, see H. Mantel, "The Development of the Oral Law during the Second Temple Period," in *World History of the Jewish People*, (Jerusalem, 1976), 7: 41–64, 325–337; Clemens Thoma, *A Christian Theology of Judaism* (New York, 1980), pp. 99f.

26. See R. Meyer, "*Pharisaios*," in Kittel, ed., *Theological Dictionary*, 9: 11–35. See also the bitter remarks in the Damascus Document, IV, 12: "the fence will be rebuilt and the bounds be far-flung," which likewise appear to be directed against the Pharisees.

27. Ibid., p. 35.

28. *Antiquitates* 17: 2, 42.

29. Ibid., 18: 1, 12–15.

30. Thoma, *Christian Theology of Judaism*, p. 65.

31. For further details see pp. 177ff.

32. See also M. J. Cook, *Mark's Treatment of the Jewish Leaders* (Leiden, 1978); M. J. Cook, "Jesus and the Pharisees—the Problem as it Stands Today," *Journal of Ecumenical Studies* 15 (1978): 441–460.

33. See also W. J. Bennett, "The Herodians of Mark's Gospel," *Novum Testamentum* 17 (1975): 9–14.

34. R. Pesch, *Das Markusevangelium* (Freiburg, 1976), 1: 376.
35. Ibid. For another view, see T. A. Burkill, "Antisemitism in the Gospel of Mark," *Novum Testamentum* 3 (1959): 34–53, and in contrast, H. W. Kuhn, "Zum Problem des Verhältnisses der markinischen Redaktion zur israelitisch-jüdischen Tradition," in *Tradition und Glaube. Festschrift für K. G. Kuhn* (Göttingen, 1972), pp. 299–309.
36. Pesch, *Das Markusevangelium*, p. 384.
37. Ibid., pp. 407ff.
38. Ibid., p. 413.
39. Ibid., p. 414.
40. Ibid., 2: 120.
41. Ibid., p. 122.
42. Ibid., p. 228.
43. See pp. 180ff.
44. A. Polag, *Die Christologie der Logienquelle* (Neukirchen, 1977), pp. 79–84.
45. See also R. Hummel, *Die Auseinandersetzung zwischen Kirche und Judentum im Matthäusevangelium*, 2d ed. (Munich, 1966), pp. 12–17.
46. W. G. Kümmel, "Die Weherufe über die Schriftgelehrten und die Pharisäer (Matthäus 23,13–16)," in Eckert et al., eds., *Antijudaismus im Neuen Testament?* pp. 135–147.
47. Ibid., p. 137.
48. Ibid., p. 146.
49. See also S. Légasse, "L'antijudaisme dans L'Evangile selon Matthieu," in *L'Evangile selon Matthieu. Redaction et théologie*, ed. M. Didier (Gembloux, 1972), pp. 417–428; T. F. Glasson, "Anti-Pharisaism in St. Matthew," *Jewish Quarterly Review* 51 (1960/61): 316–320.
50. See also J. A. Ziesler, "Luke and the Pharisees," *New Testament Studies* 25 (1978/79): 146–157.
51. H. Schürmann, *Das Lukasevangelium* (Freiburg, 1969), 1: 422.
52. In the Greek text here the imperfect (*diegoggyzon*), which indicates a continuing attitude ("the iterative imperfect"), is similar to the periphrastic construction (*ēsan eggizontes*) in 15:1 and the *pantes* ("*all* tax collectors and sinners"), which some textual witnesses have dropped as "exaggerating," both of which intend to indicate that it concerns a repeated "occurrence," naturally according to the redactional intention of the evangelist.
53. See pp. 163ff.
54. Concerning this formal application, see J. Jeremias, "Zöllner und Sünder," *Zeitschrift für die neutestamentliche Wissenschaft* 30 (1931): 293–300. Jeremias recalls the lists of professional, notorious sinners in rabbinic writings, for example, in bSanh. 25b (Bar.).
55. See also Schnider, *Die verlorenen Söhne*, pp. 89f.
56. A. Schlatter comments thus (*Das Evangelium des Lukas. Aus seinen Quellen erklärt*, 2d ed. [Stuttgart, 1960], pp. 374f.): "The (!) Pharisee thinks the search for money is innocent and is allowed even to a pious one, because in his 'heart,' in which his covetousness has arisen, he does not concern himself. . . . Pharisaic piety does not concern itself with the heart, but its goal is to present oneself as just before men. Human judgment, however, does not reject the respect for riches. When even

the pious covet it, they protect themselves with the customary self-seeking moral";
one page farther the same author writes: "Usury, betrayal, and robbery damn also
the Pharisee." Does this all really fit together?

57. What role a specific "lexicon of words of abuse" played in anti-Judaism must
yet be investigated. Perhaps the accusation of the greed for money also belongs in
this lexicon.

58. See F. Mussner, " 'Wann kommt das Reich Gottes?' Die Antwort Jesu nach
Lk 17,20b, 21," *Biblische Zeitschrift* 6 (1962): 107–111.

59. See, W. Wink, *Bibelauslegung als Interaktion. Über die Grenzen historisch-
kritischer Methode* (Stuttgart, 1976).

60. W. Grundmann, *Das Evangelium nach Lukas* (Berlin, n.d.), p. 367.

61. For specifics see p. 181, n. 104.

62. R. Bultmann, *Das Evangelium des Johannes*, 16th ed. (Göttingen, 1959), p.
57.

63. Ibid., p. 62, n. 6.

64. Ibid., p. 94, n. 2.

65. See also ibid., p. 231, n. 7.

66. See ibid., p. 209, n. 8.

67. Concerning this concept see pp. 175ff.

68. Such "leaders" who sympathized with Jesus were, according to John, Nicodemus (3:1, 7:50, 19:18) or Joseph of Arimathea (19:38).

69. R. Schnackenburg, *Das Johannesevangelium* (Freiburg, 1971), 2: 317.

70. Billerbeck, *Kommentar*, 4:212f., 293–329, 331ff.; W. Schrage, "Aposynagōgos," in Kittel, ed., *Theological Dictionary*, 7: 848–852.

71. Ibid., p. 850.

72. However, also see D. R. A. Hare, *The Theme of Jewish Persecution of
Christians in the Gospel According to Matthew* (Cambridge, 1967), pp. 39, 48ff.
According to Hare, the Birkat ha-Minim is directed above all against a "heretic"
who attempts to lead the Jewish liturgy. However, the Gospel of John doubtless
understands the term *aposynagōgos* thus: Someone who confesses Jesus as the
Messiah and Son of God will be excluded from the synagogue community. How that
concretely happened escapes our knowledge. On the problem of the "apostate
blessing," also see J. J. Petuchowski, "Jewish Prayer Texts of the Rabbinic Period,"
Lord's Prayer, ed. Petuchowski and Brocke, pp. 21–44; G. Stemberger, "Die
sogenannte 'Synode von Jabne' und das frühe Christentum," *Kairos* 29 (1977): 14–
21; and especially Thoma, *Christian Theology of Judaism*, pp. 146–150 (Thoma
comes to the conclusion: "No excommunication of Jewish Christians by all of the
rabbis ever took place. . . . Judaism considered Jewish heretics a greater evil than
non-Jewish sinners," p. 150).

73. It is interesting that in the second work of Luke, the Acts of the Apostles,
there is hardly any negative accent on the "Pharisees" (on this see K. Weiss,
"*Pharisaios*," in Kittel, ed., *Theological Dictionary*, 9: 47f.). And Paul was the son of
pharisaically inclined parents (Acts 26:4f.) and a disciple of Rabban Gamliel (Acts
5:34); in Gal. 1:13f. and especially in Phil. 3:5f. he himself speaks of his Pharisaic
past (see the excellent discussion in O. Betz, "Paulus als Pharisäer nach dem
Gesetz. Phil 3,5–6 als Beitrag zur Frage des frühen Pharisäismus," in *Treue zur
Thora. Festschrift für G. Harder*, ed. P. von der Osten-Sacken, (Berlin, 1977), pp.

296 NOTES FOR CHAPTER 5

54–64. For the rest, the Pharisees play absolutely no role in the Pauline corpus— they are never otherwise mentioned by him; his opponents were in the beginning Jews and later fellow Christians ("Judaists") who had come out of Judaism and could not identify with his theology, but rather struggled against it and the apostle.

74. See R. Meyer, "Pharisaios," in Kittel, ed., Theological Dictionary, 9: 31–35 (3: The Victory of Pharisaism); Herford, The Pharisees, pp. 147–175; Baeck, The Pharisees; C. Thoma, "Auswirkungen des jüdischen Krieges gegen Rom (66–70/73 N. Chr.) auf das rabbinische Judentum," Biblische Zeitschrift 12 (1968): 30–54, 186–210.

75. R. Meyer, "Pharisaios," p. 32. See also Thoma, Christian Theology of Judaism, pp. 44ff.

76. A. Schlatter, "Jochanan ben Zakkai, der Zeitgenosse der Apostel," in Synagoge und Kirche bis zum Barkochba-Aufstand, ed. A. Schlatter (Stuttgart, 1966), pp. 175–236; J. Neusner, A Life of Rabban Yohanan ben Zakkai, 2d ed. (Leiden, 1970); E. Janssen, Das Gottesvolk und seine Geschichte. Geschichtsbild und Selbstverständnis im palästinenischen Schrifttum von Jesus Sirach bis Jehuda ha-Nasi (Neukirchen, 1971), pp. 127–135; P. Schäfer, "Die sogenannte Synode von Jabne. Zur Trennung von Juden und Christen im 1./2. Jh. n. Chr.," in Judaica 31 (1975): 54–64, 116–124; G. Stemberger, "Die sog. 'Synode von Jabne' und das frühe Christentum," Kairos 19 (1977): 14–21 (21: "Javneh is for Judaism what the so-called 'early catholicism' is for Christianity").

77. Herford, The Pharisees, p. 237.

78. Concerning this see especially Baeck, The Pharisees.

79. On the history of the scribes, see especially E. Schürer, Geschichte des jüdischen Volkes im Zeitalter Jesu Christi, 4th ed. (Leipzig, 1901–1911), 2: 372–447; Billerbeck, Kommentar, 1: 79–82, 691–695; 2: 647–661; E. Lohse, Die Ordination im Spätjudentum und im Neuen Testament (Göttingen, 1951), pp. 28–66; E. Lohse, "Rabbi," in Kittel, ed., Theological Dictionary, 6: 961–965.

80. See also J. Neusner, From Politics to Piety: The Emergence of Pharisaic Judaism (Englewood Cliffs, 1973). Thus also Franz Rosenzweig: "This thinker deeply concerned about order, interested in the retention of Judaism . . . very definitely excluded everything messianic and left it to the Christians" (R. Meyer in a letter to the author on 1 June 1978). Likewise illuminating is the fact that nothing "messianic" is found in the Mishnah; only in the Tosephta was it brought back in (ibid.). Also in the Talmud the "messiah material" is fundamentally limited, although the messianic idea has never died out in Judaism, but rather has time and again shown itself, and shows itself, fermentive.

81. See L. Baeck, The Pharisees, pp. 72f. See also bBB 12a: "Since the day on which the Temple was destroyed prophecy was taken from the prophets and given to the sages." According to P. Schäfer it is the first Temple that is thought of, of course, Die Vorstellung vom Heiligen Geist in der rabbinischen Literatur (Munich, 1972), pp. 99f.

82. As opposed to Noth, see R. Meyer, "Die Bedeutung des Pharisäismus für Geschichte und Theologie des Judentums," Theologische Literatur Zeitung 77 (1952): 677–684.

83. Herford, The Pharisees, p. 199.

84. Ibid., p. 201.

85. On the "am-ha-aretz," see R. Meyer, "Der 'Am ha-'Ares," *Judaica* 3 (1947): 169–199; A. Oppenheimer, *The 'Am-Ha-Aretz: A Study in the Social History of the Jewish People in the Hellenistic Roman Period* (Leiden, 1977). In view of the various groups in the Judaism of that time, the most one can say is that Jesus was closer to the Pharisees than any other group; however, one cannot say with J. Klausner that Jesus of Nazareth was "in reality a Pharisee . . . who merely shifted the center of gravity of Pharisaic teaching" (*Jesus of Nazareth: His Times, His Life, and His Teaching* [New York, 1925], p. 248); this cannot be verified from the sources.

86. From the German language literature the following should be mentioned: F. Mussner, "Jesus und die Pharisäer"; Merkel, "Jesus und die Pharisäer"; Beilner, *Christus und die Pharisäer.* Further details are found in note 23. Extensive bibliography of non-German as well as German literature can be found in M. J. Cook, "Jesus and the Pharisee—The Problem as It Stands Today," *Journal of Ecumenical Studies* 15 (1978): 441–460; E. Rivkin, *A Hidden Revolution: The Pharisees Search for the Kingdom Within* (Nashville, 1978).

87. See Polag, *Die Christologie der Logienquelle,* pp. 79–84.

88. Ibid., p. 82.

89. Concerning this also see M. Hengel, "Jesus und die Tora," *Theologische Beiträge* 9 (1978): 155f. Concerning the Pharisees' attitude toward the development of that which had been handed on, see the important remarks of J. Neusner, "Die Verwendung des späteren rabbinischen Materials," pp. 307f.

90. For contrast the *Mishnah* tractate "Demai" should be read (II, 3a): "Whoever takes it upon himself to be a comrade (חבר), he may neither sell something fresh nor dry to an *am-ha-aretz,* and may buy nothing fresh from him, and may not dwell by an *am-ha-aretz* and may not put up such a person with his clothing," for otherwise he would make himself unclean; cf. also tractate "Chagiga" II, 7: The clothes of an *am-ha-aretz* are as unclean for the Pharisees. How far were these specifications and views true at the time of Jesus? This of course remains an open question.

91. Concerning this see, for example, K. Kertelge, "Die Vollmacht des Menschensohnes zur Sündenvergebung (Mk 2,10)," in *Orientierung an Jesus. Festschrift für J. Schmid,* ed. P. Hoffman (Freiburg, 1973), pp. 205–213; K. Kertelge, "Südenvergebung an Stelle Gottes. Eine neutestamentlich-theologisch Darlegung," in *Dienst der Versöhnung,* Trierer theologische Studien 31 (Trier, 1974), pp. 27–44; P. Fiedler, *Jesus und die Sünder* (Frankfurt and Bern, 1976), pp. 271–277.

92. See the rabbinic material in Billerbeck, *Kommentar,* 1: 703.

93. See specifics in W. Paschen, *Rein und Unrein. Untersuchungen zur biblischen Wortgeschichte* (Munich, 1970); J. Neusner, *The Idea of Purity in Ancient Judaism* (Leiden, 1973); J. Neusner, *A History of the Mishnaic Law of Purities,* 9 vols. (Leiden, 1974ff.); H. Hübner, *Das Gesetz in der synoptischen Tradition* (Witten, 1973); W. Bunte, *Mischna-Traktat Kelim. Text, Übersetzung und Erklärung nebst einem texkritischen Anhang* (Berlin and New York, 1972). How very much the purity of Israel lay on the heart of the Essenes can be dramatically recognized in the "Temple Scroll." Concerning it, see J. Maier, *Die Tempelrolle vom Toten Meer* (Munich and Basel, 1978)—translation and explanation.

94. Concerning this see Pesch, *Das Markusevangelium,* 1: 367–384; Merkel,

"Jesus und die Pharisäer," pp. 205–207; N. J. McFleney, "Authenticating Criteria and Mark 7:1–23," *Catholic Biblical Quarterly* 34 (1972): 431–460.

95. Hengel, "Jesus und die Tora," p. 164.

96. Concerning this see F. Mussner, "'Das Wesen des Christentums ist *synesthiein*.' Ein authentischer Kommentar," in *Mysterium der Gnade. Festschrift für J. Auer*, ed. H. Rossmann and J. Ratzinger (Regensberg, 1975), pp. 92–102.

97. Concerning this see, for example, Merkel, "Jesus und die Pharisäer," pp. 203–205; E. Lohse, "Jesu Worte über den Sabbat," in *Judentum, Urchristentum, Kirche. Festschrift für J. Jeremias*, ed. W. Eltester (Berlin, 1960), pp. 79–89.

98. One could indeed "view the dispute of Jesus with them as a special question of the Sabbath *halacha*. This manner of viewing things, however, overlooks a decisive point: a messianic-eschatological motive. The exorcisms and healings of Jesus happen as signs of the eschatological struggle against the powers of evil, which destroy the good creation of God. Because the sick are healed and demons are driven out, the Reign of God is symbolically already breaking in! . . . The Sabbath day, which images in symbolic form the coming time of salvation, was precisely predestined to the situation that in it the healings of the inbreaking Reign of God would be carried out" (Hengel, "Jesus und die Tora," p. 166).

99. See also Polag, *Die Christologie der Logienquelle*, p. 80, n. 251.

100. On this problem see the discussion on pp. 188ff.

101. However, it is also important to reflect on what Clemens Thoma has thus formulated: "For an understanding of Jesus and the New Testament it is very decisive that the disputes of Jesus with the Pharisees not be interpreted principally as anti-Pharisaism, but rather as disputes which since Old Testament times were customary within Judaism, and whose sharpness in view of the important material concerning the inbreaking Reign of God was only too understandable" (*A Christian Theology of Judaism*, p. 113).

102. And one should also not forget that the Rabbinic tradition also in part exercised a criticism of the Pharisees (cf. jEx. 84f.; jBer. IX, 7; jPeah VIII, 8; jHag. II, 7; jSot. III, 4). In bSota 22b seven types of Pharisees are distinguished: the "shoulder" Pharisee (who carries his good deeds on his shoulder); the "wait yet Pharisee"; the Pharisee "with the blue mark" (who banged his head on the wall in order to avoid looking at a woman); the "pestle Pharisee" (who is only apparently humble); the "bookkeeper Pharisee" (who keeps score on his virtues); the "fear Pharisee" (who obeys God only out of fear); the "love Pharisee" (who obeys God out of love). *And only the latter is the true Pharisee!*

103. See the overview of the neutral and negative use of the term "the Jews" in the Gospel of John in the important work by R. Leistner, *Antijudaismus im Johannesevangelium? Darstellung des Problems in der neueren Auslegungsgeschichte und Untersuchung der Leidensgeschichte* (Bern and Frankfurt, 1974), on the enclosed foldout. A similar overview and analysis was done in English somewhat earlier by Jack Epstein, "Roots of Religious Prejudice," *Journal of Ecumenical Studies* 5 (1968): 697–725.

104. In the Acts of the Apostles the term "the Jews" appears 79 times in connection with the mission work of the primitive Church, especially of Paul, as related by Luke in his second work. Concerning this see E. Haenchen, "Judentum und Christentum in der Apostelgeschichte," in *Die Bibel und Wir. Gesammelte*

Aufsätze (Tübingen, 1968), 2: 338–374; J. Jervell, "Das gespaltene Israel und die Heidenvölker. Zur Motivierung der Heidenmission in der Apostelgeschichte," *Stud. Theol.* 19 (1965): 68–96; G. Baum, *Die Juden und das Evangelium* (Einsiedeln, 1963), pp. 194–242.

105. Concerning this see J. Belser, "Der Ausdruck *hoi Ioudaioi* im Johannesevangelium," *Theologische Quartalschrift* 84 (1902): 168–222; W. Lütgert, "Die Juden im Johannes-Evangelium," in *Neutestamentliche Studien für G. Heinrici* (Leipzig, 1914), pp. 147–154; J. Jocz, "Die Juden im Johannesevangelium," *Judaica* 9 (1953): 129–142; L. Goppelt, *Christentum und Judentum im ersten und zweiten Jahrhundert* (Gütersloh, 1954), 251–259; G. Baum, *Die Juden und das Evangelium* (Einsiedeln, 1963), pp. 145–193; E. Grässer, "Die antijüdische Polemik im Johannesevangelium," *New Testament Studies* (1964/65), pp. 74–90; E. Grässer, "Die Juden als Teufelssöhne in Johannes 8,37–47," in *Antijudaismus im Neuen Testament?* (Munich, 1967), pp. 157–170; Leistner, *Antijudaismus im Johannesevangelium?* (see Note 103); M. Lowe, "Who Were the *Ioudaioi?*" *Novum Testamentum* 18 (1976): 101–130 (important!); H. E. Lona, *Abraham in Johannes 8. Ein Betrag zur Methodenfrage* (Bern, 1976); J. Beutler, "Die 'Juden' und der Tod Jesu im Johannesevangelium," in *Exodus und Kreuz im ökumenischen Dialog zwischen Juden und Christen*, ed. H. H. Henrix and M. Stöhr, (Aachen, 1978), pp. 75–93; F. Hahn, "Der Prozess Jesu nach dem Johannesevangelium. Eine redaktionsgeschichtliche Untersuchung," *Evangelisch-Katholischer Kommentar zum Neuen Testament* 2 (1970): 23–96; W. Trilling, "Gegner Jesu—Widersacher der Gemeinde—Repräsentanten der 'Welt.' Das Johannesevangelium und die Juden," in *Gottesverächter und Menschenfeinde? Juden zwischen Jesus und frühchristlicher Kirche*, ed. H. Goldstein (Düsseldorf, 1979), pp. 190–210.

106. Leistner lists the following passages: 1:19; 2:18, 20; 3:25; 5:10, 15, 16, 18; 6:41, 52; 7:1, 11, 13, 15, 35; 8:22, 31, 48, 52, 57; 9:18, 22; 10:24, 31, 33; 11:8; 13:33; 18:12, 14, 20, 31, 36, 38; 19:7, 12, 14, 21, 31, 38; 20:19. One could dispute whether some of the "Jews" passages of the Gospel of John have a neutral or negative accent (e.g., in 3:25 where moreover the manuscript tradition is divided).

107. Schnackenburg, *Das Johannesevangelium*, 1: 280f.

108. Ibid., p. 363.

109. See also Bultmann, *Das Evangelium des Johannes*, p. 182.

110. See Schnackenburg, *Das Johannesevangelium*, 2: 75, n. 1.

111. See also ibid., p. 207; "John never lists together the three groups represented in the High Council: the high priests, the elders, and the scribes. . . . The 'elders' . . . are never mentioned by him; likewise he never uses the expression *synedrion* for the institution, but only once for a gathering of the High Council (11:47). Is that connected with his distance from the time of Jesus and his own contemporaries' tendencies?" (ibid., n. 2).

112. See further Lona, *Abraham in Johannes 8.*

113. Schnackenburg, *Das Johannesevangelium*, 2: 313.

114. Ibid., p. 317. In addition see my discussion on pp. 163ff.

115. Ibid., p. 522.

116. See ibid., 3: 250–252, along with Leistner, *Antijudaismus*, pp. 81–85.

117. Schnackenburg, *Das Johannesevangelium*, 3: 251.

118. Ibid., p. 283.

119. Concerning this see note 124.

120. See Grässer, "Die Juden als Teufelssöhne," pp. 157–170.

121. Concerning this see the material in Schnackenburg, *Das Johannesevangelium*, 2: 289.

122. Leistner, *Antijudaismus*, p. 54.

123. Ibid., p. 55.

124. At the end of the first century John reflects on the occurrences which took place with Jesus and his crucifixion. However, he now places the whole thing within a "cosmic horizon," which would be more clearly seen if one were to carry out the so-called "acting-notions analysis" *(Aktantenanalyse)* of the Gospel of John (cf. concerning this A. J. Greimas, *Sémantique structurale, recherche de méthode*. [Paris, 1966]). One would then come to the following conclusions: As actors in the Gospel there are Jesus and the disciples as his "helpers," the Jewish enemies as his "opponents," who in the Gospel are said to be Pharisees and members of the Sanhedrin. John, however, reflects on this within a worldwide horizon. In this "the Jews," insofar as the term is burdened with a negative accent, become the representatives of the "world" which is hostile toward God. The evanglist means with this that "world" which does not wish to know anything of God and Christ. If one were (in the sense of Greimas) to further reduce the "actors" to "acting-notions" (*Akatanten*), one would in this reduction come upon death and life, light and darkness. These are abstract, "dualistic" terms which, as is known, play an important role in the Gospel of John and with whose help the evangelist lets us know that here we are dealing not only the historical trial against Jesus of Nazareth, but rather with a "world trial," namely of the darkness of the world against the divine light in general. One must, therefore, read the Johannine Gospel in the light of its cosmic horizon in order to be able to correctly evaluate its "anti-Judaism." The historical legitimation of seeing the trial against Jesus as a "world trial" lies in the circumstance that the representative of the Roman state, Pontius Pilate, is introduced into it. "Now . . . the trial of the world against Jesus attains its public quality; he is brought before the forum of the state" (R. Bultmann, *Das Evangelium des Johannes*, 18th ed. [Göttingen, 1964], p. 504); Bultmann probes profoundly the depth dimensions of the Johannine account of the trial of Jesus: "In the expectation of a messianic king the eschatological hope of the people is expressed; insofar as the Jews (in the Gospel of John) represent the world, their behavior means: the world in its hate against the revelation is in a position to give up its hope; even as the God-hostile world it is moved in its innermost being by the perhaps unadmitted but nevertheless indestructible knowledge of its own inadequacy, transitoriness, incompleteness. The world makes itself an inferno when it suffocates this knowledge and consciously cuts off its hope" (ibid., p. 515).

125. See Leistner, *Antijudaismus*, pp. 57–63; J. Blank, *Krisis. Untersuchungen zur johanneischen Christologie und Eschatologie* (Freiburg, 1964).

126. See Leistner, *Antijudaismus*, pp. 149f.; W. Grimm, "Das Opfer eines Menschen. Eine Auslegung von Joh 11,47–53," in *Israel hat dennoch Gott zum Trost, Festschrift für Sch. Ben-Chorin*, ed. G. Miller (Trier, 1978), pp. 61–82.

127. Thus according to corroborating exegesis of the commentators; see, for example, Schnackenburg, *Das Johannesevangelium*.

128. Leistner, *Antijudaismus*, p. 148.

129. See G. Delling, *Der Kreuzestod Jesu in der urchristlichen Verkündigung* (Berlin, 1971), p. 105.

130. See O. Michel, "*Skorpizō*," in Kittel, ed., *Theological Dictionary*, 7: 421.

131. Leistner, *Antijudaismus*, p. 150.

132. Therefore it appears that a critique of the Johannine theology of the cross is not necessary, as is announced by P. von der Osten-Sacken in his essay "Leistung und Grenze der johanneischen Kreuzestheologie," *Evangelische Theologie* 36 (1976): 154–176.

133. The poet Stefan Andres in his recollections of his youth, *Der Knabe im Brunnen*, relates that as a youth when he came across a Jew who came to his father's mill in Drohntal, he had shouted: "You Jews killed Jesus!" which made the Jew so sad that he shed bitter tears.

134. See, for example, Klausner, *Jesus of Nazareth*, pp. 333–345; D. Flusser, *Jesus* (New York, 1969), p. 120; Flusser speaks of the "chief of the temple leaders."

135. See P. Winter, *On the Trial of Jesus*, 2d ed. (Berlin, 1974); P. Winter, "Marginal Notes on the Trial of Jesus," *Zeitschrift für neutestamentliche Wissenschaft* 50 (1959): 14–33; P. Winter, "Zum Prozess Jesu," in Eckert et al., eds., *Antijudaismus im Neuen Testament?* pp. 95–104; D. Dormeyer, "Die Passion Jesu als Ergebnis seines Konflikts mit führenden Kreisen des Judentums," in Goldstein, ed., *Gottesverächter*, pp. 211–238; P. Lapide, "Jesu Tod durch Römerhand. Zur blasphemischen These vom 'Gottesmord' durch die Juden," in ibid., pp. 239–255.

136. See J. Blinzer, *Der Prozess Jesu*, 4th ed. (Regensburg, 1969); J. Blinzer, "Das Synedrium von Jerusalem und die Strafprozessordnung der Mischna," *Zeitschrift für die neutestamentliche Wissenschaft* 52 (1961): 54–65. See also G. Lindeskog, "Der Prozess Jesu im jüdisch-christlichen Religionsgespräch," in *Abraham unser Vater. Festschrift für O. Michel*, ed. O. Betz, M. Hengel, P. Schmidt (Leiden and Cologne, 1963), pp. 325–336, esp. pp. 326–328; D. R. Catchpole, *The Trial of Jesus: A Study in the Gospels and Jewish Historiography from 1770 to the Present Day* (Leiden, 1971); G. S. Sloyan, *Jesus on Trial* (Philadelphia, 1973); K. A. Speidel, *Das Urteil des Pilatus. Bilder und Berichte zur Passion Jesu* (Stuttgart, 1976); B. Klappert, "Der Verlust und die Wiedergewinnung der israelitischen Kontur der Leidensgeschichte Jesu (das Leiden, das Paschamahl, der Prozess Jesu)," in *Exodus und Kreuz im ökumenischen Dialog zwischen Juden und Christen*, ed. H. H. Henrix, M. Stöhr (Aachen, 1978), pp. 107–153; R. Kastning-Olmesdahl, "Die Passionsgeschichte im Religionsunterricht der Grundschule als Quelle antijüdischer Affekte," in ibid., pp. 45–74; R. Kastning-Olmesdahl, *Die Juden und der Tod Jesu. Antijüdische Motive in den evangelischen Büchern für die Grundschule* (Neukirchen, 1981).

137. See finally Pesch, *Das Markusevangelium* 2: 404–424 ("Der Prozess Jesu," with comprehensive bibliography). It was enough to permit decisions in a Sanhedrin procedure that "according to mishnaic law the presence of 23 members made it possible. *Holon to synedrion* (the whole Sanhedrin) in Mark 14:55 need not mean more than the whole gathering of the court that was capable of a decision" (ibid., p. 417). Therefore, by no means did all 70 members of the Sanhedrin of the chief priests have to be gathered. Concerning the historicity of the prior procedure against Jesus by the Sanhedrin under the leadership of the chief priests, what

deserves "special attention," according to Pesch, is the circumstance that the pre-Markan report of the trial "accurately describes the procedure of the Jewish trial which was based on the taking of evidence of witnesses, and that the Christian tradents had nothing legal to criticize in the conduct of the trial of the high priests" (ibid).

138. See ibid., p. 412; G. Theissen, "Die Tempelweissagung Jesu. Prophetie im Spannungsfeld von Stadt und Land," *Theologische Zeitschrift* 32 (1976): 144–158. "At the time of Jesus and of primitive Christianity the Temple was not of second rank, but rather was the specially neuralgic point of Palestinian Judaism (Martin Hengel, "Zwischen Jesus und Paulus," *Zeitschrift für Theologie und Kirche* 72 [1975]: 199, n. 149).

139. Concerning the "all" in the text of Mark, one notes the limitation which is to be read in Luke 23:50f.: "Now there was a man named Joseph from the Jewish town of Arimathea. He was a member of the council [Sanhedrin], a good and righteous man, *who had not consented to their purpose and deed.*" This refers to Joseph of Arimathea.

140. According to Pesch, *Das Markusevangelium*, pp. 442f., "the following information of the text may be judged to be historically credible:

1. Jesus was interrogated in the night of his arrest toward dawn (cf. 14:72; 15:1) at the house of the high priest and was judged by the Sanhedrin as guilty of death.

2. The chief opponents of Jesus who pressed for his death were the chief priests; on the basis of the major charge this is understandable.

3. A major charge of the witnesses alleged that Jesus had said something against the existing Temple.

4. Because of the statement about the Temple (v. 58) the chief priest, in the face of the silence of Jesus, put the question about the Messiah.

5. Jesus responded affirmatively and with a corrective threatening saying (v. 62).

6. On the basis of blasphemy Jesus was found guilty by the Sanhedrin of death and was derided as a false prophet."

141. See ibid., p. 440 (and the comprehensive literature on pp. 444–446; however, Pesch hardly deals with it).

142. Klausner, *Jesus of Nazareth*, p. 340.

143. See also O. Betz, *Was wissen wir von Jesus?* (Stuttgart and Berlin, 1965), p. 63; G. Theissen, *Urchristliche Wundergeschichten* (Gütersloh, 1974), p. 243, n. 42.

144. See pp. 234ff.

145. Concerning the "messianic consciousness" of Jesus see, for example, O. Betz, "Die Frage nach dem messianischen Bewusstsein Jesu," *Novum Testamentum* 6 (1963), pp. 20–48; N. Brox, "Das messianische Selbstverständnis des historischen Jesus," in *Vom Messias zum Christus*, ed. K. Schubert (Vienna, 1964), pp. 165–201; K. Berger, "Zum Problem der Messianität Jesu," *Zeitschrift für Theologie und Kirche* 71 (1974): 1–30.

146. J. Fitzmyer, "The Contribution of Qumran Aramaic to the Study of the New Testament," *New Testament Studies* 20 (1973/74): pp. 382–407. According to the translation and additions by Fitzmyer, the text reads: "[But your son] shall be great on the earth, [O King! All (men) shall] make [peace], and shall serve [him. He shall

be called the son of] the [G]reat [God], and by his name shall he be named. He shall be hailed (as) *the Son of God,* and they shall call him Son of the Most High. As comets (flash) to the sight, so shall be their kingdom."

147. In grammar such appositions are called "explicative appositions." See E. Mayser, *Grammatik der griech. Papyriaus der Ptolemäerzeit,* vol. 2, pt. 2 (Berlin and Leipzig, 1934) p. 111: "The *explicative* or *predicative* apposition serves as a clarification or more particular specification of a more general concept," in our case the more general concept "Messiah."

148. E. Schweizer, *Das Evangelium nach Matthäus* (Göttingen, 1973), p. 326.

149. Pesch, *Das Markusevangelium,* pp. 406–409.

150. Pesch deals hardly at all with the counterposition, as for example that of D. R. Catchpole, who attempted to show with considerable grounds that Luke had used, alongside Mark, a pre-Lukan source for his narration of the passion of Jesus.

151. Ibid., p. 124.

152. See F. Mussner's review of a book by G. Schneider in the *Biblische Zeitschrift* 17 (1973): 270–272. For the support of the thesis of Schneider concerning the second question ("you are then the Son of God?"), one could refer to the particle "therefore" *(oun).* However, one must pay close attention to the syntactic structure of verse 70: "And they all said *further (de,* which here cannot have the adversative meaning): you *therefore (su oun)* are the Son of God?" The formulation does not state: "You are therefore the Son of God" *(su oun ei),* rather the *oun* belongs to the *su,* and *su* is a taking up again of the *su* from verse 67 *(ei suei ho Christos).* The particle *oun* in verse 70, therefore, is not a syllogistical *oun,* but rather a so-called epanaleptic ("taking up again") *oun;* the *su* is taken up again. See Mayser, *Grammatik der griechischen Papyri,* vol. 2. pt. 3, p. 151.

153. R. Schnackenburg remarks concerning this *(Das Johannesevangelium,* 3: 298: "The high priests were unmasked in that their charge that Jesus was a political rebel was merely put forward. Now they must own up to it with their words since they push the death of Jesus (cf. 18:30f.) on another basis."

154. Pesch, *Das Markusevangelium,* 2: 410.

155. On the problem of the Johannine trial report see, for example, F. Hahn, "Der Prozess Jesu nach dem Johannesevangelium. Eine redaktionsgeschichtliche Untersuchung," *Evangelisch-katholischer Kommentar zum Neuen Testament* 2 (1970): 23–96; A. Dauer, *Die Passionsgeschichte im Johannesevangelium* (Munich, 1972); R. Schnackenburg, *Das Johannesevangelium,* 3: 246–309.

156. See also Pesch, *Das Markusevangelium,* 2: 419; this is especially clear in the Lukan passion narration: "And they began to accuse him [before Pilate] saying, 'We found this man perverting our nation, and forbidding us to give tribute to Caesar, and saying that he himself is Christ a king'" (Luke 23:2; cf. also 23:5, 14).

157. "There is hardly any doubt that in Rabbinic times and later, to this very day, the confession of the one or the only God of Israel and to his continuing partnership bond with the people of God, the Jews, was and is the central concern of Judaism. A denier of the uniqueness of God and his unique turning toward the people of God would therefore be called *kofer ba 'iqqar,* a denier in a major concern" (Thoma, *Christian Theology of Judaism,* p. 121, with biblographical references).

158. Pesch, *Das Markusevangelium,* 2: 421.

159. See ibid., p. 422.

160. Concerning the "foreground" and the "background" of the suffering of Jesus, see K. H. Schelkle, *Die Passion Jesu in der Verkündigung des Neuen Testaments* (Heidelberg, 1949).

161. As categories there are: admission, dispensation, disposition. The categories appearing in the New Testament itself: *boulē* ("counsel"), *prothesis* ("previous decision"), *prognōsis* ("previous knowledge"), point clearly toward "disposition": God had thus "disposed" that his Christ would have to suffer. As a motive for this the New Testament names above all the love of God (cf. above all John 3:16) whereby a "demonization" of God is rejected. One cannot say along with Lindeskog, "Der Prozess Jesu," "God himself . . . took over the responsibility for the cross of Christ."

162. For more details see pp. 152ff.

163. H. Schlier remarks concerning this statement: "Here it is emphasized that God . . . did not spare his 'own' son, which point is served by stressing the traditionally connected Isa. 53 *hyper hēmōn paredōken.* . . . The 'for us' of God shows itself in that God . . . *hyper pantōn* (!) *hēmōn* gave up, delivered, handed over his Son in an absolute sense" (*Der Römerbrief* [Freiburg, 1977], p. 277).

164. See also W. Popkes, *Christus traditus. Eine Untersuchung zum Begriff der Dahingabe im Neuen Testament* (Zurich and Stuttgart, 1967). In the New Testament the mysterious interconnection of an incomprehensible love of God with reference to the cross of Jesus is often expressed even in the divinely decreed "necessity" (*dei*) of the suffering and death of Jesus. "The son of man *must* be raised up" (John 13:14); "*Must* not the Christ have suffered this and thus enter into his glory" (Luke 24:26). Cf. also E. Fascher, "Theologische Beobachtungen zu *dei*," in *Neutestamentliche Studien für Rudolf Bultmann*, ed. W. Eltester (Berlin, 1957), pp. 228–254.

165. Pars III, cap. 5; 11.

166. "Nostra Aetate," no. 4 (end).

167. See also W. Zimmerli, "Die Schuld am Kreuz," in *Israel und die Christen, Hören und Fragen*, ed. W. Zimmerli (Neukirchen, 1964), pp. 17–30. "Thus it could happen that time and again some others would point their finger at this people and separate them from him—and not note thereby how precisely in the dark events of this people our concern, the concern of us human beings from the Gentile world, are at issue before God . . . there where it concerns the horrifying unmasking of the human being before the cross we ourselves are brought before the cross. Precisely here we also are present" (p. 24).

168. Thoma, *A Christian Theology of Judaism*, p. 118.

169. Several noteworthy textual witnesses read here: "Of the blood of this just one."

170. Thus the Jew C. G. Montefiore in his book *The Synoptic Gospels*, 2d ed. (New York, 1968), 2: 246, says concerning Matt. 27:25: "A terrible verse; a horrible invention. Note the bitter hatred which makes the Evangelist put *pas ho laos*. The whole people is supposed to be present. Hence all the atrocities which Christian rulers and peoples, sometimes, it must be freely acknowledged, with the disapproval of the Church, have wrought upon the Jews were accepted, and invoked upon their own heads, by the Jews themselves. This is one of those phrases which have been responsible for oceans of human blood, and a ceaseless stream of misery and desolation."

171. See for example: H. Graf Reventlow, "Sein Blut komme über sein Haupt," *Vetus Testamentum* 10 (1960): 311–327; K. Koch, "Der Spruch 'Sein Blut bleibe auf seinem Haupt,' und die israelitische Auffassung vom vergossenen Blut," ibid. 12 (1962): 396–416; N. A. Dahl, "Die Passionsgeschichte des Matthäus," *New Testament Studies* 11 (1955/56): 17–32; K. H. Schelkle, "Die 'Selbstverfluchung' Israels nach Matthäus 27:23–25," in Eckert et al,, eds., *Antijudaismus im Neuen Testament?*, pp. 148–156; W. Trilling, *Das wahre Israel. Studien zur Theologie des Matthäus-Evangeliums*, 3d ed. (Munich, 1964), pp. 68–73; S. van Tilborg, *The Jewish Leaders in Matthew* (Leiden, 1972); T. Mayer-Maly, "Das Auftreten der Menge im Prozess Jesu und in den ältesten Christenprozessen," *Österr. Arch. für Kirchenrecht* 6 (1955): 231–245; C. I. Foulon-Piganiol, "Le rôle du peuple dans le procès de Jésus," *Nouvelle revue théologique* 108 (1976): 627–637; R. Pfisterer, *Im Schatten des Kreuzes* (Hamburg and Bergstedt, 1966), pp. 39–46; C. Thoma, *Kirche aus Juden und Heiden* (Freiburg, 1970), pp. 70–73.

172. E. Hennecke and W. Schneemelcher, *New Testament Apocrypha* (Philadelphia, 1965), 1: 179ff.

173. Trilling, *Das wahre Israel*, p. 72.

174. Concerning this see the material presented by A. Schlatter, *Der Evangelist Matthäus* (Stuttgart, 1948), pp. 775f.

175. Trilling, *Das wahre Israel*, p. 72.

176. Ibid.

177. In this it must also be borne in mind that the appearance of the people in the reports of the trial belong to a firm topology and form in it precisely a juridical element, as Foulon-Piganiol, "Le rôle du peuple," shows.

178. "It is unimaginable that he himself would have openly demonstrated his illegal decision and the powerlessness of Rome against the pressure of the suppressed people. This move therefore belongs to the generally confirmed tendency to increasingly acquit the Romans and therefore implicate the Jews" (E. Schweizer, *Das Evangelium nach Matthäus* [Göttingen, 1973], p. 333).

179. Thoma, *Kirche aus Juden und Heiden*, p. 71.

180. See also Matt 22:7 (from the parable of the marriage feast): "The king was angry, and he sent his troops and destroyed those murderers and burned their city." See also Matt. 23:35.

181. Schelkle, "Die 'Selbstverfluchung' Israels, p. 156.

182. The literature is summarized by Pesch, *Das Markusevangelium*, 1: 325. Also see B. Mayer, "Überlieferungs- und redaktionsgeschichtliche Überlegungen zu Mk. 6:1-6a," *Biblische Zeitschrift* 22 (1978): 187–198; O. Betz, "Jesus in Nazareth. Bemerkungen zu Markus 6:1-6," in *Israel hat dennoch Gott zum Trost. Festschrift für Sch. Ben-Chorin*, ed. G. Müller (Trier, 1978), pp. 44–60.

183. For example, Pesch, *Das Markusevangelium*.

184. Schürmann, *Das Lukasevangelium*, 1: 225.

185. Ibid. See also U. Busse, *Das Nazareth-Manifest Jesu. Eine Einführung in das lukanische Jesusbild nach Lk. 4,16–30*, Stuttgarter Bibelstudien 91 (Stuttgart, 1978).

186. Schürmann, *Das Lukasevangelium*.

187. See the summary in Pesch, *Das Markusevangelium*, 1: 322.

188. Schürmann, *Das Lukasevangelium*, 1: 233.

189. Pesch, *Das Markusevangelium*, 1: 318.

190. For specifics see Schürmann, *Das Lukasevangelium*, 1: 233, with reference to B. Prete, "Prospettive messianche nell' espressione *sēmeron* dal Vangelo di Luka," in *Il Messianismo* (Brescia, 1966), pp. 269–284.

191. I shall return to this on pp. 213ff.

192. Cited in Schürmann, *Das Lukasevangelium*, 1: 236.

193. Ibid., 1: 243.

194. Pesch, *Das Markusevangelium*, 1: 317.

195. Schürmann, *Das Lukasevangelium*, 1: 136.

196. How Jesus' family arrived at this harsh judgment and exactly how they understood it can no longer be determined. In any case, their decision to "seize him" (*kratēsai*) was grounded in the fact that in their opinion "he is beside himself" (*exestē*). On this see H. Wansbrough, "Mark III.21—Was Jesus Out of His Mind?" *New Testament Studies* (1974/75), pp. 295–300. According to John 10:20 "many" of the Jews say, "He has a demon, and he is mad." Pesch, *Das Markusevangelium*, 1: 221, thinks that the relatives of Jesus were openly of the opinion that in his going public with his claims in Israel Jesus would bring damage to his family.

197. See F. Mussner, "Lk 1,48f. und die Anfänge der Marienverehrung in der Urkirche," *Catholica* 21 (1967): 287–294.

198. In harmony with this is the hardness of the demand of Jesus to break with one's own family in following him; see Luke 14:26; Matt. 10:37. See also Leonard Swidler, *Biblical Affirmations of Woman* (Philadelphia, 1979), pp. 77–79, 228, 231f., 237, 239, 241f., 257, 273f.

199. On this see also the remark of John the Evangelist: "For even his brothers did not believe in him" (John 7:5).

200. See F. Mussner, "Der 'historische' Jesus," in Mussner, ed., *Praesentia Salutis*, pp. 67–80.

201. See Pesch, *Das Markusevangelium*, 1: pp. 335f.: "The opinions of the people referred to, which reflect the attention-getting actions of Jesus in their prophetic contours, are not Christian inventions, but rather old, historically credible traditions."

202. See also J. Schmid, *Das Evangelium nach Markus*, 3d ed. (Regensburg, 1954) on Mark 6:15.

203. The report in the Gospel of John is similar; see R. Schnackenburg, "Das Messiasfrage im Johannesevanglium," in *Neutestamentliche Aufsätze. Festschrift für J. Schmid* (Regensburg, 1963), pp. 240–264; M. de Jonge, "Jewish Expectations About the 'Messiah' According to the Fourth Gospel," *New Testament Studies* 19 (1972/73): 246–270.

204. See also W. G. Kümmel, "Jesu Antwort an Johannes den Täufer. Ein Beispiel zum Methodenproblem in der Jesusforschung," in *Heilsgeschehen und Geschichte*, ed. W. G. Kümmel (Marburg, 1978), 2: 177–200.

205. See H. Frankemölle, "Jüdische Messiaserwartung und christlicher Messiasglaube. Hermeneutische Anmerkungen im Kontext des Petrusbekenntnisses Mk 8,29," *Kairos* 20 (1978): 97–109 (citation on p. 103). M. Hengel formulates the situation thus: The Messiahship of Jesus is "not to be explained with the help of traditional Jewish images of the Messiah; he himself newly defines in an unsurpassable way what Messiahship is" (*Theologische Beiträge* 9 [1978]: 157).

206. See also D. H. Hawkin, "The Incomprehension of the Disciples in the Markan Dedaction," *Journal of Biblical Literature* 91 (1972): 491–500; C. Focant, "L'incompréhension des disciples dans le deuxième évangile," *Revue Biblique* 82 (1975): 161–185.

207. Pesch, *Das Markusevangelium*, 1: 276.

208. Ibid., p. 415.

209. W. Wrede, *Das Messiasgeheimnis in den Evangelien. Zugleich ein Beitrag zum Verständnis des Markusevangeliums* (Göttingen, 1912; reprint ed., 1963).

210. The literature on the "messianic secret" is comprehensively summarized in Pesch, *Das Markusevangelium*, 1: 241; 2: 46f. Pesch himself does not put much stock in a "messianic secret of the Gospel of Mark"; according to Pesch, Mark never sketched out an "independent christological conception" (2: 41). This needs to be thoroughly looked into.

211. See also J. Gnilka, *Die Verstockung Israels. Isaias 6,9–10 in der Theologie der Synoptiker* (Munich, 1961).

212. Pesch, *Das Markusevangelium*, 1: 237.

213. This thematic is much discussed at present, having been stimulated by the modern science of literature. See T. Aurelio, *Disclosures in den Gleichnissen Jesu. Eine Anwendung der Disclosure-Theorie von I. T. Ramsey, der modernen Metaphorik und der Theorie der Sprechakte*, Regensburger Studien zur Theologie 8 (Frankfurt/Bern/Las Vegas, 1977); H. Weder, *Die Gleichnisse Jesu als Metaphern. Traditions- und redaktionsgeschichtliche Analysen und Interpretationen.* Forschungen zur Religion und Literatur des Alten und Neuen Testaments 120 (Göttingen and Münster, 1978).

214. For specifics see pp. 209ff.

215. Schürmann, *Das Lukasevangelium*, 1: 460. As Luke shows in his dual work, Israel is once again after Easter offered an opportunity to convert to the Messiah Jesus, until, as Paul preaches the gospel to the Jews in Rome, it is ultimately revealed that the most of them will remain "hardened" and the Gentiles will harken to the gospel (see Acts 28:17–28). Of course the situation at the time of composition of the Acts of the Apostles is reflected therein: Now the Church and Israel are two communities separated from one another. See also P.-G. Müller, "Die jüdische Entscheidung gegen Jesus nach der Apostelgeschichte," in *Les Actes des Apôtres. Traditions, Rédaction, Théologie* (Gembloux and Löwen, 1978), pp. 523–531.

216. Schürmann, *Das Lukasevangelium*, 1: 461.

217. For the predication "living God" in the New Testament, see W. Stenger, "Die Gottesbezeichnung 'lebendiger Gott' im Neuen Testament," *Trierer theologische Zeitschrift* 87 (1978): 61–69.

218. W. Grundmann, *Das Evangelium nach Matthäus* (Berlin, 1968), p. 386.

219. Concerning this see, for example, F. Obrist, *Echtheitsfrage und Deutung der Primatsstelle Mt 16,18f. in der deutschen protestantischen Theologie der letzten dreissig Jahre* (Münster, 1961), pp. 22–67; A. Vögtle, "Zum Problem der Herkunft von 'Mt 16,17–19,'" in *Orientierung an Jesus. Zur Theologie der Synoptiker. Festschrift für J. Schmid*, ed. P. Hoffmann (Freiburg, 1973), pp. 372–393; C. Kähler, "Zur Form- und Traditionsgeschichte von Matth XVI. 17–19," *New Testament Studies* 23 (1976/77): 36–58.

220. For specifics see F. Mussner, *Der Galaterbrief*, 3d ed. (Freiburg, 1977), pp. 83–87.

221. P⁷⁵, ℵᵃ, B, D*, W, Θ, etc.

222. See W. Grundmann, *Das Evangelium nach Lukas* (Berlin, n.d.), pp. 432f.

223. J. Ernst, *Das Evangelium nach Lukas* (Regensburg, 1977), p. 634.

224. See also David Flusser, "Der Gekreuzigte und die Juden," *Freiburger Rundbrief* 28 (1976): 152–157. Flusser shows that the Lukan account of the crucifixion is structured in a way that is much more friendly than that of Mark. He presumes correctly that in this (as also in the rest of the passion report) Mark had at his disposition an old non-Markan text.

225. E. Haenchen, *Die Apostelgeschichte*, 7th ed. (Göttingen, 1977), p. 206.

226. The "thus" (*houtōs*) refers to the events of the suffering and death of Jesus.

227. How can E. Haenchen say that v. 18 is "externally unconnected" with what precedes? In a text which is so full of difficulties the smallest lexeme must be attended to if one wishes to learn what the real content of the statement is. Here it is the particle *de*.

228. Ibid.

229. See also Acts 13:37!

230. See especially Acts 2:23: The crucified Jesus "*delivered up according to the definite plan and foreknowledge of God*"!

231. Haenchen, *Die Apostelgeschichte*, p. 206, n. 2.

232. See especially Schnackenburg, *Das Johannesevangelium*, 2: 328–346. (Exkurs 11: Selbstentscheidung und -verantwortung, Prädestination und Verstockung).

233. According to Schnackenburg, "it appears much more that the evangelist took up and applied these views which were known to him without, however, stepping over the border to a reprobation in principle that would be incapable of rejection. There is nothing to be heard in John of a determination for eternity according to which human beings are *a priori* divided up by God into two classes— the good and the evil, the chosen and the rejected. However, it cannot be denied that we are close to the edge of such an image" (ibid., p. 334). One must agree with this.

234. Bultmann, *Das Evangelium des Johannes*, p. 170.

235. Schnackenburg, *Das Johannesevangelium*, 2: 343.

236. Ibid., p. 335.

237. See again above on pp. 202ff.

238. For further details see F. Mussner, "Ursprünge und Entfaltung der neutestamentlichen Sohneschristologie. Versuch einer Rekonstruktion," in L. Scheffczyk, ed., *Grundfragen der Christologie heute*. Questiones Disputatae, 72, 2d ed. (Freiburg, 1978), pp. 77–113.

239. Further details in F. Mussner, *Die Auferstehung Jesu* (Munich, 1969), pp. 140–154.

240. See above pp. 202ff.

241. See the literature on pp. 28f., n. 131.

242. E. Käsemann remarks concerning this: "Different than with Isaac and Israel, was the case of Jacob and Esau where the matter concerned legitimate sons who in addition as twins offered no basis for a differentiating treatment. The puzzle of divine election comes more startlingly to the fore against such a background" (*An die Römer*, 3d ed. [Tübingen, 1974], p. 254).

243. See pp. 23ff.

244. Käsemann, *An die Römer*, pp. 256f.

245. The best commentary on the difficult verses Rom. 9:22f. is written, in my opinion, by F. W. Maier, *Israel in der Heilsgeschichte nach Röm 9—11* (Münster, 1926), pp. 44–53.

246. See F. Mussner, " 'Christus (ist) des Gesetzes Ende zur Gerechtigkeit für jeden, der glaubt' (Röm 10,4)," in *Paulus—Apostat oder Apostel? Jüdische und christliche Antworten*, ed. M. Barth et al. (Regensburg, 1977), pp. 31–44.

247. Käsemann, *An die Römer*, p. 269.

248. F. W. Maier remarked concerning Rom. 11:8: "God himself placed this circumstance on the one striken by him, as Paul probably believes, as a punishment for his rigid holding on to the notion of works (v. 6)" (*Israel in der Heilsgeschichte*, p. 113), but there is no mention either here or anywhere else in Rom. 9—11 of punishment! True, there is in 11:11f. reference to a "failure" (*paraptōma*) and in 11:20 to the "unbelief" of Israel, and insofar guilt is lifted up, but so as to be able to point from that perspective all the more intensely to the turning of salvation to the Gentiles and the coming saving of all Israel as proofs of the mercy of God. The tension between the guilty failure and the hardening decreed by God is not really resolved by the apostle. His doxological reference in 11:33–36 to the "depth of the riches and of the wisdom and of the knowledge of God, etc." lets one recognize all the more clearly the true inability of the apostle to resolve the tension. He "flies" in the end to the *Deus absconditus!* Nevertheless, the reference of the apostle to the "failure" and the "unbelief" of Israel also allows one to perceive that the decreed "hardening" is not determinism. How otherwise could the apostle hope that even now he could win "some" of his "flesh" for the gospel (cf. 11:14)? The freedom of the human being remains protected even when it ultimately, like the "counsel" of God, remains a mystery. Cf. concerning this also B. Mayer, *Unter Gottes Heilsratschluss. Prädestinationsaussagen bei Paulus* (Würzburg, 1974), p. 317.

249. See details on pp. 234ff.

250. Maier, *Israel in der Heilsgeschichte*, pp. 150f.

NOTES FOR CHAPTER 6

1. "It is not the narrations concerning the pre-Easter Jesus that are objectionable to Jews but rather the Christian faith in Jesus Christ" (Clemens Thoma, *A Christian Theology of Judaism* [New York, 1980], p. 120). It is not only the historical Jesus who belongs to Christianity, to the Church. There also belongs to Christianity, and indeed in a decisive way, the primitive Christian faith tradition with its fundamental statements concerning the atoning death of Christ, his resurrection as the basis of the eschatological, the end of days, salvation for those who believe in him"(U. Wilkens, "Glaube nach urchristlichem und frühjüdischem Verständnis," in *Was Juden und Christen voneinander denken*, ed. P. Lapide, F. Mussner, and U. Wilkens, [Freiburg, 1978], p. 74).

2. H.-J. Schoeps, *Paulus. Die Theologie des Apostels im Lichte der jüdischen Religionsgeschichte* (Tübingen, 1959), p. 153.

3. Ibid., p. 160.

4. Ibid., p. 163.

5. J. Klausner, *Jesus of Nazareth: His Times, His Life and His Teaching* (New York, 1925), pp. 413 f.

6. Ibid., p. 379.

7. Ibid., p. 413.

8. See G. Jasper-Bethel, *Stimmen aus dem neureligiösen Judentum in seiner Stellung zum Christentum und zu Jesus* (Hamburg and Bergstedt, 1958), pp. 81–84.

9. Klausner, *Jesus of Nazareth*, p. 380.

10. Ibid.

11. E. Fuchs, *Zur Frage nach dem historischen Jesus* (Tübingen, 1960), p. 154.

12. See F. Schnider, *Die verlorenen Söhne. Strukturanalytische und historisch-kritische Untersuchungen zu Lk 15* (Freiburg and Göttingen, 1977).

13. For details see Aurelio, *Disclosures in den Gleichnissen Jesu*, pp. 116–137, 229–258.

14. Even if the passive formulation "your sins are forgiven" should be perceived as a claim of the forgiveness of sins *by God*, which cannot be absolutely maintained, the scribes present nevertheless perceived this as an unheard-of claim, because they say: "He blasphemes God!" "With this they indicate that they understand that the word of Jesus in v. 5b is not only an attibution of the forgiveness of sins to the action of God . . . but rather its being carried out on the basis of the authority claimed by Jesus." "The silent objection of the scribes is related not to the claiming of the 'transcendent' power of God by the *human being* Jesus of Nazareth, but to the expectation of the forgiveness of sins as a specifically eschatological action of God which Jesus *de facto* undertakes ahead of time 'on earth.'" With this the *earthly Jesus* stands in the place of God, which is the God of the eschatological forgiveness of sins. See K. Kertelge, "Die Vollmacht des Menschensohnes zur Sündenvergebung (Mk 2,10)," in *Orientierung an Jesus. Festschrift für J. Schmid*, ed. P. Hoffmann (Freiburg, 1973), pp. 205–213; K. Kertelge, "Sündenvergebung an Stelle Gottes. Eine neutestamentlich-theologische Darlegung," in *Dienst der Versöhnung*, Trierer theologische Studien 31 (Trier, 1974): 27–64. See also J. Gnilke, "Das Elend vor dem Menschensohn (Mk 2,1–12)," in *Jesus und der Menschensohn. Festschrift für A. Vögtle*, ed. R. Pesch and R. Schnackenburg (Freiburg, 1975), pp. 196–209 (with bibliography); P. Fiedler, *Jesus und die Sünder* (Frankfurt and Bern, 1976), pp. 119–135. It is to be particularly noted that the words of Jesus were not in the form of a petition (*deprecatio*).

15. On this pericope see ibid., pp. 112–116; U. Wilkens, "Vergebung für die Sünderin (Lk 7,36–50)," in Hoffmann, ed., *Orientierung an Jesus*, pp. 394–424.

16. See G. F. Moore, *Judaism* (Cambridge, 1927), 1: 535; Billerbeck, *Kommentar*, 1: 495f. Whether Targum Isa. 53:5 constitutes an exception to this translation appears doubtful; see K. Koch, "Messias und Sündenvergebung in Jesaja 53-Targum," *Journal for the Study of Judaism* 3 (1972): 117–148.

17. R. Pesch, *Das Markusevangelium* (Freiburg, 1976), 1: 158f.

18. Concerning this see for example S. Safrai, "Die Stellung des Zweiten Tempels im Leben des Volkes," *Freiburger Rundbrief* 28 (1976); 158–165; J. Maier, "Tempel und Tempelkult," in *Literatur und Religion des Frühjudentums*, ed. J. Maier and J. Schreiner (Würzburg, 1973), pp. 371–390. The significance of the Temple for Jewish consciousness is especially impressively shown in the "Temple Scroll" from Qumran. "Jerusalem theology" is connected with "Temple theology";

on this see J. Schreiner, *Sion-Jerusalem. JHWHs Königssitz. Theologie der Heiligen Stadt im Alten Testament* (Munich, 1963).

19. See also Aurelio, *Disclosures in den Gleichnissen Jesu,* pp. 240–254.

20. See R. Pesch, "Über die Autorität Jesu. Eine Rückfrage anhand des Bekenner- und Verleugnerspruchs Lk 12,8f. par.," in *Die Kirche des Anfangs. Festschrift für H. Schürmann,* ed. R. Schnackenburg et al., (Leipzig, 1977), pp. 25–55.

21. Klausner, *Jesus of Nazareth,* p. 348.

22. Lohse, "Jesu Worte über den Sabbat," pp. 79-89 (89).

23. See W. G. Kümmel, " 'Das Gesetz und die Propheten gehen bis Johannes'— Lk 16,16 im Zusammenhang der heilsgeschichtlichen Theologie der Lukasschriften," in *Verborum Veritas. Festschrift für G. Stählin* (Wuppertal, 1970), pp. 89–102.

24. See. F. Mussner, " 'Wann Kommt das Reich Gottes?' Die Antwort Jesu nach Lk 17,20b.21," *Biblische Zeitschrift* 6 (1962): 107–111.

25. See F. Mussner, "Gottesherrschaft und Sendung Jesu nach Mk 1,14f. Zugleich ein Beitrag über die innere Struktur des Markusevangeliums," in *Praesentia Salutis,* ed. F. Mussner (Düsseldorf, 1967), pp. 81–98; H. Merklein, *Die Gottesherrschaft als Handlungsprinzip. Untersuchung zur Ethik Jesu* (Würzburg, 1978), pp. 155–157.

26. On the implications for ethics in this new consciousness of Jesus, see Merklein, *Die Gottesherrschaft.*

27. D. Flusser, *Jesus* (New York, 1969), p. 90.

28. See A. Polag, *Die Christologie der Logienquelle* (Neukirchen, 1977), p. 197.

29. D. Flusser, "Foreword," in Clemens Thoma, *A Christian Theology of Judaism,* p. 14.

30. See also J. Jeremias, *Jesu Verheissung für die Völker* (Stuttgart, 1956), pp. 35–39.

31. Connected with this is the fact that the really new thing that came into the world with Jesus of Nazareth *is Jesus himself!* Everything else, as for example the Church, is a consequence of this new thing. On this thematic see also J. Fr. Konrad, "Das Neue an Jesus. Eine grundsätzliche Erwägung," in *Exodus und Kreuz im ökumenischen Dialog zwischen Juden und Christen,* ed. H. H. Henrix and M. Stöhr (Aachen, 1978), pp. 154–165.

32. In this I reaffirm my essay "Vom 'Propheten' Jesus zum 'Sohn' Jesus," in *Drei Wege zu dem einen Gott,* ed. A. Falaturi et al. (Freiburg, 1976), pp. 103–116.

33. G. Friedrich, "*Prophētēs,*" in *Theological Dictionary of the New Testament,* ed. G. Kittel (Grand Rapids, 1967), 6:841.

34. See also ibid., pp. 845–847; R. Schnackenburg, "Die Erwartung des 'Propheten' nach dem Neuen Testament und den Qumran-Texten," in *Studia Evangelica. Texte und Untersuchungen* 73 (Berlin, 1959), pp. 622–639.; E. Boismard, "Jésus le Prophet par excellence, d'après Jean 10,24–39," in *Neues Testament und Kirche. Festschrift für R. Schnackenburg,* ed. J. Gnilka (Freiburg, 1974), pp. 160–171.

35. See. John 6:14; 7:40; Acts 3:22 (in a speech by Peter); 7:37 (in the speech of Stephen).

36. Friedrich, "*Prophētēs,*" p. 847.

37. On the latter see O. H. Steck, *Israel und das gewaltsame Geschick der Propheten* (Neukirchen, 1967). Concerning the whole matter also see F. Schnider, *Jesus, der Prophet,* Orbis Biblicus et Orientalis 2 (Freiburg and Göttingen, 1973).

38. See ibid., pp. 241–255; H.-J. Schoeps, *Theologie und Geschichte des Juden-christentums* (Tübingen, 1949), pp. 71–118.

39. O. Cullmann, *Christologie des Neuen Testaments* (Tübingen, 1966), pp. 34f.

40. F. Hahn, *Christologische Hoheitstitel*, 3rd ed. (Göttingen, 1966), p. 351.

41. U. Mauser, *Gottesbild und Menschwerdung. Eine Untersuchung zur Einheit des Alten und des Neuen Testaments* (Tübingen, 1971).

42. W. Zimmerli, "Verheissung und Erfüllung," *Evangelische Theologie* 12 (1952/53): 34–59, reprinted in *Probleme atl. Hermeneutik*, ed. C. Westermann (Munich, 1960), pp. 69–101; subsequent references are to the latter.

43. Mauser, *Gottesbild*, pp. 4f.

44. Zimmerli, "Verheissung," p. 90.

45. Mauser, *Gottesbild*, p. 7.

46. Ibid., p. 8.

47. Ibid., p. 15.

48. Ibid., pp. 16f.

49. Ibid., p. 17.

50. Ibid., p. 41.

51. A. J. Heschel, *Die Phophetie* (appeared in 1936); expanded American version: *The Prophets* (New York, 1962).

52. Mauser, *Gottesbild.*, p. 38.

53. J. Hempel, *Das Ethos des Alten Testaments*, 2d ed. (Berlin, 1964), p. 201.

54. Mauser, *Gottesbild*, p. 39.

55. Ibid.

56. Ibid., p. 40.

57. Ibid.

58. Ibid., p. 41.

59. Ibid., p. 42.

60. Ibid.

61. Ibid., p. 43.

62. Ibid., p. 42.

63. Ibid.

64. Ibid., p. 74.

65. Ibid., p. 76.

66. Ibid.

67. Ibid., pp. 115f.

68. Ibid., p. 116.

69. Ibid., p. 117.

70. Ibid. In this connection reference should also be made to the book by P. Kuhn, *Gottes Selbsterniedrigung in der Theologie der Rabbinen*. Studien zum AT und NT 17 (Munich, 1968). Kuhn shows with ample material what role the notion of the "pathos" of God played in Rabbinic thought; he divides his texts as follows: (1) God renounces his honor; (2) God as the servant of humanity; (3) God's gift of himself to humanity; (4) God's coming down from heaven to earth; (5) God's limiting of himself to a space in the world. See also, P. Kuhn, *Gottes Trauer und Klage in der rabbinischen Überlieferung* (Leiden, 1978); further, J. Scharbert, *Der Schmerz im Alten Testament*, Bonner Biblische Beiträge 8 (Bonn, 1955): 216 ("Der Schmerz Jahwes"); K. Kitamori, *The Theology of the Pain of God* (Richmond, 1965).

71. See M. Brocke, " 'Nachahmung Gottes' im Judentum," in Falaturi et. al., eds., *Drei Wege*, pp. 75–102, with ample bibliography.

72. See John 4:19; 9:17; 6:14; 7:40, 52; 8:52f.

73. See Schnider, *Jesus, der Prophet*, pp. 191–230; Schnackenburg, "Die Erwartung des 'Propheten,' " pp. 622–639.

74. See E. Schweizer, "Aufnahme und Korrektur jüdischer Sophiatheologie im Neuen Testament," in *Neotestamentica*, ed. E. Schweizer (Zurich and Stuttgart, 1963), pp. 110–121; A. Feuillet, "Jésus et la sagesse divine d'après les évangiles synoptiques," *Revue Biblique* 92 (1955): 161–196; A. Feuillet, *Christ, sagesse de Dieu d'après les épîtres pauliniennes* (Paris, 1966); U. Wilkens, *Weisheit und Torheit. Eine exegetisch-religionsgeschichtliche Untersuchung zu 1 Kor 2 und 3* (Tübingen, 1959); M. J. Suggs, *Wisdom, Christology and Law in Matthew's Gospel* (Cambridge, 1970); A. van Roon, "The Relation between Christ and the Wisdom of God according to Paul," *Novum Testamentum* 16 (1974): 207–239; W. Grundmann, "Weisheit im Horizont des Reiches Gottes. Eine Studie zur Verkündigung Jesu nach der Spruchüberlieferung Q," in Schnackenburg et al., eds., *Die Kirche des Anfangs*, pp. 175–199. The Shekhinah theology also was a further help to understanding for Jews (see Thoma, *Christian Theology of Judaism*, pp. 124f.; A. M. Goldberg, *Untersuchungen über die Vorstellung von der Schekhinah in der frühen rabbinischen Literatur* (Berlin, 1969).

75. A further help to Jews for the understanding of the irritating "word of the cross" and the kerygma of the crucified Messiah could be the biblical idea of the suffering just person; see L. Ruppert, "Das Skandalon eines gekreuzigten Messias und seine Überwindung mit Hilfe der geprägten Vorstellung vom leidenden Gerechten," in *Kirche und Bibel. Festschrift für Bischof Eduard Schick* (Paderborn, 1979), pp. 319–341; further, M.-L. Gubler, *Die frühesten Deutungen des Todes Jesu. Eine motivgeschichtliche Darstellung aufgrund der neueren exegetischen Forschung*, Orbis Biblicus et Orientalis 15 (Freiburg and Göttingen, 1977).

76. R. Ruether, *Faith and Fratricide* (New York, 1974); G. Baum has written an extensive introduction to the book and P. von der Osten-Sacken an afterword to the German translation, *Nächstenliebe und Brudermord* (Munich, 1978).

77. Ibid., p. 246.

78. See ibid., pp. 229–246.

79. Ibid., p. 246.

80. Ibid., p. 247.

81. Ibid., p. 248.

82. Ibid., p. 245.

83. See F. Mussner, *Der Galaterbrief*, 3d ed. (Freiburg, 1977), pp. 271f.

84. Ruether, *Faith and Fratricide*, pp. 247f.

85. On this see, for example, W. G. Kümmel, "Die Eschatologie der Evangelien," in *Heilsgeschehen und Geschichte. Gesammelte Aufsätze 1933–1964*, ed. W. G. Kümmel, (Marburg, 1965), pp. 46–66; W. G. Kümmel, "Futurische und präsentische Eschatologie im ältesten Christentum," in ibid., pp. 351–363.

86. See the documentation for this from the Gospels on p. 219. W. G. Kümmel comes to the conclusion that Jesus proclaimed the coming Reign of God, that he, however, had thoroughly borne witness also to a prior working of this Reign of God

in the present. However, this prior working out is shown alone in the person of Jesus, in his preaching, his action, his gaining disciples," "Die Eschatologie der Evangelien," p. 57.

87. See F. J. Schierse, "Oster- und Parusiefrömmigkeit im Neuen Testament," in *Strukturen christlicher Existenz. Festschrift für F. Wulf* (Würzburg, 1968), pp. 37–57.

88. See H. Schlier, "Das Ende der Zeit," in *Das Ende der Zeit. Exegetische Aufsätze und Vorträge*, ed. H. Schlier (Freiburg, 1971), 3: 67–84.

89. See F. Mussner, "Gab es eine 'galiläische Krise'?" in Hoffmann, ed., *Orientierung an Jesus*, pp. 238–252. K. Rahner remarked: "We have absolutely no possibility of standing empirically outside of the 'experimentum Christi' and seeing how it might be with the world without Christ," *Sacramentum Mundi*, 1: 1164.

90. Ruether, *Faith and Fratricide*, p. 245.

91. On this see the analyses and bibliographies on pp. 76ff.

92. See for example F. Mussner, "Proiezione o Vanificazione dei Principi Evangelici nella Storia?" in *Problemi della Chiesa, oggi* (Milan, 1976), pp. 51–58; J. Blank, *Das Evangelium als Garantie der Freiheit* (Würzburg, 1970).

93. Ruether, *Faith and Fratricide*, p. 244.

94. Ibid., p. 249.

95. Ibid., pp. 249f.

96. G. Kittel, *Die Probleme des palästinischen Spätjudentums und das Urchristentum* (Stuttgart, 1926), p. 69.

97. I have expanded this section in the *Festschrift für Scholom Ben-Chorin* (Trier, 1978), pp. 33–43.

98. I used the edition with the text, translation, and commentary by K. Marti and G. Beer (Giessen, 1927).

99. Ibid., p. 3 (commentary).

100. See ibid., pp. xxif.

101. Ibid., p. xii.

102. J. Jeremias, "*Mōysēs*," in Kittel, ed., *Theological Dictionary*, 4:853.

103. Ibid., n. 73.

104. Concerning him see especially G. Jeremias, *Der Lehrer der Gerechtigkeit* (Göttingen, 1963); G. W. Buchanan, "The Priestly Teacher of Righteousness," *Revue Qumran* 6 (1969): 553–558; P. Schulz, *Der Autoritätsanspruch des Lehrers der Gerechtigkeit in Qumran* (Meisenheim, 1974).

105. Jeremias, *Lehrer der Gerechtigkeit*, p. 273.

106. On this see the commentary in ibid., pp. 270ff.

107. See H. Braun, *Spätjüdisch-häretischer und frühchristlicher Radikalismus. Jesus von Nazareth und die essenische Qumransekte*, vol. 1, *Das Spätjudentum* (Tübingen, 1957); H. Braun, "Beobachtungen zur Toraverschärffung im häretischen Spätjudentum," *Theologische Literaturzeitung* (1954), pp. 347–352.

108. Braun, *Radikalismus*, 1:29.

109. On this see, for example, J. Neusner, "'Pharisaic-Rabbinic' Judaism: A Clarification," in: *Early Rabbinic Judaism: Historical Studies in Religion, Literature and Art*, ed. J. Neusner (Leiden, 1975), pp. 50–70. In addition see the discussion on pp. 163ff. and especially on p. 175.

110. See also B. Gerhardsson, *Die Anfänge der Evangelientradition* (Wuppertal, 1977), p. 35.

NOTES FOR CHAPTER 6

111. A. Schlatter, *Der Evangelist Matthäus* (Stuttgart, 1948), p. 670.

112. In the Gospel of Matthew, Peter "is the guarantee and tradent of the new *halacha*. With this the dissolution of the authority of the rabbis is attained, which, from the tradition represented by Matt. 23:2, was still presumed valid. This decision in principle led thereby into a relatively late stage of the primitive Christian history" (C. Kähler, "Zur Form- und Traditionsgeschichte von Matth. XVI. 17–19," *New Testament Studies* 23 [1976/77]: 36–58). See also R. Hummel, *Die Auseinandersetzung zwischen Kirche und Judentum im Matthäusevangelium*, 2d ed. (Munich, 1966), pp. 59–64.

113. Gerhardsson, *Die Anfänge der Evangelientradition*, p. 34.

114. See Braun, *Radikalismus*, 2: Die Synoptiker.

115. In his book *Jesus* (p. 72) Flusser remarks: "One could easily put together an entire Gospel from the ancient Jewish writings without a word in it stemming from Jesus." That may be true, but this "Gospel" then would then be a collection of sayings and parables from many Jewish teachers, while in the Gospels of the primitive Church we hear only the voice of a single teacher—the voice of Jesus of Nazareth. That is a decisive difference. Moreover, Flusser very correctly adds: This compilation "however, could be done only because we already in fact possess the Gospels," that is, without Jesus such a compilation would never have occurred in Judaism. "The ethical teachings of the Gospels, on the contrary, came from one man only, and are, every one, stamped with the same peculiar hallmark" (Klausner, *Jesus of Nazareth*, p. 389). "Judaism had always striven against placing a single human being in the center point" (E. L. Ehrlich, "Eine jüdische Auffassung von Jesus," in *Jesu Jude-Sein als Zugang zum Judentum*, ed. W. P. Eckert and H. H. Henrix (Aachen, 1976), pp. 35–49.

116. The restriction to a single teacher, which one could also describe as the christological "narrows," naturally had consequences as well for the understanding of the Old Testament: it became a "witness to Christ" (see especially John 5:40,46; on that see A. H. J. Gunneweg, *Vom Verstehen des Alten Testaments. Eine Hermeneutik* [Göttingen, 1977], pp. 121–145).

117. On this see, for example, K. Niederwimmer, *Der Begriff der Freiheit im Neuen Testament* (Berlin, 1966); H. Schürmann, "Die Freiheitsbotschaft des Paulus—Mitte des Evangeliums?" *Catholica* 25 (1971): 22–62; F. Mussner, *Theologie der Freiheit nach Paulus* (Freiburg, 1976).

118. See specifics on pp. 18ff.

119. See p. 134.

120. See further specifics in Mussner, *Der Galaterbrief*, pp. 188–204 (Exkurs 4: Hat Paulus das Gesetz "missverstanden"?).

121. Ruether, *Faith and Fratricide*, p. 244.

122. P. Schäfer, "Die Torah der messianischen Zeit," *Zeitschrift für die neutestamentliche Wissenschaft* 65 (1974): 27–42; see also W. D. Davies, *Torah in the Messianic Age* (Philadelphia, 1952); G. Scholem, *Über einige Grundbegriffe des Judentums* (Frankfurt, 1970), pp. 145–147.

123. See above all G. Scholem, *Die jüdische Mystik in ihren Hauptströmungen* (Frankfurt, 1957).

124. See pp. 90ff.; M.-L. Gubler, *Die Frühesten Deutungen des Todes Jesu. Eine motivgeschichtliche Darstellung aufgrund der neueren exegetischen Forschung* (Göttingen and Zurich, 1977).

125. P. Lapide names the following points of difference: "The chief difference is however that you Christians emphasize the king, and we Jews the kingdom. For you Christians the redeemer is the center of history; to us Jews redemption is more important. Not *who* brings it, but *what* it brings is for us the main point . . . *who* brings it is for us at bottom a matter of indifference" P. Lapide et al., eds., *Was Juden und Christen voneinander denken*, pp. 126f. The Christians are indifferent neither to who brings redemption or to what redemption brings. Is the content of redemption at all separable from the bringer of redemption?

126. See H. Gross, *Die Idee des ewigen und allgemeinen Weltfriedens im Alten Orient und im Alten Testament*, 2d ed. (Trier, 1967).

127. J. Moltmann, *Kirche in der Kraft des Geistes. Ein Beitrag zur messianischen Ekklesiologie* (Munich, 1975), p. 170.

128. See specifics on pp. 245ff.

129. For a more detailed exegesis of the epistle, see F. Mussner, *Christus, das All und Kirche. Studien zur Theologie des Epheserbriefs*, 2d ed. (Trier, 1968), pp. 79–107; also M. Barth, *Israel und die Kirche im Brief des Paulus an die Epheser* (Munich, 1959).

130. K. Marx, "Zur Judenfrage," in K. Marx and F. Engels, *Historisch-kritische Gesamtausgabe* (Frankfurt, 1927–32), 1: 587.

131. The French thinker and theologian G. Fessard, who in his works concerning the above-addressed problematic has reflected and written a great deal, stimulated me to these perhaps not unessential reflections. Also see M. Sales, "Die historische Bedeutung des jüdischen Volkes vor und nach Christus im Denken Gaston Fessards," *Internationale katholische Zeitschrift* 4 (1973): 302–320. However, Fessard appears to me to have overlooked important aspects of Jewish existence.

132. On this see, for example, H. Gross, "Der Universalitätsanspruch des Reiches Gottes nach dem Alten Testament," in *Kirche und Bibel. Festschrift für Bischof Eduard Schick* (Paderborn, 1979), pp. 105–119.

133. Essential reflections on this are also found in F. Rosenzweig, *Der Stern der Erlösung*, 4th ed. (Hague, 1976), pp. 378–386.

NOTES FOR CHAPTER 7

1. M. Buber, *Two Types of Faith* (New York, 1961), p. 174.

2. A great deal has already been thought and said concerning such joint tasks. Particularly profound reflections may be found in R. Friedli, "Zur Weltverantwortung der Offenbarungsreligionen," in *Drei Wege zu dem einen Gott*, ed. A. Falaturi et al. (Freiburg, 1976), pp. 218–245.

3. See H. Braun, *Spätjüdisch-häretischer und frühchristlicher Radikalismus. Jesus von Nazareth und die essenische Qumranskete* (Tübingen, 1957), 2:29ff.; "*Poiein* (to do, to realize) is practically the only word the Synoptics use to express the doing God demands of human beings" (ibid., p. 30, n. 1).

4. Ibid., p. 32.

5. See pp. 110ff.

6. For the following see especially Friedli, "Zur Weltverantwortung," pp. 221ff.

7. Ibid., pp. 223f. See also J. Moltmann, *Kirche in der Kraft des Geistes. Ein Beitrag zur messiaischen Ekklesiologie* (Munich, 1975), pp. 93–103.

8. For details see pp. 81ff.

9. Friedli, "Zur Weltverantwortung," p. 229.

10. See pp. 59ff.

11. Friedli, "Zur Weltverantwortung," p. 234.

12. See, for example, J. Scharbert, "slm im Alten Testament," in *Lex tua Veritas. Festschrift für H. Junker* (Trier, 1961), pp. 209–229; H. Gross, *Die Idee des ewigen und allgemeinen Weltfriedens im alten Orient und im Alten Testament,* 2d ed. (Trier, 1967); W. Eisenbeis, *Die Wurzel* שלם *im Alten Testament* (Berlin, 1969); H. H. Schmid, *"Frieden" im alten Orient und im Alten Testament* (Stuttgart, 1971); H. H. Schmid, *Frieden ohne Illusion. Die Bedeutung des Begriffs* schalom *als Grundlage für eine Theologie des Friedens* (Zurich, 1971); C. Westermann, "Der Frieden (shalom) im Alten Testament," in *Studien zur Friedensforschung* (Stuttgart, 1969), pp. 144–177.

13. Friedli, "Zur Weltverantwortung," p. 236.

14. Ibid., p. 237.

15. Ibid.

16. See the peace encyclical of Pope John XXIII, *Pacem in terris.*

17. Friedli, "Zur Weltverantwortung," pp. 238f.

18. Ibid., p. 240.

19. Ibid., p. 241.

20. See also S. Talmon, "Auf dem Wege zu einer die Welt umspannenden Gemeinschaft," in *Von Vorurteilen zum Verständnis,* ed. F. von Hammerstein (Frankfurt, 1976), pp. 43–55.

21. Concerning this see also pp. 81ff.

22. See also H. Arendt, *Über die Revolution* (Munich, 1963).

23. On the whole issue see also U. Hommes and J. Ratzinger, *Das Heil des Menschen. Innerweltlich-Christlich* (Munich, 1975).

24. See W. Thüsing, *Per Christum in Deum. Studien zum Verhältnis von Christozentrik und Theozentrik in den paulinischen Hauptbriefen,* 2d ed. (Münster, 1969), pp. 243–246.

25. On this also see Ze'ev W. Falk, "Israels Botschaft an die Welt," *Freiburger Rundbrief* 25 (1973): 39–43.

NOTES FOR CHAPTER 8

1. The text is above in chap. 1.

2. See also J. Oesterreicher, "Unter dem Bogen des Einen Bundes—Das Volk Gottes—Seine Zweigestalt und Einheit," in *Judentum und Kirche: Volk Gottes,* ed. C. Thoma (Zurich, 1974), pp. 27–69.

3. A. von Harnack, who indeed was no anti-Semite, has written the fatal sentences: "The rejection of the Old Testament in the second century was a mistake which the great Church justly corrected; standing by that rejection in the 16th century was a fate the Reformation was unable to avoid; however, continuing to retain it after the 19th century as a canonical document in Protestantism is the consequence of a religious and ecclesiastical crippling" (*Marcion. Das Evangelium*

vom fremden Gott, 2d ed. [Leipzig, 1924], p. 217). In reality history teaches that
the denial of the Old Testament by the Church and the almost necessary forgetting
of Israel by the Church connected with it robbed the Church of its nourishing root,
which led to its exhaustion.

   4. Thoma, *A Christian Theology of Judaism* (New York, 1980), p. 31.
   5. See pp. 38ff.
   6. See pp. 23ff.
   7. See the "Vatican Guidelines" for *Nostra Aetate*, of 3 January 1975, printed in
A. Flannery, *Vatican Council II* (Collegeville, Minn., 1975), pp. 743–749.

Subject Index

Abraham, 2, 12, 17, 68, 75, 97, 104, 122, 135, 140, 146–47, 153, 182, 205, 232, 241, 251
Abrahams, I., 292 n. 23
Acharonim, 233
Acts of the Apostles, 36, 135, 171, 192, 205, 208, 307 n. 215
Adam, 101, 143
Adam, adamah, 14
Adler, H. G., 255 n. 1
Adorno, T. W., 277 n. 132
Aeon, 78, 90, 106, 134, 138, 141, 193
Ahrendt, H., 317 n. 22
Akiba, Rabbi, 55, 62, 64, 94, 122, 191, 293 n. 25
Alexander, G., 280 n. 189
Allon, G., 292 n. 23
Am-ha-aretz, 176, 178, 297 n. 85
Amos, 9, 70, 86, 245
Am segullāh, 8
Anakephalaioutai, 130, 150
Anartung, 15
Andres, S., 301 n. 133
Angerstorfer, A., 269 n. 13
Anthropomorphism, 223–26
Antichrist, 80, 114
Antigonos of Sokho, 233
Anti-Judaism, vii, 36, 134, 137, 143, 145, 158, 160, 179–80, 184, 186–87, 196, 230
Antioch, 144, 192
Anti-Pharisaic, 167, 169, 176, 182, 184
Anti-Semitism, vii, 1, 3, 28, 36, 44, 46, 108, 227–28, 252
Aphormē, 238
Apocalypse of John, 80, 98
Apocryphal materials, 154
Apokatastasis, 37–38, 78

Apostolic Council, 9, 239
Aposunagōgoi, 174
Arab neighbors to Israel, 16, 139
Archē, 197
Arendt, H., 317 n. 22
Aron, R., 286 n. 104
Asia Minor, 156
Assimilation, 15
Atheoi, 25
Atonement, Day of, 91, 94
Augustine, 267 n. 157
Aurelio, T., 307 n. 213, 310 n. 13, 311 n. 19
Auschwitz, 43–44, 69, 105, 186, 212
Ausserhofer, B. H., 259 n. 40

Baal cult, 12, 53, 70, 245
Babylon, 13, 82
Babylonian captivity, 13, 53, 57
Bächli, O., 257 n. 17
Baeck, L., 43, 112, 114, 135–36, 261 n. 76, 266 n. 146, 280 n. 1, 282 n. 31, 287 n. 1, 288 n. 10, 292 n. 23, 296 nn. 74, 78, 81
Bagatti, B., 291 n. 5
Balthasar, H. U. von, 14, 259 n. 42, 286 n. 106
Baltzer, K., 266 n. 143
Bammel, E., 152, 290 n. 45, 292 n. 22, 293 n. 23
Baptism, 110, 131, 144
Bardtke, H., 270 n. 48
Bar Qappara, 122
Barr, J., 271 n. 58
Barrett, C. K., 262 n. 103, 265 nn. 132, 133; 293 n. 1
Barth, K., 40, 46, 130, 132, 261 n. 85, 265 n. 132, 286 nn. 102, 105, 107
Barth, M., 263 n. 119, 265 n. 132, 268 n. 174, 286 n. 1, 290 n. 50, 316 n. 129

319

Koch, K., 257 n. 13, 275 n. 115, 276 nn.
    126–27; 305 n. 171, 310 n. 16
König, E., 273 n. 98
Konrad, J. F., 311 n. 31
Kortzfleisch, S. von, 257 n. 11
"Kosher" eating, 178
Kosmala, H., 261 n. 76
Kraus, H. J., 14, 260 n. 61, 276 n. 122
Krauss, S., 29
Kreimers, H., 263 n. 118
Kruiff, T. C., 9, 258 nn. 23, 24
Kuhn, H. W., 294 n. 35
Kuhn, K. G., 270 n. 38
Kuhn, P., 312 n. 70
Kümmel, W. G., 169, 265 n. 133, 294 n.
    46, 306 n. 204, 311 n. 23, 313 nn. 85, 86
Küng, H., 49, 268 n. 164
Kuss, O., 256 n. 8, 288 nn. 19, 23
Kutsch, E., 272 n. 89

Labuschagne, C. J., 268 n. 1
Landman, L., 274 n. 98
Laos, 9
Lapide, P., 49, 268 n. 164, 271 n. 67, 275
    n. 110, 279 n. 179, 280 n. 1, 281 n. 1,
    287 n. 1, 288 n. 7, 301 n. 135, 309 n. 1,
    316 n. 125
Le Déaut, R., 278 n. 159, 279 n. 164
Légasse, S., 282 n. 41, 294 n. 49
Lehmann-Habeck, M., 180, 283 n. 41
Leistner, R., 185, 298 n. 103, 299 nn. 105,
    106, 116; 300 nn. 122, 125, 126, 128; 301
    n. 131
Lentzen-Deis, F., 282 n. 34
Levinson, N. P., 258 n. 28, 290 n. 44, 292
    n. 19
Lévi-Strauss, C., 274 n. 109
Liebeschütz, H., 267 n. 158
Liedke, G., 260 nn. 52, 62; 276 n. 126
Lietzmann, H., 150, 290 n. 41
Limbeck, M., 260 nn. 69, 70, 71; 284 n. 65
Lindars, B., 293 n. 23
Lindeskog, G., 281 n. 1, 292 n. 22, 301 n.
    136
Ljungman, H., 282 n. 41
Locus cultus, 27
Logia source, 167, 169, 174, 201, 237

Löher, M., 275 n. 112
Lohff, W., 275 n. 115, 276 n. 122
Lohfink, G., 264 nn. 125, 126; 291 n. 2
Lohfink, M., 270 n. 40
Lohfink, N., 257 nn. 12, 17; 272 n. 89, 275
    nn. 112, 117; 278 nn. 154, 156; 284 n. 61
Lohse, B., 275 n. 115, 276 n. 122, 277 nn.
    136, 138
Lohse, E., 271 n. 64, 277 nn. 136, 138; 279
    n. 167, 282 n. 41, 283 n. 50, 287 n. 1,
    296 n. 79, 298 n. 97, 311 n. 22
Lona, H. E., 299 nn. 105, 112
Loretz, O., 270 n. 25
Love, 62, 66–67, 90, 111, 116–17, 120–23,
    150, 193, 216, 225, 239, 245
Lowe, M., 299 n. 105
Löwith, K., 275 n. 112
Lührmann, D., 271 n. 66, 287 n. 7
Luke, 36–37, 120, 197–98, 221
Lütgert, W., 299 n. 105
Luz, U., 263 n. 118, 264 n. 132, 275 n.
    110, 281 n. 1, 283 n. 41

Maass, F., 277 n. 137
Maccabees, 20
McCarthy, D. J., 272 n. 89
McFleney, N. J., 298 n. 94
Mack, L., 260 n. 69
Maier, F. W., 261 n. 89, 263 n. 114, 264
    nn. 122, 132; 309 nn. 245, 248, 250
Maimonides, 104, 107
Mamorstein, A., 287 n. 1, 289 n. 36
Mantel, H., 293 n. 25
Marcuse, H., 277 n. 132
Mark, 120–21, 165, 198, 201–2, 220
Marquardt, F.-W., 50, 256 n. 8, 258 n. 29,
    263 n. 120, 267 n. 160, 268 n. 165, 286
    n. 103
Marsch, W. D., 276 n. 121
Marti, K., 314 n. 98
Martin-Achard, R., 279 n. 177
Marx, K., 45, 49, 78, 85, 106, 242, 276 n.
    118, 280 n. 190, 316 n. 130
Marxism, 46, 79, 81, 85
Mass conversion, 33–34
Matthew, 120, 195, 199, 239
Maur, H. auf der, 272 n. 70

Scripture Index